Sport and Social Exclusion

D1685184

Tackling social exclusion should be a central aim of social policy. In this fully revised and updated new edition of his groundbreaking study, Sport and Social Exclusion, Mike Collins has assembled a vast array of evidence from a range of global sources to demonstrate how the effects of social exclusion are as evident in sport as they are in any area of society.

The book uses sport as an important case study for critical reflection on existing social policy and explores sport's role as a source of new initiatives for tackling exclusion. It examines key topics such as:

- What we mean by 'social exclusion'.
- How social exclusion affects citizenship and the chance to play sport.
- How exclusion from sport is linked to poverty, class, age, gender, ethnicity, disability, and involvement in youth delinquency.
- How exclusion is linked to concepts of personal and communal social capital.

Sport and Social Exclusion features a wealth of original research data, including new and previously unpublished material, as well as a range of important new studies of social exclusion policy and practice in the UK and elsewhere. This revised edition surveys all of the most important changes in the policy landscape since first publication in 2002 and, crucially, explores the likely impact of the coalition government and of the London Olympic Games on sport policy in the UK. The book concludes with some typically forthright recommendations from the author regarding the success of existing policies and the best way to tackle exclusion from sport and society in the future. Relating current policy to new research, this is an essential guidebook for students, academics and policymakers working in sport policy and development.

Mike Collins was a Senior Lecturer in Recreation Management at Loughborough University for over ten years before retiring. Prior to this, he was Head of Research Strategy and Planning at the Sports Council from its founding, and active in the Council of Europe and what is now the Countryside Recreation Network. He edited *Examining Sports Development* (Routledge, 2008). He is currently Professor of Sports Development at the University of Gloucestershire, and still active in the new Chartered Institute for the Management of Sport and Physical Activity.

Tess Kay lectured at Loughborough and researched in women and youth sport and is now Professor of Sport & Social Sciences at Brunel University, where she founded and directs the Centre for Sport Health and Wellbeing. She edited *Fathering through Sport and Leisure* (Routledge, 2009) and is also co-author of *Localizing Global Sport for Development* (2014, Bloomsbury)

2520

Sport and Social Exclusion
2nd Edition

Mike Collins with Tess Kay

Routledge
Taylor & Francis Group

LONDON AND NEW YORK

First edition published 2003
by Routledge

Second edition published 2014
by Routledge
2 Park Square, Milton Park, Abingdon, Oxon, OX14 4RN

and by Routledge
711 Third Avenue, New York, NY 10017

Routledge is an imprint of the Taylor & Francis Group, an informa business

British Library Cataloguing in Publication Data
A catalogue record for this book is available from the British Library

Library of Congress Cataloging-in-Publication Data
Collins, Michael F. (Michael Frank)
Sport and social exclusion / by Mike Collins and Tess Kay. -- Second
edition.
pages cm
ISBN 978-0-415-56880-7 (hardback) -- ISBN 978-0-415-56881-4 (pbk.)
-- ISBN 978-0-203-85972-8 (ebook) 1. Sports--Social aspects--Great
Britain. I. Great Britain. Department for Culture, Media and Sport. II.
Great Britain. Cabinet Office. Policy Action Team 10. III. Title.
GV706.5.C645 2014
306.4'83--dc23
2013048803

ISBN13: 978-0-415-56880-7 (hbk)
ISBN13: 978-0-415-56881-4 (pbk)
ISBN13: 978-0-203-85972-8 (ebk)

Typeset in Times New Roman
by Saxon Graphics Ltd

This edition is again dedicated to three people: two friends and colleagues who have been models of intellectual integrity in social research and policy application – Allan Patmore and the late Sue Glyptis – and my wife Sue, who has loved, fed and watered and supported me now for forty-seven years, and who is my severest critic!

Contents

Figures

Tables

Foreword

Mike Collins was at the heart of sports policy in Britain for more than thirty years, first as Head of Research and Planning at the erstwhile Sports Council, and then, since 1989, at Loughborough University as founder Director of the Institute of Sports Planning and Management and a lecturer and researcher. His impact has been immense, far more than any simple record of publication might suggest. At the Sports Council, not only was he the inspiration and mentor behind a huge body of research projects (over 500), but he also used his legendary energies to see research concepts tested in the field and become an inherent part of the delivery of national sports policy and funding. At Loughborough, his energies have been undiminished, as much in the stimulation of others as in purely personal achievement. Generous almost to a fault with his time, he is so often the first point of contact of any writer and researcher with ideas to test and explore.

It is due in no small measure to Mike Collins that British sports policy has been deeply concerned with so much more than the simple provision of sports facilities or the financial support of elite athletes and their coaches. For him, the slogan 'Sport for All' has been a tenet of belief – not just a belief springing from simple emotion, but one founded on a practical concern with tested outcomes. He is clear that sport should never be funded only as an adjunct to greater national prestige and national glory; he is far more concerned with the deep-rooted benefits that widespread participation in sport can bring to health, enjoyment and well-being across the whole of society.

He is not alone, of course, in this belief, but he has long felt that there should be an accessible but uncompromising review of the evidence for the social impact of sport, as a firmer foundation for formulating sports policy at both national and local levels. This volume is that foundation, the happy outcome of the urgings so many have made of its author. Its range and grasp are magisterial. The bibliography alone will be a treasure for contemporary workers. Almost all references are to material less than a decade old and he ranges with easy familiarity over British, American and European sources. But this book is not simply – or even primarily – an evidential review. The evidence is used, carefully and convincingly, to test the links between the benefits of sport and the well-being of those who have less than average economic and social capital, to challenge much contemporary thinking, and to leave – as ever – a legacy of fresh ideas in the spending of hard-won public resources.

At the heart of the book lies the contemporary concept of social exclusion. The term is itself of French derivation (Tunstall et al., 2002) and is perhaps best described in the 1997 Social Exclusion Unit's words as 'a shorthand term for what can happen when people or areas suffer from a combination of linked problems such as unemployment, poor skills, low income, poor housing, high crime environments, bad health and family breakdown'. The concept is more fully explored in Chapter 2, but this description will suffice the present purpose. It is a complex phenomenon with complex roots: the essence of the debate in this book is to explore how far such exclusion may be ameliorated, or even overcome, by sports participation and sporting provision.

Inevitably, the answers – or perhaps the pointers towards answers – are much more complex than the definition. Social exclusion, as both concept and phenomenon, has many facets, facets explored in succeeding chapters. It is not the purpose of this foreword to anticipate arguments or conclusions, but from the very beginning it is clear that the evidence for the impact of sport on differing themes within social exclusion varies greatly both in extent and quality. The variation may perhaps be most simply expressed in the length of the successive chapters of the book, but it still on occasion surprises. Compare, for example, the very full discussion in relation to education and young people's sport (Chapter 5) with the necessarily meagre debate on sport's relation to older people (Chapter 6), which is a greater and growing segment of the population as a whole.

The messages from the debates within the book are complex. But in wrestling with them a couple of cautious notes may be helpful from the outset. The first, of course, is that sport, or provision for sport, is no panacea in itself for the problems stemming from social exclusion. It must not be forgotten that a prime characteristic of sport, as with all other leisure activities, is the element of choice. Even when all barriers to participation have been removed by the public purse – or the private and voluntary sectors – the individual has the obvious personal right to refuse to participate. Indeed the right to accept, whatever the evidence of benefits, remains a right and not a duty!

It is beyond the remit of the book, in considering how to tackle social exclusion, to weigh the relative worth of investment in sport with investment in other forms of recreation, or indeed with far more basic programmes of health, housing and education. But the comment is made only to keep the whole issue of sport in necessary perspective and not to suggest in any way that the debate on the role of investment in sport in all its facets is neither worthy nor worthwhile!

The second comment is one of equal but differing caution. Accepting that initiatives in the field of sport may have a valuable – even a vital – role to play in helping to overcome social exclusion, it is dangerous to move too far in the other direction, to pursue a wide range of differing (if equally valuable) initiatives, yet to pursue none long enough for its significance and effects to be fully and fairly assessed. As politicians and managers change, each in turn locked into a personal quest for distinctive policies 'to make a difference' and to carry their individual stamp for wider approbation, so programmes are all too often terminated long before their impact or success can be perceived or measured. The tendency to indulge in what Mike Collins calls 'initiativitis' is dangerous and counter-productive in trying to tackle social exclusion. 'Sustainability' should be an exhortation to funders as much as to the funded.

These points are basic to profiling the riches of this study, for sport alone can never be a panacea to countering social exclusion, and programmes need time as well as funds and staff to become effective. But with these cautions in mind, there remains a great range of concept, of policy, of theory and of practice to be explored before truly sound funding decisions can be made. In this context, academics and pragmatists, policymakers and practitioners owe Mike Collins a great debt for having done so much of their thinking – and reading – for them. But though the intended audience may be diverse, the heart of this book is simple and clearly focused: in sport there is a suite of powerful tools to tackle and ameliorate some of the varied and painful ills of social exclusion in the developed societies of the twenty-first century. It is rooted in a profound and overt belief that sport can become an agent rather than a mirror of change in society.

Allan Patmore

Reference

Tunstall, R. et al. (2002) *Targeting social exclusion: CASE report to the New Opportunities Fund* London: CASE, London School of Economics.

Author's preface and acknowledgements

After seventeen years of fascinating and challenging work as Head of Research, Planning (both town and strategic) and sometimes Information at the Sports Council (now Sport England) I went to academia, first to Loughborough, as founder Director of the Institute of Sport Planning and Management (now the Institute of Sport and Leisure Policy) and subsequently as a lecturer in sport and leisure management. Here the research was almost as varied as the more than 500 projects I managed in London. Now I am semi-retired, with a new set of challenges in a virtually untouched field in the Centre for Sport Spirituality and Religion at the University of Gloucestershire. Sport has provided me with over forty years of enjoyable intellectual stimulation.

Since 1972 I have seen several major switches of politics, seven different directors and nine chairmen of the Sports Council/English Sports Council/Sport England and even more different sports ministers of varying energy, imagination and competence, considerable professionalisation of sports occupations, the rapid growth of sponsorship and then of commercial operations in sport, three transformations of how sport is delivered through local government.

There were two overriding things I learned from my Sports Council work. First, one had to find ways of making real the policy challenges to all the parts of the fragmented sports system. Second, there are two roles that the public agencies cannot duck and which they must fulfil to serve the citizens whose taxes pay for their salaries and operations: that of co-ordinating all the parts including voluntary and commercial partners, and that of serving those who have less than average economic and social capital. For these lessons I have much to thank Walter Winterbottom, Gordon Cherry and Allan Patmore for, and to George Walker, secretary to many Council of Europe committees for sport, with whom it was a pleasure to work over that same period.

In my other guises as Methodist preacher and youth leader, school governor, Community Health Council chairman, and secretary to various professional and voluntary bodies, I had long been aware of the often-hidden phenomenon of inequality of resources and opportunities in British society. This was driven home in a new and graphic way when I was commissioned by the Department of Culture Media and Sport (DCMS) to review social exclusion in sport for the Policy Action Team 10. I am grateful to Paul Bolt, Director of Policy and Information, and to

Phyllida Shaw who shared the work in focussing on the arts, and gave me new insights into that facet of leisure.

I am especially grateful to colleagues and PhD students who have shared the burden of working with me on the eight case studies in the book – Guy Jackson, Chris Kennett, Fiona McCormack, Karen Jerwood, Ceris Anderson and Jim Buller. Likewise, I thank Tess Kay whose great experience in gender and sport issues made her a better author of Chapter 5 than I could be, and whose friendship has been a pleasure. I acknowledge with thanks permission to reproduce Figure 2.1 by the Crown, Exclusion Task Force, Figure 2.2 by the Equality Trust, Figure 3.4 by the City of Birmingham, Figure 10.1 by Sport England (Nick Rowe), Figure 11.1 by Professor Fred Coalter, Figures 11.2 and 11.3 by Professor Ken Roberts, Figures 11.5 and 11.6 by Ceris Anderson (Street Games), and Figure 14.1 by the Office of National Statistics.

That too-rapid review of what I knew and gathering of much new material convinced me that this issue needed a book to set it out. I am pleased that Routledge thought it worth a second edition which is much (and painfully!) revised. The editing of the text was delayed by a long spell of hospitalisation and recuperating; I am grateful for the advice of an anonymous reader and the patience of Tess Kay and Simon Whitmore and Joshua Wells from Routledge. Throughout the writing, I am grateful to the many people, too many to list, in the UK, Europe, North America and other parts of the world who have given me information and advice. I hope I have made good and accurate use, quotation, summary and reference to what many people told and sent me, but of course errors and omissions are mine, and not yours.

Shepshed, November 2013

Glossary

APS	Anti-Poverty Strategy
CA/CRC	Countryside Agency (formerly CC Countryside Commission) now Commission for Rural Communities
CCPR/SRA	Central Council for Physical Recreation (now Sport and Recreation Alliance)
CIPFA	Chartered Institute for Public Finance and Accountancy
CLR	Centre for Leisure Research (Edinburgh University)
DCMS	Department of Culture Media and Sport
DETR	Department of Environment Transport and the Regions (now DTR)
DfEE	Department for Education and Employment (predecessor to DfES)
DfES/DfE	Department for Education and Skills (now Department for Education)
DNH	Department of National Heritage (predecessor to DCMS)
DSS/DWP	Department of Social Services (now Department of Work and Pensions)
EC/EU	European Commission/European Union
ESC/SC	English Sports Council (preceded by the Sports Council – SC) (now Sport England – SE)
HEA	Health Education Authority
HMG	Her Majesty's Government
ILAM/ISPAL /CIMSPA	Institute of Leisure and Amenity Management, later Institute for Sport Parks and Leisure, superseded by Chartered Institute for the Management of Sport & Physical Activity
ISRM	Institute of Sport and Recreation Management
LA(s)	Local authority (-ies)
LC	Leisure Card (or Passport to Leisure)
LGA	Local Government Association
NGB	National Governing Bodies
NPFA	National Playing Fields Association
NSTS	Nottinghamshire Sports Training Scheme
ODPM	Office of the Deputy Prime Minister

ONS	Office of National Statistics
PA	Physical Activity
PAT10	Policy Action Team 10 (on Sport, arts and social exclusion)
SAZ	Sports Action Zone
SE	Sport England (successor to ESC)
SEU	Social Exclusion Unit (in the Cabinet Office)
SEx	Social Exclusion
SS	Street Sport, Stoke-on-Trent
SSC	Solent Sports Counselling
UKS	UK Sport

1 Introduction

This second edition, like the first, is intended for both academic and professional audiences. It is not a 'cookbook', nor even a guide to good practice, though it does include some of the latter. The first part of the chapter summarises very briefly constraints on playing sport and the benefits when one does, both summarising a small mountain of material.

Constraints on playing sport

Goodale and Witt (1989) and Jackson (1988) reviewed current research into barriers faced and constraints experienced by would-be recreationalists, and the latter (Jackson, 1991) criticised it for the following: for being limited to barriers to using public resources, for concentrating on groups subjectively identified as constrained, and for using 'rudimentary' item-by-item analysis. Subsequently, Jackson identified moves from recreation to leisure, to a wider range of activities and groups, and to other points of constraint, in lapsing, preferences and satisfactions. He also distinguished (Jackson, 1990a,b) between *antecedent* or *structural* constraints (influencing preference formation, divided into intrapersonal and interpersonal) and *intervening* or *direct* ones (affecting which preferences turn into participation). Kay and Jackson (1991) reported high levels of constraint on lower social groups in their Stoke-on-Trent sample, but also constraints on affluent groups who wished to participate in more activities or more frequently, virtually everyone being constrained relative to their dream/ideal lifestyle.

Having reviewed over fifty studies affecting particular groups, Collins, Henry and Houlihan (1999) produced Table 1.1, later with detailed weighting modified by new work, but its utility has been proven several times. It distinguishes three groups of constraints. The first, comprising rows 1–4, is labelled *structural/environmental* factors – the nexus of economic, physical and social factors that lead to identifying 'problem estates' and neighbourhoods in cities so graphically described in *Bringing Britain Together*, but which present in a more dispersed and concealed form in rural areas (Chapter 10). At the other end of the scale in the lower six rows is the *personal/internal psychological* group – seeing some activities as 'not for me' because of feeling powerless and unfit, 'unsporty', or lacking the money, skills or educational and social capital to take part. As Harland et al. (nd) showed, these are just as effective as poverty, lack of transport, and managers who are blind to or prejudiced about some particular clients. Between these two groups lie the *mediating* factors of 'gatekeepers' like facility managers, coaches, sports development officers, teachers, or club officers who select who is 'in' and who is 'out' of groups, and of society's representatives who label people as 'different' (an issue explored in both Chapter 7 on ethnic groups and Chapter 9 on disabled people). This arrangement has some echoes of structure and agency issues in sociology. The columns of the Table 1.1 cover the main groups in society that may be considered excluded, and about whom the evidence is displayed in Chapters 3 to 9.

The number of +++ indicates the estimated strength/salience of a particular factor for a particular group. Presenting this material in this manner brings out:

- The large numbers of people *affected by one or more* factors (looking across the rows). Thus improving the design of buses and buildings for access for wheelchair users also benefits others with mobility problems, like older people using walking sticks, and mothers with pushchairs, toddlers and lots of shopping bags.
- Many groups are *multiply constrained* (looking down the columns). So implementing an inherently good single policy to attack a particular constraint, like leisure/loyalty cards with discounts to combat poverty (Chapter 3) or of adapting access for physical disability, have no effect on exclusion if managers do not proactively market and make their facilities or services known to particular groups, or if the target population feel insecure in going to certain venues (females, ethnic minorities, aged and disabled citizens at night and in secluded places). Releasing one constraint merely gives another prominence. Here is the permanent ground and justification for better partnerships and 'joined-up' thinking, and client-centred policies.

Poverty adds an extra intensity to each of the other factors in terms of 'locking people in' and accentuating their feeling that they are not autonomous agents, capable of bringing change to their lives (Chapter 3). Even for the community as a whole, money is listed as the most significant constraint; the second, time, is quoted by rich and poor alike, even by retired people; the chronic unemployed is the group with the greatest problems of time structuring (Kay and Jackson, 1990, 1991). As we see in much of the rest of this book, there are combinations of exclusions that can be said to lead to double deprivation – e.g., being elderly or from an ethnic minority and in lower social groups.

As evidenced in Chapter 4 and elsewhere, if exclusion is prolonged in youth, it tends to affect the rest of the life trajectory, and only a few determined people break through, often for short periods, while some can also slide down the social ladders, especially during unemployment or single parenthood (Walker, 1995). It can affect opportunities to play recreationally and to socialise but also chances of competing and achieving at elite level (see pp 76–9).

Table 1.1 Multiple constraints and exclusion in sport and leisure

Group excluded	Youth			Poor/ unemployed	Women	Older people	Ethnic minor	People disabled/ learn difficulties
	Child	Young people	Young delinq.					
Structural factors								
Poor phys/ soc environment	+	+	++	++	+	+	++	+
Poor facilities/ community capacity	+	+	++	++	+	+	+	++
Poor support network	+	+	++	++	+	+	+	++
Poor transport	++	++	++	++	++	++	+	+++
Managers' policies attitudes	+	+	++	++	+	+	++	++
Labelling by society	+	++	+++	+	+	+	+++	++
Personal factors								
Lack of time structure	+	+	++	+++		+		+
Lack of income	+	+	++	+++	+	++	++	++
Lack of skills/personal social capital	+	+	+++	+++	+	+	++	++
Fears of safety	++	++	++	++	+++	++++	++	++
Powerlessness	++	++	+++	+++	++	++	++++	++
Poor self/body image	+	+	++	++	+	+	++	++

Note: The number of +s shows the severity of particular constraints for particular groups

Benefits claimed for playing sport

Reviews of the benefits of sport have grown, beginning in the US where Driver and Bruns (1999) listed 105 different benefits for individuals, particular groups and the whole community. They argued for using it practically in Benefits-Based Management (BBM), and it was adopted by the Parks and Recreation Federation of Ontario in a condensed form as shown in Table 1.2. The Council of Europe (Vuori et al., 1995, Patrickkson, 1995, Dorricott, 1998) undertook a similar review. In Britain the mental health benefits of visiting natural spaces and of 'green exercise' has become a new theme (Semour, 2003; CABEspace, 2009; Hillsdon, Jones and Coombes, 2011; Pretty et al., nd), though in its *Position Statement on Health & Wellbeing* Natural England (2008: 1) admitted that the evidence base was 'of insufficient quality to convince the medical fraternity.' The Forestry Commission has produced evidence and advocacy specifically for forests (URGP, 2010; Tabbush and O'Brien, 2003; O'Brien, 2005), the latter endorsed by the Chief Medical Officer. BHFNC (2013) updated the physical activity benefits, claiming it could:

- greatly reduce the £900m a year spent by the NHS on stroke and heart disease, type 2 diabetes, colorectal and breast cancer, and £103–129bn on other illnesses;
- avoid 17% of premature deaths if all sedentary people took activity;
- delay the growing costs of elderly care, reduce the costs of social inequality (bringing 285m years of healthy life if death & disability for all were reduced to those of the most well-off 10% (Marmot, 2005).

The Mental Health Foundation (2013) added numerous other well-being benefits. Coalter (2013a) provided the latest summary of social benefits.

Crompton and colleagues drove forward the idea of claiming benefits, arguing that US recreation services had been downgraded in the public's eyes to merely another utility, and the wider benefits to society foundational to the professional parks and recreation movement of the late nineteenth century had been forgotten. Thus, a conscious marketing and information effort was needed to 'reposition' the services and the profession (Witt and Crompton, 1997). Such a move was made in the UK by Sport England (Sport England, 1999) and the Local Government Association (LGA) through review and consultation on the Value of Sport (Sport England, 1999a–d). Subsequently, the LGA commissioned CLR to evaluate evidence of benefits in the form of outputs and outcomes for all aspects of culture, including sport (Coalter, 2001a). Long and Sanderson (2001) decided to see how far local authority leisure department staffs believed such evidence: credence was greatest for personal development (96%), followed by cohesion and social benefits (57–66%), then empowerment and capacity-building (40 and 51%), but less for economic benefits (17 and 23%). Neither Bovaird, Nichols and Taylor's (1997) nor Foster et al.'s (2005) models of barriers and benefits have been taken up, their apparent simplicity hiding their data-hungriness.

Table 1.2 Benefits of sports participation: coverage of selected reviews

Form of benefit	PRFO review[a]	HC review[b]	SpE review[c]	LGA review
1. Personal				
1 aiding a full/meaningful life	*	*	*	
2 ensuring health	*		*	*
3 helping stress management	*		*	*
4 giving self-esteem/image	*	*		*
5 offering balance/achievement/life satisfaction	*		*	
6 play and human development	*	*		
7 positive lifestyle choices	*	*		
8 open spaces and quality of life	*			
9 better academic performance			*	*
2. Social				
1 strengthening communities	*	*	*	*
2 reducing alienation/loneliness/anti-social behaviour	*	*	*	*
3 promoting ethnic/cultural harmony	*	*	*	
4 strengthening families	*	*		
5 community involvement/ownership/empowerment	*	*	*	*
6 access for disabled/disadvantaged	*		*	
7 promoting community pride	*	*		*
8 protection for latch-key children	*			
9 ethical behaviour models (cheating/drugs/violence)		*		
3. Economic				
1 cost-effective health prevention	*		*	*
2 fitness for productive workforces	*		*	
3 small sums/large economic returns	*			
4 attracting new/growing businesses	*			
5 reducing cost of vandalism/crime	*		*	
6 catalyst for tourism	*			
7 funding environmental protection	*		*	
8 regeneration of jobs/communities			*	*
4. Environmental				
1 aiding environmental health	*		*	
2 protect/rehabilitate environments	*		*	*
3 increasing property values	*			
4 ensuring a sustainable environment	*		*	
5. National				
1 integration/cultural cohesion		*		
2 pride		*	*	
3 trade balance/marketing		*		
4 international influence/representation			*	

Sources: a. Parks and Recreation Federation of Ontario, 1992; b. Sullivan, 1998 for the Hillary Commission; c. Sport England, 1999a, b

It might be thought that the overwhelming benefits confirmed between exercise and health (e.g., Allied Dunbar National Fitness Survey [SC/HEA, 1992], Coalter, 2001a, Chief Medical Officer, 2004, BHF, 2009) and the equally definitive links between poor health, poor diet, poverty and low participation in sport (e.g., HEA, 1999) would have lead to more joint programmes. That was the plan until 1995 when Ian Sproat, Minister for Sport, broke an established partnership between the Health Education Authority and the Sports Council, saying it was not the latter's business. (This linkage is strong throughout Europe and the world, but is still maintained by the Coalition, even though health is now an LA function, requiring partnership linkages to be made and maintained, and is a function built into the new Chartered Institute for the Management of Sport and Physical Activity. It has been said often that Britain's National Health Service concentrates on treatment to the neglect of prevention; Gratton and Taylor (2000: 107) commented that this 'may be an expensive mistake'.

Coalter (2001a) summarised the quality of evidence for benefits as patchy and often situation-specific, dependent on small, sometimes self-selected samples, frequently *post-hoc* and dependent on uncorroborated self-report, commonly lacking baselines, longitudinal and control group data, and often concerned with intermediate outputs rather than final outcomes of the sort that interest and influence politicians, media and the general public. Six years later, reiterating these weaknesses, Coalter (2007) concluded on five major areas of benefit other than health:

- *sport and social regeneration, and social capital,* focussed on clubs, he used Pawson's (2004) words to describe them as 'ill-defined interventions with hard-to-follow outcomes';
- *sports-in-(overseas) development,* describing striking changes, often in 'chaotic circumstances'; he later produced evidence of participation benefits for particular groups (Coalter, 2008);
- *sport and educational performance,* where the most he could say was 'at least it does no harm';
- *sport and crime prevention,* where good news stories and anecdotes abounded, but good evidence was still weak; he called this 'plus sport', working as part of wider personal and social development programmes of participants (Chapter 9);
- *economic impact, job creation and regeneration,* where political pressure and business coalitions and lobbies pressed for simple and supportive answers, amid much dispute over measurement.

Outline of the book

After a long spell in government, New Labour lost its way, believed its own rhetoric, stopped listening to its citizens, and deservedly lost the 2010 election. Gordon Brown played a leading role in combating the international debacle of greedy and ill-regulated bankers but coped less well at home, having inherited an economy already on the downturn in 2004–5 (see Chapter 3), overborrowing, and under-taxing the rich for fear of offence. In came a Tory-led coalition determined by slash and burn in the public sector to right the ship of state. The postlude to Chapter 12 covers the most recent of the welter of changes, which have combined to set back moves to equality, and lead to my pessimistic conclusions. The other, ironic context is that with the award of London 2012, sport has had its greatest political salience since the 1948 Olympics, but while the legacy plans are pursued with some energy, they do not seem powerful or well co-ordinated enough to be effectual.

This book intends is to issue a clarion call to researchers and policymakers to:

- the scale and deep-rootedness of inequality and exclusion issues, and the slowness of strategic change which politicians will not admit, and the swiftness of knee-jerk policy reactions;
- the dangers of succumbing to 'initiative overload' from governments and their agencies, or to compassion-fatigue;
- persuade them to commit to policies and practices to increase inclusion despite the whims of politics, the changing winds of financial and human resources, the waywardness of colleagues and partner organisations, and the sporadic interest of the media and general public.

It seeks, for each facet of exclusion, to: summarise the evidence of it in society generally; to draw together coherently the scattered research evidence from the UK and elsewhere of how it is manifested in sport and leisure; and to provide a description of current policy context, the actions to combat it and research results where these are available. The eight case studies used are attempts at evidence-based work, imperfect because they were done usually in hindsight and so depend on recall stimulated by postal and telephone questionnaires/interviews, with incomplete corroboration from records rarely gathered for monitoring and evaluation purposes.

The thread of the book unrolls as follows. In the next chapter, I show how the concepts around poverty have developed from a simple measure of the basic staples of life – *absolute* poverty – through the ideas of the poverty of some groups in twentieth century society *relative* to what the majority had and expected in terms of a wider range of goods and services including leisure and culture, to the wider idea and process of exclusion from the main spheres of involvement in contemporary society.

Chapter 3 looks at the links between poverty, exclusion and sport, exploring my belief that poverty is the core of exclusion; only a few affluent people are excluded by the other factors; so this is reflected wherever possible in relation to other facets of exclusion, in Chapters 4–10 I illustrate it with one case study of the introduction of systematic discounts through Leisure Cards, contrasting the cities of Leicester and Oxford, and a second of a recent successful social marketing project in Birmingham.

Chapter 4 examines the differing chances of children from their early experiences of sport and PE mediated in primary and secondary school and in clubs and community. The third case study covers the resurgence of school and youth sport through a sustained cross-Departmental strategy in the 'noughties.' The fourth case study is of the differential access and take-up of opportunities to try new sports and develop skills in Nottinghamshire.

In Chapter 5 Tess Kay looks at the evidence of perhaps the longest-lasting and most studied of exclusions – of gender, especially for young women. Women have been trying to equalise opportunities to play, teach, coach and administer, but as she shows, are still some way from that position despite equal opportunity laws. Women are, however, slowly finding ways to empowerment.

In Chapter 6 I look at how sports opportunities and take-up diminish with age, except for the richest and best educated, but also how other countries engender more inclusion, whether because of history, sports structure and finance, or a different philosophy of active citizenship through sport.

Chapters 7 and 8 cover aspects where Britain has enacted legislation to bolster and encourage equal opportunities for two minority groups – people from ethnic minorities and who are disabled. The majority of the first group are indisputably multiply deprived to a degree that threatens to ghettoise them, even in their second and third generation's residence in Britain. Many of the disabled are dependent on welfare and are thereby poor because of the relatively modest level of welfare payments in the UK. Both groups were allocated priority programmes by both The Department of Culture Media and Sport (DCMS) and Sport England (SE), and the English Federation of Disability Sport (EFDS) may become a source of real empowerment. Case Study 5 shows how Leicester approached disability issues.

Chapter 9 delves into the still-growing mountain of reviews and studies of sport and recreation being used as preventive or rehabilitative means for at-risk youth. Using Case Study 6 of primary (preventative) recreational work amongst young teenagers in Stoke-on-Trent and of rehabilitative work amongst young adult offenders in Hampshire, it attempts to unravel the problem of the youngsters' impoverished leisure lives as impoverished as in other aspects and so not easily or quickly remedied. Such schemes are often ridiculed by the popular press as 'holidays for hooligans' which deters politicians from supporting them. With sustained funding, Case Study 7 of Positive Futures confirms other findings.

Chapter 10 demonstrates that social exclusion manifests itself equally in town and country, giving the lie to Power's (1997: 1) strong assertion that it is 'almost entirely an urban problem and an urban agenda.' But it *is* much more strongly concentrated in cities and manifestly correlated with poor housing, poor health and crime. Consequently it has been much more studied and attacked by grant aid and public policy programmes in cities, than in the countryside, even though the now-demised Commission for Rural Communities persisted in drawing rural inequalities to HMG's attention.

Explicit governmental social inclusion policies and programmes are still relatively new, too new to yield many reliable accounts of best practice let alone researched and considered critiques of outcomes, so Chapter 11 draws together two threads: suggestions for more effective delivery (mainly through less novelty, better resourcing, more commitment, a closer focus, and less impatience); and a consideration of the role of sports clubs as a form of civic action and social capital in the mixed economy of modern governance, re-branded by the Coalition as part of the Big Society. Case Study 8 on Street Games shows how a non-governmental agency can grasp a moment of opportunity.

After summarising previous findings of chapters, Chapter 13 draws some conclusions:

- Participation does not equal exclusion, but time and time again the poor have low or narrow participation in sport but also in a much wider range of leisure, and this is even more true if they are female, non-white and disabled. Is it credible to believe that they repeatedly restrict their leisure in this way by choice? Exclusion is widespread, established early (see the gendered attitudes to sport by the age of 9 or 10 exhibited in Chapters 4 and 5), persistent and difficult to overcome. At its core is poverty. Moreover, such differences are repeated in other European countries and in the US, even though they are nuanced by differing income and class gradients.
- Evaluation has been rare, skimpy and under-resourced. Difficult as it is, politicians, the media and the public expect – and are being led increasingly to look for – evidence that relates not to narrow, more easily measured outputs, but to the broad, complex, overlapping, slippery and sometimes contradictory outcomes. But these take time to develop, and neither officials nor politicians show any understanding of exercising patience or resisting bandwagoning programmes at the first sign of positive news of take up or popularity.
- Evidence for benefits to cardiovascular health from vigorous exercise and to other ailments from moderate exercise, and to self-confidence and self-esteem are continually confirmed, but for most other claims evidence is patchy, anecdotal or open to question in methodology (Coalter, 2007). Above all better explanatory, longitudinal data is needed. For sport this is patchy and not specifically designed; Sport England has not grasped the opportunity in the huge Active People survey to remedy this crucial knowledge gap.
- On the one hand, sport can rarely yield economic, environmental, health, safety or social benefits acting alone; it needs to be a partner, often a minor one, with those promoting other mainstream policies; but it will, I believe, betray its potential if it fails to strive and colludes with sustaining the current unequal *status quo*. On the other hand, DCMS and Sport England among others must beware of making claims that cannot be supported by good evidence, and of being open to claims of exaggeration or prematurity.

The postlude to Chapter 12 sets out some of the latest effects of Coalition policies manifesting themselves during the second editing process. Though the government protests that it is trying to protect poor families, it certainly seems to have it in for anyone registered as disabled, and overall will bring about greater social exclusion for a period whose length is shrouded in unknowingness.

2   From absolute poverty to social exclusion

From absolute and relative poverty to social exclusion

Poverty is a contested concept, as Alcock (1997: 3) commented 'there is no correct, scientific, agreed definition because poverty is inevitably a political concept, and thus inherently is a contested one.' Documented studies of poverty date from the late nineteenth century, with Booth (1882) and Rowntree (1901) who set a threshold below which people were said to be *absolutely poor*. Rowntree distinguished those in 'primary' poverty, not having the basic food, clothing, housing or warmth for 'physical efficiency', and others in 'secondary' poverty, caused by waste or lack of knowledge. Booth was scathing about the latter, calling them loafers, feckless, near-criminals. Both arguments have developed a tradition. Booth's line was followed by Charles Murray's (1990) denigration of an 'underclass' in the US and Britain, by John Moore (Secretary of State for Social Security) in 1989 (cited in Levitas, 1998) and by Peter Lilley (1996) who all denied the existence of (absolute) poverty in 'affluent' Britain.

There are two flaws to the absolute definition. First, its determination, according to the architect of the British Welfare State, is 'a matter of judgement' (Beveridge, 1942) and levels of subsistence change over time, as do people's expectations; second, it takes no account of socio-cultural needs, which is one of the things that can be seen as a luxury in one era, but later as a necessity (Donnison, 1982).

So emerged a *relative* definition, going beyond subsistence and defining poverty in relation to the accepted standard of living in a society, or 'the custom of the country,' as Adam Smith called it as long ago as 1812. This was echoed by Townsend (1979: 60) who wrote that people are poor when 'they lack the resources to obtain the types of diet, participate in the activities…which are customary, or at least widely encouraged or approved, in the societies to which they belong'. He recognised leisure as part of this – 'deprivation can arise…in different spheres of life, such as at work, at home, in travel, and in leisure time activities' (1979: 271). Apart from housing, and food, he included the following items in his Deprivation Index:

* no holiday away form home in last year;
* no visit to or from a friend or relative for a meal in last month (adults);

- no friend to play or to tea in last month, no party on last birthday (children under 15);
- no afternoon or evening out in last two weeks.

Thus in terms of a broader look at lifestyle, Townsend (1987: 125) summarised what he called deprivation as 'a state of observable and demonstrable disadvantage relative to the local community or the wider society or nation.' Holman (1978) and Oppenheim and Harker (1996) followed this relative line.

Critics claimed this approach is subjective, but Townsend had stated in 1979 that 'subjectivity was inevitable in social scientists' definitions. More substantive arguments claim that a relative definition means that the numbers seen as poor would not change if living standards fell evenly (Roll, 1992), and that it takes the moral element from poverty (McGregor, 1981), likening people who go to Butlins on holiday to those who go to an upmarket villa in Tuscany, while others starve.

Lister (1990) and Scott (1994) developed Townsend's arguments to say that poverty can be understood as *exclusion* from aspects of citizenship. The EC's Poverty III programme was concerned to integrate the 'least privileged' into society, and before its completion, the rhetoric had moved to a concept of 'social exclusion' (hereafter SEx). It had become an accepted term, according to Tricart, an officer in the European Commission's DGV, responsible for social affairs:

> Today, the concept of social exclusion is taking over from poverty, which is more static...and seen far more often as exclusively monetary poverty... Social exclusion does not only mean sufficient income, and it even goes beyond participation in working life.
>
> (Rigeaux, European Commission, 1994: 12)

The term originated in France, and is usually attributed to René Lenoir, Secretary of State for Social Action to the Chirac government, who published in 1974 *Les Exclus: Un Français sur dix*, concerned with the breakdown of structural, cultural and moral ties (Levitas, 1998: 21) and a *contract d'insertion* focussed on job seeking but also other forms of social participation. Room (1993) said this involved three social shifts – from income to multi-dimensional disadvantage; from a state to a process; and from a focus on individuals or households to local communities. Berghman (1995) argued that both terms could be process *and* outcome, suggesting using 'poverty and deprivation to denote the outcome...and impoverishment and SEx to refer to the process.' Room et al. (1995) suggested that whereas poverty is *distributional*, exclusion is *relational*, a strong reason for needing 'joined-up' policies to tackle it. If exclusion is a process, who is doing the excluding? Well sometimes it is wider structures in society and community, sometimes it is people in positions of power, and sometimes it is citizens themselves.

Commins (1993), focussing on Ireland, further suggested that SEx had to involve belonging to four of society's systems:

- the democratic and legal system, which promotes civic integration;
- the labour market, which promotes economic integration;
- the welfare system, which promotes social integration;
- the family and community system, which promotes interpersonal integration.

He argued (1993: 4) that '*when one or two* (of these) are weak, the others need to be strong. And the worst off are those for whom all systems have failed.' Berghman (1995: 19) spoke of a 'denial or non-realisation of citizenship rights.' The Eurobarometer study by Rigaux (1994) showed clearly that a majority of Europeans thought income disparity and SEx had increased since 1976.

In the most intensive Europe-wide study of SEx to date, exclusion was seen as a consequence of unemployment and low income (Roche and Annesley, 1998), leading to exclusion from a fair share of social goods and capital in the forms of recognition, income and work. The UK was seen as a liberal welfare regime, following Esping-Anderson's (1990) classification, who identified three main causes of social change in welfare: mass unemployment and insecure employment; family restructuring with a rapid growth of one-parent families and workless households; and a growing inequality with a group of really poor separated from the rest – an economic underclass. The groups most at risk were the young, unskilled, lone parents, the jobless, and children (disproportionately in poor households). In terms of inclusionary policies, in the UK:

> welfare provision is increasingly contractual, emphasising rights and duties of the providers and recipients...and welfare provision comes from an increasing mixed range of resources. It operates through a lightly regulated labour market (in European terms), a mild form of workfare in the New Deal, and targeting in terms of the Jobseeker's Allowance involving evidence of willingness to work.
>
> (Roche and Annesley, 1998: 98)

The argument against this line, which in many ways the Blair/Brown governments followed from 1997 to 2010, is that employment is the answer to many people's exclusion, an argument I shall return to later.

Room et al. (1993) suggested that Anglo-Saxon, liberal concepts of poverty became fused with conservative, European concerns about moral integration and social order, and so no single discourse emerged. Levitas (1998) clearly laid out under three headings the main forms of discourse and related policy responses – RED (redistribution), MUD (moral underclass), and SID (social inclusion).

RED: social exclusion, redistribution and critical public policy

The roots of this lay in Britain, in Townsend's analysis of deprivation and his preferred solution of redistribution through benefits given as of right, rather than through means-testing. In the eighteen years of Tory government following his analysis, inequality, unemployment and poverty increased, with the only redistribution being to the richer citizens (see the Rowntree Commission and HBAI statistics below), and no evidence of the 'trickle-down' effects that were supposed to benefit low-income people. Tories attacked RED as immoral, a totalitarian imposition of uniformity, and a brake on economic growth through unnecessary taxation, and evidence of a 'nanny' state.

The Child Poverty Action Group (CPAG) published *Britain divided: The growth of social exclusion* in the 1980s and 1990s (Walker and Walker, 1997), and hopes were raised when Shadow Chancellor Gordon Brown recognised the need to reduce inequality in his John Smith Memorial Lecture (cited in Lister, 1998). Building on T.H. Marshall's 1950s model of citizenship, Goodin (1996) argued that this idea was more egalitarian than the insider/outsider aspects of inclusion, though Marshall was criticised for overlooking aspects of gender and ethnic inequalities. Lister (1990: 68) related poverty, SEx and citizenship thus: 'poverty spells exclusion from the full rights of citizenship in each of these (civil, political and social) spheres and undermines people's ability to fulfil the private and public obligations of citizenship.'

MUD: a dependent underclass

The Conservative Government responded to rising unemployment by reducing and tightening eligibilities for benefits, eventually blaming the poor for their circumstances, while reducing public expenditure, especially by local authorities. 'Benefits dependency,' 'giro culture,' and 'the underclass' became commonplace terms, but this rhetoric was linked with a neo-Conservative policy line of strengthening the moral order. So the poor were either deserving and needful of help, or 'feckless/scroungers' and undeserving. The American Charles Murray (1990: 3) described himself as 'a visitor from a plague area come to see if the disease (of people rejecting the ethics of work and family) is spreading.' He supported the underclass idea on the basis of illegitimacy, crime and dropping out from the labour force. Later (Murray, 1994), he was even more extreme in a gendered labelling – delinquent males were wilfully idle and criminally anti-social, while delinquent women were sexually irresponsible single parents whose benefits should be cut.

Those espousing RED reacted strongly to what they saw as an argument without evidence, blaming the poor for their poverty, and with policies being punitive rather than supportive (Oppenheim and Harker, 1996). But the concept of an underclass allowed the persistence of poverty to be recognised, while absolving the government of at least some blame, and it became a term used in the media and by politicians, including Tony Blair, and Labour MP Frank Field (1990). Also it gave one moral expression to the distancing and alienation of the poor from the rest of society (Duffy, 1995; Adonis and Pollard, 1997). Like Galbraith (1992) in the US, Lister has fought for the empowerment of poor people, and lives of respect and value, quoting Beresford and Croft (1995: 9) that 'it is poor people's powerlessness which lies at the heart of their exclusion from the poverty debate.'

SID: social exclusion and integration in Europe

SID is distinguished from the earlier versions in its emphasis on exclusion from paid work. Throughout the European discourse, SEx and exclusion from work were used interchangeably, as in Roche and Annesley (1998). Part of this rhetoric, however, includes ideas of recognition and non-financial income. Recognition involves status, respect and trust (as in Giddens, 1991; Beck, 1992). Income means primarily money, but may include goods and services provided through a welfare state, informal work or volunteering. Levitas (1998: 6) commented SID 'reduced the social to the economic.'

Levitas' criticism of all three is that they neglect unpaid work, so disadvantaging women in their non-employed roles. All have a moral element, especially MUD, but all differ on what the socially excluded need, bowdlerised by Shucksmith, 2001a) as 'no work,' 'no money,' and 'no morals' respectively MUD neglects the social and political, SID largely ignores the political and cultural; RED is broader, but the discourses overlap, as shown in Table 2.1 based on Kennett's (2002) summary.

The 'new contract for welfare', said the Department of Social Security (1998: 20), should provide 'public services of a high quality to the whole community, as well as cash benefits.' So, what is exclusion about? It is more than the simple condition of being equal. In any case, even equality is slippery and can be defined several ways (Palfrey et al., 1992). Is the interest in equal use, equal opportunities or equal outcomes? People are not equally endowed – neither with intellect, physique nor the world's goods; as a result, the New Right could claim 'inequality is seen as an inevitable and tolerable result of social freedom and personal initiative' (Nankivell, 1988). Unequal treatment of equal access to resources will

Table 2.1 The three discourses of social exclusion

Redistribution	Moral Underclass	Social Insertion
• emphasises poverty as the prime cause • implies better benefits as the solution • could valorise unpaid work • if inclusion=citizenship, not a minimalist model • goes beyond materialism in addressing social/ cultural/political spheres • focuses on processes of • impoverishment • implies radical redistrib- • ution of power and resources	• underclass are seen as distinct from mainstream of society • focuses on behaviour of individuals, not structures • implies benefits encourage dependency, and are bad for recipients • inequalities in the rest of society are ignored • gender-stereotyped argument about young male criminals and immoral single mothers	• narrows definition to paid work • neglects why people not in paid work are poor • obscures inequalities between employees • ignores women's low pay/ poorer jobs • neglects differences between workers and those with capital • fails to address unpaid work, and undermines its legitimacy

Source: Based on Kennett, 2002

not lead to equal use. In 1985, the World Health Organisation sought a simple outcome: the narrowing of the gap between the most and least healthy countries by 25% by 2000. But few equity targets can be so simply specified.

The philosopher Rawls (1971) sought a different aim: to provide the best possible position for the poorest (the principle of 'maximin'), and many public policies in health, employment, education, housing, crime prevention, and sport and leisure have sought something like this, while accepting that there will still be diversity. In the context of physical education, Penney eloquently and idealistically spoke of equity being:

> concerned with giving value to, and celebrating social and cultural difference of individuals and society...as a source of enrichment to all. To be concerned with equity is thus to be concerned with social justice, and specifically, the matters of dignity, privileges and power that all individuals are entitled to.
>
> (Penney, 2000: 0)

More pragmatically, Sport England (2001a) produced guidance for sports governing bodies in writing their equity plans in the following terms:

> 'sports equity' is about fairness in sport, equality of access, recognising inequalities and taking steps to address them. It is about changing the structure of sport to ensure that it becomes equally accessible to all members of society, whatever their age, gender, race, ethnicity, sexuality, or socio-economic status.
>
> (Sport England, 2001a)

Equity and exclusion are slippery concepts, and measurement is approximate and contended. But governments, depending on their ideology, have tried to use taxes on income as a means of closing the financial gaps between the richest and poorest. In recent years the edge of this weapon has been blunted by a move to indirect taxes on services and transactions, which tend to be regressive, penalising the poor, and an unwillingness to raise taxes on the richest. In the following chapters I examine the reality of the gaps regarding sport for various social groups.

Measuring poverty and social exclusion

We have seen above that Townsend developed a set of indicators of deprivation in 1979; Mack and Lansley (1985) extended his twelve to thirty-five; but arguments continued amongst researchers and policymakers about the value of such relative as opposed to absolute measures. The Blair Government's new Social Exclusion Unit (SEU) described rather than defined SEx as:

> a shorthand label for what can happen when individuals or areas suffer a combination of linked problems such as unemployment, poor skills, low incomes, poor housing, high crime environments, bad health and family breakdown.
>
> (Social Exclusion Unit, 1998)

More recently, after reviewing much data and new thinking on the multiple interrelated dimensions of exclusion, Levitas et al. devised the following more mature and inclusive definitions:

> SEx is a complex and multidimensional process. It involves the lack or denial of resources, rights, goods and services, and the inability to participate in normal relationships and activities, available to the majority in a society, whether in economic, social, cultural or political arenas. It affects both the quality of life of individuals and the equity and cohesion of society as whole.
>
> Deep exclusion refers to exclusion across more than one domain or dimension of disadvantage, resulting in severe negative consequences for quality of life, well-being and future life chances.
>
> (Levitas et al., 2007: 9)

They devised the Bristol Social Exclusion matrix with three resource domains, four participation domains and three quality of life domains, whose relationships are shown in Figure 2.1.

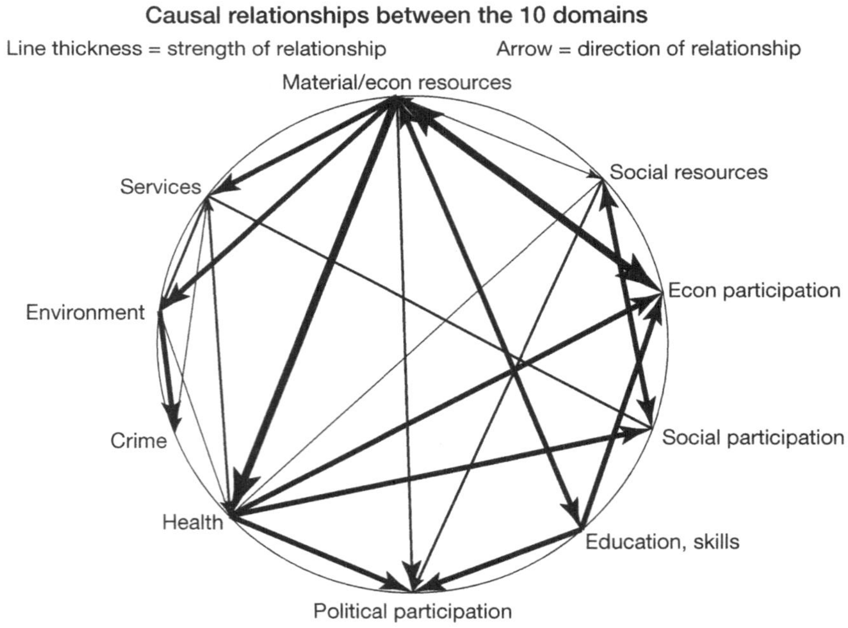

Source: Levitas et al 2007, Fig 6.1

Figure 2.1 The domains of social exclusion: the Bristol matrix

Levitas et al. used this analysis for the Social Exclusion Unit Task Force (SEUTF) on youth, working age families with and without dependent children and older people, and findings relating to the first and last are on pp 57–8 and pp 109–10. These studies involved identifying risk markers for increased likelihood of exclusion for individuals, families or areas, for example:

Resources	*	access to services – no bank account, private or public transport;
	*	social resources – no telephone/internet; no one to turn to in times of need;
Participation	*	economic – unemployment, carer, low skilled work;
	*	culture/education/skills – no qualifications; cannot afford to attend events;
Quality of life	*	living environment – overcrowded/poor quality housing, deprived locality;
	*	heath/wellbeing – limiting illness, poor mental health.

(SEUTF, 2008)

'Households below Average Income' (HBAI) is a frequent measure of poverty, used by the SEU and the Child Poverty Action Group as a main indicator, with the advantage of enabling comparisons with other EC states. In 1998, the Statistical Program Committee of the European Commission suggested a 60% threshold should be used for international comparisons. This translated to a median income of £440 in 2011–12, £367 after housing costs (Office of National Statistics (ONS), 2013). By this measure 23% of the UK population was poor in 1992–93, a stark increase from nine per cent since the Tory government took over in 1979, and in 2007–8, after all Labour's efforts, 11m were below this median before and 13.5m after housing costs. As Table 2.2 shows, New Labour achieved substantial falls in all three groups but after 2003–4 trends first flattened out then went into reverse. Tony Blair promised to eliminate child poverty, but stated that it would take 20 years – ten of which would halve child poverty, a target not reached. The recession with its benefit cuts and cost of living rises above inflation clearly set back progress considerably by 2011–12 (Alzubadi et al., 2013), with a new feature of high poverty rates amongst working age adults rather than pensioners, and most strongly amongst the under-35s (38%). These form what has become known as the 'precariat.' So, the new poor were working age adults (45%), lone parents (25%), single people (13%), childless couples (9%) and pensioners (8%). Aldridge et al. (2011) commented that the coalition was repeating the mistakes of New Labour. Monetary poverty brings in its train fuel poverty (affecting 16% of urban and 18% of rural households {DEFRA, 2013}, but 85% of the poorest tenth, and 5.5m [a fifth] of households – Macalister, T. *Guardian* 15 July 2011: 11) and transport poverty (which while not officially recognised is a high risk for 1.5m people, notably in Fenland, Devon, Cumbria, North York Moors and the north Pennines (Sustrans, 2012: 194).

Table 2.2 Poor children, adults, and pensioners 1994–5 to 2011–12 (% and 'relative income' – number below 0.6 median after housing costs, in real terms)

	Working age adults		Children		Pensioners	
	%	No (millions)	%	No (millions	%	No (millions
1994–5	23	7.5	37	4.7	36	3.6
1997–8	20	6.7	34	4.4	31	2.9
2003–4	14	5.0	20	2.5	10	1.1
2007–8	14	5.2	19	2.5	9	1.0
2011–12	21	7.9	17	3.5	14	1.6
Change 1998–9 to 2011–12	+2	1.3	–7	–0.9	–1	–0.1

Source: ONS, 2013

2011–2 HBAI after housing cost figures provided details:

* 28% of children were in poor households, but only 14% in workless households (2m);
* 62% of low-income households were in rented housing;
* 43% of lone parents were poor, 31% in the lowest income quintile;
* the highest levels of poor households were in London (because of housing costs), West Midlands and Yorks & Humber;
* ethnic minorities were overwhelmingly more likely to be in the lowest than the highest income quintile than whites (29% black, 35% Asian vs 19% for whites) but especially Pakistani/Bangladeshi groups (49/51%);
* 24% of disabled people in lowest quintile.

There are also subjective measures of poverty; consensus measures for the whole population can be seen by poor people as stigmatising. For example, policy measures exist that require poor people to produce evidence of eligibility for discounts, as they often still have to in appearing at leisure venues, unless operators have moved to swipe/smart cards where the confidential data can be hidden in the magnetic strip or chip (see Chapter 3).

Hills, Sefton and Stewart (2009, especially 342–59) clearly showed that certain policy areas responded to New Labour initiatives: tax redistribution to the poor, early years and schools programmes, New Deal and Pathway to Work employment measures, and programmes for poor neighbourhoods. But some were too small for the problems they faced, and above all, the richest tenth (rapidly getting much richer) were allowed to go without proportionate tax demands, thereby affecting the median threshold and sucking up finance to sustain those already just over the poverty threshold, leaving too little to 'pull up' some of those still poor.

The dynamics of poverty are important. From 1979 to 1994/5 the poorest tenth of the population suffered a fall in real income of eight per cent, while the average increased by 40%, and those of the top tenth by 68%. The Joseph Rowntree

Inquiry into Income and Wealth commented that the poorest three-tenths of people had failed to benefit from economic growth. Subsequently it claimed strikingly that while the richest fifty people in the UK were worth £3.4bn, it took 3.4m of the poorest to accumulate the same amount (Barclay, 1995).

Duration of poverty is an important issue, only recently researched. The British Household Panel Survey demonstrated a core of people with persistent low income – six per cent being in the lowest tenth of income for all five years between 1991 and 1995, and 12% in the bottom three. These were more likely to be lone parents and single State pensioners, living in public rented housing, in workless households, and without qualifications (Walker and Park, 1997).

Of course, the great bulk of research and policy reports focussed on people below the HBAI threshold, but in a neglected study Barry (2002: 17) suggested there is an upper threshold, less neat to define, for the affluent: 'the lower divides those who habitually participate in the mainstream institutions from those who are outside them…the upper is the one that divides those in the middle from those who can detach themselves'. These are the people who in sport can afford and choose private sports and fitness clubs and specialist holidays for themselves and their children, to obtain privacy and avoid crowding, to get specialist personal coaching and attention. As a result of both Tory and New Labour policies, this group has grown, and are the most active and highest spending, but little is known about them, because they and their suppliers are coy about spending and especially profit, and virtually all research is proprietary. Exceptionally, Warde and Bennett (2008) examined the cultural consumption of managerial and professional groups; for example, 31% of those with degrees practiced sport compared to only 15% of those with no qualification; equivalent figures for going to art galleries were 38% and 13%. When it came to the very rich, the top one per cent, in 2004 their spending on sports goods was 20.6 times the average, on sports admissions 8.5 times, on sports subscriptions 10.8 times, and on leisure services 5.8 times (Majima and Warde, 2008).

It is worth re-iterating what Becker and Boreham (2009: 1) wrote: 'SEx means being unable to access the things in life that most of society takes for granted. It's not just about having enough money.' As Atkinson (2000) commented, one of the problems of using income as a proxy for exclusion is that it is easy to neglect the relational and spatial aspects. Only recently have small area analyses of incomes and welfare payments begun.

The Universities of York and Loughborough pioneered a Minimum Income Standard which was 'more than food, clothes and shelter. It's about having what you need in order to have the opportunities and choices necessary to participate in society' (Padley and Hirsch, 2013: 6), and can be calculated for 107 types of household. Table 2.3 shows the expenditure on recreation and culture as part of budgets for four types of household.

Recreation and culture weekly expenditure also showed regional disparities from a UK average of £59.80 (between £50.50 in the NE and £71.40 in the SE) and between urban (£57.20 and 13% of total) and rural areas (£68.80 and 14%).

Table 2.3 Family expenditure on recreation 2011

Type of household/£ per week	Single adult working age	Pensioner couple	Couple with 2 children	Lone parent, one baby 0–1
Total (excl housing, childcare)	241	303	706	767
Social & cultural spending (%)	44	49	109	56
MIS excluding rent/childcare £	201	241	471	284
Disposable income as % of MIS on Minimum wage*	72	NA	84	87
MIS as % of median income	82	58	82	85
Lacking Minimum Income Standard, million (% of group)	1.35 (34)	0.8 (8)	1.84 (23)	0.83 (57)

Sources: Hirsch, 2011, Padley & Hirsch, 2013

* After council tax, rent & any childcare costs

After a slow creep in its importance to 2002–3, weekly spending on leisure goods and services fell back in the recession in absolute terms (Horsfield, 2012):

£/week (% of 2011 prices)	1995–6	2002–3	2011
Leisure goods	22.60 (5)	27.10 (5)	18.00 (5)
Leisure services	51.30 (11)	71.00 (13)	71.10 (15)

The geography of exclusion

Exclusion can be experienced by persons or groups and by places, neighbourhoods or communities (Healey, 1998; Walker, 1995). Interventions are aimed at both levels – welfare payments at the first, City Challenge and Single Regeneration Budget schemes, etc. at the second. The SEU's Neighbourhood Strategy implied interventions should be spatially targeted at the 3,000 worst areas. But not all its Policy Action Teams used a common definition of social exclusion or poverty, and Alcock and Craig (1998) recorded 63 local surveys of poverty but no common definition, where only one local authority in three with a strategy had any form of evaluation, so being 'data-rich but information-poor.'

Dorling et al. (2007) produced an atlas of poverty and wealth, dividing the population into five groups, the first two poor, the fourth and fifth wealthy by income or assets (the last being the one that Barry, 2002 referred to above as being above a second threshold). In Table 2.4, columns 5 and 6 show that while the core poor shrank, the breadline group grew, and the exclusive wealthy grew even more; moreover, the concentration of the latter was marked (columns 2 to 4). They demonstrated a marked north–south divide. Trends since increased the dissimilarities (confirmed by Fahmy et al., 2011).

Table 2.4 Indices of dissimilarity between rich and poor 1970–2000

| | Dissimilarity indices[a] | | | % of GB population | |
	1970	1990	2000	1990	2000
Core poor (income poor, materially deprived, subjectively poor)	12.3	15.3	14.1	14.3	11.2
Breadline poor (below BB index[b], excluded from society's norms)	14.7	17.1	18.3	21.3	27.0
Non-poor, non-wealthy (not in other 4 groups)		16.7	19.8	55.7	50.4
Asset wealthy (estimated by housing wealth/inheritance tax)		34.5	40.1	23.0	22.6
Exclusive wealthy (sufficient wealth to exclude themselves from society's norms)		60.6	59.7	3.5	5.6

Source: Dorling et al., 2007

Notes: a) Dissimilarity index shows % of people who would have to move to even out the distribution; b) Breadline Britain Index see Gordon and Forrest, in Gordon and Pantazis, 1997

A major debate regarding deprivation and poverty was how far area-based strategies are relevant. Is there an independent effect of living in an area, or is this merely a concatenation of different societal/national trends and influences? Rowntree's and Booth's early studies described in graphic Dickensian terms the lived experiences of poverty between various neighbourhoods. Marx and Engels did likewise, and so did Stedman-Jones in his careful (1971: 36) study of Victorian 'outcast (socially excluded?) London':

> as the Webbs later admitted, the First World War showed that the existence of the casual poor had not been the effect of some mutation induced by the degenerating effects of city life. The casual poor were shown to have been a social and not a biological creation...once decent and regular employment was available, the 'unemployables' proved impossible to find.
>
> (Stedman-Jones, 1971: 36, Peregrine edition)

Glennerster et al. (1999: 3) commented that 'this could be taken as a classic Keynsian view as well as a New Left one. A high enough tide of full employment will float off all poverty-stricken areas. Get the macro economy right and area policy will look after itself.'

Townsend was positive there was no area effect, after studying four especially poor areas in Glasgow, Salford, Neath and Belfast:

> however we try to define economically or socially deprived areas, unless we include over half the areas in the country, there will be more poor persons and poor children living outside them than in them...the pattern of inequality is set nationally.
>
> (Townsend, 1979: 60)

This has been repeatedly found since, whether the measures have been of income, poor housing, unemployment or poor health. Townsend did, however, speak of 'cardinal' policies needing to be national, leaving space for secondary, area-based ones.

Economists argue that cities have areas of growth and decline, and trying to intervene to slow or stop a downward spiral of the former will merely trap communities in a low but subsidised existence. Some American sociologists (e.g., Park in 1952 and Burgess in 1967) have argued that such areas are needed to provide transition zones where newcomers can find cheap housing, low paid starter jobs, and cheap premises for the new and innovating businesses any city needs.

But in recent decades the growth of poverty has resulted in more evident and frequent concentrations of urban poverty. This led politicians and social and physical planners to pragmatically devise area-based policies to attack the problems, typified in the SEU's focus on the 3,000 worst housing estates in England. Thus arose the Urban Programme, the Single Regeneration Budget, and under the Blair Government the proliferation of Action Zones (see pp 34, 208, 214). There was never adequate recognition of the equivalent rural problem (see Chapter 11), because though the levels were no less, the absolute numbers were smaller and scattered, and never commanded the same political response. The Rural Development Areas were based on narrower, mainly economic criteria, and consequently were more tightly drawn.

But some will now argue strongly that while city-wide employment changes may trigger these differences, once set in motion they become self-reinforcing, with better skilled and better paid workers choosing to move out. This was Jargowsky's (1996) thesis, based on studying Milwaukee, concluding that one-fifth of the poverty could be attributed to area effects. In the UK, recent economic theory suggested that one reason that the economy cannot run at full capacity is because there are pools of people outside the labour market (Layard, 1997), and that the Bank of England chooses to exercise anti-inflationary checks on economic growth before it reaches a level that would involve these people.

Poor management of public housing, and the sale of Council houses under the Thatcher regimes also meant that public housing increasingly became a refuge of the old, the disabled and mentally and physically ill, ex-prisoners, and the very poor (Power, 1997). Fitzpatrick (2004) was clear that place poverty is matter of social justice, at its most extreme in London, and that the housing market is at its heart. There is little data available and few attempts yet to explain how these factors interact. Despite evidence that area-based policies do not hit the majority of the poor (Oatley, 1998) and may not have long-term benefits, the Blair government introduced separately defined Education and Health Action Zones, and Sport England followed suit with 35 Sport Action Zones, based on the Index of Multiple deprivation (DETR, 1998).

In the late 1970s/early 1980s there was much debate and an ESRC programme on transmitted deprivation (whereby successive generations remain locked in poverty), and while there were intergenerational effects, scepticism about a cycle in which people became trapped (Brown and Madge, 1982). More recently, however, analysis of people born in 1958 and studied regularly until they were 33 years old showed clearly that poverty, family disruption, and contact with the police resulted in lower earnings, which were also influenced by lower social class and poor school performance:

> Thus there is little doubt that social exclusion, as captured by the adult outcomes and childhood factors used here, is transmitted through the generations and through the life-course...But it is essential to emphasize that all these associations capture here are just aggregate tendencies observed and in no sense determinist...Thus, there is huge scope for many, if not most, individuals to escape from the patterns and tendencies observed.
>
> (Hobcraft, 1998: 95)

Hobcraft therefore argued strongly for better investigation of those who get out of the trap. The area effects and particular exclusion problems and attempted remedies will be examined in Chapter 10 for both urban and rural areas.

Sport, social class and exclusion

Debates rage in sociology as to whether social class boundaries have dissolved and 'we are all middle class now', whether processes of individualisation are breaking up the identity of social classes and inequalities, making other differences personal, and so non-class coalitions are formed, often briefly, when threats appear (Beck, 1992: 00–01; see also Savage, 2000). Roberts concurred with this view, saying that currently there is a:

> leisure democracy in the sense that members of all social strata do similar things in their leisure, but democracy is not the same as equality: the privileged classes are distinguished by their ability to do more, which they exercise in virtually all areas of out-of-home leisure. Money is now at the root of the main differences between the use of leisure in different social strata, and the leisure differences between them are basically and blatantly inequalities rather than alternative ways of life.
>
> (Roberts, 1999: 7)

Marshall (1997: 6) refuted such arguments as 'no less premature than their predecessors,' using data from the International Social Justice projects showing the chances for working-class children in Britain of becoming a member of the 'salariat' as 5–6 to 1, compared to 3–4 to 1 in the US, and 4–5 to 1 in West Germany. Adonis and Pollard (1997: ix) went further, stating Britain's 'class system separates its people as clinically today as it did half a century ago – far from diminishing, class divisions are intensifying as the distance between the top and bottom widens and the classes at both extremes grow in size and identity' and (1997: 44), 'far from leisure being in the vanguard of the classless society, the way we live our lives is a daily, hourly testament to our place in Britain's class structure.' Roberts (2013) examined the effect of the recession on participation spending and class, discovering:

- participation in sport was stable (based on *Active People* survey)
- it was unresponsive to changes in unemployment
- spending on leisure services in 2011 was 101% of 2007 but on leisure goods 79%, indicating people not exchanging/trading up or delaying buying sports equipment, caravans and boats
- people have been going out less frequently and spending less per occasion
- regarding social class small participation decreases in the noughties did not reflect widening income disparities, though still large

Group	GHS 1977		GHS 2002	Active People Survey 2008–9 (at least 30 min moderate intensity)	Household spend £	
	Outdoor	Indoor	All		2004–5	2011
					Recreation & culture	
Large employer/ higher manager	38	24	59	55	100.6	15.3
Intermediate	28	19	43	49	52.2	61.0
Routine	14	11	30	29	62.3	46.8

He concluded: in leisure 'most people seem to use their exceptional scope for choice [of activity and provider] to stick to routines. Leisure supplies reliabilities and continuities in lives during recessions...when much else is in flux' (2013: 16).

Other sociologists of sport also doubted the disappearance of class. Bourdieu (1978, 1985) argued for early socialisation in structuring individual choices and preferences, and then of the social environment, which he called 'habitus' in shaping youth and adult practices. Kew (1997: 49) said he provided 'compelling evidence for the saliency of social class in structuring if not determining a person's choice and preferences in sport'. Atkinson (2007) comprehensively rejected Beck's idea that individualisation made people masters of their own fate. Using National Child Development Study data on the impact father's social class and academic rankings at age 11 had on social class destinations at age 33, Savage and Egerton (1997) clearly showed that sons of people in the service class are very strongly likely to end there, especially in professions, depending on material advantages. Elsewhere, Sugden and Tomlinson said:

> For Bourdieu, then, sport...acts as a kind of badge of social exclusivity and cultural distinctiveness for the dominant classes; it operates as a means of control or containment of the working or popular classes; it is represented as a potential source of escape and mobility for talented working-class performers...; it articulates the fractional status distinctions that exist within

the ranks of larger class groupings; and it reveals the capacity of the body to express social principles and cultural meanings, for physical capital to connect with forms of economic and cultural capital.

(Sugden and Tomlinson, 2000: 19)

Using cohort data, Savage (2011) found that in the 2000's there were groups with very different chances of being upwardly and downwardly mobile:

Upwardly	Downwardly
men 40%	permanent part-timers 87%
professionals 55% cf. managers	people without a degree 37%
London	SW 83% NE 73%
	79% if any significant joblessness

For Bourdieu, sport was a social arena, where, as Jarvie and Maguire argued (1994: 97) 'different classes derive different kinds of profit from sport in terms of health, slimness, relaxation and social relationships,' according to the 'capital' they possess, not just economic but also cultural (e.g., education, knowledge of high culture and art) and symbolic (presentation of self-demeanour). Social capital in personal terms comprises the education and skills they possess, not just for work but for political and social participation including in sport and leisure, but also the confidence to seek out opportunities, and the ability to organise one's time, friends and companions, childcare and transport to make participation real. Scores of site surveys and some home interviews make it clear that these are not equally distributed. Horne, Tomlinson and Whannel (1999: 107) said 'in contemporary sports cultures class categories...continue to influence participation and activity,' and they confirmed Tomlinson's view from over a decade earlier (1986) about 'issues of access and exclusion...still at the heart of British sports cultures' (1999: 109). Reviewing trends in sports participation, Sport England's Head of Research (Rowe et al., 2004: 9) wrote 'sport in England has continued to be characterised by considerable social inequities.'

Exclusion, sport and citizenship

Marshall (1950) provided a foundation for modern concepts of citizenship, defining it as having three areas of rights, to: equality before the law, universal franchise in politics, and access to services and welfare benefits. Liberals have interpreted citizenship as the right to control their own activities and own property in leisure as much as other life spheres – what Byrne (2001) called 'possessive individualism.' In the US it led to 'blaming the poor' for their poverty, a version of the Moral Underclass discourse. Conservatives interpreted it as status-based control, in leisure and other public services, as benevolent paternalism in providing what leaders thought citizens should have. Socialists saw it as solidarity, leading to Keynesian provision, including leisure, to offer citizens choices, what Coalter (1998) called a 'welfarist approach'.

Coalter attributed a 'strong' version of welfarism to Ravenscroft (1993), who opined that the state has a social responsibility, regardless of its dominant economic ideology, to provide for the basic leisure needs of society. Ravenscroft described the shift from a basic welfare view of sports services under the Thatcher government as a response to scepticism about what he called (1993: 5) 'the overplayed and unsubstantiated' external/social benefits long claimed for sport. With a bias to male and middle-income users (Audit Commission, 1989) and as one of only a few face-to-face charged municipal services, sports services were ripe for marketisation under Compulsory Competitive Tendering (see Chapter 3).

Ravenscroft (1993: 2) argued that in sport the higher-order individual human needs for esteem and self-actualisation became emphasised over the lower-order communal ones of consumption for health, quality of life and social benefits through affiliation, and yet access had been restricted by ability to pay to 'the "good" citizen at the expense of deprivation, rejection, and suppression of the "deviant" citizen,' who were respectively leisure 'gainers' and 'losers.' The losers were supplied only through legal necessity or social expediency, and represented a policy shift from local democracy in which 'the politics of choice was replaced by the politics of means.' Subsequently, he argued (Ravenscroft, 1996: 71) that sport and leisure as a form of consumption and experience was central to the New Right politics.

But while CCT improved efficiency in reducing costs through breaking the unionisation of much labour, and promoted popular, revenue-earning activities, it almost certainly held down or reduced usage by poor and already under-represented groups like the disabled, ethnic minorities, and one-parent families for whom such public services were intended (McIntosh and Charlton, 1985; Taylor and Page, 1994). Dustin, More and McAvoy (2000) made the same arguments about US National and State parks in relation to extended charging. Thus Blair's introduction of measuring success by Best Value retained the efficiency objective but added that of quality and customer satisfaction through involving citizens in planning and monitoring provision. Ravenscroft (1998: 49–51) doubted this would change the political map and hoped local authorities and their professionals would 'remain committed to the needs of the community rather than embracing euphemistic notions of consumer focus,' as indeed most did.

Coalter (1998) described Roberts' (1978) approach as a 'weak' version of welfarist ideology when he suggested the state might be interested in distributive justice, though 'recreation...interests are too diverse to make their satisfaction into rights of citizenship' and, within a pluralist view, felt the market was an effective participatory mechanism. Coalter (2007) argued that leisure professionals have failed to produce output and especially outcome measures, and leisure researchers to define needs and to show how citizens' obligations and responsibilities are delivered. Earlier, he had said (Coalter, 1989a: 27) there was 'a lack of a coherent philosophy or politics of "recreational welfare" with which to resist consumerist definitions and managerialist practices.' For members of clubs and governing bodies this was clearer than for individuals and consumers.

In the case studies in Chapters 4, 5, 9 and 10, I make a small start in empirical work on this.

The European Foundation for the Improvement of Living and Working Conditions (1995: 4) wrote 'improving access and increasing consumer involvement in public services is not a substitute for promoting equal rights, treatment and opportunities for users of welfare services.' Coalter (1990) thought consumer involvement might be a strong defence and political justification for public leisure services. In 2000, he developed this idea that leisure studies had been too pro-public and anti-commercial in its views, blaming it on a loose mixture of Marxism and Methodism! (Coalter, 2000: 64). He set out various perspectives:

- *Pessimistic Marxism,* represented by Clarke and Critcher (1985) – consumerism as false consciousness, where the ability to produce sport as a series of products is its political validation, and it develops a hold over its customers and constant innovation is needed to maintain consumption.
- *Pessimistic elitism,* represented by Tomlinson (1991), who spoke of shallow products and exchanges pandering to the 'whims' of consumers in contrast to the [unexplained] 'interests' of citizens.
- *Optimistic Marxism,* ever-widening desires can never be adequately met and consumers always want for more, or where some, often youths, seek to subvert the market.
- *Productionism,* a weak version of the alienation in pessimistic Marxism, where some value is gained but consumers are passive (as argued by Parker, 1997) or where serious leisure is like work (according to Stebbins, 1997).

He went on to argue that if there is anything in the concept of social citizenship, then SEx needs to be theorised in terms of which groups are excluded and on what basis. I come back to this argument in Chapter 11.

Sport was seen by the Labour government of the 1970s as 'part of the fabric of the social services' (Dept of the Environment, 1977), and Coalter, Duffield and Long (1986) spoke of a policy shift from 'Recreation as Welfare' (of participants) to 'Recreation for Welfare', as instrumental benefits of health and self esteem and constructively using the time of unemployed youth. In the 1980s and 1990s economic concerns overrode social ones, and sport, like the arts, became a means of regenerating towns, and of creating income and jobs. Then, as critiques of these approaches grew, a wider concept of citizenship appeared, and Ravenscroft (1993) argued for access to leisure and recreation to be seen as part of 'inclusive citizenship' (Healey, 1998), reflecting Commins' systems mentioned above.

Veit-Wilson distinguished between weak and strong concepts of social exclusion:

> in the weak version, the solutions lie in altering the excluded people's handicaps and character and integrating them into the dominant society;

[the stronger form involves identifying] the role of those who are doing the excluding and therefore aim for solutions which reduce the power of exclusion.

(Veit-Wilson, 1998: 5)

Social inclusion became a mantra for the Blair government; but, as several commentators have remarked, it is repeated against a background of shifting views about the role of the welfare state from being a prop to passive recipients in need of help, to a springboard for improving conditions of life and especially work. Thus New Ambitions for Our Country: A New Contract for Welfare stated:

> The new welfare state should help and encourage people of working age to work where they are capable of doing so. The government's aim is to rebuild the welfare state around work.
>   Our ambition is nothing less than a change of culture among benefit claimants, employers and public servants – with rights and responsibilities on all sides. Those making the shift from welfare into work will be provided with positive assistance, not just a welfare payment.

(Dept of Social Security, 1998: 23–4)

Chancellor Gordon Brown, drove this home in a 1996 speech:

> For far too long we have used the tax and benefit system to compensate people for their poverty rather than doing something more fundamental – tackling the root causes of poverty and inequality…the road to equal opportunity starts not with tax rates but with jobs, education, and the reform of the welfare state and redistributing existing resources more efficiently and equitably.

(quoted by Powell, 1999: 18–9)

Minister Peter Mandelson described poverty and social exclusion as 'a scourge and waste' and 'the greatest social crisis of our times' (Mandelson, 1997: 6, 9).

Consequently, Giddens argued that New Labour equated equality with inclusion and inequality with exclusion (1998: 02), and Levitas (1996) and Lister (1998) stressed that the inclusive mechanisms for Blair were education and employment. Also the new politics changed the view of citizenship from 'dutiless rights' to 'conditional welfare' (Powell, 1999: 9), or again in Giddens' words (1998: 5), 'a prime motto for the new politics, no rights without responsibilities.' The 1998 Labour conference document stated 'work for those who can; security for those who cannot.' (p. 67). Since the number of working age households where no one was working had increased from 8.2% in 1979 to 20.3% in 1996–7 and 17.1% (3.5m) in 2012 (ONS, 2013), this priority was not to be wondered at.

What inferences can one take from this set of policy attitudes and aspirations?

• first, that the belief that work will provide the income, status and self-esteem to make recipients into active citizens, exercising their political and consumer rights, cannot be achieved quickly;
• it will also depend on the jobs being decently skilled and paid;
• in the meantime the secondary support from welfare payments will be necessary.

It is also worth remarking that New Labour's early rhetoric did not mention sport and leisure (other than fleetingly in the SEU's Bringing Britain Together, 1998: 9, 58, 70), nor did the major discussion papers (Levitas, 1998, Lister 1998, Powell, 1999). Nonetheless, there was stress on building up community capacity and social capital, this time in the communal rather than the individual sense, particularly in areas needing economic regeneration. This was seen as strengthening civic networks and infrastructure, a sense of local/neighbourhood identity, a level of participation and solidarity, and in Putnam's (2000) use of the term also trust and reciprocity between citizens and their civic institutions. Ironically, when the Conservative–Liberal coalition squeaked into power in 2010, a new mantra appeared of the Big Society, where local self-organised activism would replace an overbearing and inefficient state apparatus, much cut back. Meanwhile, the rich continued to get the lion's share of wealth and income (Chapters 3 and 12).

MacDonald and Leary (2005) confirmed that marked SEx and its associated guilt, shame, loneliness from lack of support, could produce real pain just as much as physical illnesses, because the mechanisms were the same. Several studies suggested that more egalitarian societies are healthier because of their social cohesion and smaller inequalities (Wilkinson, 1998). In 2009 Wilkinson and Prickett produced their influential Spirit Level, relating over twenty international validated sets of social data to income inequality for 21 advanced nations, which produced a consistent picture, with the Scandinavian countries and Japan at the equal end and the UK and US at the unequal end of the scale (Figure 2.2). Coalter (2013b) agreed that the Scandinavian comparison is inappropriate and points to the severe limitations of sports policy. Updating the 1999 COMPASS project comparing sports participation, Gratton, Rowe and Veal (2011: 15) confirmed that the strongest correlation was with income inequity, above population age structure, GDP and hours of work. Vanhuysse's (2013) 4-dimensional index of intergenerational justice (considering policy outcomes for child poverty, social spending on old people, national debt per child, ecological footprint) and showed UK as 11th of 29 OECD states (ranging from Estonia as the most just and US as the least.

In Chapter 12, I explain why the policy choice from 2002 onwards to raise English sports participation to the level of Finland's (one of the highest in the world) was neither logical nor feasible because of the huge gulf in inequality. Glyn and Miliband (1994) and Osberg (1995) argued more equal societies grow faster, which would make sense intuitively; a human analogy is that inequities cause tensions and friction in a body politic as much as in families or friendship circles. In the EU 27 states, the UK ranked eighth highest in terms of social exclusion, with people with minimal secondary education, single parents, housing tenants and retired and unemployed people all above the EU averages (Eurostat, 2010).

Line thickness = strength of relationship

Source: Wilkinson and Pickett, 2009. Reproduced by permission of the Equality Trust

Figure 2.2 Income inequality: the UK-Finland gap

A healthy society is one of social inclusion, and the policy to secure it, defined by the European Commission (2005) as:

> a process which ensures that those at risk of poverty and social exclusion gain the opportunities and resources necessary to participate fully in economic, social and cultural life and to enjoy a standard of living and well-being that is considered normal in the society in which they live. It ensures that they have a greater participation in decision making which affects their lives and access to their fundamental rights.
>
> (European Commission, 2005)

Lister (1999) spoke of SEx as multidimensional, where individual factors reinforce each other – sexism, ageism, disablism, poverty, geography, to which paid work was not the whole solution without substantial income redistribution. In Chapter 3, I look at poverty, which I still consider the core of exclusion from sport and leisure as well as many other aspects of life, and at these other dimensions. Looking back over three generations, Townsend's (2010) judgement was that 'we seem to have convinced ourselves that there is almost no poverty in Britain. In fact there seems to be a substantial amount and more, by any reasonable criterion, than we care to admit.'

3 Poverty

The core of exclusion

Jesus is recorded as saying *the poor you will have among you always, and you can help them whenever you like*.

Mark 14.7 Revised English Bible (1989: NT 44)

Introduction: why we know so little about the economic gradient in sport and leisure

We have seen in Chapter 2 that social exclusion has many faces, and that unemployment, disability, single parenthood, and race have strong influences on exclusion. But for me, poverty *is* the core of exclusion, as a factor in itself and compounding the others just mentioned. In this section, I look at why we have so little data on leisure and poverty and why we often use social class as a surrogate measure. In the next section, I set the context for policy since the 1970s. Then I review evidence of the influence of price/cost on sports and recreation participation, the growth of local authority anti-poverty strategies and Leisure Cards/Passports to Leisure. Next, are case studies of early, successful Leisure Cards in Leicester and Oxford, followed by another of a Birmingham project in collaboration with the Primary Care Trusts devised after careful social marketing. Byrne (2001: 10) stated: 'although income is only a proxy for exclusion....we can get a grip on processes that are central to exclusion in relation to exploitation.'

Leisure studies as a new academic field has been criticised for many shortcomings, but curiously not for ignoring poverty. Four features make this chapter difficult to write. First, leisure studies have produced only a few discussions of income and poverty, and mainstream poverty studies have mainly ignored or neglected leisure issues. Second, lack of income data means that major sociological texts on leisure and sport have focused on the more difficult to define concept of class (e.g., Horne, Tomlinson and Whannel, 1999; Sleap, 1998; Polley, 1997, Kew, 1997). With the growth of social mobility, Roberts did mention income, while then going on at greater length to discuss class:

Pay has always been the most plausible explanation of why the higher occupational strata do more. Income is the source of the clearest, widest, and most consistent leisure contrasts...income effects are so powerful that they override what, all other things being equal, would presumably be the negative leisure effects of relatively long work hours. These effects are long-standing and show no signs of diminishing.

(Roberts, 1999: 95–6)

But see his modified ideas from 2013, p 243. Third, most analyses of sports and leisure participation are by Socio-Economic Group or Social Class (as used by the Market Research industry), which relate to income in a loose fashion. Fourth, none of the 'mainstream' poverty analyses discuss impacts on sport and leisure patterns. Despite extensive background research on poverty and SEx by Collins, Henry and Houlihan (1999), even Policy Action Team 10's report on *Sport and Arts* (in SEx) concentrated on ethnic groups and disability, saying only about economic disparities: 'people from lower socio-economic categories tend in general to participate less in the arts/sport and therefore to benefit less from Government support for the arts/sport.' (DCMS, 1999: 95–6)

The context of anti-poverty policies and leisure

Chapter 2 charted the movement from the concept of absolute through relative poverty to that of social exclusion. The post-war Keynsian economy was paralleled by the development of a welfare state based on virtually full employment and free health and pension systems. While public agencies were set up for broadcasting, national parks and the arts, it was not until the early 1970s, under the direction of the newly-formed Sports Council, that local authorities were urged and grant-aided to make a provision of sports facilities in all areas. Urban deprivation, however, only became an issue after urban unrest late in that decade. Townsend and Abel Smith reminded society that poverty had not gone away, suggesting in 1965 that 14% of people were poor. In the US, Kaplan (1975) suggested that the poor included the 'leisure poor,' comprising low-paid workers, the long-term unemployed, and unskilled young people unable to forge a career. Townsend (1979) and Mack and Lansley (1985) included leisure activities in definitions of poverty.

During the 1970s, local authority leisure services grew. While sports halls and swimming pools had encouraged middle-income people to participate more than the poor (Grimshaw and Prescott-Clarke, 1978; Collins 1979 in Henry, 1993), across-the-board concessions were intended to keep prices low and encourage participation, especially for children and pensioners. Gratton and Taylor (1985) argued they benefited the higher socio-economic groups who were well-informed and mobile enough to use them without social barriers, that is, that many were what economists call 'free riders' in no need of subsidy.

As crises developed in capitalism and unemployment grew, government grants became focussed on regenerating old urban areas. Sports policy followed suit,

Houlihan (1991) suggesting that the Sports Council's Sport for All campaign had been transmuted into 'sport for the disadvantaged' and for 'inner city youth', or as Coalter (1989a) described it, 'sport as welfare.' The Sports Council (1982) identified in its strategy *Sport in the Community* several target groups, none specifically poor, though Action Sport schemes were aimed at promoting involvement amongst inner city youngsters. Glyptis (1989: 42) commented on a dual purpose for public leisure provision, of enjoyment and a belief that it could *contain* 'urban problems, build a sense of community and...overcome class and other social inequalities.'

Later, a Tory party in power determined to reduce public spending and increase its efficiency would see public leisure services, with their emphasis on marketing and direct delivery to customers, as a likely candidate for Compulsory Competitive Tendering. However, obsession with reducing costs and maximising income, rather than quality and equity, meant encouraging popular activities and regular users, at the cost of protecting social/sports development objectives of serving deprived and low participant groups (Collins, 1997). As a discretionary service, municipal sport and leisure have gone on taking disproportionate financial cuts. In those towns they controlled, the urban New Left reacted by producing anti-poverty strategies. They also used sport, arts and leisure, first as a tool to tackle inequalities in direct provision (including Leisure Cards), and second as a means to support local groups and events, some explicitly poor, others like disabled and ethnic minorities with a high share of poverty.

More narrowly, the Sports Council saw 'two distinct markets' for sport –

> the larger being composed of generally affluent people who are in work, healthy and well-educated, the smaller being people who are less healthy, often unemployed and concentrated in urban and rural areas with a poor economic base.
>
> (Sports Council, 1988: 3)

Its strategy went on to say of these markets: 'the former group provides considerable opportunities for the private and voluntary sectors, while the public sector must play a leading role in meeting the needs of the latter.' This begins to hint at the idea of a two-tier society, of consumer rights for those rewarded with the financial power to exercise them, and of citizen's needs to be met for those who do not.

John Major's rhetoric after 1991 was of 'one nation' Conservatism. However, the 1995 White Paper, *Sport: Raising the Game* (DNH, 1995), concentrated on a supposed decline in school sport and on overcoming Britain's lack of success in elite/international competition. Introducing the National Lottery initially benefited local sport greatly, but an increasing proportion was directed to excellence after 1997, when no reference was made to encouraging people in disadvantaged groups, other than the disabled. Also, virtually no mention was made of the local authorities' role (Collins, 1996, Houlihan and Lindsey, 2013). These positions were repeated in the English Sports Council's strategy *England: The sporting nation* (ESC, 1997a).

The Blair government took office in 1997 with a new rhetoric of SEx and of providing a high quality modernised local government. The demanding Best Value regime, while removing the 'C' representing compulsion in tendering, required public authorities to demonstrate that they were providing the services all groups of residents and local business wanted, efficiently and to high quality. After the publication of *Bringing Britain Together*, it required all the agencies and Lottery funds to have a policy for combating SEx. This was all done, however, with a self-imposed spending limit until 1999, and a stress on improving employability as the main way out of deprivation (Levitas' SI Discourse, 1998).

A governmental sport strategy *England: A Sporting Future for all* (DCMS, 2000) partly reflected Levitas' Moral Underclass discourse, harking back to Glyptis' (1989) dual role for sport. In its more significant *Game Plan* (DCMS, 2002: 89), it said that interventions should 'focus on the most economically disadvantaged groups.' The ESC had already changed to its Lottery rules to encourage applications from deprived communities by designating Priority Areas (defined according to DETR statistics) whereby local contributions to schemes would be reduced from 35% to 20%.

In 2000, Sport England launched Sport Action Zones as priority areas, and within its Active Communities scheme, showcase projects aimed at youth and some excluded groups. Yet in its *Framework* report (2004: 13) it mentioned simplistically 'lack of transport is often the biggest issue in rural areas, whilst money is more commonly a barrier in urban priority areas' (Chapter 10 gives the lie to this analysis); SEx did not get a mention, either in the Henley Centre's 'drivers of change' in the social value of sport section, or in Lord Carter's (2005) evidence report. A drastic move from 'sport for [wider social] good' to 'sport for sport's sake' was encapsulated in the next *Strategy 2008–11* (Sport England, 2008a: 1), describing the goal as 'maximising English sporting success in all its forms', focussing solely on sport and leaving issues like transport and health to the Departments. So, once again, under-participation by gender, disability and ethnic group was mentioned with no context of income or disadvantage.

Sport and poverty, and prices

Wilkinson (1998) confirmed Townsend's analysis that poverty and exclusion have correlations with crime, suicide, fat- and sugar-rich diets, high rates of smoking and overall poorer health, and feelings of powerlessness over life: 'in Britain overall crime rates are so closely related to measures of deprivation that it is difficult to distinguish between maps of crime and maps of deprivation.' He demonstrated a strong correlation of income inequality and:

> having control over one's work and domestic circumstances, job security, a regular income, social support, the absence of long-term difficulties and life threatening events, quality of parenting and lack of family conflict early in life, all appear unexpectedly successful in explaining differences in physical disease.
>
> (Wilkinson, 1998: 78)

The Health Education Authority (1999) recorded lower physical activity by unskilled manual workers, people with fewer than five GCSE 'O' level qualifications, with disabilities, in ethnic minorities, over 65 years of age, and living in council housing.

Poverty affects access to leisure: apart from a few happy hermits or those who have opted out of mainstream society, there can be virtually no one who is poor and not excluded from leisure and culture, for much of leisure is now commodified and has to be paid for directly, or indirectly though transport, parking fees or food and drink associated with many activities. Dawson, from Canada two decades ago, opined 'that to be without access to or opportunity for leisure, is to be poor' (1988: 230).

Based on broad arguments, Polley indicated that, since the Second World War, choice of sport has still been seen as a signifier of lifestyle and indirectly of status, but that:

> what has been notable is the fluidity of this process, linked to disposable income, private transport and the growth of the white-collar workforce. Here, previously restricted sports have become more mixed, and the ownership and control of certain sports has been contested in class terms.
>
> (Polley, 1997: 113–4)

For a minority, sport has also been a ladder to social status, and even more a means to gaining high incomes and professional advancement (Holt, 1990).

I have said there was a tradition of keeping public leisure services as cheap as possible in the UK, and Gratton and Taylor (1994) were convinced that for many in society demand was elastic, i.e., that price increases would be absorbed by users because the value of sport to them was sufficient. As Competitive Tendering loomed, the Audit Commission (1989) argued for more facility costs to be borne by users, because most were more affluent groups, and too much of the burden fell on poorer groups who made less or no use of them. In the 1980s prices increased steadily above inflation, so that the costs recovered increased from 27% to 44% for sports halls and from 12% to 36% for swimming pools By 1998–99 the recovery rate was 30% in England and Wales, but 40% in non-Metropolitan districts for halls and pools combined (CIPFA, 1999).

Despite such policy discourse, there was no empirical test of the elasticity of demand and underlying factors until the Scottish Sports Council commissioned CLR (1993) and Gratton and Taylor (1994) to investigate the impact of pricing experiments in four authorities in Scotland, subsidising the experiments, involving:

- increases in charges for most users of two Edinburgh leisure centres, to be offset by introducing a Leisure Card for needy groups;
- increases in prices by 36–100% from a low base in Biggar's sports centre, in rural Clydesdale;

- pricing a new fitness suite in East Kilbride to break-even, while increasing other prices;
- Most radically, abolishing charges for eight months at Port Glasgow's swimming pool, and then re-introducing charges.

Table 3.1 shows the changes in price, use and revenue, the reaction of users to the increases, and how far users (U), general sports participants (P) and non-participants (N) in the facility catchments thought price and time were constraints on their sports participation.

As the Table shows, there was:

- no great resistance to the price increases;
- no great loss of use except at one of the Edinburgh centres; while those who had stopped were mainly young men, at school or unemployed;
- free use at Port Glasgow pool led to 15% more use, because one in three existing users went more often rather than new users being attracted, or diverted from the nearest pool;
- price was a constraint on one in ten users but far fewer residents, in contrast to two or three times as many who saw time as a problem.

Of 1,795 residents, 955 spent £3.42 a week on sport, with entry prices comprising only a third of this; meanwhile, PIEDA (1991) found them to be only 16% of all Scottish sports expenditure. So, time seemed to be a greater constraint than price

Table 3.1 Consumer reactions to four Scottish pricing experiments

Authority	% Changes in			Attitude to new price % 'too high'	% Constrained by	
	price	use	revenue		price	time
E Kilbride	+10			11	U 11	U 4
New fitness	+15	+134	+120	24	P 6	P 16
Old fitness	+13	+3	+19	8	N 1	N 23
Edinburgh					U 9	U 3
No1	+70	−37	+11	13	P 6	P 24
No2	+31			12	N 1	N 25
Clydesdale	+71	+9	+39	12	U 10	U 6
	(+31–+100				P{ 1	P 15
	for various				N 1	N 25
	groups)					
Inverclyde	−100 then	+15	−54[a]	na	U 0	U 9
pool	reinstated				P 1	P 11
					N 1	N 22

Source: Gratton & Taylor, 1994

Note: Revenue for Inverclyde is for other than admission

to playing sport, as indicated by Kay and Jackson (1991) and Coalter (1991). Gratton and Taylor commented (1994: 4) 'it is likely that the price of time is rising relative to the price of goods.' But these surveys did not differentiate samples of poor people. The day-to-day experience of sports centre managers in general was often different: those on limited incomes, youngsters, unemployed people, single parents, many old age pensioners – were income inelastic (CLR, 1993). Compared to working adults, they looked to older, cheaper swimming pools to get as many swims as possible for a given sum, and reduced the frequency of attendance when prices increased.

In contrast, Glasgow City Council introduced free swimming for young people via two cards – Young Scot Glasgow Card for 16–35s and the Kidz Card for under-12s. Within months, attendances had increased by 26% (Macdonald, 2001). In 2009–11 in the hope of driving up participation, New Labour Sports Minister Gerry Sutcliffe promoted free swimming for over 60s and under 16s, as already been tried in Wales and Glasgow. There was a surge of use by both groups in Wales (Bolton, 2010), while PWC (2010) estimated for England:

• for under 16s, 5.5m more swims and a net 115,000 more swimmers;
• for over 60s,1.5m more swims and only 23,000 new swimmers.

These figures were low because in both groups but particularly the over 60s, many already had access to free or reduced-price swimming. Sutcliffe's successor, Tory minister Hugh Robertson, cancelled it, saying 'the programme is a luxury we can no longer afford' (*Guardian* 16 June 2010). O'Brien (2013) saw it as an economistic result of growing Treasury control, allowing it to be presented as a non-political decision.

In Finland, Puranaho (2000) showed how, even in such a high-income society, the costs of sports training for regular young competitors could comprise a social problem, and most parents wanted costs cut. For example, young soccer players spent between £460 a year (when aged 8) and £2,300 (aged 16), while ice hockey players spent £400 and £2,860 respectively. More and Stevens (2000: 349) found entrance fee increases over a period of five years for public outdoor recreation areas in Vermont and New Hampshire lead to 23% of low-income users reducing their use or going elsewhere compared to 11% of high income users.

In contrast, McCabe (1993) and colleagues attempted to construct a 'Modest-but-Adequate' (MbA) family budget for six household types, and also set a Low Cost (LC) budget, (using public transport rather than cars, consuming no alcohol or cigarettes, taking a day trip rather than a holiday, trips to the cinema and stately homes only twice a year, and little or no regular sports participation). Table 3.2 shows that, even accepting the unrealistic assumption about smoking and drinking, for those on the LC budget in 1992 income support was inadequate to cover the needs of three of the four groups. For the MbA budgets the leisure figures were less than the medians found in the Family Expenditure Survey for most households.

Table 3.2 Modest-but-adequate and low cost family leisure budgets 1992 (£ a week)

Family type	MBA leisure budget[a]	MBA total budget	Family type	Low cost leisure budget	Low cost total budget	Income support
Single male, 30	16.46	150.34	–	–	–	–
Single female, 72 years	12.63	119.30	Lone pensioner/ own-occupier	4.42	67.06	57.15
2 adults	28.19	210.87	Lone pensioner/ LA tenant[b]	2.81	53.16	57.15
2 adults + 2 children 4 & 10	32.24	316.50	2 adult+2 children, 4 & 10/ LA tenant	13.97	141.40	105.00
2 adults + 2 children, 10 & 16	37.19	322.23		–	–	–
Lone parent + 2 children 4 & 10	27.64	296.04	Lone parent/LA tenant	11.76	110.72	85.60

Sources: McCabe, 1995 updated for inflation from 1991in Barclay, 1995

Notes: a) MBA=Modest-but-adequate; b   LA =local authority

We now turn to Leisure Cards as a common form of intervention, but it is notable that compared to general clothing and food retailing, while there are premium brands in expensive tailor-made sports clothing, equipment and exclusive clubs, especially in golf, sailing and fitness, there is little provision for budget brands except in cheap clothing and trainers, and 'back-street' gyms/fitness clubs.

Local authority anti-poverty strategies and leisure cards/ passports

The Urban Programme and Community Development Projects and other anti-deprivation schemes were criticised for being adventitious (Alcock and Craig, 1998) or having no strategic pattern being based on bidding rather than planning (Oatley, 1998). This lack of central direction drove authorities, mainly large, urban, and Labour-controlled initially, to review policies for poor people. By 1995, Alcock et al. showed one in two were engaged in some anti-poverty activity, in urban and rural areas, and under all forms of political control. Of these, a third had a formal strategy. They associated Anti-Poverty Strategies (APS) with decentralised service delivery, reduced/remitted charges, welfare rights promotion, debt advice and support including credit unions. Scottish authorities followed a more strategic framework, but more slowly, Higgins and Ball (1999) discovering that 25% had APSs. Anti-poverty strategies were linked to other equal opportunities work, for women, disabled on BME groups.

Moving from concepts of poverty to SEx allowed a wider view of equal opps work: by 2001 over half of authorities had a structure to deal with SEx, and dedicated staff. Initial policy responses were to introduce discounts, first for Old Age Pensioners, then for unemployed and people with impairments, and then for a wider range of disadvantages, making them numerous and very complex for staff and customers alike. Then, the Audit Commission asked local authorities not only to market leisure provision more cost effectively, but also to target subsidies better. Leisure Cards (LCs) or 'Passports to Leisure' were introduced. These were generally cheap to buy, and provided one, two or three levels of discount:

- the highest for deprived/poor people;
- the second for other groups given some priority, e.g., students;
- and another for all residents (which are being transmuted into municipal Loyalty Cards, analogous to those issued by supermarkets and major stores).

Collins and Kennett's (1998) postal survey of British local authorities yielded a 52% response. Just over half of authorities had LCs, more with populations over 100,000, those with above-average spending on sport and arts, with above average numbers of benefit claimants, and ranking highly on the DETR's index of deprivation. Fifty-five per cent were for concessionary groups only, while 41% had other tiers of charging, e.g., for all citizens. Perhaps most marked was the correlation with authorities having an APS: 48% with a card, compared to 14% without, indicating a corporate approach to poverty.

Cards were introduced overwhelmingly for political or managerial reasons of encouraging low-income people in sport (56%), and an ideological commitment to low-income people (24%, see Fig 3.1). Collins and Kennett hypothesised that economic (such as filling empty off-peak space) or managerial reasons (like simplifying complex discounts) might be significant, but these were of minor importance, though they may have helped get the card idea accepted. Market research prior to launching was sketchy, often limited to contacting a sample of operating schemes, leading to much 'copy cat' management.

Early Leisure Cards were concentrated in metropolitan authorities, but later spread to smaller towns and rural areas. From 1999 to 2009 the Chartered Institute of Public Finance gathered data on cards in England and Wales (CIPFA, 1999, 2010). Table 3.3 shows the results over this period, suggesting that the numbers grew until 2005–6 but afterwards declined. Virtually all the cards offered sport, but only 32% offered public arts and only 28% commercial leisure and retail services. This meant that LAs were missing out on a large part of three markets – women, older people and non-sporty individuals, the latter 38% according to the Allied Dunbar National Fitness Survey (SC/HEA, 1992).

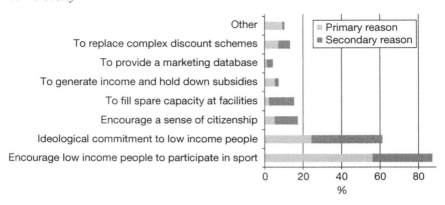

Figure 3.1 Reasons for establishing leisure card schemes

Table 3.3 Local authorities with leisure and loyalty cards: 1999, 2005–6, 2008–9

	1999	2005–6			2008–9			
	Total	Total	Average membership 000(%)	Average low income/ benefit membership 000(%)	Total	Incl sport	Incl arts	Incl comm
London boroughs	20	27	17.2 (13.7)	3.9 (3.3)[1]	24	22	9	8
Metropolitan boroughs	27	39	15.6 (9.0)	9.4 (6.8)[2]	23	22	10	9
Unitary authorities	30	36	15.6 (12.6)	2.9 (4.2)[3]	29	28	13	8
Non Met authorities	108	127	7.7 (6.5)	1.9 (1.8)[4]	76	73	19	19
Welsh authorities	8	12	12.6 (7.9)	1.0 –[5]	9	9	1	1
Total % RESPONSE	193	241	2,239.6	606.7	161	154 (96%)	52 (32%)	45 (28%)
		60			60			

Sources: Collins, 2008a, CIPFA, 2010

Notes:
1 Averages in brackets exclude Greenwich, Westminster and Waltham Forest
2 Averages in brackets exclude Wigan, Liverpool, Birmingham and Leeds
3 Averages in brackets exclude Nottingham, Peterborough and Plymouth   } see Table 3.5
4 Averages in brackets exclude Derbyshire Dales, Rushcliffe
5 Averages in brackets exclude Conwy

For ease of operation, card operators selected target groups directly related to categories of welfare beneficiaries; subsequently, Sport England (2000) showed that 79% of English leisure centres had reduced prices for eligible people, 35% had a passport scheme for all citizens, 30% an access card only for low-income groups, and 19% had some other membership scheme. Table 3.4 shows the situation in 2008–9, where over half the LAs provided discounts for their obese and sick referred by GPs, two in five for local elite athletes, but relatively few for lone parents, mostly poor. The biggest issues over targeting are whether to include part-time students who may be working, all pensioners or only those on benefits, carers for disabled people and the dependants of cardholders.

In terms of services offered, virtually all LAs discounted municipal sports provision at 30 to 50%, two in five public arts and culture, and less than one in three private leisure and other commercial operations discounted at 10 to15% (notably cinemas and some professional soccer clubs. It also included taxis, photographers, sports and arts equipment retailers, florists, steam railways, zoos etc., a good and cheap way to help small businesses – Chester for example, had no deprived scheme but over 300 partner businesses).

In terms of access, many cards could only be purchased at town halls and leisure centres, but Cardiff used Post Offices, the facility most used by poor people, while Leicester and a few other employed marketing staff who used outreach methods to reach target groups (see below). Marketing was very conventional, through low impact leaflets, council newsletters and websites, Council Tax mailings and posters on council hoardings and buses, but little use was made of paid advertising or local radio/TV. The more substantial schemes

Table 3.4 Concessionary groups in leisure cards 2008–9

Group	% of 161 responding authorities	Group	% of 161 responding authorities
Young people		*Low income groups*	
• Schoolchildren	60	• Income Support recipients	83
• HE/FE students – Full time	82	• Housing Benefit recipients	80
• HE/FE students – Part time	48	• Family tax Credit recipients	55
• Children in care	7	*Unemployed*	
• Foster carers	3	• Job Seekers Allowance	
Disabled		recipients	84
• Disabled Living Allowance		*Elite athletes*	41
recipients	85	*GP referral patients*	55
• Dependents of DLA		*LA & PCT employees*	2
recipients	40	*Asylum seekers*	4
• Carers of DLA recipients	60	*One parent families*	17
Senior citizens			
• All seniors	80		
• Seniors on Benefits	82		

Source: CIPFA, 2010

sent members a regular magazine advertising new services and special offers, or a directory of outlets, as in Chester's and Windsor and Maidenhead. In 2004, Kidz Cards were launched in Scottish cities but eight years later, only 28% of parents in a Glasgow sample thought their children held cards; in the last year, two thirds had used it for swimming and two-fifths for cinema (CelloMRUK, 2010).

Two other marketing issues were whether to limit card use to off-peak hours; some LAs did so openly to fill unused space, others because they feared losing peak trade. Others objected on the grounds that disadvantaged people should be able to enjoy their leisure at these times as much as anyone else: an Oxford manager said 'it's an appalling assumption that just because people are unemployed that they can only come between 9 and 5.' The Audit Commission cited an authority that excluded concessionary users, mistakenly believing they would crowd out full-price swimmers, when in fact the pool was only half full, commenting 'low income families were being unnecessarily excluded, and potential additional income was being lost' (1999: 27).

While some groups did not change status and eligibility much (like disabled and retired people), others who are unemployed and on low incomes because of low skills get short-term jobs and go on and off of benefits (Walker and Park, 1997) which created expensive bureaucracy in removal and re-registration. So, authorities started to offer longer memberships to the former groups and shorter ones to the latter, to reduce administrative costs and 'free riders', respectively. A Leisure Card is essentially a membership scheme and needs the same care and attention to retention and marketing that commercial fitness chains like David Lloyd and Fitness First give. Neglect means waste: Cardiff did little follow up in 1995–6 and only four of 1,439 lapsed members renewed! Some LAs thought introducing cards under CCT rules would create difficulties for contractors and later Trusts, but the few problems were solved by renegotiation, or specific payments.

In fact, card resources and budgets were very limited:

- 29% of authorities had no staff dedicated to managing and marketing and only 18% had two or more;
- one in four had NO budget for operating their cards, and another one in seven under £5,000 annually; their small scale was demonstrated by a third receiving under £500 in revenue. Only one in seven earned more than £40,000. This was partly because prices were kept low: 37% of concession cards were free, and the same share again cost £3 a year or less for adults.

With the advent of better IT, Kennett (2002) suggested that one part-time staff member would be needed for every 5,000 members.

So the lack of money and staff went some way to explaining but not excusing the low level of promotion. Indeed, only one authority in three had set a target for the penetration of its card sales, and one in four had no target for usage. It also meant that monitoring and review were not rigorous and systematic, only two in five conducting an annual review, and despite computerisation of membership records, and of facility ticket sales, many had no one with the necessary skills to reduce the data mountain to informative indicators.

The success of schemes can be judged by the extent of take-up, the accuracy of targeting, and the degree of use and income to facilities. Thus in Collins and Kennett's sample, one in three concession schemes had fewer than 1,000 members compared to one in twelve multi-tier, whereas one in three multi-tier schemes had more than 10,000 members compared to only one in seven concessions. The CIPFA data (Table 3.3) showed an average membership of only 2,300 and 600 deprived people, skewed by large numbers of small schemes in small LAs. Roughly what this means is that by 2006–7 there were some 3.9m cardholders in England and Wales (Collins, 2011) with some 1.1m people receiving discounts. Curiously, I never found an Audit Commission Inspection report criticising a Leisure Card.

But some larger authorities did better (Table 3.5, see Collins, 2008b). Even in this small sample there was substantial variation. Windsor and Maidenhead had nine out of ten residents signed up for its card, made attractive by its wide range

Table 3.5 Selected larger leisure card/passport schemes 2006–7

	Population 000	*Total card-holders 000*	*% of population*	*Concession holders 000*	*% of population*[a]
London Boroughs					
Greenwich	234	57	24	16	7
Westminster	286	72	28	3	1
Barking & Dagenham	165	47	29	3	5
Tower Hamlets	213	35	15	9	4
Waltham Forest	226	34	16	13	6
Metropolitan Boroughs					
Wigan	307	54	18	2	1
Liverpool	439	73	19	23	5
Wirral	327	75	23	3	1
Leeds	733	164	22	14	2
Birmingham	1003	?	?	40	4
Unitary Authorities					
Leicester	288	56	19	9	3
Nottingham	279	62	22	34	12
Swindon	182	44	21	22	12
Windsor & Maiden'd	136	122	90	1	1

Source: Collins, 2008

Notes: a) for take up from eligible groups multiply roughly by 3

of commercial offers, but only a thousand in its concession tier. By contrast, Nottingham and Swindon attracted 12% of residents to their concession tiers – probably a third of all their deprived groups, not a minor achievement in the varied and fragmented supermarket of leisure choice, which other authorities would do well to emulate.

Like many bicycles bought with good intentions of exercising, many of which remain in sheds and hung on walls, ownership of a card does not equal use. Only with the advent of integrated management information systems and the use of swipe or smart cards can the disparate site data be brought together with the membership data at Headquarters. Thus holders used their cards about six times a year in Leicester, twenty in Cardiff and between twelve and forty in Oxford. Card use can vary greatly by facility according to its catchment – 38 and 68% of total use at two Coventry sports centres, just under half at the four Oxford facilities. Wood, Downer and Toberman (2011) reviewed smart cards in LAs for the DWP; six of their seven case studies used them for leisure and libraries, while Bolton MDC extended social inclusion by allowing people without bank accounts to book tickets for events.

If one in two authorities had cards, why had not others taken one up? Collins and Kennett hypothesised that it was because some authorities believed they had no poverty/deprivation problem and thus no need for a card (which turned out to apply to only one in five), or that these authorities lacked a strong core of leisure services with which to implement such programmes (which hardly anyone admitted to), or that the costs of administration or subsidy were too great (both identified by one in three). Small size need not prevent running a Leisure Card programme. Tynedale, the geographically largest English district with one of the smallest populations (37,000 people) – it has only two staff members in its Leisure Department and five small facilities – runs a successful card. Brighton and Hove is a large authority (245,000 people) with a major deprivation problem, fairly limited leisure facilities run by three separate contractors, an Anti-poverty staff team, but no card. A Leisure Services officer considered LCs 'a scattergun approach…a bureaucratic nightmare…ineffective in increasing participation'.

Case study 1: leisure cards in Leicester and Oxford

Leicester

Leicester launched its Leisure Pass early, in 1985, with the following objectives: encourage and make accessible sports participation amongst low-income and disadvantaged groups; increasing use in both peak and off-peak times; minimising income loss by negotiated discounts, and encouraging take-up by a range of attractive concessions (LCC, 1985). Its clients incorporated previously targeted groups of unemployed, disabled, full-time students aged 16–17 and Youth Training Scheme trainees, but added single parents, senior citizens, low-income groups and their dependants. Carers of disabled people were added in 1991.

The cards were free, and offered 50% discounts for municipal sport; soon other municipal arts services were added, and events like the Leicester show and private retail, cinema, zoo, steam railway, and other outlets, a total of 95 by 1997. The philosophy was to maximise take up and this, said the responsible officer, involved offering a range 'from Veg to Verdi.' In fact, four of the five most popular services were commercial.

By 1987 membership reached 6,800, but doubled to 14,000 by 1988, and so did administrative staff, from one to two; adjacent authorities were invited to buy cards and subsidise them or re-charge eligible citizens, five districts and five parishes purchasing over 900 passes. A focused campaign on students was the main feature behind the increase to 21,700 members by 1992. This group was recruited by taking photo-card laminating machines to colleges during autumn registration, and then to other venues – job centres for the unemployed, clubs for women, disabled people, ethnic groups. In 1996 the composition of passholders was:

Group	%
People aged 60+	45
Young people	20
Income Support/low-income recipients	12
Unemployed	9
Disabled	9
Single parents	3
Carers	1

The budget in 1996–7 was £44,500, including £7,000 for marketing; since the only direct income was the sale of cards outside the city (£10,100), the deficit was £34,400, or £1 per passholder. A significant reduction in budget in 1998 raised the question of whether to charge for the Pass, though officers were reluctant, saying 'it would be met with resistance...it would put people off...it could be costly.' In a 1996 user survey, one in three of low-income groups and students said they would give up if they had to pay for the cards, confirming the narrow margins and importance of incentivising subsidies for poor people. Crompton (2011) suggested that in pricing with reference to other providers, to work discounts needed to be in the 30–50% zone. Leicester has one of the highest concentrations of ethnic minorities in Britain, at 39% of the population; passholders were almost representative at 34% of the total (30% of them Asian). At this time, Leicester reached 11% of all its 270,000 citizens.

But membership peaked at 30,071 in 1995. Once Leicester was a unitary authority, the rateable value of some affluent suburbs fell outside the city boundary; successive cuts had to be made in its leisure budget, and after some years of protection, this meant the loss of dedicated administrative and marketing card staff. The Assistant Director said this was 'sad, but not a sad as the alternative of closing facilities…we will maintain the scheme as far as we can, but we won't be able to market it in the way we have in the past…to a degree it will have to become self-marketing.' No example of self-marketing operations can be found in marketing textbooks, and anyone who discovered one would soon be wealthy! Once those staff and marketing activity was been reduced by third, the Leisure Pass lost 10,000, or one third of its members (Figure 3.2).

After the financial cuts, the Assistant Director believed the emphasis should be 'on not how many people have a Pass but how many people use their Pass.' Use of leisure centres had doubled in the previous five years, partly as a result of the individual annual average of visits moving from 5.2 in 1992–3 to 6.5 in 1996–7. Low-income members made most frequent use, with one in five attending once a week. Swimming was by far the most popular activity for nine out of ten passholders, while cultural activities came second to sport:

	%
Sports facilities	92 one swim a week, saving £50 a year
Libraries	59
Museums	53
Odeon cinema	43 one showing a week, saving £60 a year
Haymarket theatre	40
De Montfort concert hall	40, saving £15 a year
Bonfire night (Abbey Park)	27
Twycross Zoo	23, saving £1 per adult ticket
Leicester City FC	12, saving £125 a year on a season ticket

Having postcodes for Leicester's passholders allowed Kennett (2002) to relate them to deprivation as measured by the DETR's (2000a) index, by a laborious analysis using the PC2ED programme to convert 7,000 postcodes into census

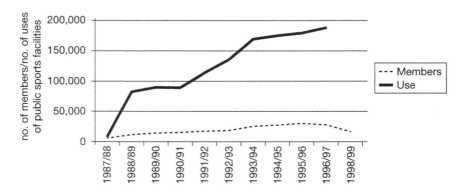

Figure 3.2 Use of Leicester Leisure Pass, compared with membership 1987–98

Enumeration Districts, entering them into the database; and calculating from the figures for constituent EDs a Postcode Deprivation Index, and finally entering over 20,000 passholders' addresses. Spearman's rank order coefficient showed no statistical significance between level of deprivation and the number of cardholders (r=0.12 (n=31), perhaps because of the small number and large size of postcodes and their mix of both affluent and deprived housing areas.

Figure 3.3 shows the take-up of Leisure Passes by postcode for Leicester (in italics) superimposed on a map of wards with the deprivation index by shading. Leicester was then the 32nd most deprived LA in England. The take up was higher in the least deprived wards/postcodes LE2 3 and LE5 6 in the south and east, and in LE2 6, LE2 8, LE3 6; LE3 9; and LE4 7. The most deprived areas were in the centre of the city, the north and the outlying western wards, and here there were lower levels of take-up. From this analysis, there was a clear need to increase take-up in the more deprived areas.

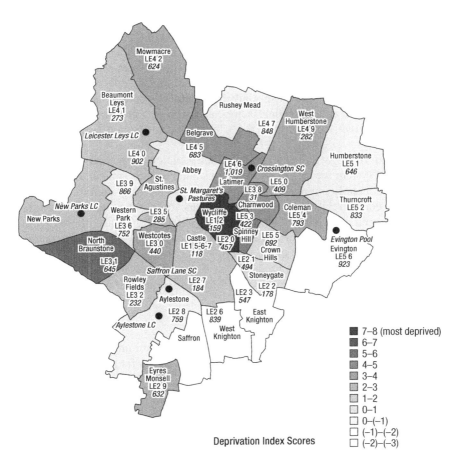

Figure 3.3 Geographic take-up of Leicester's Leisure Pass

After a time in the doldrums, the scheme was re-launched, with some free activities (e.g., swimming for several groups and everything free for 2,800 foster families). It gained new members rapidly, reaching 56,000 in 2006–7, and 254,000 by 2009 (130,000 adults and 124,000 over 60s), and with 25,000 from the county districts. Short-term membership of six months was offered to 11,000 people referred by GPs, and of 18 months for 19,000 people on cardiac rehabilitation programmes. Of 2.1m users at seven Leisure Centres, two pools and a tennis centre in 2009–10, 61% were by cardholders (of these, 24% by Black and Ethnic Minorities, five per cent by disabled people, and 54% by women) (*pers comm.* Dorde 'George' Vranges, 12 September 2009).

Oxford

Oxford had a Leisure Card attracting only 4,000 people, three out of five being concessionaires and getting it free; nine out of ten holders used it only for swimming; it had failed to attract young people aged 15–25, retirees and ethnic minorities, and only half the population had heard of it (OCC, 1998). So, in 1997–8 it re-launched its re-named Slice Card, with objectives to: increase income so as to be able to subsidise targeted groups, as the Client Services Manager said, 'on the Robin Hood principle'; and to increase use and income overall; and to target groups without discrimination, especially low-income people. This was a mixture of social, economic and marketing factors, and seen as a corporate rather than a Departmental initiative, involving the Chief Executive's and Social Services departments.

It decided on a swipe card, and its introduction coincided with a new computerised system for all its leisure centres and pools capable of yielding tiny details of use, greatly improving the capacity for monitoring. Oxford decided to have three commercial and two concessionary tiers. Membership exceeded expectations, and attracted 14,000 of Oxford's 110,000 residents after only nine months of operation. In contrast to Leicester, concessionary Bonus Slice holders used their cards less often than the others – once a month compared to 2.6 for Aqua and 3.1 for Active slice holders. The Audit Commission (1999: 56) cited Oxford as 'a neat example of how one tariff tool can be priced for a range of target groups and segment the market.'

The 2011–2 offers and prices were:

> *Cool Slice* – unlimited access for ice skating, swimming, sauna, aerobics/ fitness, racket sports, creche from £44 to £47 a month for adults; £29 for off-peak option.

> *Active Slice* – as for Cool slice but without skating, price from £38 to £41 a month for adults.

> *Aqua Slice* – unlimited access to swimming and sauna and free squash or badminton, price from £28 to £29 a month.

Bonus Slice – concessions of 33–70% for unemployed, disabled, people on Income Support/ Housing Benefit/Family Credit/Council Tax rebate, price £2 for a year partners or children 50p for 6 months.

(City Executive Board paper, 12 January 2011)

In 2010, Free Access to National Sportspeople (FANS) was introduced for competitive athletes. In 2009, the city decided to let a 10-year contract for management to a not-for-profit trust, Fusion Leisure; in 2010–11 Fusion achieved increases of 63–65% in users from under 15s and over 50s, people from deprived communities and Bonus Slice users overall, and 183% from ethnic minorities, admittedly from a modest base (Partnership Board paper 20, June 2011).

Kennett (2002: 278) suggested that the early waves of cards showed 'Fordist' features, unresponsive to users, poorly researched, marketed and resourced and hence inefficient, concluding: 'the majority of [card] schemes seemed to be like a favourite toy kept into adulthood – fondly and zealously preserved, but out of date.' In the new generation of cards typified by Oxford, he saw post-Fordist tendencies, notably flexible production processes, flatter organisational structures, increased market research and technological investment, and better interdepartmental cooperation. He judged, though, that cards were struggling to reach their potential. The new technology of smart cards was spreading. Southampton undertook a three-year experiment with Gothenberg and other continental cities; York and Bath have, with London, schemes with the Leisure Pass Group. After looking at the feasibility of a card shared by the City of Derby and all county districts, Collins and Enoch (2006) opined that it was only cost-effective if part of a corporate scheme (covering, e.g., transport, school and social services, as in Nottingham) and swipe technology being adequate for leisure and library operations.

Many tourist cities offer incentive discounts to attractions, but fewer have schemes for residents; exceptionally Holland has them in at least thirteen cities, the Rotterdampas having 80–85,000 passholders (about 11% of the population), three-quarters on low incomes or state benefits, and half using their Passes once a month or more often (E. Reitsma, *pers comm* 7 March 2000, www.rotterdampas. nl.algemeen/ accessed 8 June 2000).

Collins (2011) concluded that Leisure Cards need both commercial and social marketing, and I turn now to a case study of a large, successful, prize-winning social marketing programme for sport and health promotion.

Case study 2: gym for free/be active, Birmingham

Background

The City Council and Heart of Birmingham PCT (HOB) shared concerns about the Ladywood area with high proportions of poor people, BME minorities (totalling 62%) and other hard-to-reach groups, suffering obesity, health and physical inactivity, and specifically:

- 48% of households had incomes below £15,000 pa, compared to a city average of £25,600;
- male residents had a life expectancy of 71 years compared to 79 in Sutton Coldfield;
- unemployment and crime levels were both high.

So they agreed to tackle health inequalities by social marketing actions related to Local Area Agreement targets:

- removing price barriers by offering free gym, swimming and fitness classes;
- encouraging regular physical activity (PA) (joiners had to agree to attend at least four times a month) (target N18);
- linking PA with health, community wellbeing & cohesion (targets N1, N15);
- improving life expectancy (target N120);
- encouraging partnership.

HOB used Mosaic to segment household types, and the three largest of twelve groups in Ladywood were:

E Families with children living in low-values terraced houses	12.3%
F Diverse, large families, mainly from South Asia living in terraces, privately rented	32.6%
H Diverse younger people with uncertain employment living in social housing estates	23.7%

It was known each had a preferred mix of communication means – telemarketing for F&H, community associations for E&F (including religious groups for F), internet for F, ITV/direct mail and leaflets/posters for H, and Working Men's Clubs for E.

Pilot launch

The pilot was launched on Valentine's Day 2008 with a mail drop offering an initial one-year free gym membership, banners and posters near gyms, material placed with community groups, and as many word-of-mouth messages as could be generated. In October this was reinforced for all 300,000 residents with Boxer Frank Bruno heading a TV and radio campaign, and co-branding publicity with the Department of Health's national Change4Life advertising. Monitoring was aided by venues having swipe cards with membership profile data and independent evaluation by Birmingham City University (Rabiee, Robbins & Khan, 2008).

The visitor profile was:

- 45% were female, high for an area so heavily immigrant and Asian;
- 41% were Asian and 33% Afro-Caribbean;

- 42% were in jobs, 27% unemployed and 23% students;
- 27% were overweight and 15% obese;
- more than 30% had never previously used one of the centres;
- users recorded weight loss, increased energy levels, healthier diets, increased confidence and reduced depression, more social capital (getting out of the house and making new friends);
- it produced a take up of some 40,000 people at cost of £4 per head per month;
- it generated 33,000 new members for the Leisure Pass scheme, and 362,000 visits to the facilities.

Many said they could not have afforded the £50 a month gym fees. The greatest requests were for more staff/instructors, more equipment, and more nutrition advice. So the scheme was meeting the LAA targets, getting to the target groups and producing changes in lifestyle that would be beneficial if sustained. The only problem was that the gyms became very over-crowded at peak times.

Extending the scheme city-wide, as Be Active

With this experience, a proposal was made by a new partnership board comprising the city, all three PCTS (the others being Birmingham East & North – BEN, and South Birmingham – SB) and three Partnerships (Health & Wellbeing, Sport & PA, and Culture) to extend the scheme to serve all 1.1m citizens for two years. Of a national group of eight Core Cities, Birmingham had the least physically active population (16.9%), the highest incidence of type II diabetes (4.6%), and the second highest rate of obesity among school Year 6 children (21.5%) (BHWP, 2009). The DOH estimated that inactivity cost the city £13.2m a year, so there were high stakes to play for. The cost was estimated at £9.3m, of which £2.7m would come from the committed Free Swimming scheme, £2.8m from an existing commitment to Gym for Free, and £1.9m from the 3 PCTs (excluding the city's revenue subsidy of £14.7m to its 48 sport and leisure centres). Besides the aims sought by Ladywood's pilot, it was intended to:

- recruit train and use 300 volunteers, and retrain BCC Leisure and PCT staffs;
- offer targeted support to older people with mobility problems, and overweight; smokers;
- increase activity participation by 7.3%;
- save between 150 and 175 lives a year.

Extending the scheme brought in three more market segments (Jerwood & Cook, 2010):

I *Low income families* living in suburban social housing
J *Mostly white families* in homes bought from social landlords, and
K *older, vulnerable white adults* mostly living in social housing.

These combined to 'dilute' the proportion of ethnic minorities to 37%, but raised the female share to 54%, and spread users almost equally across income quintiles (Be Active analysis 01 September 2009 to 31 May 2010). Figure 3.4 shows the take-up in the three PCT areas by segment against targets, with only the well-educated group G in South Birmingham greatly out of line with the target (but this is the group most swift and able to take up opportunities in any market).

The gyms were free until 5pm to avoid the crowding, the pools were free at all times and a programme of walks and runs was organised. In the event the unreceptive media channels were the internet, newspapers and leaflets.

The outcomes were:

- 100,000 people signed up, and by 2013 370,000 were active members;
- average usage reached 2.8 trips a month, one-third swimming, two-thirds doing fitness, and six per cent aerobics;
- BCC's customer knowledge database and the PCT's marketing tools reached six key customer segments, and highlighted high density areas for targeted marketing;
- 22 full-time leisure posts were created by the extra demand of 10% increases in swimming, gym use and fitness classes.

The continuing tasks were to:

- develop a sense of value in a free scheme;
- extend opportunities for women;
- exploit the fact that several groups were keen in their use of open spaces;
- ensure that exercise became habitual, routine and frequent.

The scheme won nine awards including from AHC Communicating Health & *Health Service Journal* for best social marketing, and as Secretary of State's overall winner, *Local Government Chronicle* in health & wellbeing category, *Guardian* Public Service for diversity, and a *World Leisure* innovation award

On the termination of the Free Swimming scheme after only a year (see pp 37, 51 and 114) funding was re-negotiated at a cost of £2.5 m for 2011–2. More recent budget cuts meant also that the city will not be boosting its Active People sample as hitherto, so inferior monitoring data will be available on population subgroups. By 2013, there were over 300,000 members, active in parks, tennis and rounders as well as indoors. They had to have a Leisure Card and be referred by a GP or Practice nurse for three months, thereafter they were offered a fitness programme and followed up after three and six months to see if they were still active (see www.birmingham.gov.uk beactiveplus, accessed 12 October 2013).

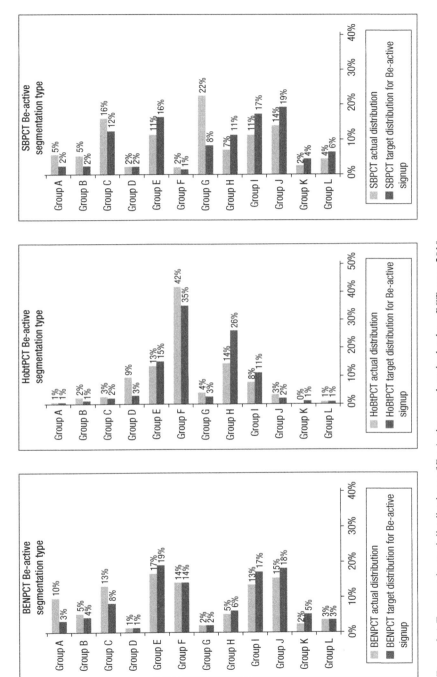

Figure 3.4 Target and actual distributions of Be Active members in the three PCT areas 2010

Evaluation

This was an attempt to overcome the short-term, small-scale, temporary-funded and unevidenced nature of most health and PA interventions (Bentley, 2008). Gym for Free was feasible because there was more unused capacity than in pools and leisure centres. Also the free scheme unlocked substantial use amongst hard-to-reach and needy groups, who were willing to travel some distance to participate.

What can we conclude about leisure and loyalty cards? They are a flexible mechanism, which can be targeted and marketing in ways that are suitable to and can be designed by local officers and members. With modern swipe/smart card systems any stigma of identification can be removed (especially for those unemployed), and close monitoring of use can be done by facility, time, space, activity or target group and place of residence. One could go so far as to say that they are a managerialist mechanism that can help implement social-democratic equality and inclusion policies.

However, in present circumstances they are often poorly designed, managed and monitored, operated as political tokens, often in isolation as a leisure policy and under great restraints, and are under-performing both as a social policy action and a management tool. Yet the great majority of politicians and managers want their scheme to be a redistributive policy tool, but cannot demonstrate its unit cost-efficiency or its effectiveness. Coalter (2000) criticised Collins and Kennett (1998) for presenting Leisure Cards as unproblematic attempts to combat social exclusion, failing to confront the fact of low take up. I reject this in the explanations set out above. Adapting Chesterton's wry comment about Christianity, Leisure Cards have been tried and found difficult, and mostly left as insensitive, under-resourced and tokenistic attempts at anti-poverty and inclusion policies.

Conclusions

Ferragini, Tomlinson and Walker (2013: 4–5) extended Townsend's half-century old analysis using Structural Equation Modelling on three major databases, defining 'participation as a combination of freedom from material deprivation, active social participation and trust'. They discovered:

- sport was one of four factors underpinning the deprivation component, with a coefficient of 0.91;
- insufficient data to verify whether higher participation amongst Asian and Caribbean minorities compensated for greater material deprivation;
- participation fell in line with poverty to a 'floor' for the poorest 30% where they have to choose 'between basic necessities and between fulfilling one social expectation or another';
- for children, lower income is related to less parental involvement and poorer educational attainment.

Ferragini, Tomlinson and Walker concluded, 'the existence of such different worlds helps to explain the gulf in understanding and the high level of mistrust... between those who are in poverty and those who are not'

The literature on poverty and inequality is huge and growing; for much detail on its distribution, intergenerational effects and impact on health see Hills et al., (2010), and Marmot (2010); Field (2010) commented to the Prime Minister that 'poverty is a much more subtle enemy than pure lack of money.' With limitations due to the lack of specific data on money and leisure behaviour, I have tried to show how poverty limits and excludes people from leisure. There are others excluded by factors of racism, ageism, gender-blindness, disability, and geographic isolation, as we shall see in Chapters 4 to 10, but the bulk of people thus excluded are also poor. The SID discourse of social insertion in European, French and UK policy would argue that getting an adequate income through work is the most logical and effective action to combat poverty. Bauman (1998) criticised Blair's Third Way, arguing that it is not work which is the means of social integration, it is money, the means to participate in a modern consumer society. I agree, and:

- this is not possible overnight, so there is a major transition period to come, extended greatly by the recession;
- to date many of the jobs created have been part-time, low-skilled and low-paid, and training can improve personal skills but the jobs have to be there, which currently they are not in the north and west, Wales, or parts of Scotland;
- still there will be people who will not be able to work at all or for enough hours or at pay rates which will lift them above the poverty threshold, for whom policies to offer sport and leisure as part of an adequate quality of life will still be needed. Be Active shows what concerted action and careful marketing can achieve.

4   Exclusion, education and young people's sport

Introduction: children and poverty

This chapter will investigate whether inequality starts where sport starts – in childhood – and flourishes – in youth. According to a Chancellor of the Exchequer 'child poverty is a scar on the soul of Britain' (Brown, 1999). The Prime Minister had said 'poverty should not be a birthright. Being poor should not be a life sentence. We need to break the cycle of disadvantage' (Blair, 1999), and he pledged to eradicate it in 20 years. But Oakley and Tinsley (2013) showed that while households in relative income poverty (Chapter 3) fell from 25% to 17.5% the 2020 target would not be met, even without the recession; they criticised government policy for focussing too narrowly, ignoring job creation, instantiating that more than half of two-parent poor households worked a total of under 40 hours together, whereas half of non-poor households worked 64 hours or more. Severely poor children averaged 13%, rising to over 24% in Leicester, Newham, Tower Hamlets, Manchester, and even Westminster, said Charity *Save the Children* (Hansen, et al., 2010) and Brewer, Browne and Joyce (2011) forecast an increase from 19.7% of children in relative poverty in 2009 to 22.2% in 2015 and 24.4% in 2020.

Poverty affected 34% of children in 1997–8 compared to 10% in 1979, and was the highest in the EU. Children do cost: the LV= annual survey for 2009 showed an average cost from birth to 21 years of £201,800, ranging £187,000 in Yorks to £221,000 in London (Smithers, R. *Guardian* 23 February 2010: 11). Looking at the dynamics, Hill and Jenkins (2000) found that 14% of pre-school and eight per cent of primary age children were poor in every year 1991–96 compared to 6.7% of the whole population. In the poorest fifth of households this meant that there had been no real increase in their spending on toys, children's clothing, shoes and fresh fruit and vegetables over three decades (Gregg, Harkness and Machin, 1999). Obesity is linked to income (via diet – 15.8% in the poorest group compared to 13.3% in the richest), areas of residence (16.4% most deprived, 11.2% least deprived) and parental example (19.8% where both parents were overweight/obese, 8.4% where one and 6.75 where neither) (DoH, 2006).

Analysing the interaction of factors in home and childhood is immensely complex; using the National Child Development Study 1958 cohort, Hobcraft

(2000) looked at outcomes at ages 23 and 33. He came to some striking conclusions, when we relate them to the facts about poverty above and in Chapters 2 and 3, and to the persistence or fragility in sports interests below:

- educational qualifications showed a strong relationship with every measure of disadvantage at both 23 and 33, after controlling for all sorts of factors;
- the most frequent predictor of negative adult outcomes was childhood poverty;
- mother's interest in education was more salient for young women, father's for men;
- low parental interest in school, frequent absence from school, and low educational test scores were quite influential on subsequent disadvantage;
- the father being in Social Classes IV and V was a clear predictor of males growing up in the same class at 23 or 33, net of all other factors.

Platt (2009) showed that compared to an average of 21% of children in poverty, in 2004–7 BME groups had higher rates – Caribbean 26%, Indian 27%, black African 35%, and Pakistani and Bangladeshi over 50%, but much higher where there were lone or disabled parents or no workers (e.g., 39% for Caribbean, 66% for Bangladeshis, 62% for black Africans). Using data from seven waves of the European Community Household Panel from 1994, Mendola, Busetta and Aassve (2008) constructed a model of persistent youth poverty, and compared to the 11-country average, the UK in the 1990s was slightly better off, despite domestic concerns:

	Average (%)	UK (%)
Never poor	64	69
Socially vulnerable (in and out – never more than three years poor)	26	20
Permanently poor	11	11

Cooper and Stewart (2013) reviewed 34 studies from six countries, showing regular effects of (especially persistent) low income on children's cognitive development and school attainments, health and social/emotional lives, with evidence of stress and maternal depression compared to the ability of higher income households to invest in their children's lives. Save the Children (2011a) claimed that more expensive utilities, insurance and having to use usurious doorstep lenders rather than banks made for a poverty premium of £1,280 a year, up by 28% from 2007, while the Office of Budget Responsibility envisaged average household indebtedness rising from £58,000 in 2010 to £77,300 by 2015 (i.e., from 1.6 to 1.75 times income – Helm, T. & Boffey, D. *Observer* 3 April 2011: 1,6).

None of the studies mentioned so far incorporate leisure or sport, no doubt partly because they were seen as marginal, but also because there was no effective longitudinal data. (e.g., in the National Child Development, British Birth Cohort studies and Active People).

Children at high risk of poverty were:

- in workless families;
- in BME communities;
- with one or more disabled adults in the household;
- had three or more siblings;
- in inner London.

(HM Treasury et al., 2008)

Deprivation is linked with low educational attainment, which is concentrated not just in inner cities but also East Anglia and the SW; and in turn this is linked with aspirations, which as SEUTF (2008: 24) said, is influenced by their social networks. Child poverty costs some £12bn a year, three-fifths for personal social services, benefit payment, reduced tax revenues, and lost earnings add another £13bn (Hirsch, 2008). Sport England (2006) reviewed sport's potential to meet the broad aims of the national *Every Child Matters* framework, with nine examples of successful schemes. In Wales 35% of children in schools with the highest quartile of free school meals played extra-curricular sport three times a week or more compared to 46% of those more affluent, in the lowest quartile (SCW, 2013). The current effect of income on children's sport is shown in Figure 11.4.

The remainder of this chapter looks at children's successive involvements with sport – in play and primary schools, secondary schools, sports clubs and out-of-school clubs, and before dealing with higher levels of performance, with one case study of the PE and Youth Sport Strategy and one of school-club links. I do not deal here with the use of sport to integrate disaffected youth, or to prevent/treat delinquency, covered in Chapter 9.

The early years: home, play and primary schooling

Children play and in doing so learn about the environment, themselves, their friends and adults. Many playworkers argue play is essential to human development and worthwhile in its own right. Because play develops motor and other physical, cognitive and affective abilities, it is delivered against a host of disciplinary theories (Child, 1985, Lester and Russell, 2008) and by professionals and volunteers in various settings, including schools, homes, workplaces, and hospitals (Moore, 1986), by public, commercial and voluntary agencies. Local authorities deliver play services through housing, education, social and leisure services. Many after-school clubs do not promote equality of opportunity in terms of gender, race, or disability (Smith, 2000).

Although there were two short-term attempts at having a central advisory agency similar to Sport England or the Arts Council, both were terminated by government because of management shortcomings; the central vacuum (Collins, 1994) was filled partly by a voluntary Children's Play Council (CPC), and then by

Play England, which proved an active agency. Candler (1999) displayed models of provision and policy across the world, in his view, all failing to give play the status the United Nations wished in its Charter for the Rights of the Child.

Fear of 'stranger danger' and of traffic accidents means that the range and *milieux* of play has become more limited and home-centred since the 1950s, especially for young children and girls until their mid teens (MORI, 2000). Sutton (2008) showed that children from more affluent households had more structured and organised play, calling for protection of open space in deprived areas. A classic study of the effects of play on children's development was by Schweinhart and Weikart (1997) who traced Americans to their early 20s, claiming better school and work outcomes for those with rich play lives. Drawing partly on this, the CPC (2000: 13) listed the effects on children of a deprived play life as poorer abilities in motor tasks, physical activities, dealing with trauma or stress, assessing and managing risks, and social skills (relationships, and dealing with conflicts and cultural differences). Several recent studies underlined the myth that living in the countryside confers better play opportunities than in towns; Smith and Barker (2001: 175) arguing that they are limited 'owing to geographical isolation from other children, the privatisation of rural land, and fears over children's unsupervised use of public spaces.' So only 70% of boys and 59% of girls played actively on five or more days a week, and for only 8.5 and 7.5 hours (BHF, 2009). In 2004 DCSF re-invented community use of schools as Extended Schools (ES), though for twenty years sport had been the most common activity in out-of-school hours. While not distinguishing sport, Wallace et al. (2009) reviewed ES' progress:

Service	% of schools providing	% use in last school term
Child care	94	58
After school	91	53
Before school	?	16

Then Secretary of State for Culture, Media and Sport, Chris Smith, claimed his Department was the 'champion of play,' but under the Blair government there were no less than twelve sources of funding from the DfEE. Their main aim was to free mothers and male single parents to work; so while child minders declined (possibly because of higher standards for facilities and staffing), day nurseries and out-of-school clubs grew substantially until the current recession, while there are concerns of over-emphasis on cognitive and social care objectives, judging play too narrowly.

Children move from play to primary school and learn generic running, jumping, throwing and catching skills. Unlike many countries, Britain has never had a tradition of specialist primary Physical Education teachers; in 1999 only one in twenty schools had a full-time specialist teacher and 14% a part-timer (MORI, 2000). Some question whether this slows the development of specific sports skills in the two years before transfer to secondary schools. Also, the most common facilities were multi-purpose halls and playgrounds, though a tenth didn't have these, and one in seven did not have an outdoor pitch or sports field, a situation Campbell (2000: 23) called 'close to being a crime.' Things have improved with some Local Education Authorities (LEAs) providing specialist spaces in joint schemes with district and parish councils with public use in the evenings and weekends, but only one in three teachers thought them adequate in 1999, three quarters having access to a pool but only one in seven to a sports hall. The Space for Sport and Arts programme alleviated this situation somewhat.

A broad aspiration of the PE profession was to have two hours or more a week in lessons for PE and sports, but between 1994 and 1999 there was a sharp reverse, with a decline from 32% to 11% (MORI, 2001a). It lead Sue Campbell, then Chief Executive of the Youth Sport Trust, to say 'primary school PE should be the foundation for lifelong health and sporting excellence. It is no good pumping millions of pounds into top sport when the base is crumbling away' (Campbell, 2000: 22). In 1994, a new National Curriculum order reduced the compulsory areas, and school budgets were reduced, resources having been 'directed at numeracy and literacy strategies.'

Table 4.1 gives some basic data on sport in and out of school for children in years 2–6, at the Millennium, showing:

*   a stable situation in range of activity, with a greater focus on individual rather than team activities;
*   a widening range of out-of-school activity, on average 6.5 hours a week, with some increase in extra-curricular and competitive sport;
*   club membership dominated by soccer and swimming;
*   a high level of enjoyment and wish to do well;
*   a gendered difference appearing, with more girls not seeing themselves as sporty; getting parental encouragement and disliking aspects of sport.

What this survey did not measure, however, was the intensity of exercise; moderate or vigorous being necessary to get health and fitness benefits. ISRM (2000) summarised evidence for emergence of a generation of 'couch potatoes':

*   children becoming fatter;
*   the proportion of children under 17 walking to school falling to one in two in 1986–96, and only 1% cycled;
*   96% of intense activity for 6–10s lasting less than 15 seconds, while a quarter of 11–16 year olds spent more than four hours a day watching TV, and one in ten boys of this age spent more than ten hours a week on computer games.

In Nestlé's Family Monitor survey (MORI, 2000) four in five parents agreed sport was a vital part of a child's development, but almost as many felt that contemporary children were less active than they had been, despite three out of five agreeing that opportunities had increased in the last thirty years. More of DE groups agreed that academic subjects always should take precedence over PE than AB groups

Table 4.1 Sport for children of primary age, 1999

Item	Boys	Girls	change 1994–99
In lessons			
Average number of sports at least once in year	7.4	7.6	+0.1
Average number of sports 10+ times a year	3.3	3.5	none
Out of school			
Average number of sports done at least once in year	10.1	9.5	+0.3
Average number of sports done 10+ times a year	4.7	4.5	+0.2
Place %			
• Extra curricular at school	45	38	+9
• Sports club outside school	52	32	+4
• Youth club/other organisation	46	51	–2
Competition, against %			
• Other schools	28	25	+4
• Between clubs	28	10	+5
• National/international	3	3	+5
Attitudes % agree strongly			
I enjoy PE and games lessons in school	71	64	none
I enjoy sport and games in my leisure time	77	63	+1
I am better at PE/games than most subjects	30	17	+1
I want to be successful at sport	70	47	+1
My family encourage me in sport/exercise	60	50	+4
I am a 'sporty' type of person	56	36	+3
Named sporting heroes	81	52	na
Attitudes % mind a lot			
Getting cold and wet	12	21	–2
Getting hot, sweaty, dirty	7	18	+1
Having to change in/out of sports clothes	8	14	none
Going outside in bad weather	14	29	–3

Source: MORI, 2000

(74% compared to 59%). In a Cochrane systematic review, Dobbins et al. (2009) showed that physical activity in school *did:*

• increase time spent in PE (confirmed in English schools by Quick et al. (2010);
• increase oxygen uptake and cardiovascular capacity;
• reduce blood cholesterol;
• have some effect on lifestyles.

But *did not:*

• reduce heart rate or Body Mass Index (BMI);
• reduce time spent watching TV, except in the short term for primary pupils;
• increase time spent on PA outside school.

The reduction of curricular PE alarmed members of what used to be Speednet, the consortium of UK PE organisations:

> The indicators are loud and clear that more children may be literate and computer literate, but many more than usual will remain physically illiterate.
>
> (British Association of Advisors and Lecturers in PE)

> We are in danger of changing the old quotation to read 'a healthy mind in an unhealthy body'.
>
> (Pat Smith, National Council for School Sport)

In primary school sport is seen by most children to be about fun, becoming more serious at secondary level, while gender inequity emerges (as explored by Kay in Chapter 5). Too many clubs still expressed interest only in those with marked talents (Hutson, Thomas and Sutton, 1995). Sport England commented (MORI, 2001a: foreword) 'the decline in PE curriculum time...will affect children from less well off backgrounds the most...who will be least likely to be able to take up the opportunities offered by extra-curricular and club sport.' Sport England, The Association of Physical Education and the Sport and Recreation Alliance were still pressing the Education Select committee for specialist primary teacher training (www.bbc.co.uk/school report 14 May 2013). The Chief Medical Officer (2012) reported that obesity affected 12% of toddlers, (10% of primary reception children and 19% of Year 6), with 20-year costs of £588–686m, yet an annual payback of 6–105 on interventions, physical activity helping not only academic performance but also satisfaction with school and connectedness.

Developing sports interests: secondary schools

Youth is seen often as a transition from school and childhood to work and adulthood, and those who struggle or drop out of work are seen as deviant or even an 'underclass' (Chapter 3). The contributors to MacDonald (1997) on youth and social exclusion overwhelmingly rejected this view as labelling and demeaning youth's rights of citizenship, speaking of structural influences on opportunities, especially for young people in care and disabled.

Rees and Miracle began a challenging review of sport and education literature thus:

> Sport in schools has been credited with teaching values of sportsmanship and fair play to participants, increasing athletes' educational aspirations, developing a sense of community and group cohesion amongst students, helping to reduce dropout rates, and giving poor and minority youth access to higher education.
>
> (Rees and Miracle, 2000: 277)

They accepted evidence that sport reinforced academic progress and reduced drop-out from High Schools, but that results for career development (whether academic or sporting), and equality of opportunity by race, gender and class were much more ambiguous at college and university.

Sport flowers from physical recreation in childhood and youth, and throughout the world thereafter declines in terms of penetration in the population. In consequence, sport is more often associated in government with youth and education than any other function. Sport has become increasingly entrenched in school curricula in England, Australia, Ireland, Canada, and the US, with the growth of programmes like the National Junior Sports Programme and Aussie Sport in the first two countries. Meanwhile, PE has not been able to establish a clear role for itself, having not resolved the competing aims of preparation for competitive sport, developing interest in recreational lifetime activity or in health-related exercise (Houlihan, 1997).

Hardman and Marshall (2000: 66) reviewed the state of PE around the world, and their summary was gloomy: at the very least in many countries, PE has been pushed into a defensive position, suffering from:

- decreasing curriculum time allocation;
- budgetary controls with inadequate financial, material and personnel resources;
- low subject status and esteem, occupying a tenuous place in the school curriculum, and not accepted on a par with seemingly superior academic subjects concerned with developing a child's intellect;
- marginalisation and under-valuation by authorities.

So far as inclusion was concerned, four out of five countries thought it had been achieved for gender but barely half for disability. Ethnicity was not covered.

In an update, Hardman (2008) found:

- continuing shortfalls in implementation of policy in one in ten European countries;
- variations in curriculum time from 30–120 minutes in UK primary and 6–120 minutes in secondary schools;
- 28% of respondents felt PE teachers had lower status than others;
- 63% of countries found PE lessons cancelled when sports space was needed for concerts, ceremonies, and dining;
- in Europe a majority found maintenance of PE facilities below adequate.

A positive step was the EU's resolution on sport in education (European Commission 2007/20686NI) as 'the only school subject which seeks to prepare children for a healthy lifestyle [and] among the most important tools of social integration,' but he wanted it to be more than a promise.

An English update survey of 1995 (Mason) in 1999 (MORI, 2000) showed that all secondary schools had at least one full-time specialist PE teacher (and usually

Table 4.2 Sport for children of secondary age, 1999

Item	Boys	Girls	Change 1994–99
In lessons			
Av no of sports at least once in year	9.3	9.4	+0.1
Av no of sports 10+ times a year	3.7	4.0	none
Out of school			
Av no of sports done at least once in year	11.3	10.3	+0.3
Av no of sports done 10+ times a year	4.8	3.6	+0.2
Place %	36	41	+9
• – Extra curricular school	35	36	+4
• – Sports club outside school	53	50	–2
• – Youth club/other organisation			
Competition , against %			
• – Other schools	38	29	+4
• – Between clubs	31	18	+5
• – National/international	19	9	+5
Attitudes % agree strongly			
I enjoy PE and games lessons in school	62	42	none
I enjoy sport and games in my leisure time	71	45	+1
I am better at PE/games than most subjects	38	20	+1
I want to be successful at sport	60	37	+1
My family encourage me in sport/exercise	41	29	+4
I am a 'sporty' type of person	52	28	+3
Named sporting heroes	80	64	N/A
Attitudes % mind a lot			
Getting cold and wet	10	20	–2
Getting hot, sweaty, dirty	11	23	+1
Having to change in/out of sports clothes	10	14	none
Going outside in bad weather	17	32	–3

Source: MORI, 2000

three or four), only seven in ten had access to an indoor sports hall, and two in five to an indoor pool. The equivalent data for sports participation and attitudes already discussed for primary schools is shown for secondary ages in Table 4.2.

This shows a wider range of sports in secondary school and a similar small increase since 1994. The increases in out-of-school sport were likewise larger. The gap in attitudes between girls and boys became more marked, including the issue of sporting heroes/role models. Flintoff and Scraton (2001: 18) pointed out that for girls 'many activity contexts, such as mixed PE classes, remained controlled largely by men and boys,' that there was much macho, destructive male behaviour in PE, and that there was a gap between school programmes and young women's active lifestyles out of school. Addressing teaching and management issues for girl-friendly PE, Kirk et al. (2000) suggested this entailed:

• changing traditional teacher-learner interactions;
• changing subject matter to support task-oriented rather than competitive/ego-oriented styles;

- tangible support from colleagues and managers;
- planning, commitment, flexibility, and effort by teachers.

Penney and Evans (1999, 124) were very strong in judging the National Curriculum as continuing to feature 'disproportionate attention to a narrow range of competitive team games, sex differentiated programmes, and teaching characterised by a limited range of teaching methods and strategies'. In Wales 86% of schools claimed to teach health-related fitness in 1997–8 (up from 70% in 1993–4) (SCW, nd), but the Sports Council for Wales expressed similar concerns about timetables, facilities, lack of extra curricular provision and budgets. Kirk (2005a) was convinced a sport-based curriculum limited continuing participation, and to be effective the 'sampling' of sports in secondary Key Stage 3 should happen in primary KS2 (Kirk, 2005b). Green, Smith and Roberts (2005) felt that the partial introduction of 'lifestyle sports' more likely to be continued in adulthood was constrained by the National Curriculum.

In later school years interest in sport starts to diverge; casual participation drops off for boys and girls in and out of school; range of serious participation is sustained for boys but drops more markedly for girls, as the 1999 data showed:

	Boys		Girls	
	Years 7–9	*Years 10–11*	*Years 7–9*	*Years 10–11*
In school				
10 times in last year	3.7	3.8	4.3	3.5
Out of school				
At least once in last year	11.7	10.5	10.7	9.4
10 times in last year	4.6	5.0	3.7	3.3

Sport England's (2005) *Sport Equity Index* (Table 4.3 on page 66) showed the widening gender gap by Key Stages 3 and 4, and its increase from 1994, while children from ethnic minorities had narrowed the gap with white children, if anything things had become slightly worse for disabled children since mainstreaming in non-specialist schools was introduced.

Part of this divergence of interest by gender may be due to the growth in popularity of Physical Education/sports studies as examination subjects in England, Joint Qualification Council results gave the following figures:

	2001			*2010*			*2013*		
Level	*Boys*	*Girls*	*Total*	*Boys*	*Girls*	*Total*	*Boys*	*Girls*	*Total*
GCSE 000s entering		N/A		72	39	112	62	32	95
% A*–C (cf all students)	53	56	54 (57)	68	69	68 (69)	69	72	70 (70)
A level 000s entering	9.7	5.7	15.4	12.3	6.4	18.7	8.6	4.6	13.1
% A*–B (cf all students)	21	34	25 (37)	31	48	39 (52)	32	49	38 (61)

Table 4.3 The effects of gender, disability, ethnicity and class on children's sport

Young people's (6–16) index	1E (at least ten times a year outside school)		2E (3 sports at least 10 times a year excluding walking)	
	1994	2002	1994	2002
Key stage 1 (aged 5–7)	104	102	108	109
Male	102	103	106	109
White	102	101	102	102
Benchmark, all young people	*100*	*100*	*100*	*100*
Key stage 2 (aged 7–11)	99	97	92	93
Key stage 3 (aged 11–14)	97	101	98	106
Female	98	97	91	91
Key Stage 4 (aged 14–16)	95	97	93	90
Black & Ethnic minority	83	90	72	82
Disabled	67	60	39	37

Source: Sport England, 2005

It can be seen that numbers entering have declined, notably since the Coalition stressed numeracy and literacy subjects; boys are in the majority but girls show better results, particularly at A Level.

Apart from the constraints already mentioned, young people (in Scotland – CLR, 1999) mentioned foremost the same lack of time that adults offered – 26% for boys, but 33% for girls, the latter indicating greater responsibilities for housework and childcare. Both sexes mentioned homework and part time jobs, essential to the economy of poorer households, though much of the work was low-skill, low paid and even illegal (Mizen et al., 2000). They also mentioned 'nowhere near home to play' (one in four), and 'costs too much' (one in eight).

So far as PE time in the secondary curriculum was concerned, 61% of Year 7–9 children had two or more hours, but this dropped to only 34% for Years 10–11 as academic demands grew, reductions since 1994 of 5% and 2% respectively. In 2001, the government agreed that every child should have access to two hours of activity a week in total, in and out of school.

Nonetheless, Sport England (MORI, 2001a: 14) assessed the situation as 'a solid platform for promoting the value of sport and exercise among young people,' but attributed the girls' reduced interest to lack of family support and role models, less confidence in their own ability, less interest in competition, and features they disliked, as listed in Tables 4.1 and 4.2.

Does the area of residence or the type of school make a difference? Educationalists in the UK have voiced concerns that the more open market for parents to enrol children in school and the publication of league tables of exam results will lead to social polarisation. Two accepted measures of this are the percentage of children obtaining free school meals and the percentage awarded five or more GCSE passes at grade C or above: while the national aggregate figures showed improvements, Gibson and Asthana used local catchment figures for schools to demonstrate that:

within local markets...high status schools are drawing to themselves the most socially advantaged pupils within their catchment areas and that this will in due course, and perhaps already does, mean that they are able to improve their GCSE results faster than their local 'competitors.

(Gibson and Asthana, 1999: 315)

For sport and PE, again there was no good data on geographical, social class or cultural differences.

The UK has one of the lowest levels of educational qualification in Europe. Two schemes were devised to use the attraction of sport and leisure to encourage participation in education, aimed particularly at those who are under-performing or truanting. *Playing for Success* set up study support centres for pupils at Key Stages 2 and 3 (10 to 14 years) at professional sports clubs, where in six four-hour sessions a week they could learn literacy, numeracy, IT, and link soccer to geography and European studies. Sharp et al. (1999) monitored clubs operating in the first year, who together took 4,934 pupils from 209 schools, just under a third with special educational needs, and discovered:

- most pupils attended more than four-fifths of sessions, and to fill the lists was no problem;
- there was nothing they did not enjoy, and their schools would be glad to take part again;
- self-confidence, self-esteem and attitudes to learning improved and on average reading scores were improved by six months for primary and eight months for secondary pupils.

Following up to see if there were effects on educational attainment, Sharp, Schagen and Scott (2004) showed that lower-attaining children made up two months on KS2 tests and three months at KS3 over non-attenders. Getting sponsorship and involving professional players proved problematic, but PFS reached its target group and achieved its aims. Consequently, it has been extended to lower division soccer clubs and professional cricket, rugby union and league, and basketball clubs.

Connexions (DfEE, 2000) was a wide-ranging programme to support learning for 16–19s, including individual mentoring. For every course a young person attended, they could accumulate credits that could then be traded against training or materials costs. Connexions set up a smart card for leisure goods or services, for which DfEE sought national sponsors; however, it overlapped hugely with local Leisure Card schemes (Chapter 3); of one million issued only 145,000 were used, with no direct impact on learning outcomes (Rodger and Cowen, 2006), and Connexions was scrapped in 2006.

Dropping out or sustaining interest? Sports clubs and out-of-school schemes

When moving into the adult community, young people need information and confidence to access opportunities; they also have less purchasing power than adults. Thus, in 1997 (Sport England, 2000):

*   76% of authorities had a policy in leisure management contracts regarding young people, but only 19% specified targets for throughput;
*   73% of sports halls and swimming pools in England offered concessions to full-time students, and 67% to under 16s;
*   33% of hall space and only 19% of pool space was programmed for schools and under 19s and less than 3% of users were youth with discount cards.

A main concern of the Wolfenden report (CCPR, 1960) that led to setting up the Sports Council and introducing the Sport for All programmes was that provision for youth sport was poorer than in many European states, and that getting further education and training, and getting married and having children, led to drop-out and a 'post-school gap' – 'a manifest break' between school and adult participation. Subsequent research showed that the position was more complex than this, but that there were many constraints on the transition to adult sport. Nevertheless, dropout in adolescence 'is reported from all countries where researchers have studied the phenomenon,' recorded de Knop et al. (1996a) in studies from nineteen countries.

The Sports Council provided two experiments to help sustain participation and its health and social benefits. First, information, coaching, tournaments and taster sessions for local sports were provided in Streatham and Hastings. Wade (1987) showed that these had an immediate effect, but could not be sustained without new resources. In Active Lifestyles, coaches in Coventry were brought into schools, and the curriculum widened to include health-related fitness. Follow-up surveys showed participation in existing sports was substantially sustained as school-leavers hoped, but that far fewer new sports were started than had been intended (Sports Council/Coventry City Council, 1989). For the Health Education Authority, targets for promoting physical activity were girls aged 12–18, youth of low socio-economic status, and adolescents aged 16–18, including from ethnic minorities, with disabilities, or clinical conditions like obesity, diabetes or depression (HEA, 1998a: 6).

Undoubtedly, involvement of out-of-school sport grew substantially from 1970 (CLR, 1999). Issues about girls' opportunities and the quality of much participation experience remain, especially in deprived areas. Roberts and Brodie (1992: 81) clearly showed in six cities that 'the number of sports played when young was the best predictor of whether individuals would continue to play into adulthood,' i.e., having a portfolio of skills and interests is the best preparation for overcoming the changes and constraints of adulthood, and a broad-based curriculum is the best way to ensure this. This also was the consensus of a Carnegie

Corporation conference in the US (Poinsett, 1996: 117). In a 38-year follow-up of Swedish 15 year-olds, Engstrom (2008) found that the amount of time spent and club membership at 15 had no influence on middle-aged sport, but breadth of interests did, and even more high social status-people with high cultural capital were five times more likely to be playing than those with low. But the Qualifications and Curriculum Authority (1999: 3) reported that in many schemes of school PE 'little attention is given to the needs of the least and most able pupils.' In Germany, Anders (1982) reported a much larger drop-out from sport among lower social class youth. Roberts and Fagan (1999) examined youth leisure in three post-Communist East European states, and found that traditional class and gender divisions survived, even with reduced incomes and opportunities, indicating their strength of influence.

Youth has been called 'the dangerous years,' and were the focus of the Action Sport projects that launched the sports development sub-profession (Rigg, 1986). Initially, they focussed on young people, especially those unemployed, and involved three principles

- getting into young people's peer network rather than expecting them to come to publicly provided venues;
- working with new partners (not necessarily for sport) linked to youth and later to other target groups;
- using sites and buildings already available in communities.

Later schemes were aimed at women, ethnic minorities, older people, workers, health-at-risk groups, PE teachers and their pupils, and disabled people (McDonald and Tungatt, 1991). Similar Roving Leader programmes were run in Chicago in the 1930s, New York, San Francisco, Los Angeles, Buffalo, and other cities in the 1960s, and San Antonio in the 1990s (Crompton and Witt, 1997).

Schemes in Leicester, Birmingham and Derwentside for young unemployed people were evaluated by Glyptis, whose conclusions coincided with Rigg's:

> the idea that sport can contribute substantially to the lives of most unemployed people is unfounded. The idea that leisure in general can contribute is more plausible. From the evidence to date leading a full life demands a source of structure. Leisure cannot provide it. Leisure can, however, fulfil its present role as part of a balanced lifestyle, if a source of structure and purpose exists alongside it. If work in the conventional employment sense cannot survive in sufficient measure for all, then work is the concept to be examined.
>
> (Glyptis, 1989: 159,161)

Nine years later, from Australia, Lobo (1998: 8) came to similar conclusions:

> many young people live with deprivation, impermanence and temporary relation-ships in new ways. Emergent lifestyles include intermittent employment, the establishment of middle term careers, welfare claimant

'careers', extended full-time education, pre-marital cohabitational arrangements, and single parenthood.

(Lobo, 1998: 8)

One of the constraints to post-school sport is that until recently many sports clubs were interested only in the few talented young people who found their own way in, or were spotted as a result of high performances in school or junior competitions. Now many governing bodies make a much greater attempt to set up 'youth-friendly' clubs (de Knop et al. 1995). Many Welsh young people stated that they found sports clubs 'intimidating' and 'unwelcoming' places. Few clubs actively recruited junior members; most having been introduced only through parents already members, or sport teachers associated with particular clubs. Only 47% of 11–16s belonged to youth organisations, and half that number to sports clubs. SCW concluded that:

> this level of membership indicates that where community links do exist, the base for children's involvement appears to be very small and narrow. If continuity of participation is to be achieved when children leave school then the strengthening of the children's section within clubs will be a necessary condition.

(SCW, nd: 28)

DCMS (1999) floated the idea that there should be 'hub' and 'satellite' clubs, but imposing this, even with the 'bribery' of grants would be anathema to Britain's fiercely parochial, independent single-sport club system. Only the Civil service and often-defunct workers sports clubs, notably in coal or railways, were multi-sport, compared to the continental tradition, springing from urban or rural workers' or religious movements where sport was part of the social contract (Riordan and Kruger, 1996). The British workers' movement was pre-occupied with hours of work, holidays, pay and occupational health (Jones, 1988). Such clubs have to grow organically, and cannot be 'manufactured'; in the noughties, Sport England sought to promote 'hub clubs' with very modest success, but, after another strategy continuing to focus on national governing bodies (NGBs), and by inference, clubs (Sport England, 2012), in 2012 it (Sport England, nd) allocated £49m of Lottery money to set up 'satellite' clubs on school college and community sites, with the aim of creating 6,000 by 2017; aided by a Maker in each County Sports Partnership, by 2013 1,000 had formed.

In Belgium, although memberships were being sustained, de Knop et al. (1995) suggested there was a crisis in clubs from shortage of volunteers, small numbers of professional staff, and competition from other forms of leisure including commercial sports and fitness providers. Drawing on Dutch experience, de Knop and Martelaer (2001) suggested clubs must ensure more varied and quality-assured staff and programmes designed for youth's objectives, and with youth input. *Running Sport* was Sport England's voluntary and less formal version of this.

But such involvement is easier in Denmark (Thomson, 1998) or Germany (Heinemann and Schwab, 1999) where municipal support is more generous and better guaranteed than in Britain. These much larger clubs (averaging 300 but sometimes reaching 3,000 or more members) means that youth leaders, coaches and mentors can be more easily found and dedicated to youth work than in Britain's small clubs, averaging only about 43 members. Many, such as single-side soccer and most table tennis clubs, are smaller than this. Larger size allows specialisation of roles, but also makes the clubs a more secure place to invest public money in facilities and especially professionals – German clubs in the largest category may have 8–10 paid workers, as managers, coaches, groundsmen and animateurs. In Finland there is a long tradition of involvement of parents in sports clubs which has a strong influence on children (Seppanen, 1982, and Heinila, 1989).

The value of sport in diversion and 'character-building', explored in Chapter 9 in relation to delinquency, is evidenced in its role in summer play schemes and, especially in America, in the growing number of after-school clubs demanded as more household have both parents working by choice or necessity. Martinek and Hellison (1997) spent a career developing using PE and physical activity as a means of building resiliency and moral values in young people. The use of individual, team and outdoor adventure sports to work with underprivileged youth has been likewise documented in France (Anstett and Sachs, 1995; Charrier, 1997, Hindermeyer, 1998) and Belgium (Stassen, 1996) including those with alcohol, drug, or other health problems, and with a focus sometimes on migrant communities (de Knop et al., 1997, Spaaij, 2011 in Australia, Brazil and Netherlands).

The voluntary youth movement and statutory Youth Service had a strong role in sport traditionally (Stead and Swain, 1987), but suffered financial cuts in the mid 1990s and since. The overwhelming majority of a large number of English schemes submitted to Policy Action Team 10 claimed benefits to youth, but few had any data on outcomes. There is no link between youth and sport in EU policy.

To summarise this section, Roberts (1983: 176) believed it must be accepted that no single form of leisure provision will voluntarily attract all young people: 'There is no 'right' club or centre which, once…marketed will capture and retain all the 11–21 year olds, or any other age span.' Understanding of why and how teenagers either resist or co-operate with efforts from the adult world remains incomplete. What is clear, however, is that co-ordination between sectors is necessary if youth provision is to be enhanced. White and Rowe summed up this issue:

> Although there are many imaginative and innovative schemes for promoting youth sport in England, provision is variable and the development of sport for young people has been hampered by a lack of vision and poor co-ordination between different ages.
>
> (White and Rowe, in de Knop et al., 1996a: 124)

Thus whether or not there is a participation 'gap' or just a slide, there is undoubtedly an institutional gap on leaving school. Most children are taught to change a fuse, use a bank, fill in tax returns and attend unemployment offices or job centres, but few are given consumer skills to find their way through the sport and leisure maze, with its gaps and tenuous links. Analysis of Active People 1–3 results (Hart and Kung, 2011) showed statistically significant declines overall of 1% among 16–19s, and in football, swimming and rugby league; most of the increases were in minor sports, individual and gym-based. Before looking at the Nottinghamshire case study intended to bridge over the gap between schools and clubs, and to provide a continuing pathway for young sportspeople, we chart a sudden but foreshortened recovery in sport and PE's status and resourcing.

Case study 3: the rise (and premature demise) of the PE, School Sport, Club Links/Young People's Strategy

After initial collaboration over community use of schools in evenings, weekends and school holidays and shared investment with LAs on school sites (*A Chance to share* – DES, 1964), once the Sports Council was put under Departments responsible for the environment/local government, it was virtually warned off any collaboration, except between the architects in both bodies responsible for designing the sports facilities that often comprised a tenth of a secondary school's costs. Also, as we have seen, many teachers of academic subjects looked down on PE, and teachers were disunited about PE's purpose.

So, PE went through a rapid series of phases (Houlihan and Green, 2006):

1   *From disdain to neglect* (1960s–early 1990s);
2   *From neglect to moral panic* (about children's fitness, the loss of school playing fields, and debates about games in the 1992 National Curriculum);
3   *From panic to priority* (the development of a multi-strand programme within New Labour's high priority education programmes, to which I now turn).

Houlihan and Green argued that the weakness of the PE lobby, the influence of Sue Campbell as a policy entrepreneur, the accumulation of evidence influencing sceptical DfES ministers and officials support a 'multiple streams' (Kingdon, 1995) explanation of this particular policy change.

In the late 1990s, the Department of Education started to take a greater interest in school PE, perhaps stirred by curricular debates, accusations that the burdens of paperwork and accounting had taken non-specialist teachers from voluntary helping in extra-curricular sport, intimations that children had become less fit and fatter, and the Youth Sport Trust's TOP programmes had shown a need and appetite for training and support in primary schools. Suddenly, there was a whole change of tone and relationship; for a short while Sue Campbell was in a unique position as advisor to both sports and education ministers. Later she moved to chair UK Sport and was given a seat in the House of Lords for her national and international work for children and elite athletes, and their coaches.

So, under New Labour was born the multi-strand £7bn PE, SS, CL programme (DES, 2003) with its infrastructure of secondary Specialist Colleges at the centre of School Sport Partnerships linking up primary schools. Its cumulative success was headed by exceeding its prime target of 90% of schools offering two hours a week of 'high quality' (self-defined) PE and sport in and out of school (from 25% in 2002); some of the others are listed in Table 4.4. Prime Minister Tony Blair called school sport a 'hidden success' (speech to Sports Colleges conference, 1 February 2007, Telford). Though there was no formal evaluation, the target for quality PE and sport was raised to a 'five hour offer' in 2008 (Sport England et al., 2009), partly through offering activities on Friday/Saturday nights (DSCF/DCMS, 2010). France raised its sights from two hours of PE and sport a week to four by 2011, but teachers attacked the scheme because the extra hours were voluntary, and only likely to be taken up by keen pupils (European Information Service, 5 September 2007).

Table 4.4 PE, School Sport, Club Links and PE & sport strategy for young people programmes 2003–9

DfEE 2003 elements (1)	*Developments and PESSYP 2008 (2)*
• PSA targets from 62% in 2003 of 75% of children having 2 hours high quality PE & sport a week by 2006, 85% by 2008; £1.5bn 2003–8	• Exceeded – 90% by 2007–8 ; but only 71% and 66% in Years 10 and 11 (3); a five hour target is being set (DCSF, 2008) with £755m for 2008–11
• 400 Specialist Sport Colleges (SSCs) by 2005	• DFEE say exam results improved; still struggle between PA, competitive and lifelong recreation; help raise the floor rather than raising the ceiling (4); SSCs obtain above average GCSE scores for 5 subjects graded A*–C (6)
• 450 School Sport Partnerships (SSPs) involving virtually all state schools	• SSPs *do* develop networks, help teacher development , & focus on neglected primary PE (5,7); £30m for coaches in SSPs 2008–11
• 3,200 School Sport coordinators (SSCos) by 2006, linked to 18,000 primary teachers	• Appoint FE college coordinators (FESCOs) linked to SSPs
• increase proportion entering clubs	• Club links increase from 5 to 7.6 per school 2003–7, and volunteers from 12% to 16%
• gifted and talented development programmes including talent camps	• Those registered as G&T rise from 3% to 7%
• Step into Sport to encourage youth volunteering in 200 SSPs	• SSCs developing interest in sports leadership
	• £45m for *Playing with Success* schemes with professional clubs to increase numeracy/literacy
	• Create at least one multi-sport club for disabled children in each SSP

Sources: (1) DfES 2003; (2) DCSF, 2008; (3) Quick et al. 2008; (4) Houlihan and Wong, 2005; (5) Loughborough Partnership, 2005; (6) YST, 2000 (7) Smith and Leech, 2010

PESSCL's title was changed to end with 'Youth Strategy (DSCF, 2008) and £0.7bn committed for two more years. PESSYP was supported by a £750m Lottery fund for improving sport and PE facilities (Neville et al., 2008). But Waring and Mason (2010) pointed out that physical access needed full-time staff and a social infrastructure to become real for excluded youth, a lesson learned from Action Sport. School sport, which Houlihan (1999) called 'a crowded policy space', has become even more crowded! In another attempt to widen young people's choices a three-year programme called Sport Unlimited was launched via the County Sports Partnerships (Chapter XX), offering 10-week taster courses; by its penultimate term it had engaged 785,000 youngsters, and the Sport Industry Research Centre monitoring reported girls were 48% of participants, and two out of five had taken up a new activity (www.sportengland.org, accessed 02 August 2011). But of the nine sports targeted to prevent post-school dropout by Sport England, only three (football, basketball and tennis) were in the top ten choices of a sample of year 12–13 boys, and only two for girls (tennis and badminton). The other, mainly team games – rugby union and league, hockey and netball – just did not figure; maybe SE and the Coalition need to talk more with youth, as Bullough (2011) suggested.

The Coalition singled out PESSYP as a spending cut, on the unevidenced grounds that its administration through the County Sports Partnerships was expensive, and that it would give schools the freedom and clarity to focus on competitive sport and building a 'lasting legacy of competitive sport in schools' (DCMS/Sport England, 2012). This brought howls of protest from head teachers (*Observer* 28 November 2010: 5), PE teachers (Compass group letter to Michael Gove, 29 November 2010), sports interests, local and education authorities, and children (*Observer* 5 December 2010: 12, 19) headed by Baroness Campbell (letter to Secretary of State Michael Gove 20 October 2010, pointing out that the scheme had been exported to India, for 2.8m teachers and 22m children). Many called it 'hasty', 'ill-considered', and 'an act of vandalism'. Gove relented (u-turned?), announcing that SSPs could complete that academic year, at a cost of £47m, while £65m was available for each secondary school to release a teacher as co-ordinator for one day (rather than two days) a week until 2012–3, and relieving schools of some requirements 'so that they may have the 'clarity and freedom to concentrate on competitive school sports' (DE *Press Statement* 21 December 2011). It did show the fragility of the school sport coalition (Philpotts, 2013).

The impact on the schools and the children's sport over the ten years is shown in Table 4.5, in terms of minutes of participation, choice of sports, membership of clubs, taking part in competition and volunteering and the school's attainment of two or three hours' provision and provision for gifted and talented children. Continuation of School Sport coordinators will depend on schools allocating money from their own budgets. The gendered and ethnicised nature of volunteering is shown in the Street Games Case Study 8 and Figure 11.5.

Table 4.5 Data from School Sport surveys 2003–4 and 2009–10

All=years 1–11	2003–4			2009–10			Comments
	1y	All	2y	1y	All	2y	
Participation 2hrs/week %	52		73		86		boys 53% girls 37% mixed 56% just 22% yrs 12–13
3hrs/week %					64	46	60% rural, 54% urban lower where high free school meals, 50% BME, high IoMD*
Curricular time mins/wk	101		113	127		107	increases only 3% yrs 10,11;7% extra curricular top-up yrs 1–9
Internal Competition %	23		28	B 81		72	virtually all hold sports days
Inter-school pupils	35		32	G 80 B 60 G 58		67 40 30	by years 12–3 gender gap large–24% boys, 11% girls
No of sports		15			19		Girls traditional offers plus cheerleading 64%, yoga 35%
Club links no % pupils 1 or more club	4 28		10 16	8.3	33	13.8	now defined as community, dance or multi-skill clubs
Gifted and talented %		5			8		
Volunteering %		9			24		peaks in yrs 5,6

Note: *=Index of multiple deprivation

Source: Quick et al., 2010

School sport coordinators had been introduced to Further Education Colleges (FESCOs); a 2009–10 survey showed that:

- 23% of 16–19 full-time pupils had taken part in a session, up 7% in a year;
- 12% took part in internal competitions, up from 7%;
- 19 activities on average were on offer, up from 16;
- links with schools were up to 37% from 25%.

But this money was cut after only two years (as was the TNS annual surveys, after a series of eight).

The value of young volunteers has been recognised by Sport England; for example, in partnership with the Co-operative Society, Street Games had 4,000 new volunteers aged 16–25, of whom a third were female, a fifth BME, and a quarter NEETS (not in education or training, Walpole 2012). Now thirty years old, Charity Sports Leaders UK trains 200,000 young people a year; Mawson and Parker (2013) analysed data on 76,000 candidates 2004–9, revealing a profile of 91% aged 16–25, 40% female, 11% non-white and only 0.4% disabled. Three-fifths had previous experience of volunteering, more likely if they were women, had attended an FE College (numerous BTEC sports courses included SLUK awards), and came from a higher socio-economic group.

Much of youth leisure is outside school and little is known, for example, about countryside recreation; Mulder, Shibli and Hale (2005) examined activities of 1,000 Hampshire schoolchildren; use depended on access via family (93%), friends (58%) or schools (44%); popular activities required no special equipment, and depended more on preference. But overall, only a quarter of children visited a natural site weekly (compared with twice as many of their parents when young). And so in 2009 Natural England launched *A Million Children Outdoors*, a target to be reached in three years, with a £23m grant fund for children from deprived communities (NE *Press Release* 2 April 2009).

Developing commitments: sports performance and excellence

Leisure is an important part of youth lifestyle, consuming 14% of household expenditures for under 25s, but unequally: 37% for males and 23% for females (Mathieson and Summerfield, 2000). For sport, Hendry (1992: 71) suggested that 'school sports will be most liked by pupils who are highly skilled, competitive and achievement-oriented.' Performance and Excellence in Nottingham Sport (PENS, see below) and schemes that multiplied under the Lottery-funded World Class Start programmes were about structured talent identification and nurture, and not only formed a more professional cadre of coaches but also specialised sports scientists, in what has been called a global sporting arms race (de Bosscher et al., 2008).

Bailey, Morley and Dismore (2009) from a sample of 535 schools, discovered that nine out of ten had a gifted and talented whole school policy; 63% identified G&T children by current performances, 20% considered their potential; subject leaders reported expertise in games (86%), athletics (45%), and gymnastics (31%), but only one in ten felt they had had significant impact.

The much-vaunted programmes of the Eastern bloc in the Cold War era were as much attributable to hard training and harder competition as to science and were not backed up by longitudinal studies (Thomson and Beavis, 1985), but with the Institutes of Sport in Australia, Canada, West Germany and the UK more similarities are becoming evident (Oakley and Green, 2000, also Houlihan and Green 2008):

- good formal co-ordination between administrators, coaches and scientists in an athlete-centred model, including lifestyle support and preparation for retirement from competition;
- effective identification and monitoring of athletes;

- well-structured competitive programmes with continual international exposure;
- accessible and specialised facility provision;
- adequate funding for people and infrastructure.

As Gratton (1996) remarked, Britain seeks to support excellence in a wide range of sports, as it does in participation, which may explain its relative decline in Olympic fortunes. In the 1980s and 1990s Australia, Canada, Italy, Spain, and the Netherlands made strategic investments in identifying and preparing athletes. In the UK, after decades of resisting specialist provision in schools for other than for drama and music, in the 1990s the Department for Education supported programmes for specialist sport, arts, and technology colleges, providing money for extra staff (teaching or coaching), and for programmes to extend participation and improve performance. A report on the first 26 colleges demonstrated:

- improved links with feeder primary/high schools and sports clubs;
- in-service training of teachers and coaches;
- improved examination results.

When students get into full time Further and Higher Education, they are in a privileged environment, with subsidised or free facilities, and opportunities to take part in self-organised specialist clubs. Loughborough University is possibly the most developed example with 60 clubs in its Athletic Union and substantial community involvement (Thorpe and Collins, 2010). For students, it is not surprising in 1996 that both sports activity rates – at 76.3% in the last four weeks compared to 62.5% for all 16–19s (excluding walking) – and sports club membership (at 18.1% compared to 8.1%) were the highest in the population. Nonetheless, at these ages in the population as a whole, a gap between doing enough moderate or vigorous activity to gain health benefits and actual participation had already appeared – 53% against 66% for 16–9 year-old men and 29% against 44% for women (Mathieson and Summerfield, 2000).

Higher Education is becoming, as in America, a base for elite sports training with the bulk of the specialist facilities for the UK Institute of Sport at HEIs, with £120m of investment on facilities, already surpassing Sir Roger Bannister's prediction that one in three elite athletes would come from HE. But access to higher education is socio-economically biased (Platt, W. *Guardian* 13 August 2000: 13):

%	Professional	Skilled	Semi/unskilled
15–19s with two A levels	40	12	8
with 2 A levels going to University	82	78	71

This bias is reflected geographically in the affluence of households in an area (HEFCE, 1997).

In Britain, Searle (1993: 5) reported 'on gaps which leave even gold medallists in debt or dependent on parental or spouse support.' Of the 1992 Olympic squad 45% were in debt to an average of £5,000 because of sports costs, only 38% had ever obtained prize money or sponsorship and those that did only averaged £1,000 a year. In the late 1990s, the Lottery gave British athletes the sort of 'broken time' payments in lieu of salary and support costs via NGBs that had been common elsewhere for years. This investment takes time to materialise, but there were great successes in Olympic and Paralympic sport in Sydney and Beijing and London; by then, UK Sport was driving a payment-by-results set of rules, wanting 'no compromise' in training to promised medal targets, and seeking to capitalise on 'home advantage'(UKS, 2009) to reach fourth in the London 2012 medal table.' With an average subsistence award of £7,000, nine in ten athletes agreed that WCPP 'had made a significant difference to their ability to train and compete,' but nearly half felt it was still insufficient (UKS, 2001).

We will see in the Nottinghamshire case study how social area and household differences divided opportunities unevenly for the performance squads (Buller 1998, Collins and Buller, 2003). Unless there is a sustained redistribution, the next generation of sports performers will reproduce current inequalities. The *Development of Sporting Talent* study (ESC, 1998a) showed that 38% of the members of elite squads in twelve sports studied were from professional and managerial groups compared to 19% in the whole population (Fig 4.1). Only rugby league with 22% AB came anywhere near the population average, and some like swimming at 83% had four fifths of their squads from privileged backgrounds.

Interestingly, the proportions were reversed when it came to employment in professional sport with 25% of C2DEs compared to 14% of ABC1s. The English Sports Council concluded that:

> the opportunity to realise sporting potential is significantly influenced by an individual's social background. So for example, a precociously talented

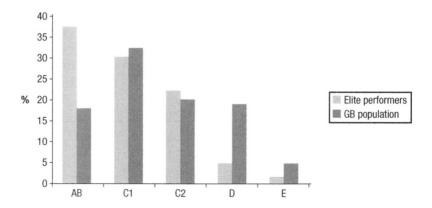

Figure 4.1 Social class of elite performers in the DOST study

youngster born in an affluent family with sport-loving parents, one of whom has (probably) achieved high levels of sporting success, and attending an independent/ private school, has a 'first-class' ticket to the sporting podium. His or her counterpart, equally talented but born in a less favoured social circumstances has, at best a third class ticket and at worst no ticket at all. The chances of the former achieving high levels of sporting success are very good while the chances of the latter are minimal. The differences in opportunity clearly affect the country's ability to compete and win in international competition.

(ESC, 1998a: 13)

Lord Killanin of the International Olympic Committee, said it should be possible for everyone, in spite of very different beginnings, to have an equal chance to obtain the standards of high level international competitions. Kay (2000: 166) showed just how much time, moral support, transport and money, and sacrifice by parents and/or siblings was involved in having an elite athlete as a member of a family, concluding the absence of such support may exclude such children from realising their own talent. This is very much a first world/third world problem, but as we have seen still bedevils developed societies like Britain.

Case study 4: sport for secondary schoolchildren: go for gold and Champion Coaching in Nottinghamshire

White and Rowe argued there was a gap in integrated functioning between school PE and adult sports clubs, such that:

> There is no unified network or programme which provides opportunities for young people to participate in sport and develop their sporting potential. Provision is uneven and fragmented and much depends on the locality in which young people live, their family circumstances, their gender and their ability level.

(White and Rowe, in de Knop et al., 1996a: 115)

In Britain, the 1980s saw a growing awareness of the importance of more technically proficient and ethically aware amateur coaches in the wake of setting up the National Coaching Foundation (NCF). It launched the Champion Coaching (CC) scheme in 1991 with the sole target of developing an after-school sports programme with a mission to: 'promote quality assured youth sport coaching for performance motivated children within a co-ordinated community structure' (NCF, 1996: 3).

In the first two years it developed 24 pilot schemes across England, each co-ordinated by a part-time/volunteer Youth Sports Manager. By 1996, 105 local authorities were CC partners, and Geoff Cooke, NCF's third Chief Executive, could claim CC as 'the success story of the decade [having] provided quality coaching for more than 25,000 young people [and] an excellent vehicle for recruiting and developing over 2,000 coaches' (NCF, 1996: 1).

Nottinghamshire, unusually for England, had a county-based leisure service and inter-district. It had a buoyant mixed economy in the south, but successive pit closures in the 1980s and 1990s removed its coal industry, leading to high unemployment in the north. By 1989, Nottinghamshire's Leisure Services Committee had established the Nottinghamshire Sports Training Scheme (NSTS) with a £200,000 grant from the Sports Council, to 'increase the number of young people participating in sport.' This was elaborated into four principles, to 'meet the needs of participants at all levels of ability; be phased and achievable; represent a long-term county commitment to sports development, and to recognise that support and co-operation of a large number of organisations...were essential'. The last was perhaps the key to NSTS' success.

NSTS used the PE, club and governing body systems as well as education, municipal, and voluntary club facilities in all District Councils, irrespective of local politics. The original NSTS set three levels through which children could progress:

Taster → Improver → Advanced

Selection for 'taster' courses was on a strictly first-come-first-served basis, primarily referred through schools. Children could only progress to 'improver' and 'advanced' courses by invitation from one of 200 registered coaches. Prices were set at a matter of pence per session to prevent cost being a barrier.

In 1991, with another Sports Council grant, the Performance and Excellence in Nottinghamshire Sport scheme (PENS) was added as a stage following CC, allowing children identified as talented to progress into top-level clubs or into county, regional and national squads (NCC, 1993). The county also organised a pre-CC programme called Go for Gold (GfG) for 9–17 year olds for children of any ability, two weeks shorter to fit into school terms, cheaper if paid in advance, and where youngsters could move sideways to another GfG course.

The initial success of NSTS was striking, with some 2,600 children in 1990, but numbers dwindled over the next three years, and taster entrants fell from three-fifths to just under half. Another problem became evident: it was intended that participants not progressing to improver or advanced courses would be directed to existing voluntary clubs with junior sections, or to a junior club set up by NSTS. Hoping to overcome these problems, NSTS was re-launched in 1993 when the three streams were incorporated into a 'new' Scheme, now with five objectives, to:

- effectively cover the stages of the Sports Development Continuum;
- provide a clear and accessible performance pathway for talented youngsters;
- increase the number of junior clubs;
- maximise the effectiveness of coaches employed; and to
- complement work in schools.

In 1994–8 NSTS underwent further changes. The 'PENS' performance work was revamped as Performance Resources (PR), to support the county Governing Bodies of Sport and School Sports Associations, presaging a Nottinghamshire Active Sports partnership in 2000.

As a result of its innovation, scale and coherent management, NSTS set the pace for pioneering youth sport development work throughout England, but while CC's monitoring of registered players and coaches proceeded, the *Champion Coaching Guide* (NCF, 1996) dealt only briefly with evaluation, a deficiency remedied in this case study. Telephone and face-to-face questionnaires for young users yielded robust and reliable responses of 39% for CC, 38% for PR, and 31% for GfG, from children ranging from 10 to 118 years; in CC boys were half of CC's sample, and two-fifths in GfG. In-depth interviews were held with chief coaches and secretaries of clubs popular with the youngsters. I look at four outcomes for NSTS:

1   How satisfied were the children and their parents?
2   What sport did children do after NSTS?
3   What was the take up of Performance Resources?
4   Did NSTS demonstrate social inclusion or exclusion?

Outcome 1: children's and parents' satisfactions with NSTS courses

Very encouragingly for Nottinghamshire CC, 96% of CC and 95% of GfG users had enjoyed their courses. Of the few who did not, five found it 'too basic', three claimed it was 'monotonous or boring,' and only three mentioned unfriendliness of the group or the coach. Perhaps unsurprisingly, they highlighted enjoying the games most, followed by being coached:

%	*Champion Coaching*	*Go for Gold*
Playing the games	27	31
Coaching	21	23
Learning new skills	23	18
Making friends	12	16

Interestingly, the girls found the games and meeting new friends more appealing than boys. Boys enjoyed competition more than girls, thus supporting Hendry's (1993) and Mason's (1995) characterisations of male sport as more competitive, and female as more social.

Forty-four different Nottinghamshire venues were used in CC's nine sports. Only a handful of CC youngsters, mostly girls, encountered access problems, of distance, poor transport, and parents not free to provide lifts. Asked about satisfaction with coaching staff regarding friendliness, helpfulness, quality of organisation and punctuality, the first three responses showed very high satisfaction – from 89 to 96% for both schemes – and the fourth only a little lower, at 80 and 83%.

When the children were asked whether they received information about local clubs or other opportunities to continue playing after their course (in CC jargon 'exit routes'), only 60% for CC and 56% for GfG said yes. Even allowing for forgetfulness, this figure was too low to be satisfactory for this key objective, emphasized because it decreased every year from 1994.

Outcome 2: children's sports participation after NSTS

This issue is illustrated in Table 4.6, showing the largest group carrying on with their chosen sport as recreation, compared to only one in three or four who joined a local club, perhaps again reflecting inadequate information. Once again, there were concerns: one in eight children gave up their sport entirely, mainly for lack of time, inadequate facilities, and not enjoying it. Providers could do something only about the second reason. Analysis demonstrated that team players were more likely to continue than individual players (85 compared to 77%), but the latter seemed more likely to progress higher –10% joined a county squad, compared to only 4% in team sports.

The children were also asked whether they currently belonged to a sports club, one to four years after their course. Three-fifths of CC respondents were members of at least one club, covering 21 sports in 97 clubs, while 136 GfG children joined 68 clubs in 15 sports. Six out of seven CC members felt junior sections were strong, they were offered coaching, and were kept busy. More encouraging was that children who joined clubs found them rewarding (24% in team, and 44% in individual sports). Ninety-seven per cent stated their 'club was friendly'. GfG figures were very similar (Table 4.7).

Table 4.6 Children's sports activity after attending the Nottinghamshire Sports Training Scheme

Type of participation %	Go for Gold	Champion Coaching
Give up	–	12
Recreational	52	46
Club	31	25
County	11	17
Regional	5	–
National	1	–

Table 4.7 Residents and performance participants living in areas of social need in Nottinghamshire

Level of social need	% of Go for Gold registrants	% Champion Coaching Registrants	% of Performance Resources registrants	% of Nottinghamshire residents
Below Average	92	87	92	71.3
Moderate	5	4	4	11.1
Serious	2	7	4	10.2
Extreme	1	2	0.3	7.3
Base	951 in basketball, cricket, netball, orienteering 1994–8	751 in 9 sports 1994–8	315 in cricket, table tennis, squash 1995–9	994,000

Two thirds of volunteered comments were positive, such as:

> CC helped me progress and carry on in the sport.
>
> (Hockey, anon, 17)

> CC has a very friendly atmosphere between coach and trainee.
>
> (Squash, boy aged 14)

> CC was enjoyable and made me think about my skills, so therefore I can play netball a lot better than I used to.
>
> (Netball, anon)

Parents of CC children were asked to rate their satisfaction on a scale of 1 to 5, and the averages of 310 answers were:

Standard of coaching	4.22
Organisation of sessions	4.03
Parental contacts by coaches	3.03
Administration from centre	3.59
Enjoyment of child(ren)	4.38

Three-fifths of parents rated enjoyment as 'excellent,' but amount of contact received the most criticism, and lack of information was volunteered as a problem. For example:

> More information and suggestions for when course ends. Didn't really have a chance to talk to coach about further courses/clubs – no follow-up, so child lost interest. Coaching was first class!! Well worth the small cost.
>
> (Parent)

That this situation was class-linked was confirmed by the Nestlé Family Monitor (MORI, 2000) where AB parents said they used all forms of information more than DEs, except word-of-mouth from friends and family, and especially from teachers (26 compared to 17%) and clubs (27 compared to 13%).

As a form of triangulation, the views of NSTS and the young players they referred were checked out in interviews. Coaches and secretaries confirmed the importance of NSTS to recruitment, as two examples showed:

> Without the NSTS running central organised activities to send the kids to, our membership would be considerably depleted.
>
> (D. Dreycote, Keyworth Table tennis club, 9 Aug 98, 40 juniors)

> ...integral to the success of the club...we need all the assistance we can get!
>
> (Secretary, Trent Bridge Squash Club, 25 juniors)

Trent Bridge SC took a proactive approach by having a 'junior friendly' membership fee and an 'adopt-a-junior' programme whereby adults were encouraged to pay the junior players' membership fees. The Sports Council (1995) stressed the importance of youth-friendly clubs. Thus nothing appeared to be wrong with the clubs acting as exit routes and the wide range of clubs Nottinghamshire offered provided much-praised and appreciated services to juniors.

Outcome 3: take up of Performance Resources

As with CC and GfG, PR children gave high scores for enjoyment, the quality of the sessions, facilities and coaches (from 7.4 to 8.4 out of ten). When asked about the highest level of participation they reached prior to attending, two out of three had entered from GfG or CC, and nearly one in two was involved in county or higher level competitions. This suggested the pathways provided were appropriate and successful. Suggestions for improvements included smaller squads to allow more individual attention, and changing times of sessions to avoid evening rush hour traffic.

Outcome 4: social inclusion or exclusion in NSTS?

CC was organised by Governing Body partners, to be available to all youngsters but not to take specific affirmative actions amongst poor children. GfG managers hoped their local knowledge would make it more sensitive to social need. To examine NSTS' effectiveness in outreach, the addresses of children registered were related to deprivation ratings (NCC, 1994: 4). In 1991, across the county almost a third of the population lived in areas defined as having some social need. Table 4.7 provides definitive evidence that a disproportionate share of children from non-deprived areas took part in NSTS. Put another way, only eight per cent of GfG and PR participants and 13% of CC's came from areas of moderate, serious or extreme social need compared with 29% of the population.

Table 4.8 Likelihood ratios of young people getting involved in Champion Coaching according to social need

District	Pop. aged 5–17	% in 1–3	1. Extreme	2. Serious	3. Moderate	4. Below average
Ashfield	17,100	18	N/A	0	1 in 455	1 in 379
Bassetlaw	16,500	19	0	N/A	0	1 in 2,668
Broxtowe	16,200	0	N/A	N/A	N/A	1 in 376
Gedling	17,400	3	N/A	N/A	1 in 186	1 in 91
Mansfield	16,700	55	1 in ,1250	1 in 483	1 in 250	1 in 133
Newark	16,800	16	N/A	1 in 364	1 in 408	1 in 164
Rushcliffe	15,400	0	N/A	N/A	N/A	1 in 350
Nottingham City	41,100	70	1 in 839	1 in 261	1 in 789	1 in 187

Thus, participants were not representative of the population. Put most starkly, as in Figure 4.2:

• For GfG in four major sports over five years only eight per cent of children registered from only 19 areas of social need. Thus 56 areas of need registered no-one, though Nottingham City took only a small part in this scheme.
• In CC 13% came from 25 areas of need, leaving 42 from which no-one registered; only two children came from the six most deprived areas, all in the city.
• For PR eight per cent came from 25 different areas, leaving 50 areas of social need where there had been no participants since its introduction in 1995.

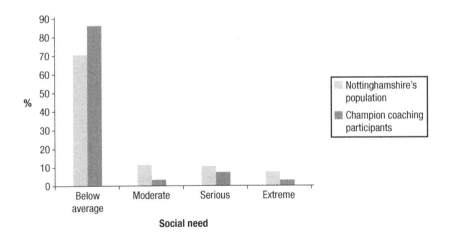

Figure 4.2 Distribution of population and Champion Coaching participants in Nottinghamshire

It is clear that there is a social gradient in take-up, related to income/social class, but also to physical opportunity. Rushcliffe in southern Nottinghamshire, one of the most affluent districts in England, had eight NSTS venues, no zones in social need, and registered 240 (one in four) of PR registrants. This was clearly a serious issue, especially given NSTS' aim to 'be organised to meet the needs of *all* participants at all level of ability.' Using NCC's (1994) document and the 1991 census data for all 5–17 year olds, one can calculate a 'likelihood ratio' for each District of a child becoming involved in NSTS. The results for CC are shown in Table 4.8.

It clearly shows the low chances of children in Bassetlaw and Mansfield. Buller (1998) showed the vast majority of Nottinghamshire's population lived within three kilometres of a CC venue and there was a strong relationship between venues and areas where large numbers of CC participants originated. For example, 44 and 49 CC participants resided in just two Enumeration Districts in Bingham and Retford near six venues. In contrast, Bassetlaw District with a youth population of 16,533 had only two venues and five CC participants.

This analysis of the four outcomes shows that children in well-off areas had a much higher chance of becoming NSTS participants than those from places with social need. This situation was true of every District, and particularly in Mansfield and Nottingham with the largest needy populations. This suggests the social inequalities were structural rather than circumstantial. One can understand that some parents in deprived areas could not manage or afford to get their children to a venue (though once there, the low average cost of 50p a session could be waived on application), or they might not have seen CC as 'for them'. But why were referral rates so low; what were the PE teachers in these areas doing? This demands close analysis of referral routes in sports schemes.

Despite criticisms of NSTS, the overriding picture from the participants, their parents, the coaches, and a selection of club secretaries, was that it was a resounding success. As young participants said

> I felt it has made me a better player and it has made me aware of the other organisations that I can join.
>
> (Squash, girl aged 13)

> I really enjoyed taking part in the course and it improved my skills dramatically, I really hope that my younger sister and her friends can take part in a few years.
>
> (Hockey, anon)

Was experience of CC elsewhere the same? Using Pawson's (2006) scientific realism, Bell (2010) sought to replicate and extend analysis of CC in two Merseyside boroughs. She found that youngsters here were also clearly helped in regular sports participation and club membership, but the exit routes were not always sustained. Venues encouraged a more even spread of participation in Knowsley (21% in most deprived wards, the same as the share of population) but in St Helens it was clearly skewed to more affluent areas (13% of participants compared to 27%). Coaches clearly had their confidence and expertise raised, but also unevenly sustained with a three-year timescale.

Conclusions

Even though sport has been synonymous with school-age children in English history, there is remarkably little cross-sectional and no longitudinal data on participation, and little on its physical, psychological or social effects. The balance of opinion is that, besides intrinsic enjoyment, sport helps academic performance, though Lindner (1999) quoted by Coalter, Allison and Taylor (2000) believed the evidence was more ambiguous. It seems to work as an instrumental aid to learning when linked to the glamour of professional sport, as in *Playing for Success*. The best data is the retrospective reconstruction of Roberts and Brodie (1992: 80–82) which showed a long term growth of involvement.

Although there are studies of what children like and dislike, we do not have typologies of youth lifestyles for educational or sporting policy purposes. In a not-dissimilar society, slightly less affluent, and with more concentrated poverty, but with a similar range of sports, would we replicate the typology discovered in a factor/cluster analysis of 4,000 13–21-year-old Germans, where Brettschneider (1990) identified five types:

1   *No sports* (5%) – slightly overweight, good family relations, but interested in computers, music, or other leisure;
2   *Activity/motion* (4%) – interested in body image, using sport and exercise; relations more with friends/peers than adults; no clear future plans;
3   *Negative body concept* (17%) – would like to be more active, but have delicate health/experience physical discomfort;
4   *Stylistic hedonism* (13%) – absorbed in promoting a personal style (in sport, slimming/fitness, fashion, music), not close to parents or concerned about the future;
5   *Balanced lifestyle* (61%) – a surprisingly large group of inconspicuous adolescents, looking for both fun and achievement in sport, satisfied with their body images, on good terms with parents and peers and with a positive outlook on life.

From the limited survey data and the international research literature, the following is clear: there is a social and income gradient in youth sports participation, girls' choices are not as wide as boys, and, despite high levels of enjoyment, there are several points at which dropping out can occur, when:

*   PE becomes optional and/or children become involved in intensive study for career-forming exams (in England, GCSEs);
*   getting involved in vocational study or full time work;
*   getting married/cohabiting, and having children, especially the first;
*   moving house or job and breaking up social networks.

In 2011, it was clear also that Coalition Ministers educated in public schools want to go back to a masculine, games-driven competitive sport model, and London 2012 provided a cloak for this, if not an excuse.

Poor households have little money for leisure (Chapter 4), but their children do need money to be able participate in sport alongside their more fortunate peers. The potential for Sport for All can be epitomised amongst Higher Education students who mostly have local cheap or free facilities, fairly flexible timetables and the highest participation rates in the country (75%); but relatively few poor and deprived children make it into HE.

Introducing the MORI survey, Sport England's chairman, wrote:

> the costs to individuals and society of this declining commitment to primary school PE may not be felt now. They will, however, be measured in the years to come in terms of heart disease and increasing obesity, osteoporosis and stroke... in addition, we must not forget the potential waste of sporting talent and missed medal opportunities.
>
> (MORI, 2001a)

Public sector sports planners can do more in making facilities more physically accessible, and managers could be more welcoming and open, but for young people it needs first the understanding of encouragement of parents, teachers and coaches, next the reinforcement of peers, and then the support of youth-friendly clubs where parents are active. While there are structural factors of class, gender, disability, geography and to a lesser extent race, it would seem that what may be needed is what in vocational training, Rudd and Edwards (1998) called *structured individualisation*, that is, tailoring provision to individual needs. We shall see in Chapter 9 that this can make a considerable difference in counselling schemes for young delinquents, and as far as it was possible, so it did in NSTS. Such services are not cheap, but nor are area initiatives if a high proportion of the benefit is devoured by active, informed, mobile, and more affluent residents.

Roberts and Parsell (1994) argued that social class divisions in leisure were becoming more blurred, but confirmed Hendry's findings that participation in sport was likely to be higher in middle than working-class settings. By 1996, Roberts, reviewing Mason's and two other studies of youth sport, opined dryly that

> Sport and leisure are fields in which the wills of policy makers are rarely decisive. Shakespeare and religion have not soared as popular leisure passtimes through their promotion in schools. Competitive team sports are likely to fare similarly whatever governments pronounce and schools promote if young people prefer other activities. Leisure effects in education are often unintentional. Breaking down class divisions in leisure was not among the principal reasons why the 11-plus was abandoned in Britain, or why postcompulsory education was expanded. The 1988 Education Reform Act seems to have persuaded schools to upgrade their sports facilities and publicise these provisions not via the National PE Curriculum but by extending parental

choice. Sport and leisure policies are always most likely to succeed when they flow with and harness broader tides.

(Roberts, 1996: 56)

Coalter came to similar conclusions:

there has been a relative decline in more 'traditional' team and partner sports, accompanied by increased participation in a more diversified range of activities...one conclusion might be that the key policy issue is to encourage current, committed participants to increase their frequency of participation rather than commit resources in an attempt to expand the base of (possibly reluctant) participants.

(Coalter, 1999: 36)

Scheerder et al. (2005), looking over thirty years of youth sport's evolution from 1969 in Flanders, identified individualisation and a longer period of peer influences, a reduction in social class differentiation, the effect of mass media, but stuck with age, gender, school programme and parental involvement as enduring influences.

YouGov (2012) for Sport England identified a regular commitment amongst 25–34s to sport in general rather than a particular sport, but half of regular participants (more than once a week – 39%) said that it did not depend on school experiences aged 11–16, whereas half taking part less often (once a month or less – 24%) thought they would have been taking part more if they had had better experiences. Half their active sample played two or three main sports and a seventh a variety compared to two-fifths and a quarter of the inactive respectively, which would appear, to pour cold water on sustaining a broader choice, which Engstrom (2008) and Telama et al. (2006) and Roberts and Brodie (pp 216–8) found likely to support lifelong participation.

There is still much to be done also about unhealthy diets, and addiction to passive computer games (BHF, 2009). Once the aura of London 2012 has faded, it is likely that the issue of childhood obesity and sloth, and the problems they store up will resurge, from current levels where at 10–11 years 14% are overweight and 17% obese (Rudolf, nd). *End Child Poverty* (2011) showed that compared to a national average of 21.3% below the poverty line 20 local authorities (in London, Liverpool, Birmingham, Manchester Leicester, Nottingham and Middlesbrough and Leeds) had rates of 34 to 57%, and six of these were suffering the greatest cut in spending power via the 2010–12 Rate Support Grant. Reflecting on the causes of the 2010 urban riots, Baroness Lister opined 'addressing the social deficit must involve confronting the rampant inequality and materialism that disfigure our society' (letter, *Guardian* 13 September 2011: 33). OFSTED (2013) reported that a quarter of both primary and secondary school PE teaching was less than good; there is still much to do.

5   Gender, sport and social exclusion

Tess Kay

Introduction: sport and the gendered experience of social exclusion

When writing this chapter first in 2001, the links between gender, sport and inclusion were relatively under-explored. There had been little reason for analysts of female experiences of SEx to address sport: sport was generally less prominent in girls' and women's lives than in boys' and men's, and particularly so in the case of those most affected by poverty. In gender analyses of sport, more attention had been paid to the general under-representation of females in sport than to the situations of those who were most disadvantaged.

In the first decade of the twenty-first century the situation has changed as linkages between sport and inclusion have developed, in two ways. Firstly, efforts to involve girls and women in sport – i.e., gender inclusion *in* sport – have increased, either through targeted initiatives, or through their inclusion as targets for wider sports provision. Secondly, efforts to use sport to facilitate wider inclusion for girls and women – inclusion *through* sport – have also grown in number and scope, with sport now being used to empower girls and women in economically advanced nations, and also in international development contexts (e.g., Kay, 2009a; Saveedra, 2009). How sport has been linked with SEx has therefore become wider, more varied, more complex, and in some cases better documented through research.

But these changes are accompanied by some very marked continuities. The position of women and girls has not been transformed, either in sport or in inclusion: in society generally, a pervasive gender ideology discriminates against females of all ages, and this is replicated and reinforced in sport. In the public sphere, females remain disadvantaged in education, the labour market and welfare state; and in the private sphere through the persistence of resilient inequitable gender relations played out in the home. The positioning of women as primary carers and domestic workers can start young, consigning females to roles valued and rewarded less than paid work. In sport, expectations of sex-appropriate behaviour remain strongly influential and contribute to broader gender ideology. Sport is uniquely positioned to reinforce the idea that women are less powerful and therefore 'inferior' to men, and that these differences are natural phenomena rather than the products of social processes. This, however, does make sport an important area for contesting women's subordination.

This chapter tries to reflect this mixture of continuity and change. It first considers how women and girls experience exclusion. Attention then turns to the sport and inclusion relationship. The analysis focuses on girls' and women's under-representation in sport, and on efforts to involve them more fully, so that sport itself becomes a site for inclusion rather than exclusion. It also considers attempts to use sport as a vehicle for women's and girls' broader empowerment and inclusion.

Throughout the chapter no specific attempt is made to define 'socially-excluded' women. It is not just that the measures are too imprecise and the group too diverse, but also that women's lives are too dynamic. At any one time, for example, around one-fifth of mothers in Britain are lone parents, which carries one of the highest risks of being poor – but many others have experienced lone parenthood previously and more will do so in future. Whether lone parenthood will actually lead to exclusion will, in any case, vary according to individual women's wider circumstances. Not surprisingly, their main barriers to participation are cost of playing, of transport, of suitable childcare and having the confidence to take part, especially if they have done little sport hitherto (GfK NOP, 2006).

In later life, many women who previously had adequate resources will first encounter poverty and exclusion when they enter old age, especially if they join the growing number of 'old old' women aged 75 and over, who depend long-term on a state pension. For others still, exclusion may not be primarily linked to poverty or specific life stages, but in discriminatory practices surrounding identities, such as membership of minority ethnic groups, or disability. This chapter, therefore, takes the approach that a very diverse, large and fluid proportion of women will for different reasons be classed as socially excluded at different times in their lives. Other dimensions of their experiences of disadvantage are dealt with elsewhere in the book, including older women (Chapter 6), women from racial minorities (Chapter 7), and disabled women (Chapter 8).

Female experiences of poverty and social exclusion

> Women's issues are intrinsically linked with poverty, and poverty carries a woman's face. Three fourths of the poorest billion people of the world are women. In many countries, women own nothing, inherit nothing and earn nothing. Poverty leads to ill-health and additional strain on already over-stretched households, and ill-health intensifies poverty.
>
> (Brundtland, 2003)

Exclusion is not defined solely in terms of income, yet poverty remains its most prominent cause and symptom. With the 'feminization' of poverty recognised worldwide, poverty is especially relevant to women's experiences. Across centuries rich with social, economic, political and industrial transformations, women's greater vulnerability to being poor is a constant. The brunt of deprivation is not only borne by women in poorer countries, but also in western industrialised states operating extensive welfare systems. Rather than protecting women from poverty, many welfare practices institutionalize gender inequity.

Britain is one example of a social and economic system where being a woman increases the likelihood of being dependent on welfare assistance, and this increases the risk of being poor. In 2009, benefits composed 21% of the average woman's income but just 8% of the average man's, and one in five single women pensioners was at risk of being in poverty in retirement (Fawcett Society, 2010). As in other industrialised democracies, contemporary welfare fits women's life patterns less well than men's, and is a key contributor to gendering poverty. As the Fawcett Society warned, in the UK 'poverty...has a female face' (2010). Recently the female: male earnings gap widened to 17% for full-time and 37% for part-time jobs (Addey, E. and Rendage, R. *Guardian* 15 Nov 2008: 10).

Some dimensions of gender difference have reduced – for example, more women are active in the labour market than from previous generations, and fewer now live out their adult years in full economic dependency as unpaid wives and mothers. Nonetheless, marked differences remain in the lifetime experiences of men and women, with implications for their access to welfare support. Burchell and Rubery (1994) coined the term 'general domestic interference' to describe how the demands of servicing the home and family constrain women's labour market participation. The impact is particularly strong for certain women, including those in lower socio-economic groups, many ethnic minorities, and women heading a household alone. Notwithstanding women's improved access to educational and professional qualifications, their employment histories continue to be more fragmented than men's, damaging both their capacity to earn income, and their entitlement to welfare. As a result, many women can only access minimum levels of insurance-based key welfare types, including unemployment benefit and pensions, in contrast to higher entitlements for their male counterparts.

In 2010, women in the UK remained economically disadvantaged compared to men, but better positioned than ten years earlier. Since the Millennium, the 'gender gap' in the proportion of men and women classed as being on low income more than halved, from five percentage points to two (The Poverty Site, 2010). This came about because low-income households reduced in two significant population groups where women predominate – single pensioners and lone parents. Thus, by early 2010, women were only a little more likely than men to live in low-income households (21 compared with 19%), although there was a larger gap between single women and single men (29 compared with 24%) (The Poverty Site, 2010).

Welfare strategies made major contributions to these gains for women. Bellamy and Rake (2005: 6) showed that New Labour's post-1997 policies were significant in improving women's economic welfare and with a 'striking' impact on their lives. Mostly, however, the reforms from which women had benefitted were not aimed at improving their situation *per se*; rather, they had gained from a wider commitment to reducing poverty, and especially from measures designed to benefit low-income families. Despite their improved situation, overall they were still more vulnerable to poverty than men: 'women predominate among the low paid, they are more reliant on benefits than men, particularly means-tested as opposed to contributory benefits, and women are the majority of poor pensioners and parents of poor children,' said Bellamy and Rake (2005: 1).

The continued reliance of many women on welfare is likely to disadvantage them when policies are less supportive. In 2010, Britain's Con-Dem coalition government responded to the global recession by approving an immediate emergency budget to reduce welfare spending, with deeper cuts to come. Commentators across the political spectrum were quick to highlight its gendered impact. The Shadow Welfare secretary, Yvette Cooper, argued that 72% of the reduction in welfare support would fall on women and described the coalition's financial plans as 'the worst for women since the creation of the welfare state.' The Fawcett Society, a women's advocacy and rights organisation, bid for a judicial review to have the budget declared unlawful (*Guardian* 8 August 2010). The judge, opining this was a matter for the Equality and Human Rights Commission; and the Home Secretary and minister responsible for equality in the coalition government, Theresa May, warned colleagues that they faced a 'real risk' of a successful legal challenge if it could be shown that equality issues had not been fully considered.

This is the context for the following account of girls' and women's inclusion in and through sport. During the first decade of the twenty-first century the UK offered a relatively (but only relatively) favourable policy environment; as the decade drew to a close a much less auspicious social, political and economic climate was taking hold (see Chapter 12).

Girls, women, sport and exclusion

Women's disadvantaged position in the welfare state reflects the inequities of the gender order. Sport contributes to these unequal social relations, by elevating male experience over female in particularly powerful and visible ways. Sport is an arena where traditional gender identities are constructed, reinforced and contested (Humberstone, 2002). It is therefore a site where the unequal social relations that underpin women's experience of SEx are persuasively reproduced.

Taking part in sport regularly is a minority activity for British girls and women. Data compiled by the Women's Sport and Fitness Foundation (WSSF, 2010) showed that just a quarter of girls took part in 60 minutes of physical activity every day compared with a third of boys, and the proportion of girls taking part in recommended levels of activity a week declined with age, particularly after age ten. In sport, school-age girls were less likely than boys to take part in any organised sport a week – 73 compared with 80% – and as girls aged, their participation fell dramatically. Between the ages of 5–8 and 17–19, girls' activity dropped by two-thirds (from 91 to 31%), while for boys it was less than half (from 91 to 49 % – WSSF, 2010). Low participation levels continued in adulthood, so that in 2008–09, only 12.7% of women aged 16 or over took part in regular sport at least once a week, compared to 20.6% of men (Sport England, 2009). The greatest difference was at age 18, when more than double the proportion of men than women did sport regularly. Women's sports participation is far more affected than men's by lifestyle changes and the growth of family responsibilities, with particularly strong constraints on women's sports participation when their household includes a child aged under five. With the ageing of the population, the Future Foundation (nd) forecast participation changes to 2017 from at best only +1.3%, and at worst, −5.5%, before taking the recession into account.

Patterns of gender inequality in sport vary between subgroups of women, correlating strongly with variations in women's exposure to poverty and SEx. There is a stronger social class effect on women's participation than on men's: in the lowest group, women's participation rate is only two-thirds of men's (Table 5.1), and only one in ten in disadvantaged communities. As a result, Sport England launched an Active Women Programme, with £10m from Lottery money, aimed at women with children and in deprived areas (summarised in Table 5.2). In other words, women's sports participation appears more vulnerable than men's to the impact of other social structural constraints. Only women who are relatively favourably positioned in the social structure come close to closing the sports participation gap with men.

Table 5.1 English sports participation rates by sex and income, 2008–9 (% participating in regular sport at least once a week)

%	Men aged over 16	Women aged over 16
Up to £15,599	10.6	7.8
£15,600–£25,999	14.9	11.6
£26,000–£36,399	20.1	15.3
£36,400–£45,799	23.3	16.5
£45,800+	27.8	23.0

Source: Sport England, Active People Survey 2008–9

Table 5.2 Active Women projects 2011–14

Project name	Areas	Value £m
Major projects National Framework for Doorstep sport (Streetsport & partners)	Aimed at 30,000 women in various places including Wigan, Liverpool, Hastings, Northumberland, Milton Keynes, Hammersmith; 200 events & festivals, training & qualifications for 1,700 leaders	2.29
Netball in the city (English Netball)	For 12,000 women in Bristol, London, Manchester, Newcastle, Nottingham & Wolverhampton	1.0
National Women's Cycling network (British Cycling)	Aimed at 80,000 women; nine mass events, & rides led by champions; leaders recruited to teach basic skills	0.99

Project name	Areas	Value £m
Women Get Active (Liverpool Sport & Activity Alliance)	Seven or more activities for 1,800 women in seven deprived neighbourhoods, with upgrade of three city fitness suites, leaders/buddies & the chance to qualify	0.49
Active Women in Leicester (B-Inspired [Braunstone] & partners)	For women from deprived communities including carers for children	0.50
Minor projects Fit, Free & Fabulous	Fitness for sufferers of abuse, Hyndburn Lancs	0.15
Active Luton	Swimming and multi-sport sessions for 3,000 women from deprived areas	0.25
Oxfordshire Active Women (Oxon Sports Partnership)	For 6,000 women from deprived areas of the City & four Districts, including chances to volunteer & coach	0.37
Women's Sporting Champions (sportessex)	For 2,000 women in disadvantaged areas, lead by self-appointed 'champions'	0.20
East Durham Belles (Wingate & Station Town Family Centre)	For 1,500 women from four disadvantaged settlements in a range of sports	0.21
Hastings & Rother Active Women (2 local authorities, NHS, & Housing Association)	To give 3,000 mothers and women confidence to participate, volunteers and coach in eight sports	0.27
Active Women in Hull (City Council & partners)	1,200 women from disadvantaged areas; various sports and childcare	0.30
Catch 22, Southampton	Introducing boxercise, badminton, canoeing, swimming at low cost and with childcare	0.15
Sandwell Active Women (Sandwell Leisure Trust & partners)	Accessible sessions for mothers & women from low income, deprived areas; six or more sports & child-care	0.09
North London women playing (Tottenham Hotspur Foundation)	Badminton, exercise and dance for women from four London Boroughs	0.16
Catch-22 (Southampton)	To remove barriers of accessibility, cost & childcare for 1,800 women, including ethnic minorities	0.14
Active Women Nottingham (City Health & Wellbeing Partnership)	To support mothers and women and boost emotional wellbeing	0.18
Active Women (Leeds City Council & partners)	For 900 women from disadvantaged communities, 5 or more activities	0.07
Active Women 4Life (LB of Barking & Dagenham	For 1,500 women in LB's leisure centres, in various sports plus training opportunities	0.08

Source: Sport England *press notice*, 10 January 2011

However, while sport plays a smaller role in women's lives than men's, trends suggest that it is nonetheless a growing role. Levels of female sport participation are higher than in the 1970s and there has been a broadening of the range of activities which females take, with more females now playing sports formerly considered male preserves, such as rugby, football and cricket. Some of these sports have been particularly successful at attracting large numbers of girls and women: for example, football is now the most popular participant sport for them, having seen a huge rise in numbers – from 80 affiliated teams in 1993 to over 8,000 in 2005 (FIFA, 2006).

Yet, women's sports participation remains low in absolute as well as relative terms. Despite the relative popularity of health and fitness activities, few women lead active lifestyles and most have physical activity levels below the threshold required for optimum health benefits. Women and girls appear particularly disaffected from the commodified sports products of the contemporary global economy – the high-profile, competitive, commercial and professional world of sport that dominates media. And within this general picture, it is the least powerful women in society who are most distanced from sport.

The marked differences between men's and women's relationship with sport mirror the broader pattern of social relations in which sport is situated. Female participation in sport is very much in line with the model of the less powerful female, and stems from a female socialisation process that perpetuates the ideology of women as nurturers and carers that is entrenched in welfare policy. Sport appears to provide evidence that these traditional views remain valid. Many sports are still seen as less suitable for women than men, and female participation in the activities women have traditionally played (e.g., tennis, netball, gymnastics) is generally seen as more compatible with femininity than 'male' sports (e.g., football, rugby, cricket), notwithstanding the rise in participation in the latter.

The gender socialisation process that underpins this begins early, instilling different sports-related experiences and attitudes from the very start. Even as babies, girls are encouraged to be less independent and adventurous, and this sex typing becomes more explicit as children grow older (Greendorfer, 1983). By the time children reach school age, a link has been made between sport and masculinity, and a distance established between sport and 'feminine' behaviour. During adolescence many girls turn away decisively from sport, and the proportion who enjoy PE in school declines. As shown in Chapter 3, girls are also much less likely to play sport outside school than boys, less likely than boys to be frequent participants, and more likely to be non-participants. At the end of their school careers, young women's post-school participation declines more rapidly than young men's.

Much of the blame for this has been laid at the door of secondary school PE experiences, but there are other influences on adolescents from outside school. Many girls do not associate sport and physical activity with femininity, and sport is more likely to be seen as typical of 'unfeminine' girls. Sport sits uneasily with the experiences and aspirations of teenage girls, and is more likely to be seen as something to be left behind as part of the transition to female adulthood than continued. Women prefer to adopt more 'appropriate' feminine behaviours, and to express their sexuality through attractive appearance, with the female body presented as decorative rather than active. The growth in forms of fitness and exercise confirms the over-riding importance given to their physical appearance. Although there has been some loosening of such restrictive views of femininity, most forms of sport seem irrelevant to many young women's priorities. Moreover, irrespective of their commitment to sport, young women find that life transitions (like school to college, or education to paid work) put increased pressures on their time, money, and energy for taking part (Cox et al., 2006).

Societal constraints on women's involvement in sport are reinforced within sport. Institutionalised sport is strongly masculine in culture and organisation. Media coverage of sport reinforces its masculine image and is highly influential in promoting a view of sport that limits its appeal to women. The over-riding message is that 'real' sport is still not something for 'real' women.

Substantial efforts have been made to combat gender inequity in sport. In the UK, after initially focussing solely on women as participants, policymakers began to recognise female under-representation in sports organisations as a fundamental barrier to gender equity and advocated greater women's involvement in all aspects and all levels of sports participation, provision and management (e.g., the Sports Councils/WSSFF establishing a Framework Strategy for women in sport in 2003). However, in sport as elsewhere, formal policies do not guarantee effective action, as McKay's (1997) in-depth analysis of resistance to 'affirmative actions' in sports organisations in Australia, Canada and New Zealand showed. Policies to promote gender equity have often foundered in the face of organisational and societal cultures where gender differentiation was entrenched.

Obstacles to female involvement in sport, therefore, continue to be widespread. They also continue to be potentially most significant for women amongst whom traditional female roles remain most influential, many of whom are also vulnerable to SEx. Engaging women in sport and through sport has required specially targeted policies.

Girls' and women's empowerment through sport

Collectively, girls and women identify with sport far less than do boys and men. Sport also seems to be least valued among women most vulnerable to SEx, including those from lower social classes, from non-white populations, and from disabled and elderly groups. So, while sport may seem an obvious way to reach out to men who have become distanced from other social institutions, it appears less appropriate for engaging girls and women. Why then should we concern ourselves with the notion of sports-based interventions for women who experience poverty and SEx?

The simple answer is that women can derive as significant benefits as men from participating in sport. Rather than detracting from their personal development, sports participation appears to offer women substantial gains (e.g., Talbot, 1989). Like men, women who are involved in sport report positive changes in self-esteem and sense of 'self', and increased physical power and well-being. For women experiencing SEx, the everyday practicalities of taking part in sport outside their home environment may also have multiple individual and social values – for example, by providing opportunities to get out of the house, engage in physical exercise, have some social contact, and participate in personally meaningful, enjoyable and relaxing activity.

It has also been argued that encouraging women's involvement in sport has a more fundamental contribution to make to their lives. Contemporary sport is a highly visible social institution, global in its reach, which offers a shared experience crossing national and cultural boundaries. But a shared experience is not necessarily an inclusive one, and there are many ways where sport is not unifying but divisive. In relation to gender, sport is a powerful mechanism for delivering a *non*-inclusive version of society – one that promotes white above black, male above female, physical prowess above alternative qualities, and certain body types above others. Sport therefore carries a social significance that reaches far beyond its own sphere, yet paradoxically does so while appearing to be outside 'real life'.

Theorists have argued, therefore, that, because of its significance in constructing gender relations that expose women to greater hardship than men, sport has a very direct and fundamental relevance to combating women's SEx. If sporting practices reinforce hegemony in the rest of society, then challenging them amounts to challenging gender inequity in social relations. This is an ambitious project, but one with some empirical support. Research into women's experiences of sport has shown that the gains obtained can contribute to a wider feeling of empowerment. Women reported developing a stronger sense of identity and self-direction – what Talbot (1989) described as 'being herself through sport.' By giving women the chance to discover their physical potential, test their ambitions and 'realise their ability to create their own destiny,' sport might lead them to restructure the cultural and personal boundaries shaping their lives. The very 'maleness' of sport that makes it such an oppressive arena for women also makes it an especially significant and potent site for women to challenge and contest dominant stereotypes (e.g., Scraton et al., 1999). Colwell (1999) suggested that simply by participating in sport women challenged patriarchal definitions of submissiveness, passivity and dependence, while Whitson (2002) argued that by using their bodies in sport as skilled and forceful subjects, women challenge fundamental sources of male physical power. The sense of accomplishment and confidence women gain from mastering sport skills provides them with a strong experience of empowerment. This is not to claim that women completely change gender expectations through sport, but that they can undergo a complex mix of compliance and contestation that opens up significant new experiences.

These benefits provide sufficient rationale for encouraging women's involvement. They suggest that sport is not 'unsuitable' for women, and that their absence from it results primarily from obstacles to their participation rather than an innate mismatch with sport itself. More to the point, if sport can offer positive experiences to women experiencing hardship in their lives, then to deny them these experiences is to add a further dimension to their broader SEx. So there is a strong generic argument for bridging the sporting gender gap, and this has been strengthened in the last decade by broader policies to address SEx. Sport has been used to address several dimensions of exclusion, including improving health, providing opportunities for personal development, and contributing to community cohesion. Each has strong relevance to the situation of girls and women, who score particularly poorly on health measures, are potentially major beneficiaries of strategies for personal development which may raise their aspirations and improve educational and employment outcomes, and may suffer social isolation through their more constrained and home-based lives. The remainder of the chapter looks more closely at their experiences of sport, and considers what constrains and facilitates their participation.

Girls' and women's inclusion in and through sport

If sports experiences can help women to challenge their subordination in a patriarchal society, sport is potentially of exceptional value to those women most disadvantaged. But girls and women at risk of poverty and SEx have particularly low sports participation levels. How effective are strategies to engage them in sport, and what benefits accrue?

Arguably we are in a better position to answer this question than we were ten years ago. In the last decade, targeted provision for women and girls has increased, and so has research into its impacts. This differs from the 1970s and 1980s, when the first national sports development projects were emerging, but 'gender' had yet to achieve real profile in sports policy. At this time, sport was being used to address social problems among disadvantaged groups, especially in urban areas, but was targeted primarily at disaffected young men believed to pose a threat of social disorder. Programmes such as 'Football in the Community' had resonance with male youth, but little relevance to other deprived urban dwellers such as older people or housebound young mothers.

There were of course examples of work with girls and women, such as that by the Action Sport West Midlands project. The efforts of the (male) directorate of the West Midlands' inner city Action Sport project showed how deeply gender discrimination could be embedded in even determinedly pioneering projects. As one area co-ordinator admitted, initially he and others had simply dismissed women as completely irrelevant:

> I will admit now that I never even considered women...it was well into the project – six to eight months – before we really decided to think seriously of women as participants. It all started at the co-ordinators' meetings. I suddenly realised that women did exist.
>
> (Glyptis, Kay and Murray, 1985: 2)

Although some unsympathetic views were expressed by sports leaders – one said that 'Women can find excuses for doing nothing...They should not be allowed to look for ways out e.g., children, too fat, no money, not interested' (Glyptis, Kay and Murray, 1985: 14), more sensitive approaches within the same project elicited some very positive responses:

> Most of my work is ladies' keep-fit to music sessions, which are becoming increasingly popular; however, the ladies I deal with are prepared to have a go at anything from rock-climbing and assault courses to rounders and netball.
>
> (Glyptis, Kay and Murray, 1985: 4)

These examples illustrate the ambiguous and contradictory situation of women's sport in the 1980s. This was a time when momentum was growing within the women and sport movement, in the UK and internationally: in 1984 the Women's Sport Foundation was formed in the UK, and in 1994 the first ever International Women and Sport Conference was held, attended by delegates from 82 countries, and the Brighton Declaration adopted, committing participants to advancing women in sport at all levels and in all roles. The Declaration both reflected and stimulated the growing momentum behind achieving gender equity in sport. Although there was resistance, increasing attention was beginning to be paid to developing sport for females.

Since the late 1990s there has been a discernible increase in the profile given to sports provision addressing girls' and women's situations. A number of well-publicised national initiatives have focused specifically on the challenges of engaging girls – e.g., the Nike-sponsored 'Girls in Sport' programme led by the Youth Sport Trust (YST/Nike 2001a; Kay and O'Donovan 2004), and the Women's Sport and Fitness Foundation's 'Sweat in the City' campaign (WSFF, 2009). Females have also been identified as specific target groups within wider participation strategies, such as the New Opportunities for Physical Education and Sport initiative, sportscotland's Active Schools, and the Cricket Foundation's national *Chance to shine* programme. Additionally, many smaller programmes designed for specific subgroups of girls and women have been implemented and evaluated, such as the 'Widening Access Through Sport' programme for ethnic minority young women.

It is notable, however, that this increase in provision has not removed some of the longstanding obstacles to girls and women's participation. A decade after Flintoff and Scraton (2001) argued that many girls were discouraged from participating by negative experiences within sport itself, a wide array of research into youth sport participation shows that many such problems persist. More, however, now is known about how they can be overcome, with some of the most persuasive evidence coming from Jeanes, whose in-depth work with young people has been foremost in revealing what constitutes a good and bad sport experiences for girls. Drawing on first-hand accounts from participants in several large UK research studies, her work (e.g., Jeanes, 2011; Jeanes and Kay, 2008a,b,c; Jeanes, Musson and Kay, 2009; Jeanes and Nevill, 2008) suggests that the most significant factors that contribute to poor participation experiences for girls include:

- limited opportunities for enjoyment, especially when sports sessions over-emphasize performance and achievement and underplay fun and sociability;
- lack of inclusiveness, marginalising girls with lower skills and abilities, especially when provision is structured around overly competitive opportunities that highlight poor ability;
- inappropriate provision, often offering 'traditional' ranges of sporting activities in which many girls have limited interest, and providing mixed-gender opportunities dominated by boys and especially discourage less experienced girl participants.

Jeanes' studies provided insight into how each of these factors affects girls' experiences negatively, but can be largely overcome through appropriate forms of delivery. First and foremost, she identified the simple significance of enjoyment, pointing out that girls are more likely to participate in sport when they find the experience pleasurable. In their analysis of leadership of girls' extra-curricular sport, Jeanes and Kay (2008b) noted that enjoyment was particularly significant for out-of-school activity: while there was some acceptance that teachers could be authoritarian during school PE lessons, girls expected to be treated differently in sessions they attended in their own time. There were significant negative consequences when these expectations were not met. Several girls who stopped attending sessions had done so because these replicated the environment constructed in school PE:

> There's just no point going, she tells you off all the time and is really strict, it's just 'do this, do that'. She does that in PE and I don't like that then – so I'm not going to go [to a voluntary extra-curricular session] if I don't have to.
>
> (Year 9, non-participant) (Jeanes and Kay, 2008b)

Conversely, there were dividends when teachers adapted their style to be more relaxed and informal. The girls enjoyed sessions run in this way, and appreciated the difference in how teachers related to them:

> You see another side of the teachers, they are really strict in class and when you are at the club they are dead relaxed and have a carry on with you.
>
> (Year 10, participant) (Jeanes and Kay, 2008b)

The annual evaluations of the *Chance to shine* cricket programme reinforced this message, providing many examples of coaches delivering sessions that combined fun and enjoyment with opportunities for young people to progress and develop their skills. The expertise and knowledge of the coach was recognised by pupils:

> I like doing the technical stuff but we also have fun. He does a little like kind of warm ups then he does like a match after, and then after we'll have like a little cricket relay and it's fun. We do all sorts of fun stuff. I don't like just standing there for hours just being told how you hit the ball.
>
> (Year 5, pupil) (Jeanes, Musson and Kay, 2009)

Jeanes' work emphasised the significance of the social relationships within provision for girls, and especially the importance of how leaders treated girl participants. Her evaluation of *Chance to shine* demonstrated the value of having coaches who were friendly towards girls, demonstrated a personal interest in them, and were prepared to engage in a 'laugh and joke' with them. Coaches' accessible and non-authoritarian attitudes were crucial to girls' engagement, especially for those who initially lacked confidence and were reluctant to try a new sport.

> He's just really nice and friendly. He's young and he has lots of patience. I was really scared at first that I couldn't do it but he was so nice, and he really helped me and it just made me more confident.
>
> (Girl pupils, year 6) (Jeanes, Musson and Kay, 2009)

The relationship between leaders and girl participants is an important social dimension of girls' sports experiences. Another is the opportunity that sport can provide for girls to enjoy social interactions with peers. Taking part with friends is important to girls, who welcome sport environments that offer the opportunity to socialise and interact. Coaches who allow girls to enjoy socialising in the sport setting are viewed positively:

> She (coach), she understands that we come because we want to spend time together and she lets us have a gossip and find out what's going on at the same time as doing stuff. When I went to netball it wasn't like that. The coach shouted at us all the time for talking and kept saying we weren't there to socialise but actually I was. I get to talk to lots of my friends in sport that I wouldn't normally see, that's why I like doing it.
>
> (Girl, aged 14) (Jeanes and Kay, 2008b)

Laura Hills' (2007) work on the role of friendship in girls' PE expertness, however, showed that girls' social relationships with each other in sports settings can be negative. During her ethnographic work with 12- and 13-year-old girls in a multi-ethnic, mixed comprehensive school, it became clear that girls' social relationships and networks played an important role in shaping their involvement in and enjoyment of PE lessons. In sport, girls' partly assumed roles – as teammates, partners, opponents and leaders – on the basis of already established social ties. Girls who were physically skilled and socially valued were able to exercise power and maintain their status through demonstrating competence and strategies of inclusion and exclusion (Hills, 2007: 535).

Hills' work also highlighted how practices in sports can be exclusionary and marginalising for some girls. The importance of delivering sport in an inclusive way is the second of the points raised by Jeanes. Jeanes and Kay (2008a) found that leaders who were able to integrate different abilities ensured girls had enjoyable experiences:

It's just he [football coach] is really good, he keeps us all doing things but you don't feel really stupid, like he gets us all doing stuff but he doesn't make it obvious he is making sure the girls are getting their chance. It just sort of happens.

(Year 6, participant) (Jeanes and Kay, 2008a)

Chance to Shine evaluation reports provided several further illustrations of inclusive leadership being key to girls' engagement, especially when coaches were skilled at integrating pupils of lower competences. The evaluation reports also illustrated that inclusiveness and enjoyment accompanied skill progression, rather than undermined it. Although some girls had low skills levels and were unconfident about their ability to progress, they wished to improve; in fact, girls who felt they were not learning were likely to need to continue engaging.

Mr. X has really helped me improve my skill and now football is like the main sport I play…Even now I'm much better but he still teaches me things, I know when I go I'll be able to do something else by the time I get home.

(Year 8, participant) (Jeanes and Kay, 2008b)

The third issue to consider here is whether delivering sport in particular formats makes it more attractive to girls and women – e.g., by making provision single-sex or mixed, or by carefully selecting the activities offered. At school, where early attitudes to sport are formed, single-sex provision can play a positive role in protecting girls from boys' physical dominance of activity spaces, and from unfavourable comparisons with their performances. This especially applies in traditionally 'male' sports where many boys have an established skill set. Despite the challenges, it can be particularly beneficial to nurture girls' participation in these sports, as there is some evidence that succeeding in 'male' sports can provide extra value. Overcoming restrictive gender beliefs about their capabilities in sport can have wider consequences:

It's like everyone says, 'girls can't do cricket, they are no good at boy's sports' but we are doing it and we are really good. We keep winning all the time and it has made the boys realise we can be as good as them. I didn't know I was good at cricket but I am now so when I'm in school and I think I can't do something I just think well I was like that about cricket and I did that OK.

(Year 6, pupil) (Jeanes, Musson and Kay, 2009)

The research evidence is mixed concerning the range of sports suitable for raising and retaining girls' participation. Programmes such as sportscotland's Active Schools initiative, developed in response to declining physical activity levels and launched in 2005, have offered a broad diet of activities to maximise their appeal (e.g., Kay et al., 2007). The inclusion of dance, for example, has been successful in engaging girls to whom organised sport did not appeal. Meanwhile, at the other end of the spectrum, the growth of participation in girls' football, rugby and cricket emphasises variety in girls' relationship to being active, showing that sports once regarded as 'male' can be popular with girls if delivered appropriately. As Hills (2006) reminded us, girls' experiences are diverse and are constituted in various social contexts. She found, for example, that although the working-class girls in her ethnographic study had limited involvement in organised sports, many had a range of relevant informal interests and experiences that did not always emerge in the school environment (Hills, 2006: 553). Her findings point us towards the importance of differential provision for groups of girls and women of differing characteristics, experiences of inclusion and relationships to sport.

One group that has attracted some attention from sports providers has been Muslim girls and women. Attention has focused both on what they require, and how inclusion in sport may contribute to their wider social and cultural integration. The 'Widening Access Through Sport' (WATS) project, funded by the European Social Fund in 2003–4, is an example of such a project. WATS used sport to engage young people in a combined sport and education programme, as part of a broader agenda in Europe to increase levels of youth education and training.

The project was located at a university in the English Midlands, and was mainly attended by Muslim girls from local Bangladeshi communities. It offered a range of sport and education activities providing opportunities for small groups to build study skills, enhance self-development, and experience taster sessions for academic subjects. A local Muslim female development worker was appointed to manage and deliver the core programme. Her role included reassuring the parents, individually when necessary, of the appropriateness of the activities for their daughters. It provided female-only sports, supported by experienced coaches able to adapt their teaching to the girls' interests and experience. The sport component was a special attraction, as many of the attendees were constrained by cultural restrictions from participating in mixed-sex sport provision in schools and local facilities. WATS sports activities proved so popular that several participants subsequently progressed to achieving coaching awards.

The activities offered through WATS were led by the participants in partnership with the development worker, which led to the group 'owning' the work and feeling a sense of membership of the University. At their own request, the girls made presentations to university staff to explain their culture and to demonstrate the educational and sports skills they had acquired. When they talked about the project, they commented on how much their self-confidence and sporting ability had improved, and that their interest in higher education had grown. Several also commented they wished to use their improved sporting knowledge and qualifications to work in their community and give others the same opportunities.

The WATS programme delivered a number of benefits to participants, and succeeded in its immediate aim of encouraging educational aspirations. Follow-up research conducted with nine of the ten earlier participants five years later found that all but one was attending a university, or had been accepted for the coming academic year. Holding the sport and education sessions at the university had broken down the social and cultural barriers and made it an accessible institution. The project had also run larger events promoted locally, including a sports day, a five-a-side football tournament, and cultural activities at the university's community open days. These had brought many more members of the local Muslim community to the campus and familiarised them with the university.

The follow-up research also revealed how the participants felt the programme had empowered them personally, and also brought wider benefits to their community, by showing that it could be compatible with Muslim life:

> I used to do less sport then because I didn't think it was part of a Muslim woman's life – but now I can walk down the street wearing my joggers and being proud that I do sports. Now [...], with Muslims, it's like 'yeah we can do sports now', it's a different stereotype in their mind, they'll actually take part. I think that it's really important that Muslim women actually have a chance to do sports as it gives them more confidence and it shows them that they can do other things in life.
>
> (Kay, 2009b)

Jawad, Benn and Dagkas (2011) reported similar findings from a project in Birmingham schools, providing teachers with support in dealing with issues of body modesty, especially in dance and swimming, and in helping girls to continue participating during Ramadan. The findings of these projects indicate that for some girls and women, sport may be able to help disassemble the barriers that divide social groups.

The WSFF (2008) set out some of the continuing scale of gender challenges:

- While three out of five women thought they did enough exercise to benefit their health, only one in five did so (a 'huge reality gap'), and trends in employment, obesity and aging suggested sport participation may fall by 5–10% over the next decade.
- Only one performance coach in four was a woman (but exceptionally almost half of Sports Development Officers – Pitchford and Collins, 2010), only 3% volunteered (half the rate of men), only 2% of coverage in broadsheet newspapers showed women's sport, and virtually nothing in the populist 'red tops.'

Conclusions

The gender situation in sport varies by country: in the OECD, the UK and seven other states showed a male majority, but four Scandinavian states and the Netherlands, all with high overall participation, had more women than men playing sport (van Tuyckom, Scheerder and Bracke (2010), as shown in Table 5.3. The authors pointed out that the Scandinavian figures are associated with sustained egalitarian social and sport policies overall.

Table 5.3 Sports participation by gender in five of 25 OECD countries, 2004 (odds ratios, adjusted for educational attainment)

Country	% participating regularly, M&F	Model 1 (also adjusted for age)	Model 2		
			Aged 18-34	Aged 35-54	Aged over 55
Spain	33.4	1.99	2.81	1.78	1.36
Greece	25.6	1.88	1.75	1.34	4.58
UK	41.3	1.28	1.62	1.39	0.98
Sweden	71.9	0.68	0.62	0.65	0.74
Finland	74.2	0.64	0.62	0.42	0.80

Source: Eurobarometer 62 data, in Van Tuyckom, Scheerder and Bracke, 2010

As sport has been increasingly used by governments as a tool for achieving wider social outcomes, interest in the broader social implications has been reflected in greater academic and policy research. This examines the impact of sport on diverse aspects of people's lives, from their physical activity levels and health to their behaviour in schools and communities. Many of the claimed outcomes of sport are ambitious yet hard to define; they may not be easily measurable, and even when they are, it can be difficult to demonstrate that outcomes have directly resulted from participation in sport (Coalter, 2007). There is still little research that can claim to explain how sport contributes to social inclusion.

These caveats apply fully to our understanding of the relationship between sport and inclusion for women and girls. This chapter has shown that on the one hand, sport can contribute to female SEx in sport and wider society, but on the other may also help counter it. Over the last decade substantial evidence has enhanced our understanding of how sport can be more inclusive for females, and a smaller literature how sport may also promote wider inclusion. We know how positively girls and women can respond to sport, how much they benefit from doing so, and we know more than previously about the steps required to facilitate their involvement. In particular, research from the last decade has thrown fuller light on the significance of the social processes within sports experiences to girls and young women's engagement, highlighted the importance of good leadership – but also indicated the unfortunate persistence of some poor practices. It is apparent that socially-excluded girls and women are not automatically equal beneficiaries of sports initiatives that tackle SEx, or even of those that tackle gender inequity in sport. The role of sport in countering exclusion will continue to be contingent on women's wider lifestyles.

6 Exclusion and older people in sport

Freysinger (1999: 254) commented on the lack of longitudinal studies of ageing and of studies of the leisure of those 'on the margins of society – persons with disabilities, of colour, with sexual orientation other than heterosexual, the poor, and until recently women'. Based on the assumptions being made about immigration, reducing birth rates and longer life expectancy, the old-age dependency ratio will rise from one retired person to four workers to almost 1: 1.

Introduction: trends in aging and social exclusion

Exclusion in the Third Age comes from poor health, poverty and disability, which may be further compounded by isolation and poor mobility. Patsios (2006) reckoned that of four million male and seven million female pensioners, 41–43% were poor, partly because between 22 and 36% did not claim Income Support. Isolation is a particular risk factor for older people from minority ethnic groups, those in 'rural areas and for people older than 75 who may be widowed or live alone' (ODPM, 2006a: 5). That is why maintaining physical activity with its impact on coping and mobility pays off most in this age group, shown in numerous studies since the Allied Dunbar National Fitness Survey (SC/HEA, 1992). It is clear that combating diseases is leading to continuing growth in the over 60s population, expected to outstrip the under 16s by 2014. This ageing process is more marked in remote rural areas, (Speakman and Lowe, 2006).

'Ageing is now understood to be a deleterious side effect of biological processes...the gradual accumulation of a complex, diverse and tissue-specific array of faults' (AMS, 2009: 5). As *The Who* sang in 1965, 'Hope I die before I get old'; what is important is *healthy* life expectancy. Most older people are better off and healthier than their predecessors, but the main risks are continued growth in obesity, inactivity and the gap that leaves poor people less healthy (AMS, 2009: 15, 16, 18). The life-expectancy gap between the richest and poorest of Glasgow's suburbs is now 28 years (Yates et al., 2008). A healthy 70 year-old person has a 54% chance of living until 90, but this is reduced:

- by 22% if one smokes;
- by 26% if one is obese;

- by 36% if one has hypertension;
- but by 44% if one has a sedentary lifestyle.

In the UK, the Conservative government broke the link between state pensions and average earnings in 1981, with the result that the state pension is about a fifth of average earnings, compared to about half in many other European countries. HMG promised to increase state pensions in line with earnings (Inman, P. *Guardian* 8 October 2009: 29) but investment in private pensions lags – 8m people make no provision, mostly under 35 years of age (*Foresight 2*, Visit Britain 2003).

The most authoritative material on exclusion comes from the 2002–3 *English Longitudinal Study of Ageing* (ELSA), which used Scharf, Phillipson and Smith's (2005) seven dimensions and showed:

- half not excluded on any dimension, 29% on one, 13% on two, and seven per cent (or 1.1m) on three or more;
- those at greatest risk were over 80, living in cities, alone with no living children, depressed or in poor health, in rented accommodation, with low income mainly from benefits, with no access to private transport or use of public transport, and no telephone;
- lowest quality of life was reported by people with poor access to basic services, financial, health, and cultural.

(ODPM, 2006b)

ELSA did not survey people in residential care; nor, from our point of view, did it include sporting participation.

Future trends suggested:

- from 2006 the over-80s would increase by 223,000 by 2011 and by 909,000 (including 355,000 women) by 2021, yet many people underestimate how long they would live, women aged 60–64 reckoned on 65% of reaching age 75, against a reality of 80%;
- While some will live longer with no severe disability, on the increase are obesity, arthritis, osteoporosis, stroke or diabetes, and dementia costs £23bn a year;
- numbers living alone (divorced or never married) are likely to increase;
- more will work to new retirement ages of 70 or 72 years, which may boost savings;
- while the proportion of women with basic state or second state pension rights are likely to increase, the withdrawal or limitation of employers' schemes means that for pensions policy to succeed, governments will have to vigorously encourage take up of individual private schemes;
- more baby boomers will retire after 2011, with more ethnic diversity;
- thus provision for 'active ageing' – physical activity, leisure, and learning – is important and needs to be low cost.

Becker and Boreham (2009) used ELSA data and Levitas et al.'s (2007) Bristol Social Exclusion Matrix (p16, Figure 2.1) to create 16 risk markers. Half of the over-60s experienced multiple markers, but almost three quarters of the over-80s, among whom they identified five clusters:

1 Mostly lonely and unsupported (20%, average 2.5 markers);
2 Fear of local area (24%, 2.8 markers) especially after dark;
3 Low income (32%, 3.2 markers);
4 Poor health (general and emotional – 14%, 3.7 markers); and
5 Poor access (for three quarters to transport) and with little physical activity – 10%, 5.1 markers).

Women, especially on low incomes and poor access, living alone, without qualifications, and in cities, were more likely to experience multidimensional exclusion. Physical inactivity marked only six per cent overall, but 51% in the poor access cluster and 32% in that for poor health. They also used British Household Panel survey data 1997–2005 to examine the dynamics of exclusion: on at least one occasion over four-fifths experienced multiple markers of low social support and loneliness, and two-thirds either loneliness and poor health or low income and poor transport. The one clear trigger to SEx was getting divorced or becoming widowed.

Other studies confirmed these issues and added:

* elderly deprivation can be concentrated – four million pensioners lived in the 88 most deprived wards of England, yet pensioners have four times the voting power of under 25s (Dean, nd);
* a quarter of those in remote areas, notably women, spent five of nine years in low income (Philip and Gilbert, 2007);
* Evandrou and Falkingham (2009) showed clearly the changing composition of retirement income:

%	1951	1997–8	2006–7
State benefits	42	52	44
Occupational/private pensions	15	26	29
Savings/investments	15	14	11
Employment	27	8	17

* men shunned clubs specifically for older people;
* while car manufacturers sought to make driving easier for older people (though two in five over 75s have no access to a car), many transport operators perceived them as a nuisance, partly because of free or concessionary travel (Gilhooly et al., 2002)
* 'For most [of the poor], life consisted of a dismal succession of juggling acts, typically between purchasing food and paying bills.' (Craig, 2004: 102). He showed the gains in choice, social life and independence from accepting

welfare payments (peace of mind, better mobility, better services like cleaners, hairdressers, gardeners, ability to buy capital items like mobility scooters, ability to purchase presents or attend social events;

- index-linked pensions and savings made some the most affluent-ever pensioners, and significant consumers. Higgs et al. (2009) traced changes in spending: by 2004–5 in retired households: ownership had risen from 20% in 1968 to virtually 100% for phones, and from 20% to 54% for cars; from 1988 from nil to 25% for PCs. Food spending fell from 32% to 20%. From 1993, it was the youngest/most recently retired who had most exposure to a leisured/ consumer society spending pattern, 20% compared to 10% by the oldest (born before 1910).

Patsios (2003: 453) summarised thus: 'there are two different groups: a "better-off" group, made up mostly of younger pensioners living in pensioner couple households, who experience low poverty and SEx, and a "worse-off" group, who are often female pensioners living alone, experiencing much higher levels of poverty and social exclusion'. Higgs et al. (2010: 34) judged that 'the end result is huge differences in the resources, including pension rights, with which people enter retirement'.

As people get older, more become dependent on domiciliary health and welfare services (like meals on wheels, home helps, and mobile libraries); in 1996–7 one in twelve households received intensive care (six or more visits in a week). With further frailty, they then need residential care; but public policy has cut or privatised both. The extent of leisure provision for institutionalised folk varies, but has barely been studied.

McPherson (1999: 5) stressed that while there is a decline in physical capacity with ageing, 'successful ageing and adaptation in later life is as much a social as a biological process'. Nor, he argued, is it closely linked to chronological age. The elderly, so often lumped together, comprise several cohorts, and now cover a 30–40 year span. Transport is a major issue for older people (Walker et al., 2006). Buses work well for concentrated flows – to work, school and shop – but less well for dispersed activities like leisure, and often cease early in evenings and may not operate at weekends, so customised services like taxibuses/dial-a-ride may be more appropriate (Su and Bell, 2009). So long as services are reliable, the most important issue is being close to a bus stop rather than having frequent services. From 2008, all operators had to offer free off-peak services to over 60s, and government was surprised by the rise in take up, even by car-owners, but Scottish research suggested they were of limited value in reducing SEx (Rye and Mykura, 2009).

Without contradiction, the evidence for physical and mental benefits for older individuals has strengthened since 2003, confirming American College of Sports Medicine (1998) saying that 'sedentariness appears a far more dangerous condition than activity among the old.' The British Heart Foundation (2003) recommended for three successive stages:

1   *Making activity choices*, for 50–70s (Department of Health's 'Entering old age') across a wide range for disease prevention and opportunities for recreation and social activity

2   *Increasing the circle of life*, for 65–80s ('Transitional') for reducing disability with declining body and mind functions, and maintaining mobility, independence and daily activities, and

3   *Moving in the later years*, for mainly over 75s ('Frail older people') through activity with purpose and meaning in home, community or care settings, avoiding falls and helping people with dementia.

Some main practical outcomes are:

• *strength* to lift household objects, open a jar and get in and out of the bath, on–off a bus platform;
• *flexibility* to wash hair, tie shoes;
• *balance and agility* to climb stairs;
• *co-ordination and dexterity* to open a door with a key;
• *speed* to cross the road whilst the lights are green;
• *endurance* to walk to the shops, play with the grandchildren (confirmed by Taylor et al., 2004).

The main question centres around the appropriate 'dose'. The Chief Medical Officer (2004) recommended 30 minutes of moderate activity on at least five days a week, with elements of resistance and strength training on at least two of these. The BHF suggested promoting messages like 'think of minutes spent walking each day as £s in your health bank.'

Ageing, leisure and sport

Given the ageing of European populations, the literature on leisure for older people is remarkably sparse. McGuire (2000) criticised leisure researchers' lack of attention, and their reliance on gerontology for many concepts, like 'disengagement,' and selective optimisation of activity while compensating for falling incomes and failing faculties. In the UK, Bernard (1988) catalogued local, adventurous activity schemes.

Freysinger (1999: 257) showed that for men retirement *per se* meant more continuity of past activities than disengaging or taking up a host of new interests. Older people emphasised looking for enjoyment, fitness, health, relaxation and challenge in their activities, though middle-aged men tended to view it as treatment for a condition rather than preventing poor health (Nicholson, 2004). Arkenford (2006) argued for introducing a specific motivational element into the Hillsdon's Oxford model of participation, and identified things to avoid:

• a focus on solo, serious exercise;
• avoiding any 'sport' label;

- using machines;
- anything seen as costly;
- any mixed gender activities (for older Asian women);
- anything pigeonholed as for 'oldies.'

People's preferred activity is walking; Natural England's Walking for Health Initiative reached some 40,000 people a week and aimed to quadruple this by 2012 (www.whi.org.uk accessed 19 April 10). The leisure of older women in Leeds, including ethnic minorities, was substantially home-based, and often constrained by continuing obligations to housework and grandchildren (Scraton et al., 2000; Seigenthaler and Vaughan, 1998). Age Concern, examining the social and cultural activities of older people from ethnic minorities, argued:

> becoming involved in leisure and educational activities, and meeting other older people, often enables people to find out about and benefit from other services, and entitlements.
>
> (AC/CRE, 1998, *Education and leisure*: 7)

From on-street interviews with over 50s, Sasidharan et al. (2006) showed the importance of social support in their PA and sport from friends but not family. Stanley et al. (cited in Freysinger, 1999) followed a cohort of American over 50s for 16 years, examining the effects of age, gender, and health on nine activities:

- six declined (playing sports, hobbies, civic and fraternal organisations, social and spectator activities, and travelling);
- two stayed much the same (church-going and watching TV/listening to the radio);
- one activity, reading, increased.

The BHF National Centre (2008: 13–20) gathered data on 16 schemes: one each offered cycling, dancing and Nordic walking in the countryside; six in domestic or residential homes sought to avoid falls, especially for women; one trained pharmacists to advise patients on PA.

Even in health-conscious Canada, many older women were unaware of their doctors' views on exercise (O'Brien Cousins, 1995). O'Brien Cousins (1999) and Hawkins (1999) both stressed the North American ethnic/cultural variations in sport and recreation patterns, found also in England by Verma (1994) and Rowe, and Champion (pp 127–9). Low levels of activity were found amongst women of working class and of Asian origin. Amongst the latter, deprivation and poor health was concentrated – 47% of Bangladeshi and Pakistani pensioners experienced three or more types of disadvantage compared to 42% of Caribbean pensioners, and 19% of white pensioners. Three-fifths of them struggled in the bottom fifth of the income range compared to half the Indians, a third of Caribbeans, and just over a fifth of whites (Carvel, J. *Guardian* 13 Sept 00: 11).

Learning is a form of leisure with socialising benefits. But the most recent (1999) survey by the National Institute of Adult and Continuing Education showed that a fall of up to 20% in registrations by older people (*Guardian Education* 18 May 1999: 13). For Clarke's sample of 129 older north Londoners, leisure was mostly passive and sociable: seven per cent danced monthly but 71% never; one in five did some sport, half going swimming and one in ten saying they were members of a sports club, about the same as attended a day centre or luncheon club, but 87% never went to a leisure centre. Clarke commented that familiarity was an important feature which bred 'content, comfort and security' (1993: 7).

McPherson (1991) believed social support is very important in older people's leisure, so is having a good deal of autonomy to plan and run their own programmes. From focus group research, Stead and Swain (1997) suggested that active older Scots emphasised the psychological and social aspects of activity, while exercise and health professionals tended to emphasise physiological and health benefits. Finland is reckoned to sustain one of the most active lifestyles in the developed world; following up a sample after eight years, Hirvensalo et al. (1998) found three quarters of 65–84 year olds still walked for fitness, and half did callisthenics at home. But even there, with an 'Evergreen' promotional campaign, two out of five did nothing but chores, most saying it was because of their poor health.

Retirement populations are unevenly spread; many of those who can afford to move from cities to congenial locations choosing the 'costa geriatrica' of England's south coast and Cornwall and Devon's north coast, North Wales and Lancashire coasts, Yorkshire around Whitby and Scarborough, and parts of Norfolk and Suffolk, but also the Welsh Borders and southern Lake District (Law and Warnes, 1976). Having many elderly people puts a larger demand on local health and welfare services, but also a different view of physical activity. After ten years of growth, only now is the British fitness industry recruiting older people as instructors, and providing centres that focus on older customers.

Despite the ageing of society there has been what Midwinter (1992) called a 'research gulf', and Sport England has for three decades accorded age no priority, despite the fact the its *50+ and all to play for* pack was reprinted several times since the 1980s. The data on older people's leisure and sport are both sparse. The Allied Dunbar National Fitness Survey (SC/HEA, 1992) showed the decline of vigorous and moderate exercise with age, to the point where most men and almost all women over 65 had significant arm and leg weaknesses, limiting their mobility (in getting up and down stairs, onto bus platforms and armchairs) and the extent of their walking capability; five years later only 14% were active enough to obtain health benefits (HEA, 1999, 6).

In terms of sport, the General Household Survey showed a steady increase in participation from 1987 to 1993 but a decline in the recession to 1996 – no doubt a factor linked to a reduction in the DE social groups which were a disproportionate part of the older population (Chapter 3) and a small decline in women taking walks longer than two miles. This decline was in sports, especially keep fit activities, but also in walking. Swimming, however, kept on growing – see

Table 6.1. In contrast to a strong commitment to social clubs, sports club membership dropped substantially with age (MORI, 1999: 10):

Percentage of adults who were club members in the previous four weeks, 1996			
	Total	Aged 45–59	Aged 60–69	Aged 70+
social club	2.8	2.2	2.7	1.7
sports club	8.2	7.7	6.0	2.9

A survey of management and use of sports halls and pools (Sport England, 2000) showed clear under-representation of people over 45 in both halls and pools – 26% and 31% compared to 44% of the population as a whole. But only three per cent of the programme time in sports halls and one per cent in swimming pools was allocated to them. Almost nine in ten facilities offered concessions for people aged over 60, and 72% claimed specific policies for over-50s, but only 18% had specific targets. Only four per cent of hall users and 6.7% of swimmers were senior citizens with discount cards (one in seven and one in four respectively of all card holders). The last four decades demonstrated a steady growth in sports hall users aged over 45, accelerating in the 1990s, perhaps because of the interest in fitness – four per cent in the 1960s, nine per cent in the 1970s, six per cent in the 1980s, 24% in the 1990s.

The Active People survey in 2006 showed an increase in active over 55s, but from 7.6% doing enough for health benefits (3x30 minutes a week moderate) in 2007–8, a statistically significant decrease to 7.5% was recorded in 2009–10 (Sport England, *Release* 17 Mar 2010). This was to be expected in the recession, for this and for other low-income groups. Free swimming was introduced in England in 2008, but was cancelled after only one of its two years by the Conservative-LibDem coalition as a cost saving measure; 82% of over 60s surveyed said they would have swum any way, and so additionality was only 21%, and PWC–LLB (2010) estimated a cost benefit of 0.53 for every pound invested.

Table 6.1 Sports participation amongst people aged over 45 in GB 1987–96

		Aged 45–59		Aged 60–69		Aged 70+	
At least one activity	1987	56	(92)	47	(77)	26	(43)
	1990	63	(97)	54	(83)	31	(48)
	1993	64	(100)	51	(80)	32	(52)
	1996	63	(98)	55	(86)	31	(48)
At least one activity excluding walking	1987	35	(75)	23	(51)	10	(22)
	1990	42	(88)	28	(58)	12	(25)
	1993	43	(91)	27	(60)	16	(34)
	1996	40	(87)	30	(65)	13	(28)
Bases		*4,140 to 3,686*		*2,654 to 2,024*		*2,541 to 2,305*	

Participation in active recreation and sport in all countries shows a general fall with ageing. Using data from five countries in Europe, Rodgers (1977) argued this was accentuated because many people over 50 then had had a very limited experience of sport in childhood; they had never learned the skills or ethos of sport; they were 'sports illiterate.' Harahousou (1999) showed how a new, affluent, sports-literate but minority group in Greece was moving into retirement. Nevertheless the wider school sport curricula of the 1960s onwards has equipped the baby boomers and future generations better for exercising choice. The seven-nation COMPASS Survey (UK Sport et al., 1999) demonstrated that participation fell swiftly during people's third age in all countries, even though the overall levels were much higher in Scandinavia than southern Europe. But there were significant differences for over 50s (Table 6.2):

- intensive participation remained much higher in Scandinavia and very low in Italy and Spain, even increasing after 60 in Finland and 65 in Sweden;
- the converse of this was a much lower rate of no or low participation in Scandinavia than in UK.

The reasons cannot be conclusively adduced, nor attributed to winter commuting on skis (which only a Scandinavian minority do), but socialising around an active club culture remarkable for young people's attendance with their parents is probably a factor (Seppanen,1982; Heinila, 1989), together with a widespread adoption of a healthy lifestyle in which exercise is accompanied by a 'good' diet and little smoking.

Other international comparisons are interesting. In the US only 30% of over 50s did 5×30 minutes a week moderate PA, and 34% of over 65s reported no activity, so there was an Active for Life programme in the community and care settings sponsored by the Centers for Disease Control and the 40 million members of AARP (AARP, 2002). The Netherlands has the same threshold as UK of 5×30 minutes moderate or 3×30 minutes vigorous activity; it set a target of 50% reaching this by 2010, which was achieved in 2005, with only the over 65s and

Table 6.2 Sports participation by age in three European countries (percentages)

Age Groups	Finland		UK		Italy	
	Groups 1 & 2	*Groups 6 & 7*	*Groups 1 & 2*	*Groups 6 & 7*	*Groups 1 & 2*	*Groups 6 & 7*
50–54	38	22	20	60	3	88
55–59	41	24	118	67	3	90
60–64	46	28	14	69	3	93
65+	–	–	10	82	1	97

Note: Groups 1 and 2 were involved in sport on 120-plus occasions a year; Groups 6 & 7 were involved in none or fewer than 12 occasions a year

those in poor health lagging, at 21% (Van Campen, 2008: 13, 20,65). Sports participation among 65–79s was 33% in 2007, up from eight per cent in 1979 (Tiessen-Raaphorst and Breedveld, 2007: 21), substantially higher levels than for Britain.

In Germany, Breuer and Wicker (2009) argued the traditional expectation of declining activity with age may be mistaken through confusing age-related changes with individual cohort effects. Using panel data for 1985–2005, cross-sectional data on weekly participation demonstrated the expected (1985 – eight per cent, 2005 – 20.9%, significant at one per cent). But of the 10-year cohorts, virtually all showed a decline; but all women except over 65s showed increases. This the authors attributed to more women having higher incomes and better education, more taking up sports as a health precaution, and better offers being made – i.e. some of the same factors that make older British people stronger consumers (already mentioned on p 110). What is perhaps salutary for Britain, where the situation is reversed, was that older women participated more than men, rising from 15% to 27% (for men from nine per cent to 26%, so the gender gap was being slowly closed.

While in consumer markets 'grey power' was identified in US, the same group is less vocal and less powerful in the UK. These are people with time to commit to volunteering, and they play vital roles in many welfare organisations; in sport the dominance of older people on British National Governing Bodies has been derided as being out of touch – notably in the ruling bodies of cricket and rugby union, branded as 'old farts'; a derogatory comment, a very different view of the experience of age, from that venerated in many eastern and southern cultures. But also two out of five people aged 45–54, 3.5m people, especially women, are in the 'sandwich generation,' double carers, for teenagers and older parents simultaneously (Helm, T *Observer* 6 March 20011: 8).

Conclusions

While 'veteran's' sport has increased greatly in popularity, in competitive terms this mainly means people in their 40s, except in bowls and running. Most older people's sport is for fun and socialising. But it can be a great boon to health, and for medicine, though long-term follow-up is still lacking. Whereas the costs of injuries outweigh health benefits for younger people, for every year after the mid 30s the balance of benefits over costs grows, through maintaining independence and improving body functions (Nicholl et al., 1993). Given the expected growth of the over 60s, it is almost alarming that no attention has been paid by Sport England to encouraging their participation, despite stating that it was 'imperative' to 'reduce drop out with age and extend regular participation deep into the older age groups' (Rowe et al., 2004: 119). Having been told to leave Sport for All to other agencies, notably local authorities, it has abandoned *50+ and All to Play for*, one of its cheapest and most successful promotions. The English Sports Council's 'hands-off' commentary was that the reduced spending by local authorities on parks was likely to reduce opportunities for walking, cycling and bowls, and that:

Unless the remaining subsidy for sport can be more accurately targeted towards the less wealthy, they will become increasingly disadvantaged. The divergence in incomes of the retired will be reflected in a divergence of sports participation

(ESC, 1997: 9).

Only one of Pitchford and Collins' (2010) samples of local SDOs was devoted to working with older people.

Many local authorities maintained programmes, sometimes jointly with Primary Care Trusts, 60% of GP referral programmes prescribing exercise were hosted in local leisure facilities. But much has been left to the British Heart Foundation, emphasising walking, stair climbing, dancing, swimming and cycling. Such casual activity, however, will not close the gap in sports participation between Britain and Scandinavia, which must be seen as the site of good practice, or bind future generations into a sports club network.

The global growth in numbers of people aged over 65 (Table 6.3) will be very great (McPherson, 1999: 7), magnifying the importance of social life and leisure for more of the life span, even if retirement age is raised, from eight per cent in 2010 to 13% in 2030 and 16% in 2050 (UN projections 2012 revision). Japan's retired population doubled to 14% of the total in only 26 years, compared to 115 years for France, and this is likely to be the mode for the developing world. Harada (1999) berated Japan's government for failing to set up preventive health and activity programmes on a scale to match this change. He also foresaw, in a work-dominated society, the need for programmes of adult education to 're-socialise' people into leisure. Some might argue likewise for Britain! As more people gain decent pensions, they will expect fulfilling leisure; past patterns may be little guide to future needs (Hawkins, 1999, O'Brien Cousins, 1999).

While 65–74s spend more on recreation than any other group, this is not true of the 'old old' of whom the poorest might lose 34% of their income in benefit cuts (Age UK, 2011; *Press Notice* 14 October 2010). But in the recession, 48% of those coming into the workforce in 2009 were over 65s (Hutton, W. *Observer* 6 March 2011: 9). Research by WRVS (2011) showed that in 2010, far from being a drain on the economy, over 65s, though spending power, taxes and the £10bn value of volunteers, contributed a net £40bn. By 2030, when there will be some 15m over 65s, this will rise to £70bn.

Table 6.3 Projected population over 65 years 1990–2025 (millions)

Region	1990	2005	2010	2025
World	328	475	529	822
Less developed regions	183	289	331	566
North America	35	39	57	67
Europe	68	82	122	105

7 Social exclusion and sport in a multicultural society

Introduction: from race to ethnicity, from segregation to cohesion

> Sport has the power to unite people in a way that little else can. Sport can create hope where there was once only despair. It breaks down (racial) barriers. It laughs in the face of all kinds of discrimination.
>
> Nelson Mandela, Laureus Sports Awards 2000

It is fitting that this chapter begins with Mandela's statement of faith. The non-white population of England and Wales reached 11.8% in 2011, an increase of over 50% from 2001. The issue of race in sport comes to Britain from the US where the discourse has focussed until recently around African Americans and skin colour but more recent studies have included Hispanic groups. In Britain, from the late 1970s, serious study has developed from the issue of skin colour to that of culture, though studies of South Asian, Chinese and even more white cultural minorities in sport (Irish, Polish, Ukrainian) are progressively rarer. In the US, issues have been:

- Why black people are well or over-represented in some professional sports (notably athletics, American football, basketball and baseball). In Britain these same contrasts are made between athletics, soccer and cricket and other sports; but even in 1999 the FA held a major conference into the lack of Asian players;
- The idea of 'stacking' – the placing of ethnic minority professional players in certain positions within a team;
- The use of professional sport as a route 'out of the ghetto'; and
- More recently, the unequal chances of participation by minorities in sport as recreation, including refugees and asylum seekers (see p 241).

These same issues have been raised in Britain, though with less emphasis on stacking (though Maguire 1988, 1991 and Melnick, 1988 have studied it in soccer and rugby). Collins contrasted the involvement of black professional players and coaches in Rugby League with their slow and late emergence in soccer and Rugby Union. He commented on the stacking of black players in non-decision making positions, and the lack of black supporters (1998: 152), attributing this to 'an ideology ostensibly based on meritocracy but within a wider setting shaped by business exigency and the underlying racist assumptions of British society.' Later he concluded 'Rugby League is…a deeply contradictory phenomenon…with deep-rooted racial stereotyping and estrangement from local communities' (Collins, 1998: 166). Horne, Tomlinson and Whannel (1999) dealt with the issue as a matter of black identity. Cashmore (1982, 1989, 1996) looked at the emergence of black professional elite athletes and discrimination against them. Although the political and academic discourse is about multiculturality, in the pub and the popular media it is about race (Polley, 1997).

Previous studies have to be viewed against the backdrop of society's reaction to waves of immigration from Africa and the Caribbean, East Africa, India, Pakistan and Bangladesh, Cyprus and Turkey, with steadier trickles from Hong Kong and many other places. Although black people had been coming to the UK in tiny numbers from the eighteenth century, it was the inflows from the West Indies in the 1950s and 1960s that brought concerns about competition for jobs and housing epitomised in Enoch Powell's 'rivers of blood' speech, when only three per cent of the population were not white/Caucasian. Daniel (1968) demonstrated in housing, employment and public services 'racial discrimination… varying from the massive to the substantial.' Political action led to Acts in 1965, 1968 and 1976 to outlaw such attitudes and behaviours, and to promote equality of opportunity, led by a Commission for Racial Equality (CRE). When polled about the most important problems facing Britain and Europe respectively, race relations and immigration came fourth out of ten in both cases (Bramen, *Guardian* 22 Jun 2001). By the millennial year, Black and Ethnic Minorities (BME) comprised 7.1% of the population, but 11.5% of schoolchildren; 84% lived in the four conurbations of Greater London, the West Midlands, Manchester and West Yorkshire, seven out of ten in the 88 most deprived local authorities.

In sport, the first move was probably the British Boxing Board of Control's decision in 1948 to allow anyone 'normally resident' and having lived in the UK for 10 years to hold British titles. The Anti-Apartheid movement's opposition to South African 'rebel' cricket and rugby tours and the maintenance of segregation kept the issue alive through the 1970s, as did the Government's stance on the same issue. Herman Ouseley, then chairman of the Commission for Racial Equality, commented on discrimination in 1995: 'some people think it's all over… but it hasn't gone away' (1995: 1). The Sports Council said

> In sport individuals and organisations deliberately discriminate against black and ethnic minority people. There are others who unintentionally discriminate, mainly because they fail to acknowledge how racial inequality, cultural variance, and their own organisational behaviour restrict equal opportunities. Because many people in sport have understood racism to consist only of overt and deliberate forms of discrimination, more subtle and unintentional racism is not even detected.
>
> (Sports Council, 1994a: 17)

Carrington and McDonald (2001: 12) agreed: 'sport, like many other cultural areas, is a site of contestation, resistance and struggle, whereby dominant ideologies are both maintained and challenged…this applies as much to "race" and ethnicity as it does to gender, sexuality or class.' Racist chants in football crowds and in players' remarks on the pitch led to anti-racism schemes promoted by the NGBs:

- *Let's kick racism out of football* (Commission for Racial Equality/Professional Footballers Association, 1993, later widened to include the amateur game, lack of Asians in football, European football, and discrimination in boardrooms).
- *Hit racism for six* (1996) in cricket (Long et al., 1997a).
- *Tackle it – racism in Rugby League* (1996, CRE/Rugby Football League), said to be a 'small but significant issue' (Long et al., 1995, 1997b).

In 1999, the Football Association promoted a campaign to attract more Asian players into the amateur and professional game, and produced an *Ethics and Sport Equity Strategy* (FA, 2002). But, studying five County FAs, Lusted (2011) showed they were as 'colour-blind' and racism-denying as the local cricket interests examined by Long, viewing such a strategy as a piece of centrally-imposed political correctness.

Thus stereotyping and discrimination continue, despite the growing numbers of BME players visible in professional sport, and of both mixed culture and culturally representative teams in amateur sport. Still, views exist that 'black people are not suited to managing teams or clubs,' or 'black people aren't suited physiologically to swim or play hockey,' 'Asians cannot play contact sports and can only play hockey' (Sleap, 1998: 111). Academic research has widely agreed that race is essentially a social construction and not a natural division. Hylton (2009) explored a new racism, which, he said, distanced itself in discourses about citizenship, immigration and nationhood. Through Critical Race Theory he sought to uncover 'the racism in society that privileges whiteness as it disadvantages others because of their "blackness"' (2009b: 4).

The Cabinet Office (2001: 37), extrapolating from past trends concluded that 'the most likely pattern for the future appears to be widening differences for most ethnic minority groups and most dimensions of inequality,' and no coherent policy for tackling these issues was apparent. Policy Action Team 10 (SEU, 1998) recommended sports and arts should be part of reviving deprived communities, and equal opportunities actions should be taken in local authority cultural strategies, Lottery, New Deal and other programmes, and their evaluations.

There are also stereotypes about low skill and low income amongst BMEs; Platt and Noble (1999) looked at Birmingham, where 42% of the population were non-white, 2011. Their analysis of Housing Benefit or Council Tax relief covering 270,000 people showed:

- Notable concentrations of couples with children in Bangladeshi households (55%), and lone parents amongst Afro-Caribbeans (45%)
- Ninety-four per cent of Pakistani and Bangladeshi lone parents received Income Support, whereas 24% of Black Afro-Caribbeans were working in jobs above that threshold
- Pakistanis more likely to be buying their own homes, while Bangladeshis have more people in public and Housing Association accommodation, like the white population.

Ethnicity, disadvantage, exclusion and cohesion

The work of the Social Exclusion Unit stimulated data collection, its overview concluding:

> People from minority ethnic communities are at disproportionate risk of social exclusion....are more likely than others to live in deprived areas and in unpopular and overcrowded housing. They are more likely to be poor and to be unemployed, regardless of their age, sex, qualifications and place of residence. Minority ethnic communities experience a double disadvantage. They are disproportionately concentrated in deprived areas and experience all the problems that affect other people in these areas. But...also suffer the consequences of racial discrimination: services that fail to reach them or meet their needs; and language and cultural barriers in gaining access to information and services.
>
> (Cabinet Office, 2000: 7.8)

Table 7.1 illustrates some of the features of this disadvantage.

Table 7.1 Features of ethnic disadvantage

- 56% lived in the 44 most deprived local authorities
- 34% of Chinese people lived in households with under half average incomes, 40% of Afro-Caribbean and Indian, over 80% of Pakistani and Bangladeshi (compared to 28% of the total population)
- from 1994–5 to 1997–8 Afro-Caribbean pupils were 4 to 6 times more likely to be excluded from school, though no more likely to truant than others
- ethnic minorities were 2 to 3 times more likely than white people to be unemployed
- one in seven lived in overcrowded housing compared to two in a hundred of white households
- in 1995 there were an estimated 382,000 racial incidents of which only three per cent were reported to the police
- black people were 6 times more likely to be stopped and searched and 4.3 times more likely to be arrested than whites
- 32% of Indian/Pakistani/Bangladeshi children attained 5 or more GCSEs at grades A*–C compared to half of whites

Source: Cabinet Office, 2000, 2001

Riots in Bradford, Oldham and Burnley in 2001 led to separate inquiries and an overview – the Cantle report (Home Office, 2001). This report said that white and minority communities lived 'parallel lives', supported by separate social, educational and employment patterns, with little communication, and ignorance, fear and demonisation of difference, factors also spelled out by Dorling (2010: 145–207) in what he called a new, wider racism. Cantle condemned weak community leadership and discrimination by private sector employers, and said a meaningful concept of citizenship needed to be established and championed (Home Office, 2001: 22). A parliamentary committee (House of Commons, 2004, paras 1, 3, 12 and 25) said cohesion should 'not be seen as a law and order issue,' but should be on a par with education and social services, should be dealt with by better-funded statutory youth provision. Subsequently, the ODPM (2003a, b) sought to build cohesion into local authority policies, and area-based initiatives like Housing Action Zones, then topical (Chapter 10). The Department for Schools (Rodger and Cowen 2006) laid an obligation on schools to promote community cohesion and a 'sense of belonging.' Birmingham City Council catalogued the barriers to their leisure BMEs faced (Table 7.2).

Table 7.2 Barriers faced by ethnic groups

Category	Examples of comments
Overt racism (17%)	• Abuse – called names (at swimming pool) • People from other religious groups came to cause trouble so we Hindus never get to enjoy our events • There's always tension from teenagers in the park…they think they own the parks • I go out covered and you get nasty comments (park) • English children (at Youth Centres) are racist
Service-delivery barriers (28%)	• I need to dress in a certain way so I don't go there (Muslim female) • Many Muslim women would prefer not to have music to exercise to • Harder to find women-only facilities • Hard to communicate when they are only English speaking • You feel out of place – people look at you
Political (15%)	• Don't support African-Caribbean events • More provision in white areas
Cultural (13%)	• Children are restricted in what they do more than white kids • It's frowned on if you go to the park without the family
General issues not specific to Leisure & Culture (26%)	• Frightened of attacks/muggings • Poor condition of place

Base n=4283

Source: Birmingham City Council (2003: 52)

For the Local Government Association, using sport and cultural activities as a vehicle:

> community cohesion goes beyond the concept of race equality and social inclusion…[and] a cohesive community is one where:
>
> * there is a common vision and sense of belonging for all communities;
> * the diversity of people's different backgrounds and circumstances are appreciated and positively valued;
> * those from different backgrounds have similar life opportunities;
> * strong and positive relationships are being developed in workplaces, in schools and within neighbourhoods.
>
> (LGA, 2002: 6)

Though Dorling (2010: 183) scathingly described community cohesion as 'a strangely manufactured lament reflecting some old concerns,' the term was promoted by New Labour (particularly then Home Secretary David Blunkett), and has become both a descriptor and euphemism for what some term a 'new social Darwinism.' In 2005, Trevor Phillips, then chair of the CRE, inflamed the debate by claiming the country was 'sleepwalking into segregation' (speech to Manchester Community Relations Council 22 Sept 2005), but simultaneously, an extensive review of 56 places in *The State of English Cities* (ODPM, 2006) showed that generally this was not so: in terms of employment disparities for the UK, whites were 29% more likely to be in work than non-whites, a shocking enough figure in itself; those for Luton, Bradford, Birmingham, and Tower Hamlets were higher, peaking in Blackburn (67 vs 41%); in contrast, multicultural Leicester at 64 vs 57% was a haven of equality. McCabe et al. (2013) found, regarding the role of social networks: informal 'bonding' links helped access to employment, but often limited it to low paid jobs; voluntary and faith organisations helped 'bridging' moves into multi-cultural networks (though sport was not mentioned); social class constrained linkages.

Perhaps fuelled by the terrible legacy of South African apartheid, there was an unspoken fear of segregation or 'voluntary separate development' as it if was a contagious disease, but as Cantle (2008: 18) later wrote, 'the opposite of parallel lives is not assimilation, as some commentators seem to fear. In fact, some form of clustering on the basis of distinct communities will help to maintain cultural heritage. Interaction is about shared experiences, building trust and understanding differences, not about being the same,' and Shah (2008: 64–70) added, 'cosmopolitanism is a more helpful concept than cohesion.' Also, as Gilchrist (2004) pointed out from her case studies, it takes time to move from culturally specific targeted projects to broader, bridge-building partnerships (also Amara et al., 2006).

Whereas under the Conservatives no mention was made of racism in national strategy, in the New Labour *Game Plan* (DCMS, 2002) it was debated (Carrington and McDonald, 2008). Sport England and the CRE created Sporting Equals in

Table 7.3 The Racial Equality Charter for Sport

Governing bodies and sports organisations will:

- Make a public commitment to challenge and remove racial discrimination and achieve racial equality in sport
- Encourage people from all communities to take part in sport
- Welcome employees and spectators from all communities, and protect all employees and spectators from racial abuse and harassment
- Encourage skilled and talented individuals from all communities to become involved at all levels of sports administration, management and coaching
- Develop the best possible racial equality policies and practices, and to review and update them regularly
- Celebrate diversity in sport.

Source: Sporting Equals, 2000

1998 to support and empower NSOs, which produced a charter (summarised, Table 7.3), and a standard (Sport England, 2000). Sporting Equals produced *Achieving Racial Equality: a standard for sport* (2001) as a guide for NGBs, showing ways of recording the realities of anti-racist actions. It plays an equivalent role to the Women's Sport and Fitness Foundation (Chapter 5) in gender relations. Hylton criticised some antiracist moves as naïve or incompetent, commenting (2009: 123): 'if antiracists hope to make gains…the gaps between reflexive consciousness, policy and practice must diminish, so that the dynamism of racism is met with dynamic responses.' Spracklen, Long and Hylton (2006) showed that adopting the Charter and Standard did not mean that equality rapidly seeped into daily practice at NGBs' grass roots clubs, and doubted the wisdom of rolling race, gender and disability into a single national Equality Commission.

To look at concentrations of ethnic groups, one can use the Index of Dissimilarity, showing scores above 0.7 for white-Asian differences in Blackburn, Bradford, Rochdale and Burnley, for Barnsley on white-Black, and again for Blackburn and Bradford on white-Non-white; in contrast, Leicester's scores were low – 0.62, 0.47 and 0.59, and London's 0.50, 0.51 and 0.44. *State of the Cities* clearly showed that non-whites were concentrated in deprived areas (Table 7.4) generally for Asians, but for blacks also in Manchester, Leeds and Nottingham; in Leicester black deprivation was concentrated, but not Asian.

The report concluded with a balance sheet on cohesion and segregation, thus:

- Segregation by ethnicity…declined between 1991 and 2001 in 48 out of 56 cities. It increased significantly in only two.
- Segregation by income, wealth and employment [was] greater than segregation by ethnicity.
- Higher segregation [was] associated with lower employment, lower earnings, lower education.
- participation and higher levels of deprivation.

Table 7.4 Asian and Black concentrations in deprived areas, 2001 (percentages)

	A. Asian (Black) presence in most deprived areas	B. Asian (Black) presence in all other areas %	Concentration ratio of Asian (Black) presence A: B
Bradford	42.1 (1.6)	8.3 (0.6)	5.1 (2.7)
Burnley	25.4 (0.2)	7.1 (0.1)	3.6 (2.0)
Rochdale	20.0 (0.5)	6.1 (0.3)	3.3 (1.7)
Manchester	10.3 (3.7)	3.9 (0.8)	2.6 (4.6)
Birmingham	25.8 (7.9)	9.6 (2.7)	2.7 (2.9)
Luton	34.6 (11.3)	17.9 (6.2)	1.9 (1.8)
London	15.6 (23.2)	10.4 (8.2)	1.5 (2.8)
Leicester	17.2 (5.2)	23.1 (1.7)	0.7 (3.0)

Source: Office of the Deputy Prime Minister, vol 1, 2006 Tables 5.7, 5.8 using 2001 Census figures

- Segregation [was] significantly higher in cities in the north and west of England.
- The connection between segregated minorities and deprived areas [was] critical.

(ODPM, 2005, vol 2: 153)

Billings and Holden spoke graphically of 'enclavisation' in Burnley, a more accurate description than ghettoisation, and which they thought threatened stability in disadvantaged areas of white youth, whereas in mixed white-Muslim enclaves there seemed to be a measure of protection/nurturing for tolerance. But they pointed out (2008: 5) that many young Muslims had little contact with mosques and poor knowledge of the Koran, and were torn between 'being British citizens and part of the worldwide Muslim movement (umma),' demanding urgently a new theology of being both British and Muslim.

Phillips (2009: 183) reported continued gaps in school performance measured by GCSE exam results; that between Whites and both Blacks and Pakistanis closed from 18 percentage points to seven in 1998–2007, and from 14 to one for Bangladeshis. Rutter and Latore (2009: 202–3) noted that Bangladeshis, Poles, and Sri Lankans suffered particularly in school and labour markets because of language difficulties. Tackey, Barnes and Khambhaita (2011) reported a 'possible cumulative effect' of poor educational attainment, and that at secondary school poverty is the biggest constrainer of achievement.

Sport Structures (2005) were commissioned to study BME sports employment: they formed 6.8% of the NGB workforce, but only 3.6 per cent of volunteers. In Sport England's Active People survey they were less likely to give an hour a week than whites (3.6 cf. 4.8%). Only four of fourteen groups were in senior management, and only one in eight workers was of Asian origin. Lack of senior leisure managers was raised by the Institute of Leisure and Amenity Management (Hylton, 1999), and has been taken up modestly by Sporting Equals for members of managing boards in arts, sports and heritage (*press release* 22 Feb 2009).

Sporting Equals has not focused yet on the (mis)representation of race in the media or on the 'double discrimination' of leisure opportunities for older BME people (see CRE/AC, 1998a,b). Nor has Britain followed the US route of creating a separate black coaches' association or a foundation for black women in sport. Good practices to encourage BME groups are similar to those for women – providing role models, programme space and time sympathetically, offering private/segregated sessions providing leadership and outreach workers (also de Knop et al., 1994 for Belgium), and promoting healthy walking in the countryside as an entrée to outdoor sport (in Countryside Agency's 2003 *Diversity Review*).

Issues of race have inevitably become entangled in theory, policy and practice concerned with social cohesion, and the antisocial behaviour of youth. But while there is evidence that sports schemes for youth at-risk can improve health and self-esteem, and divert from antisocial or criminal behaviour in the short term (Chapter 9), there is no longitudinal evidence or satisfactory mechanism to demonstrate long-term effects (Coalter, 2007). Putnam (2007) sought to explore whether ethnic diversity encouraged social capital formation (especially 'bridging' capital amongst different people – the 'contact hypothesis') or led to in-group links between similar people – bonding – the 'conflict hypothesis' see p 127). His initial findings seemed to support the conflict concept, but multivariate exploration showed in-group trust declined with diversity – what he called 'hunkering down', and accepted that becoming comfortable with diversity would be a slow process.

Letki used 2001 Citizenship Survey data in a multi-level individual-community model, finding no evidence of racial diversity eroding interaction and social capital, whereas poverty had a major effect. She opined strongly (2008: 121) that 'solidarity is undermined by poverty but the blame is placed on diversity' and criticised governments for downplaying multi-cultural policies, concluding (2008: 122) 'to maintain social solidarity and community cohesion twenty-first century Britain needs more social and economic equality, rather than more cultural unity.'

Sport is said to promote social cohesion, presumably by mixing people up (Cantle, 2007). The Nice Declaration of the European Council (European Council, 2000) asserted that sport 'is a factor making for integration, involvement in social life, tolerance, acceptance of difference and playing by the rules....in a sports hall or on a sports field everyone is equal.' But does this happen?

In Germany, there are nearly two million Turkish 'guestworkers', most of whom are non-citizens (unless one parent is German). They have a separate network of sports clubs, though virtually none for women (Merkel, 1999). Ackcayer (2004) described Turkish women's cultural clubs in Cologne offering dance, swimming, and other activities as 'a place to start with sports for Turkey[sic] women, who would never join a typical German sport club.' Elling et al. (2001) found lowest female participation amongst Turkish girls (18%) compared to Surinamese or Moroccans (40%), while Indonesian and indigenous girls participated most (68%); boys always participated more than girls; sports clubs were the main place to make friends for only one child in ten. But in Rotterdam BME clubs Krouwel et al. (2007) found:

1   Sport reinforced strong existing (BME) identities rather than forming new ones.
2   Mixed ethnic competitions, rather than sheltering peaceful exchanges, could easily become arenas for external issues – lack of language comprehension, verbal abuse and even violence.

The authors recommended that government pondered, because in social capital terms mono-ethnic civic involvement was better than none. Likewise, remembering two-thirds of Australians are of mixed ethnic origin, Deane and Westerbeek (1999) described highly identified ethnic origins in the national soccer league, notably by teams from the former Yugoslavia and Greece. The Soccer Federation tried to de-ethnicize soccer – requiring removal of symbols of origin in names, badges, or team shirts. Some changes were made, with small effect on teams' ethnic composition; some was strongly resisted. The authors advised the ASF to reconsider. These examples support the 'conflict hypothesis', perhaps, and provide evidence of trying to intervene too early in the settling-in process (p 126). Adair, Taylor and Darcy (2010: 307) thought that coming to terms with otherness and negotiating togetherness was something many sports bodies found difficult.

Multi-cultural participation in sport

Long et al. (2009: 59) rejected the notion of a single cause for BME groups' non-participation in sport: they may suffer racism and distancing factors as mentioned in Table 7.2; be denied opportunity by material constraints; have never received the right encouragement; be inhibited by family or community cultural traditions; or a lack of money or interest. Taylor and Toohey (2002) commented that virtually all research on BME women focussed on Muslims.

In Manchester, Verma and Darby (1994) interviewed 721 people from five Asian, African, Caribbean, and East African Asian groups, and a white group of 190, about their leisure and social and religious life. Their sports participation is shown in Table 7.5, with a smaller measure of casual participation than the contemporary General Household Survey, demonstrating how use of facilities from different providers varied – the most recently arrived groups from Bangladesh and East Africa depended more than other groups on their own community's provision. Those sports chosen by significant numbers were:

	Men (%)			*Women (%)*	
	White	*Ethnic minorities*		*White*	*Ethnic minorities*
Soccer	37	47	Badminton	22	28
Snooker	25	28	Swimming	57	23
Swimming	47	20	Keep fit	25	15
Badminton	17	14	Aerobics	22	10
Pool	18	24	Dancing	17	11

Table 7.5 Participation and use/non-use of sports facilities by ethnic groups in Manchester

	Bang (%)	Afri (%)	Carib (%)	Chin (%)	EAfA (%)	Indi (%)	Pak (%)	White (%)	Oth (%)	Total (%)
Sports										
Male	32.7	23.2	32.4	33.0	42.9	39.1	35.4	33.1	–	34.1
Female	9.9	29.0	25.9	25.1	28.1	23.5	10.9	24.1	–	21.9
Places Used										
Local authority facility	34	17	45	25	27	35	23	46	–	35
Sports Club	8	6	7	14	39	19	18	10	–	14
Own Community Centre	28	1	1	6	15	7	1	0.4	–	7
Youth Club	3	3	16	2	6	2	7	0.4	–	4
Education	6	6	8	31	–	7	19	7	–	12
Company club	6	21	10	9	3	16	17	20	–	14
Base Male	55	19	38	80	9	53	62	71	7	313
Female	49	26	80	53	12	98	81	129	9	408

Source: Verma and Derby, 1994

The 1996 General Household Survey identified ethnic origin for the first time and made clear that participation by black people was closest to white patterns overall. Bangladeshis participated much less and Indians substantially less, but interestingly, the other groups participated more. The black and South Asian groups walked for pleasure considerably less than white people. These patterns may be related to the Households below Average Income statistics displayed in Chapter 2. Small sample sizes made it impossible to describe specific sports, but Sport England undertook a separate survey (Rowe and Champion, 2000) with a sample size of 3,084 adults (Table 7.6).

Black Other groups participated more than average, notably through their men; indeed the gender gap was more marked (21–35 percentage points) than in the population as a whole (15 percentage points). Walking regularly and briskly was an important contributor to healthy lifestyles, but no group reached the population average of 44% for walking two miles or more, only one in five of the Bangladeshis doing so. Nor did BME groups take part in activities popular amongst the white majority – bowls, fishing, table tennis, squash and horse riding. Table 7.7 shows the activities that they did take part in including:

• keep fit/aerobics as the second most popular;
• snooker, slightly more so than generally;
• swimming lower than its second place for England as a whole.

This table also shows the variegated patterns of activity by group, none so strong as to sustain stereotypes like 'black people can't swim.'

Table 7.6 Participation in sport 1999–2000 by ethnic group (percentage aged over 16 undertaking one or more sports/activities in last four weeks by all aged over 16, excluding walking)

Ethnic group	Total (%)	Male (%)	Female (%)
GHS 1996 All	46	54	39
Any ethnic minority	41		
Black Caribbean	39	45	34
Black African	44	60	34
Black other	60	80	45
Indian	39	45	31
Pakistani	31	42	21
Bangladeshi	30	46	19
Chinese	45	54	39
Other	46	51	41

Source: Rowe and Champion, 2000

Table 7.7 The five most popular sports undertaken by ethnic minorities 1999–2000 (percentage in last four weeks)

	Black Carib (%)	Black Afric (%)	Black Oth (%)	India (%)	Pak (%)	Bang (%)	Chin (%)	Other (%)	GHSa 1996 (%)
Walking	34	37	36	31	24	19	28	42	44
Keep fit	19	17	24	13	9	7	16	15	15
Snooker	9	8	16	10	6	10		10	11
Swimming				11	8	8	8	15	15
Soccer	8	11	14	7	9	8		6	5
Cycling	8		14				8	6	11
Running		13						6	4
Badminton							10		2
Table tennis					6				2
Weight training	9								6

Source: Sport England, 2000

Notes: a) GHS = General Household Survey; b) some responses are too small to be calculated.

Indeed, similar variety was shown in the sports groups would like to take up:

For men	*For women*
swimming (Black Af, Pak, Chin)	swimming (Black/Af/Other, Ind, Pak, Bangla, Chin)
soccer (Black Other, Bangla)	keep fit/yoga (Black Car/Af/ Other, Ind, Pak)
badminton (Bangl, Chin)	badminton (Ind, Chin)
Self defence/martial arts (Black Other, Bangl)	netball (Black Af/other)
Tennis (Black Af/Other, Chin)	self defence/martial arts (Black Car)
Motor sports (Black Af, Chin)	

When asked what had prevented them taking part in sport during the last year, the answers were very similar to those given in surveys of mainly white users:

- home and family responsibilities ranked first, for over two in five women in all BME communities, and both men and women from India and Bangladesh;
- lack of or unsuitable facilities was quoted by 48% of Bangladeshis and 45% of Black Others;
- lack of money, cited by more Black Caribbean and Black Others (a quarter).

Finally, only six per cent said they had had a negative experience in sport arising from their ethnicity, and when asked whether they had enjoyed sport in school, two-thirds said yes, only three per cent stating something had deterred them from taking part. The authors commented:

> the results...challenge stereotypical views that suggest that low levels of participation in sport (and in certain sports in particular) by certain groups are more a reflection of culture and choice rather than other constraints such as provision, affordability and access.
>
> (Rowe and Champion, 2000: 37)

Given that the second and third generation schoolchildren in such households are taking part in National Curriculum sport and are becoming more acculturated, it is interesting to watch participation patterns evolve. By 2008, the participation of BME children in school sport was only slightly lower than of the indigenous white pupils, though more so in schools in deprived areas and where the take up of the government's two-hour a week target was lower (Quick et al., 2008). By contrast, de Knop et al. (1996b) recorded that Belgian Muslim girls sometimes did not get an adequate introduction to PE. In Leicester and Nottingham, three-quarters of Asian and Afro-Caribbean primary/middle school children said they swam regularly in classes and three-fifths regularly for recreation out of school, and enjoyed it, but only 11% of boys and 14% of girls swam in clubs, and only one and six per cent respectively took part in competition, which Collins (2002) described as a decline from 'a popular pastime to invisible sport'. Long et al. (2009: 27) commented that BME groups were encountered in only a few clubs. For adults, the Active People Survey 7 showed a statistically significant increase 2005–13, but no increase after the 2012 Olympics.

Although a 1980s outreach scheme, Action Sport, was targeted at black inner-city youth (Rigg, 1986), Carrington and Macdonald (2008) argued that other concerns for deprived areas allowed the Sports Council no policy space to focus on BME groups until the mid 1990s, when there was a policy framework (Sports Council, 1994a), and equity guidelines and statements for NGBs. In 1997, Sport England (2000) discovered BMEs were fairly represented among users in an English sample of sports halls (5.3 compared to their 5.2% share of the population), but were substantially under-represented in swimming pools, at 2.8%. But Taylor et al. 's (2004) benchmarking data showed while sports centres in deprived areas consistently attracted more low skill/income groups, unemployed and disabled people than in affluent ones, they were no better at serving BME groups. In contrast, Ravenscroft and Markwell (2000), sampling visitors to eight parks in Reading, discovered a consistently greater share of black and Asian visitors than from the neighbourhood populations, a greater segregation of groups in neighbourhood parks, and less satisfaction with the equipment and facilities by black compared to white and Asian youths.

As far as elite sport is concerned, there were again inequalities in representation. In 11 sports in 1997, two per cent were Black Caribbeans (twice the proportion in the population), and only one per cent were from Asian backgrounds (compared to three times as many in the population, English Sports Council, 1998b).

Arguments about race and ethnicity in sport, therefore, fall into three groups:

• unequal treatment relates to and cannot be separated from the *social deprivation* of many ethnic groups;
• ethnic groups make different leisure choices from the host population, reflecting different meanings and values;
• sport is a site of discrimination as much as other areas of life, emanating in poorer access to resources, expertise and power.

Sport, ethnicity and exclusion

The popular press has promulgated stories of, in particular, footballers, cricketers, boxers and athletes who have 'climbed out of the ghetto' through sport, and yet also of lack of equal opportunities and racism in sport. In Canada, Stodolska and Jackson (1998) found little 'discrimination against a Polish minority, though this may be partly due to effectively 'closed' clubs. Sport England and NGBs have sought to promote non-discriminatory attitudes to combat racism, and to open up organisations to equal opportunities. Brownhill and Thomas (1998) argued that while some resources and projects under the Urban Programme were successfully targeted at BMEs, more recent initiatives – City Challenge and Urban Development corporations – have been 'racially blind,' and failed to involve minorities in terms of 'associational democracy.' Hylton and Morpeth (2012) made the same point, being pessimistic about any legacy for the 42% non-white populations of the Olympic host boroughs.

Some argue that problems of stereotyping and lack of equal treatment begin at school. Fleming (1991), studying a comprehensive school, suggested that Asian schoolboys lived out a self-fulfilling situation where they were expected not to do well in sport, valuing sport less and having few role models. De Knop et al. (1996b) recorded in Muslim countries the introduction of PE for boys but not always for girls. Meanwhile, Asian girls in the UK and Western Europe live under a strong cultural pressure about revealing their bodies. In contrast, Leaman and Carrington (1985) found sport a means of self-expression and recognition for Afro-Caribbean pupils, something they did not always get in 'academic' subjects. Carroll and Hollinshead (1993) argued that in mixed culture situations, teachers have a dilemma of time and resources to acknowledge cultural minority authenticity. Bayliss (1989: 1) argued that superficial responses like separate showering and activities for Asian girls are inadequate, and schools should ask four questions:

• *Entitlement* – are the school's aims rooted in individual needs?
• *PE* – does the Department have multicultural aims that relate to cross-curricular themes?

- *Delivery* – do teaching styles, grouping, attitudes and expertise reconcile the needs of all groups?
- *Monitoring* – is there regular evaluation to see how ethnic issues are addressed?

Scott Porter's (2001a) qualitative research in Scotland showed Asian people: heavily influenced by parents and 'significant others;' the problem of training during Ramadan's fasting, and also by the issue of modesty for girls. They divided their sample into: the *security seekers*, least likely to play sport and only then in safe, segregated settings; the *harmony seekers,* who sought to reconcile their sport with cultural and religious expectations; and *independents*, who saw themselves first as Scots citizens, and wanted to share the culture of their indigenous neighbours. They found few community-specific barriers, the largest by far being 'an experience or fear of racial discrimination [which is about]...institutional racism' (2001a: 32), which most had suffered.

Segregated transport and sessions were successful in supporting participation in the short term – like swimming schemes for Asian girls and women, such as Sitara fitness and health in Batley, Blackburn, Leeds, Birmingham and in Belgium (de Knop et al., 1994) and in other places. Jones (1998) stressed their fears of harassment and assault, but also their frustrations at a home-centred lifestyle. In the post-apartheid 'Rainbow society' in South Africa, participation was severely restricted by poor infrastructure, and participation and leadership very much related to educational attainments (Wilson and Hattingh, 1992), but Burnett and Hollander (1999) demonstrated that the government concentrated resources on elite facilities and players rather than Sport for All, continuing to until 2010 FIFA Football World Cup at a cost of over £2bn in a country, and running costs for new and refurbished stadia.

The Sports Council's demonstration project in Scunthorpe suggested that a stronger lifestyle link of leisure to health and education was a helpful precursor to promoting sports programmes (McDonald and Tungatt, 1991). In Germany, guestworkers (*gastarbeiter*) cannot have citizenship unless one of their parents is German, and in particular the 28% (1.92 million) from Turkey have by law – and discrimination – remained a separate group in sport. There is a network of separate Turkish sports clubs, virtually all male, with little participation by girls in PE and almost none in sport (Merkel, 1999). Studying exercise amongst BMEs in the US, Taylor et al. (1998) 45% of their sample of African American women sustained weight loss six months after exercise classes, and 55% three months after aerobics classes, but pointed out more work was needed amongst Latinos, native Indians, and Asian immigrants.

In countryside recreation, lower BME participation shown in national surveys was attributed, on limited evidence, to: lower average incomes and car ownership, concentrations in inner cities distant from countryside, and a lack of cultural tradition of countryside day trips. This was only explored from 2003 (by the Countryside Agency), showing a need for a cultural change by many providers, and better offers to young people, to establish habits of visiting. Getaway Girls in

Leeds and the Wild Outdoor Women project in Kirklees aimed to encourage outdoor sports participation by inner city women white, ethnic minority, and disabled (Glyptis et al., 1995). In the US, Floyd et al. (1993) found less countryside visiting by Latino citizens, and Johnson et al. (1998) by poor blacks. Baas et al. (1993) found that in the Mojave Desert, Mexican and US-born Hispanics desired equipped sites (with toilets, picnic areas, garbage disposal, marked trails) and favoured team games and picnicking, while Anglo visitors preferred informal sites and trails, and walking and backpacking.

Interventions

BMEs were a target of English sports policy after 1982, leading to the installation of BME managers and Sports Development Officers, especially in inner cities. By 2005, Pitchford found one in seven frontline SDOs but only four in 100 managers from BMEs (Pitchford and Collins, 2010: 265–9). When the marketing device of targeting fell out of favour on the (undemonstrated) grounds that it was stigmatising, a new racial equality policy was introduced 'to work towards the elimination of racial disadvantage and discrimination' (Sports Council, 1994c: 7).

Case studies of good practice in promoting sports, especially cricket, and awareness training and courses for BME members to become coaches, officials and administrators were included in each Sports Council (NW, 1991 and Y&H, 1995a). Symbolically, the English Sports Council (1997b) gave examples of good practice for local authorities in:

- policy planning for multiculturalism (Leicester City);
- the use of Race Relations advisors and customer care (Birmingham and Southwark);
- employment schemes (Watford);
- recognition of the issue in Compulsory Competitive Tendering (Newham);
- inclusion in sports development programmes (Oldham and Watford), and leadership training (Kirklees).

Its National Demonstration Scunthorpe project (McDonald and Tungatt, 1991) demonstrated ways of linking sport with other actions, such as:

- more publicity and information in BME languages (just as needed for housing, social services, and citizens' advice);
- involving and empowering local BME groups (as seen in CARE, below);
- better awareness training for staff and volunteers;
- linking sport to cultural/religious festivals like Diwali, the Festival of Lights, as also in Leicester;
- linking with health promotion and anti-poverty work.

Racial abuse by spectators at professional matches has become widespread; the Sir Norman Chester Research Centre at Leicester discovered 36% of spectators at

Rangers matches and 38% at Everton hearing such abuse, compared to 11% at Wimbledon and 12% at Charlton Athletic (Brown, P. and Chaudhury, V. *Guardian* 7 Jan 2000: 5). The problem even extends to amateur and junior soccer, leading the Football Association to launch the 'Let's kick racism out of football' campaign. In West Riding soccer, with 2,300 clubs, no member of any county committee was African, Caribbean or Asian, only 2.4% of referees, and in half the leagues three-quarters or more of teams had no black players. The Centre for Leisure and Sport Research (2001: 8) recorded that all the black players 'had experienced racism in physical and verbal forms as well as what they interpreted as institutional forms (e.g., differential treatment by officialdom).'

Cricket followed suit with 'Hit racism for six.' Long and Hylton (2000) recorded 46% of Rugby League spectators having heard racial abuse directed at players. Long (2000: 2), examining the issue in rugby league and amateur West Yorkshire cricket, demonstrated Riggins' 'discourse of othering.' He recorded examples of denial of prejudice, of defensiveness about practices ('we don't get good enough black players', 'look at the (few) black stars'), concluding 'because of the privileges bestowed by whiteness, moving in and out of identities is in fact easier for whites than it is for blacks.' Only a third of the League clubs had an Equal Opportunities policy. Having examined both professional and amateur cricket, Carrington and McDonald (2001: 67) judged that, if reforms were implemented, the League 'has the potential to be used as a model for a modern, democratic and multicultural society rather than being seen as the last cultural vestige of a pre-modern, imperial cultural formation.'

While awareness training for staff is now widespread, including amongst volunteers through the Running Sport programme, it is clear that many local sports clubs have not yet taken action to broaden their cultural base (Collins, Henry and Houlihan, 1999). The advent of local Cultural Strategies in 2000 should have brought together interests in BME arts and sport much more closely, but evidence of this is sparse. MacGowan (1997) described the belated but extensive promotion of sport for Aboriginal people in Australia; Taylor and Toohey (1996) pointed out that women from any ethnic minority were invisible in Australian sport – as much because of expected gender and family roles as of discrimination. The Australian government (Commonwealth of Australia, 1999: 55) stated that 'in a multicultural society like Australia, sport is an important mechanism for bringing diverse groups closer together.' Maxwell, Taylor and Foley (2011) gave three examples of including Muslim women and girls: in a club in a western Sydney suburb with 14% Islamic population, life-saving programmes across New South Wales and Victoria, and a national surf life-saving programme. The Hillary Commission recently implemented an extended Maori sports programme involving extensive grass roots development actions (HC, 1998) but evaluation of outcomes is absent.

Immigrants bring cultures that often include indigenous sports. The imposition of the British Empire and its educational and cultural values on many countries brought British forms of sport and its values to different parts of the world. So soccer, rugby, cricket, badminton, hockey, and squash in particular became part of the sports scene in Africa, South Asia and Australasia, and helped the acculturation of immigrant sport. But only in the last decade have national games like kabbadi, carramboard and gulli danda been accepted and established in cities with major ethnic population concentrations – notably in Birmingham with the Birmingham Pakistani Sports Forum after the 1985 Handsworth riots.

Arnaud (1996) compared 'second city' sport and recreation interventions in deprived BME neighbourhoods in Birmingham with Lyon: in Birmingham, all City Council policies were scrutinised for impacts on BMEs; Lyon reflected French national policy, focusing on economic problems at the expense of ethnic issues. Both cities developed substantial Sports Development programmes, but while in Birmingham BMEs were seen by officers as a market with grants to back community action after consultations, in Lyon it was seen as part of the City's and Region's joint attack on poor housing, jobs and environments programmes for *sports du quartier* (neighbourhood sports). Although projects were grant-aided they subject to strict supervision from the regional office of the Ministry of Youth and Sports

Conclusions

Barnard and Turner (2011) showed how the 'intersectionality' of a host of social factors means that the kaleidoscope of communities argues for local knowledge and policy design. As newcomers, immigrant minorities spend much of their first generation finding a workplace and a home; leisure and sport concerns only gradually become more important; there is a balance between maintaining authentic 'home' culture and adopting host culture. This is more starkly seen in the arts than in sport where the influence of Empire had long since introduced European sports to colonies and trading partners. There is a theoretical debate as to how far sport and culture for ethnic communities are structured by race and discrimination, by poverty/income, or by subcultures (Taylor, 1992). In Britain, at the beginning of the twenty-first century, all of these are influences: racism, sexism and ageism all affect BMEs and need combating; concentrations of poverty coincide with minority communities and need a similar complex of policies as for the majority population.

Interventions to overcome exclusion have to encompass:

- sensitive provision in PE classes, drawing on the wish of children to participate because sport is fun, and in youth work, especially as a safe site for Muslim girls;
- working to persuade parents of the benefits of sport and physical activity, even where there might be cultural resistance, as in some Islamic households (Collins, Henry and Houlihan, 1999);
- training all leisure services workers in race awareness, and operating mentoring schemes to overcome the shortage of black leisure managers, a shortage;

- providing dedicated BME youth, community and sports development workers, discount schemes, targeted programmes and separate transport, coaching/participation sessions, at least for a prolonged transitional period;
- not forcing public or club providers to false integration (integration for its own sake, not wished by the parties), especially when they have genuine local community roots.

Several reports outlined good practices. The PAT 10 report (DCMS, 1999: 100–2) extensively covered a multi-agency, 'bottom-up' scheme: the Charlton Athletic Race Equality Partnership (CARE). Instigated by the London Borough of Greenwich, using Single Regeneration Budget funds, CARE was relocated to the new Valley ground in 1992 and its local partners were the local University and Higher Education College, the Metropolitan Police and local multifaith, victim support groups. Employing three full time workers, its initiatives included:

- a newsletter, the *Equaliser*;
- home match tickets at less than half price for CARE members;
- *Show Racism the Red card* and *Roots of Racism* education packs;
- Face Value project for 10–16s in schools exploring exclusion, peer pressure, prejudice, racist violence and mixed race relationships; carnival costumes and music for primary schoolchildren; PATH theatre and summer play-scheme for 16–21s
- mini-soccer for primary girls; Plumstead Common sports festival;
- a study centre for 10–14s to help with homework, literacy, numeracy and computing.

But, while all the frameworks connected with CARE and similar schemes seem to offer positive signs of positive outcomes, no pre-establishment baseline studies were done, and no evaluations set up. Although the PAT 10 report concentrated on BME groups, the European SEx rhetoric has not recognised the multicultural reality of many West European states now with numerous sizeable minorities. An EU study identified incidents of racism, anti-Semitism and anti-Gypsyism in football and basketball, with experts warning rightwing extremists were becoming active, especially in German and Italian amateur leagues. Almost no data were available for other sports. Ten governments monitored racist events, though mostly in football and little attention was paid to under-representation of BME persons. The Council of Europe's Commission against Racism and Intolerance commented on 'a level of denial' from some federations and clubs (FRA, 2010: 7, 45–7, 58).

Gramann and Allison (1999) speculated about the ethnic future of the US where immigration and high birth rates mean that large areas will have non-white majorities. Reflecting deaths in two World Wars and lower-than-replacement birth rates mean that much of Western Europe will import large numbers of workers from the former USSR, Turkey and North Africa. For third and fourth generation citizens of black and Asian extraction, acculturation processes will pull in one direction and deliberate attempts to rediscover or re-invent authentic cultures and personal identities will pull in another, in sport as much as in other social spheres. So, there is still a long way to go, even in Scandinavian states that have travelled furthest regarding gender equity (e.g., Ottesen et al., 2010). Sport England (2013: 22) characterised the BME market as 'growing but complex' with the largest challenges among black and Asian women and Chinese men. Structural social changes involving ethnic issues may take a couple of generations to resolve, frustrating politicians and lobby groups (Collins, 2010a). Difference will continue to attract attention, whether admiring or abusive; what matters is how society and individual citizens deal with it.

8 Sport and exclusion by disability

Introduction: attitudes, policies and structures regarding disability and sport

In 1999, The Disability Rights Task Force reported:

> there is a common misconception that disabled people are only those with mobility difficulties or sensory impairments, such as deafness or blindness. In reality, people with a very wide range of impairments and chronic or recurring health conditions can be disabled. For example, people with mental health problems, asthma, diabetes or epilepsy might be disabled. The failure to appreciate the diversity of disabled people means that not all of them benefit from new policies.
>
> (DRTF, 1999: 6)

The Task Force recommended extending the definition to include people with HIV and serious cancer. Historically, disability has been misunderstood and vilified; in biblical times it was seen as the result of a person's wrongdoing, or that of their parents. Nixon said disabled people have been accustomed to being

> treated as members of a deviant minority group. Deviant status has meant that disabled persons have been relegated to a position outside the mainstream. Minority status has meant that disabled persons as a stereotyped and stigmatised category or group have been accorded degraded status, little power, and few opportunities for economic advancement or success.
>
> (Nixon, 2000: 423)

Even in 2007 popular British perception focussed still on visible physical symptoms, like wheelchairs and crutches – only 44% regarding older people with hearing aids and 48% sufferers from schizophrenia as disabled (Rigg, 2006). As Dattilo and Williams (1999: 452) commented, a person's disability is not the origin of a stigma or deviancy. Rather, society assigns stigma and 'deviant' labels to people with 'undesirable' differences.

For centuries societies preferred disabled members of communities to be kept 'out of sight, and out of mind,' many in closed institutions. As medical science grew, the 'medical model' appeared, that saw disability as a pathology happening to passive victims, needing treatment and rehabilitation, and required disabled people to do their best to adapt their behaviour in a predominantly non-disabled world. As Oliver (1996a: 30) wrote: 'the assumption is, in health terms, that disability is a pathology and, in welfare terms, that disability is a social problem.'

Education and social science have come to see things differently, in the 'social model' many disabled people are in situations partly determined by social structures, policies and 'disabling attitudes' (West, 1984). Conversely, Thomas and Smith (2009: 14) suggested the 1970 Chronically Sick and Disabled Persons Act made disabled people more dependent on state benefits. Poverty adds restrictions on mobility and in its train reduces social voluntary and political involvement (Beresford, 1996). This was pithily encapsulated in the BBC Radio 4 programme title 'Does he take sugar?' – implying disabled people are often ignored by visitors who speak to their families and carers as if they were absent or incapable of speaking for themselves, and not independent persons. Even in 'mainstream' school situations, disabled students are often under strong surveillance, made to sit together in class and lunch rooms, and often cannot share leisure settings with their non-disabled peers because they don't feel they can ask their friends to push their wheelchairs all the time. Then there was bullying – 'we all get picked on' (Watson et al., 2000: 12). Brittain (2004) examined how 2000 Paralympic athletes regarded their disabilities: some adopted the medical model, and saw their disability as a major factor in their identity; many hoped that improved media coverage would move perceptions towards the social model.

The social model considers many factors – family circumstances and finances, education, employment, environment, housing, and transport (Barnes et al., 1999: 11–37). But it also includes issues of empowerment, and increasingly, disabled people are organising themselves as citizens and participants, coaches, administrators and volunteers in sport. Campaigning and lobbying by disability pressure groups have become significant activities (Beresford, 1996). Wheelchair users and people with acquired rather than congenital disabilities have been in the vanguard of these movements, using their prior knowledge of how networks of influence work – what Goodley (2000) called 'self-advocacy.' Paterson and Hughes (2000: 30, 35) went farther, arguing disability has 'been transformed from an individual or medical problem into a civil rights issue…conceptualised…not as an outcome of physical impairment but as an effect of social exclusion and discrimination.'

Healey (1998: 62) stressed the importance of leisure provision and transport as part of the local social worlds 'for those with limited mobility and access to work and leisure opportunities.' Sport England (1999b: 12) sought to persuade local planning authorities to take account of the sporting needs of disabled people and enhance access to built facilities and natural resources in their development plans. The nationwide Inclusive Fitness Initiative (IFI) (nd) aims, by 2012, to have 1,000 facilities accredited, and 7,500 instructors specifically trained in marketing and managing exercise for disabled customers (2,000 trained by 2008. But Miller et al. (2006: 35) found that:

- four out of five leisure venues did not provide proper access, and only 39% had an useable toilet;
- two-thirds of disabled children felt unable to do the same leisure activities as their non-disabled friends, and two-thirds of families with disabled children did not use leisure facilities because they felt uncomfortable;
- despite the IFI, only two of the eight largest fitness chains had disabled access to all their gyms;
- on average disabled youth spent only 3.4 hours a week on sport compared to 7.5 hours by non-disabled;
- half of sports clubs said they had no disabled members because 'disabled people do not play our sport.

Hall (2004) described how spatial/social contexts of living, working and leisure can be 'safe' and inclusive for people with Learning Diffciulties, or sites of discrimination abuse or rejection. Later, the Office for Disability Issues (2010a) reported restrictions on participation of impaired adults as follows:

Activity	Impaired adults %	Other adults %
Visiting friends	48	38
Going on holiday	66	55
Playing sport	72	52

Barnes et al. (1999: 210) wrote: 'historically, images of disability have been generated by non-disabled people, and have been more about the prejudices and decisions of mainstream society than the reality of the disabled experience.' The media can work in conflicting ways in its representation of disabled people – by under-representing them in popular features like soaps, and picturing them as victims, not attractive and not powerful. Thomas and Smith (2009: 150–1) commented that usually, coverage has 'focussed on particular athletes, with particular impairments, competing in particular sports.' Some of the most powerful people in disabled sports organisations have not been disabled, as in other voluntary organisations (Drake, 1994). The British Social Attitudes Survey 1998 showed that 3 in 4 Britons thought there was prejudice against disabled people.

Alternatively, the media can show them as active, free agents or even heroes. For sport, TV coverage of the Paralympics and of wheelchair sports people in world-famous marathons has made disabled sport an accepted element of sport overall; but even this can reify the trained athletic body over the average recreational one. The HEA (1998a) identified the lack of prominent role models for disabled people; Dame Tanni Gray's success in wheelchair marathons for Britain was a first move in changing this.

The International Year of Disabled People in 1970 coincided with the Chronically Sick and Disabled Persons Act, which required public buildings to be made accessible for disabled people 'so far as reasonably practicable.' Despite progress, the continuing deficit combined with a realisation through research and lobbying about continuing neglect and discrimination in paid work opportunities led to the Disability Discrimination Act 1995 (DDA) (ILAM, 1997; Wetherby, 1998). This Act enshrined new rights of access to goods, services and facilities, in buying or renting premises and in employment, requiring suppliers and employers to respond by the year 2000. There are now numerous advisory guides on design for disability in sports venues (e.g., Sports Council, 1994b; BSAD, 1994) and Access Groups are active through the Centre for Accessible Environments.

Identified shortcomings in this Act led the Blair government to set up a Disability Rights Task Force (DRTF, 1999), and in response to its interim report, to legislate for a Disability Rights Commission in 2000. The DRTF wanted to bring sports clubs' premises and operating practices under scrutiny for fair access under the DDA. In 2007, disability was rolled into a single Equality and Human Rights Commission (EHRC), including gender, age, sexual orientation, race, and religion, and a new Public Service Agreement (PSA 15) committed the government to equality in all public services. An Office for Disability Issues (ODI) was also set up, as a watchdog to ensure the EHRC used its enforcement powers when needed.

The concept of segregated physical activity and competition was first established by the British Deaf Sport Council in 1930, but brought to public notice by the neurosurgeon Ludwig Guttman who organised the first International Wheelchair Games at Stoke Mandeville Hospital to coincide with the 1948 London Olympics. 'Although a single-minded autocrat and maverick' (B. Atha, quoted by Thomas and Houlihan, 2000), he inspired the disabled sports movement in Britain. A national organisation for paraplegics was set up in 1948, an organisation for blind sportspeople in 1960, for amputees in 1978, mentally handicapped and Cerebral Palsy sufferers in 1981. An umbrella body, the British Sports Association for the Disabled (BSAD), was formed in 1961, and developed a regional network. The first Paralympics was held in Rome in 1960 and has become a huge event. By the time the Beijing Olympics were held, in 2008, there were 4,200 competitors from 148 countries and 165 national committees. The medical and functional classifications are labyrinthine (leading to 700 events compared with 350 in the Olympics), and subject to increasing disputes over the fairness of officials' judgements (Thomas and Smith 2009, 116–33), as TV coverage has brought fame with medals. Notable was the exclusion of Oscar Pistorius from the Beijing Games, because his carbon-fibre leg prostheses extended his height and stride length over what they would naturally be.

Barnes et al. (1999: 180) said the burgeoning of disability groups and organisations could be theorised as 'a new social movement or as a liberation struggle'. Oliver (1996b: 117–8) cast these organisations into four types:

1   *Partnership/patronage* – operating *for* disabled people in providing services or consultation/ advice e.g., Royal National Institute for the Blind, SCOPE.

2   *Economic/parliamentarian* – operating *for* disabled people as single issue research/campaigning groups e.g., Disability Income Group, Disability Alliance.
3   *Consumerist/self help* – organisations *of* disabled, sometimes campaigning nationally or locally e.g., Spinal Injuries Association, British Blind Sport.
4   *Populist/activist* – organisations *of* disabled for personal/political action, consciousness raising e.g., British Deaf Association, Union of the Physically Impaired against Segregation. They may be less keen on partnership actions.

Most sports organisations are of the third type, though some have altruistic/welfare aims to benefit others e.g., Riding for the Disabled. Even though the Paralympics are held in the same city and venues as the summer Olympics, the International Olympic Committee (IOC) and the International Paralympic (IPC) remain separate, highlighting abled-disabled segregation. In the US, the Olympic Committee was declared the umbrella body for Paralympic sports, and it remains to be seen if this gap can be bridged (Hums et al., 2000). As interest in sport by disabled people has grown, the Sports Council (later ESC and SE) prioritised support for them continually since 1982.

Current arrangements in England are:

- English Federation of Disability Sport (EFDS) – a charitable company, in 2010 relocated to the Loughborough sportpark, with a board of eight members (reduced from 16), to provide a 'united voice...effective partnership working... and co-ordination of diverse activities,' through 'Empowerment, Funding, Deliverers, and Strategy' (EFDS, 2004: 6 and 17).
- National Disability Sports Organisations (NSDOs) – representing the 11m disabled people in England; including British Amputee and Les Autres Sports associations, British Blind Sport, Cerebral Palsy Sport, Dwarf Athletics, Mencap Sport, Special Olympics GB, UK Deaf Sport and British Wheelchair Sport.
- Ten regions – mirroring the national, each served by an EFDS manager, working with CSPs, local and education authorities.

While EFDS links the former BSAD regions and the 'vertical' management lines of disability-specific NSDOs, giving them one voice and a sizeable budget, only time will tell if it can influence the over 300 sport-specific governing bodies, many of which have given the issue much attention or priority (Thomas and Houlihan, 2000). Thomas and Smith (2009: 23) still saw disabled sport as a 'largely marginal aspect' of sport as a whole.

But, as NGBs develop their disability awareness, so competitions with adapted rules, equipment and specialised coaching evolve: thirty-two sports have disability committees or Associations, beyond those expected to do so like angling, archery, basketball, bowls, swimming and riding. The EFDS (2001) had 12 priority sports – athletics, basketball, boccia, cricket, football, goalball, hockey, netball, rugby union, swimming, table tennis, and tennis. Thomas and Smith (2009: 96–7) reckoned progress had more to do with committed individuals rather than policy interventions – EFDS was instrumental in Association Football's progress, but not in tennis, Sport England in wheelchair basketball, but not tennis or swimming. They concluded (*ibid*, 157) that 'mainstreaming disability sport will remain nothing other than peripheral to the core activities' of many NGBs. Numerous local initiatives are proceeding, though it is too early to judge mature outcomes; there were 45 county, city or district disability officers in 2004, soon to grow to 60 (EFDS, 2004), as in Leicester (see Case Study 5 below). Integrated children's play schemes are more common.

According to a Minister's Review Group, some local authorities were 'pursuing their obligations with diligence imagination and generosity' and others 'doing little more than paying lip-service' (MSRG, 1989: 23). Thomas and Smith (2009: 56) suggested the lack of focus on municipal provision after *Raising the Game* in 1995 inevitably sidelined disability provision, and their case studies contrasted services in Kent with more limited provision in Nottinghamshire and Cumbria.

Meanwhile, after the European Year of People with Disabilities 2003, the French Ministry of Youth and Sport developed a national hub at its research centre at Bourges, appointed a national co-ordinator and 19 technical posts to work with the two multi-sport federations with increased budgets, and a 'responsible' in each of the 60 'able-bodied' NGBs (www.jeunes.gouv.fr, accessed 30 January 2013).

Disability, poverty and social exclusion

The Department of Social Security suggested 9.4m adults and 0.6m children are affected by disabilities or serious limiting chronic illness, half over 65 and including 72% of women over 60. Of these, two million were the largely ignored people with Learning Disabilities, who can be very good at both recreational and competitive sport. Disability often incurs extra living, travel and care costs, and consequently, many disabled people and their families depend on welfare benefits; Martin and White (1998) estimated this to be as high as three in four; Disabled Income Support recipients rose from 8.5 to 14% in 1991–6 (DSS, 1997). Thus many are poor – almost half of severely impaired women compared to one in five of non-disabled (Townsend 1979: 733–4). In 1999–2000, the Blair government, believing that paid work is the core means of preventing poverty, sought to means test disability benefits previously given as of right. Opponents claimed this would make disabled people even poorer and more dependent. The British Council of Disabled People (BCODP) criticised Ministers for sticking to the 'individual tragedy' rather than the social model (*Guardian Society Extra* 3 Nov 1999, p ii–iii). Burchardt (2006) graphically demonstrated the poverty gap for households including a disabled person using 1996–7 figures (when extra data was available), as shown below:

Individuals in...	Poverty rate % based on unadjusted income	Income net of extra costs/benefits	% of all individuals fully equivalised for disability
Households with disabled person	31.8	38.2	55.8
Households with no disabled person	22.7	22.2	18.7

Clearly, benefits did not close the gap, and the real costs of disability in the third column as calculated by Zaidi and Burchardt (2003) more than doubled the vulnerable group compared to their share of the population.

Reviewing policy since 1997, Hills et al. (2009: 23) said relatively little about incomes and disability; expenditure on disability-related benefits almost trebled in 1974–97, and its share of welfare costs increased from 16% to 27% during 1979–97. Yet benefits increased only in line with prices, and from April 2010 all Incapacity Benefit claimants will have to undergo a Work Capability Assessment; those more severely disabled will receive a higher benefit, the others will receive help to find employment and may apply for Job Seekers Allowance (*ibid*: 93, 96–7). Then the ConDem coalition announced that they wished to reduce DLA expenditure by a fifth, making tests for a new Personal Independence Payment even tighter. Often the work that disabled people get to do is poorly paid, low skilled and part-time (as Walker, 1982 called it – 'underemployment').

A year later, in *Anatomy of Economic Inequality*, Hills et al. (2010: 19–20) summarised the situation regarding inequality and disability as:

> nearly half of those reporting 'work-limiting' and DDA disability have no or only low qualifications, twice the proportion of those who are not disabled. Their paid employment rates are less than half those who are not disabled. When employed, disabled people have median hourly earnings 20 per cent lower for men and 12 per cent lower for women. The disability employment 'penalty' has grown steadily over the last quarter century...Disabled men with higher qualifications had employment rates of 93 per cent in 1974–6, and 75 per cent in 2001–3, whereas those with no qualifications had 77 and 38 per cent respectively...the net income of disabled people is reduced by more than 10 per cent, and their poverty rate would be more than 30 per cent.

Disability, mental illness and learning difficulties and sport

There is no good data on participation in sport by disabled people as a whole; in 1997 Sport England surveyed 155 sports centres and swimming pools and showed low use by disabled people – only seven per cent in sports halls and 11% in swimming pools compared to 22% of the population having a long-term illness or disability limiting daily activities (Sport England, 2000). With the recession, Sport England's *Active People* survey showed a decrease in health-conveying 3x30 minutes a week moderate exertion from 6.7 to 6.1% from 2006 to 2008 (compared to a small increase for non-disabled adults from 18.2 to 18.5%), and DCMS' *Taking Part* survey 2009 showed a significant decline in monthly participation from 2005–6 to 2007–8 from 32.3 to 30.1%.

Sport England's only detailed survey of 6,500 disabled adults (Gatward and Burrell, 2001) showed, for people with a long-term limiting disability:

- lower and much less frequent participation in sport over a month and a year, with and without walking (Table 8.1);
- nine of the ten most popular activities were individual, football being the exception (in contrast to team sports at school);
- seven per cent belonged to a sports club, and five per cent to a fitness centre (compared to 11 and five per cent for non-disabled), and one per cent to a specialist disabled sports club;
- a social participation gradient similar to non-disabled sport, but with disabled people about a third or more lower:

Selected socio-economic groups:	Professional	Skilled manual	Unskilled manual	Student
% with limiting disability	61	34	33	59
% not disabled	72	60	37	77
(at least one activity in a month)				

These figures also show the privileged position of full-time students.

- four-fifths of disabled people enjoyed school sport (the same as their counterparts);
- one in five would like to do more, with swimming most popular (35%);
- having credible information and someone to go with would help most;
- one in seven felt constrained by their health/disability, or lack of time.

Scottish data for 2012 (SHS, 2013) showed only 20% of those with a disability/ health problem playing sport once a month or more often and 32% walking for 30 minutes, compared to 59% and 65% of those without.

EFDS (Spring, 2013) surveyed 476 disabled people (including learning disabled) and confirmed many other findings, including:

- exercise and swimming are the most popular activities (for 46%), more by men, 14–25s, and youth at special schools;
- only 51% had enjoyed PE in school;
- most wanted fun and social activities.

Table 8.1 Sports participation among disabled and non-disabled adults 1996, 2000 (per cent in columns 2–5)

Sport	Participating once or more a month		Participating once or more a year		Frequency per participant in 4 weeks		Frequency per adult in 12 months	
	2000	1996	2000	1996	2000	1996	2000	1996
Walking	26	50	47	75	–	–	–	–
Swimming	13	19	31	51	4	4	7.4	9.9
Cue sports	8	15	16	26	5	5	4.8	9.1
Cycling	7	15	14	29	8	8	7.0	15.3
Keepfit/ aerobics/ yoga	5	16	10	27	7	6	3.1	13.2
Gym/ gymnastics	4	0	7	6	7	1	1.4	0.2
Darts	3	–	8	11	–	–	–	–
Golf/pitch & putt	3	6	8	14	4	3	1.4	2.6
Football	3	8	6	13	5	4	1.7	5.1
10 pin bowls/ skittles	3	5	10	22	2	2	0.6	1.1

Note: figures in italics are comparable data for people without a longstanding limiting disability from the 1996 General Household Survey

Rowe (2001) demonstrated the additive effects of gender and class on disabled people's participation compared with males aged 16+ as the benchmark:

Males with a disability	–47%
Females with a disability	–59%
Classes AB with a disability	–39%
Classes DE with a disability	–65%

The practical outcomes of sports programmes for disabled people have been little studied; Case Study 3 looks at the efforts of a typical English city, Leicester, as it attempted to meet the law's requirements, and the needs and wishes of its disabled citizens. From benchmarking data on 386 sports centres 2005–9, Taylor and Kung (2010) showed that disabled people were underrepresented, at 0.71 compared to their share of population, and even more so in areas with more than 20% of the population in the two lowest socio-economic classes, at 0.69.

Aitchison (2003) opined that proliferating studies on leisure inequality generally omitted 'any explicit discussion of disability.' Those concerning physiology showed many people with disabilities are sedentary and obese. Kitchin (1998) argued disability is socio-spatially constructed; 'disablist' attitudes traditionally disadvantaged and segregated people with disabilities and learning difficulties in schools, in workplaces (as 'unproductive'), on public transport, and in public buildings and spaces (as marginal customers). Proactive policies need to go further than the changes to buildings and spaces achieved since the 1970 Act. Public transport is important, and all operators offer concessions to disabled people, but not all take them up, and Scottish research suggests limited help in reducing exclusion (Rye and Mykura, 2009).

Modell (1997) showed seven in ten leisure activities of American children with learning difficulties were family-based, only a fifth included disabled members, but those in more integrated settings participated significantly more than those in segregated ones. Anderson et al. (1982) compared the activities of 119 disabled and 33 non-disabled teenagers and rated two in five of the disabled youngsters as having a 'severely restricted' social life compared to three per cent of the others. They discovered the former spent more time in passive, solitary pastimes like watching TV and listening to music and were less likely to see their school friends after school hours. Indeed, the reality of disability was and 'is hard for friends to confront' (Morris, 1989: 105). Barnes et al. (2000) showed how disabled children in both special and mainstream schools spent much time under adult surveillance and much less time than children in general with other children, circumscribing their scope and style of play.

Aitchison (2003) claimed the needs of disabled children and their families had been neglected in both research and policy. Their costs are three times that of their non-disabled counterparts (Dobson and Middleton, 1998), and often they lived in isolation (Audit Commission, 2003). Jeanes (2010) and Jeanes and Magee (2012) monitored the development of a playground on the site of three special schools provided by a group of parents in partnership with the local Education and Library Board, whom they praised for having the trust and patience to allow a community development, bottom-up approach. In 2008–9 there were 15,000 users. The benefits to all the families were great; one said 'it allows us to be a 'normal' family.' It enabled them to develop bonding social capital with other families, both with and without disabled children

In the UK, 'mainstreaming' has been the policy since the 1980s and especially since the Special Educational Needs Strategy (DES, 2004), predicated on the assumption that schools should not refuse SEN or disabled pupils because of their needs, requiring modifying buildings, obtaining equipment, and providing trained teachers and support staff, and leaving a much smaller number of special schools for those who cannot cope in mainstreamed situations. Sport England's (2001b) survey of 2,293 children aged 6–16 showed much lower sport participation than among other youngsters – in school, in clubs and in the community (Table 8.2).

Table 8.2 Sports participation among disabled and all 6–16 year olds (per cent unless stated)

	Disabled children, 2000	All children, 1999
NOT playing frequently in school (10+ times a year)	26	6
No of frequently played sports	2	4
Less than three hours a week secondary PE	20	53
Time playing in summer holidays		
• 15 hours a week or more	10	29
• 1 hour or none	32	10
Popular sports for disabled		
• swimming	37	30
• horse riding	6	1
Members of clubs outside school	12	46

Source: Sport England 2001

The children mentioned constraints on their taking part as:

		%
1	Cost (probably including transport)	37
2	Health issues	37
3	Unsuitable local facilities	37
4	No local sports facilities	34
5	Unwelcoming staff and clubs	32
6	Difficulties with transport	32
7	Clubs do not provide for my disability	32

Constraints numbers 1, 3–5 and 6 imply a large gap between policy aims and delivery. With 45% spending one hour a week or less in PE lessons compared to 18% of the whole school population, and with a narrower range of activities (the top five activities being swimming, soccer, gymnastics, athletics and other games), and game-based activity dominating inside and outside the curriculum; 36% did not take part 'regularly'. Sadly, the annual PE and School Sport surveys commissioned by DCSF omit any data on disability. Often it seemed disabled and SEN pupils were having to 'fit into' existing planned curricula; cost and availability of transport limited off-site activities. Teachers received training unequally, and felt that they did not always get the support they wished from Learning Support Assistants. CLR (1995: 22) confirmed similar paradoxical outcomes. So, Thomas and Smith (2009: 107–15) concluded these were unintended and unforeseen outcomes of a policy with inclusive intent, not meeting the aspirations of the regulatory body OFSTED or of UNESCO (1994). Hodge et al. (2004) expressed similar concerns from the US.

Brittain (2004) went further, arguing that inclusion policies were making it difficult to identify talented disabled youth, weakening Britain's competitive strength. Examining provision for Gifted and Talented children in 15 Specialist Sports Colleges, Fitzgerald and Kay (2005) found:

- provision and methods varied, and several Colleges wanted more government support;
- some pupils had bad experiences, but this did not deter their out-of-school participation;
- parents often acted separately from schools, but felt they should be working closer.

Most studies are practical, showing how to serve these groups (e.g., BHF National Centre, 2008); de Pauw and Gavron (1995: 11) described the barriers as similar to those for women – lack of organised programmes and informal early experiences, of role models, of access, and of economic, physiological and social factors. They also said (1995: 223) 'the original therapeutic purpose through sport has given way to sport for sport's sake, and competition for competition's sake.' Cavet (1995: 60) wrote 'there is now an increasing focus upon community involvement and learning in community settings rather than training for leisure prior to introduction to the real leisure environment,' which would involve greater public understanding and volunteer support. Reviewing 28 schemes in six European countries, she (1995: 61) identified three (not exclusive) philosophical emphases, on:

- social role valorisation, normalisation, an ordinary lifestyle and integration;
- education and the development potential of people with learning difficulty;
- leisure, relaxation and enjoyment as valid ends in their own right.

Scott Porter Research and Marketing (2001b) classified their Scottish sample into:

- *Dependents* – with the lowest sports participation, needing others to help with transport, changing, companionship and emotional support;
- *Independents* – were happy to try anything their non-disabled neighbours played, and in unsegregated settings;
- *Unconfidents* – needing some support and likely to seek, initially at least, segregated settings.

They provided 41 other UK examples of current practice. In a similar way, interviewing a small sample of American disabled people in mainly non-disabled groups in various leisure settings, Devine concluded:

Some felt inclusive leisure facilities facilitated social acceptance and definitions of disability were given new meaning; adaptive equipment meant independence, executing recreation skills in a non-traditional way meant uniqueness, and encouragement meant acceptance. Others felt traditional definitions of disability were revealed during leisure. In these cases, a disability was a devalued role; a hierarchy...meant that some disabilities were more acceptable than others; and inclusive participation meant over-protection.

(Devine, 2004: 156)

The (English) Sports Council supported the development of national bodies for disability sport and the appointment of specialised regional and local Development Officers. With the advent of Sport England, funding focussed on the EFDS framework and on targets for activity, e.g., in the Active Sports programme and the county-based Millennium Youth Games. This network is still new; studies describe good practice in improving social involvement, participation for recreation and competition (e.g., Collins et al., 1995; McConkey and McGinley, 1990), and Everybody Active project in Tyne and Wearside (Tungatt, 1990, Williams, 1988). The last clearly pointed out needs with these groups for:

- generating confidence and trust in a lifelong counselling context; such programmes cannot be 'hit and run';
- undertaking positive, long-term, committed outreach;
- involving and encouraging ownership by the client groups, and on 'mainstreaming' disability.

Messent et al. (1996) and Borrett et al. (1996) reminded readers that many people with disabilities and learning difficulties are obese and relatively sedentary, but showed they enjoy, benefit and achieve as much as any other citizens in a hierarchy of sports competitions leading to the Paralympics, so long as appropriate activity, help with transport and support to gain confidence were provided.

The author agrees with Cavet's (1995: 25) conclusion that 'research studies into the results of making changes in the environment of people with profound and multiple disabilities often appear too short term and not sufficiently fine grained,' and presumably that any new research should address racial issues. Doll-Tepper et al. (1994) identified a huge research agenda for the International Paralympic Committee.

The Sports Council (Y&H, 1995a) showed good practice in NGB schemes in table tennis, canoeing and gymnastics, and in programmes and training provided by local authorities in Leeds, Kirklees and the then Humberside county; Collins et al. (1994) highlighted schemes enabled by the East Midlands Initiative Trust in netball and powerlifting. The Open Country project in Harrogate brought together the resources of LAs, the Yorks Health Authority, The Fieldfare Trust, The Countryside Commission, Powergen and the Yorks Field Studies Trust in a partnership to provide countryside visits for local disabled people (numbering some 29–30,000 – Glyptis et al., 1995). Kent Sportslink (KSDU, 1999) promoted disabled use of leisure centres effectively – the Cascades centre received only 70 users in the year before the project; by 1996–7, 7,800 had attended. The Kent report also quoted Phillips saying (1996: 2) 'the creation of accessible facilities can attract new business'.

After reviewing provision for informal recreation in the countryside, the Countryside Agency (2000) recommended greater attention to design to accessibility of routes, and especially to gates and alternatives to stiles, and much better information for intending disabled visitors, especially to National Trails (lately via the internet). Two workshop participants made telling comments:

Disabled people should be able to decide what is an acceptable risk.

Disabled people have become used to being excluded, therefore they need to know it is for them.

Three major constraints were mentioned in the *Making Connections* survey (Stoneham, 2001): physical barriers (by more than half), lack of information and insufficient toilets (by two in five), confirmed in the subsequent Diversity Review (OPENspace, 2003).

Relatively few studies have examined the therapeutic benefits of exercise and sport in helping people with mental illness. Dishman's (1995) review concluded that:

- small-to-moderate decreases in self-rated anxiety and depression accompanied acute and chronic exercise, according to numerous studies with small, non-clinical samples;
- the few population studies showed stronger relationships;
- increased aerobic fitness did not appear necessary to achieve these reductions;
- various psychological, biochemical, and physiological mechanisms had been suggested but not researched.

Taylor et al. (1998) criticised exercise studies for focusing on people with cystic fibrosis, chronic low back pain, osteoarthritis and pulmonary disease, and neglecting paraplegia and quadriplegia, poliomyelitis, and visual/hearing/learning disabilities. Focussing on outdoor recreation, Levitt (1991) came to similar conclusions, while on the basis of numerous field studies, Barton et al. (2010) summarised the benefits as physical (reduced stress, obesity), psychological well-being (better mood and self-esteem, reduced depression, anger and tension) and social (via networking and socialising, building social capital), notably for people with mental illness. Greenfield and Senecal (1995) demonstrated how recreational family groups at a day centre had involved unwilling parents to help their children suffering from attention deficit disorder with hyperactivity, reducing family conflict and improving the adults' parenting skills. Denyer (1997) showed how guided walks in the Peak District organised by the National Park and local Health Authorities helped both low-income families and those recovering from mental illness: 'getting away from it' in beautiful landscapes was one feature, but another important aspect was socialising. With such groups, however, the transition to independent leisure practice is slow; withdrawal of organising, support staff and free transport would lead to a loss of benefits, and a major feature of these people's social lives, so continuing subsidy, painfully gathered, is essential.

So far as volunteering by disabled people is concerned, there are environmental, organisational and attitudinal barriers which limit them in all fields including sport (Active People 2006 suggested only 4.5% played compared to 7.3% of non-disabled, Fitzgerald and Lang 2009). The cerebral palsy charity SCOPE (2005) suggested all agencies taking volunteers needed Disability Equality Training, and obtained Big Lottery funding to establish courses.

Case study 5: disability and sport and leisure in Leicester

Background

The Arts and Leisure Department (ALD) of Leicester City Council (LCC) spent two decades investing to improve its buildings, signage, staff training, and support for community organisations with information and grants. It wished to establish: the current and desired use of its facilities and services; what barriers disabled citizens faced, and to review provision and customers' satisfaction. So, Collins et al. (1999) asked 639 disabled Leisure Pass holders (see Case Study 1 in Chapter 4) about their use and problems with the card, audited seventeen ALD sites and interviewed 18 city and voluntary managers. Where possible, comparisons were drawn with Community Consultants' earlier (1989) survey of 489 Leicester residents.

Leicester City Council's policies and activities regarding disability and leisure

ESC's (1998b) guide to good practice in race relations provides a useful analogue for disability, under seven headings:

1   *Policy* – there must be a vision of what could be, and for Leicester this was stated as:

    Leisure is essential to everyone's health and feeling of well-being. Our purpose is to make Leicester a city unparalleled for leisure activities and experiences...'; 'We will do this by ensuring equality of access for all cultures, with particular regard to groups and individuals experiencing social or economic exclusion

    (M. Frith, *pers comm*, 5 March 1999)

2   *Dedicated staff* – unfortunately, budget cuts reduced the complement from three posts for race, gender and disability to one
3   *Training of staff* – Staff awareness of disability issues and customer care was believed to vary greatly

4   *Employment of disabled people* – several disabled people were employed in ALD
5   *Information and communications* – means such as minicoms, language leaflets, video/audio tapes, and special signage were common, but not universal; only eight sites had minicoms
6   *Physical adaptations* – LCC had made many adaptations e.g., ramps/lifts, doors, toilets, and parking. Nonetheless, of 52 facilities listed in ALD's (1998) Access Guide, nine had no parking, and fourteen no Orange Badge spaces
7   *Voluntary organisations* – over 30 disability-specific groups operated in Leicester (VAL, 1998). Grants regularly supported nearly 40 schemes covering children's play, arts, outdoor activities, a city farm, ethnic groups, and community centres.

Additionally, the city, county and Rutland education authorities were committed to a joint *Sport through Education* Strategy, and with the East Midlands Initiative Trust had audited schools' and special schools' provisions for disability (LCC, 1999), discovering:

• most special schools and units wished to see further specialist INSET training for PE teachers, curriculum support through links with clubs, and competitions between schools at Key Stages 3 & 4;
• day centres highlighted the need to support their sports sessions with coach education, better information on upcoming events, and links with clubs;
• disability clubs needed to strengthen their competitions, coach development, and sports development know-how, e.g., on equity training, Lottery Awards for All, and
• All schools, centres and clubs wanted to develop particular priority sports, viz

Special schools	Day centres	Disability sport clubs
Swimming	Bowls (inc. ten-pin, short	Swimming
Football	mat)	Athletics
Athletics	Boccia	Football
Basketball	Unihoc	Boccia
Gymnastics	Snooker	Bowling (indoor)
Multi-sport	Pool	Equestrian
	Table Games	Fishing
	Multi-sport	

Current leisure participation, aspirations and barriers

The respondents took part in 98 leisure and 29 sports activities. Figure 8.1 shows that most frequent were visiting parks, swimming, visiting libraries and cinemas, and shopping for fun. Compared with 1989, it was obvious that disabled people's

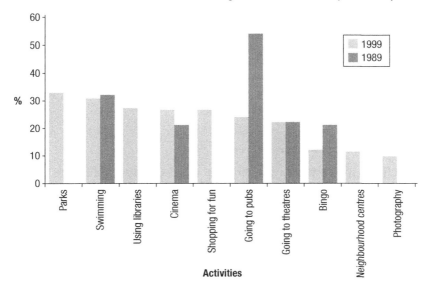

Figure 8.1 Top ten activities for people with disabilities in Leicester in 1999 compared to 1989

participation had almost doubled, with four in five undertaking their favourite activity weekly. While two in five in 1989 said they would like to go out more, in 1999 a quarter said there were activities they would like to do – notably swimming, health and fitness, and more Day Centre activities.

Five major issues were identified in the Leicester interviews and discussions – transport, physical barriers, staff training, information and communications. As Leishman (1996) pointed out, such improvements for disabled people benefit many other groups, especially pregnant mothers, those with small children, and older people.

Transport problems

As mentioned above, mobility and independent travel are major everyday issues for the disabled (Heiser, 1995). Sharkey (1996: 18) said 'getting to a building can often be more of a problem for handicapped people than actually using it.' All 52 ALD facilities were on at least one bus route, but that said nothing about frequency of service outside peak hours. The three most common barriers to using public transport were said to be cost, infrequency (especially in the evenings and at weekends), and lack of information about services, notably for people with physical and multiple disabilities and learning difficulties. Staff awareness was often poor e.g., bus drivers failing to stop, driving off, and giving disabled people inadequate attention.

> I don't like buses much as they tend to drive off before you sit down. They also get ruffled because it takes me so long to get off. I tend to use taxis but can't afford that many.
>
> (Physically disabled respondent)

When the Leisure Pass was set up, for some technical legal reason it was said not to be possible to include transport discounts.

Physical and human barriers to access

Four in five respondents found no problem with LCC sport and leisure facilities. Apart from ramps and lifts, signs were difficult for both visually impaired and learning difficulty groups; when having to ask what was written because signs were too small or unclear, one visually disabled person saying, 'Why am I forced to let everybody know I am disabled?' (David, Scott, Leicester Society for the Blind, nd). Swipe cards for Leisure Card schemes, of course, conceal such differences from other customers and onlookers. Regarding staff, seven in ten said the staff at their most frequented facility were helpful, but numerous problems were mentioned, especially by people with learning difficulties.

Programming

Three-quarters of respondents were happy with the scope of their activities, but there was concern about the lack of opportunities for disabled children, and poor follow up to taster programmes. The provision of new services was complicated by the fact that equal numbers of people wished to go on their own, with a helper, in groups with the same or other disability, or via integrated sessions. Leicester had a Leisure Plus One card giving accompanying helpers discounted access.

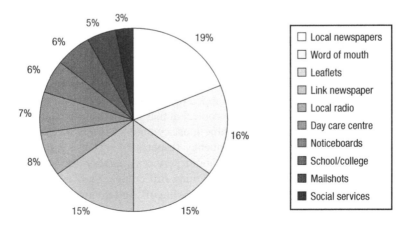

Figure 8.2 How disabled respondents found out about leisure events/opportunities

Information

The main ways disabled people found out about leisure events/opportunities are shown in Figure 8.2. Although the daily *Leicester Mercury* was most popular, the fact that word of mouth came second means that these people relied on friends and relatives to discover what was on. Half would like mailshots, compared to the one in seven who said they received them. Leisure Pass holders received regular news of events and offers; in 1989 42% of respondents said they had a Pass and 34% used it; while in 1999 84% said they had one.

Implications

LCC had tried hard to improve the quality of leisure lives of its disabled citizens, but clearly there was scope for improvement on each issue.

- *Transport* – Frequency and late night running are part of a general policy issue of improving public transport. Issues of bus and bus stop design (e.g., talking bus stops) were in part dealt with in PSV Regulations from December 2000 (*DETR News Release 494*, 22 July 2000). The most common issue for all disabled groups was lack of understanding and empathy in bus crews.
- *Physical* access – Observation audits and reports highlighted no major problems with ramps, doors, lifts etc., although convenient parking was problematic. A common complaint that could be dealt with at reasonable cost was the difficulty of reading crowded, wordy and ill-designed signs.
- *Access:* Human resources – Although ALD was generally perceived as helpful, client groups saw it as lacking awareness, especially for people with visual, hearing and learning difficulties. Awareness training should be provided for existing staff who had not had it, and for all new staff during induction. This is vital for leisure centre and library assistants, where there is significant turnover.
- *Programming* – Taster days and special events were good ways of opening up new activities, but clients perceived a lack of follow up; some would like to be involved as volunteers in such events. They also thought better links between schools, LCC facilities, clubs and day care centres would extend options. They believed more tailor-made sessions for particular groups would be popular, arguing that not every session has to be integrated. Choice in this is crucial, to encompass the needs of the confident and reticent, the slightly and severely impaired.
- *Information and consultation* – No method of communication is infallible, and this was a concern for all client groups. Their preferred method was mail-shots, which can be costly and usually engender a low response; and a regular newsletter was suggested for marketing regular and special services, with a section targeted at disabled groups, copies going to the Day Centres, and the Leicester Centres for the Deaf and Visually Impaired to target those without Leisure Passes, and including Braille, large print or tapes versions. Other

media avenues could be implemented – returnable audiotapes, PC disks and email versions of the Leisure Card News, along with features in the Leicester Mercury and on Radio Leicester. Clients commented on the short times often allowed by LCC for consultations, not allowing that it is less easy for disabled groups to co-ordinate their views. The authors felt a new Disability Network might aid these processes, and one was set up for the City, County and Rutland linked to the main Sports Forum.

- *Monitoring and review* – Continuous monitoring is crucial, but must involve citizen and client groups and partners, which the Network could do. New computerised tills should provide a more detailed usage and marketing database (which they did, as Case Study 1 demonstrated).

In conclusion, the overall level of satisfaction amongst Leicester's disabled users was fairly high, and activity choices had been extended over the previous ten years. Therefore, as far as the Arts and Leisure Department was concerned, the challenge was neither huge nor costly, except for adapting the buses. Perhaps the most urgent, as part of improving social inclusion, was the training of ALD and bus staff to ensure that disabled people did not perceive themselves as different or separate from other customers.

But regarding the City Council as a corporate whole, a larger challenge needed to be met. In one of Britain's most multicultural cities, disability has a corporate dimension. Issues of concern include transport and communication. Transport is possibly the major factor limiting many disabled people's leisure activity, as discovered also in Coventry by French and Hainsworth (2001: 146), to the extent of 'an extensive mismatch between policy development and the experience of disabled people.' Partnership with increasingly strong local groups is also essential. Thus, despite policy commitment, continuous (if constrained) investment, and dedicated staff, LCC still faced substantial challenges.

Conclusions

Internationally, Riordan and Kruger (1999: 185) judged that biographies and case studies, rather than research literature, stressed inclusion and contributing to more enlightened and tolerant attitudes. Disabled sport is now a high-profile issue for Sport England, trying to ensure disability is included in NGB strategic planning, coach development, and youth sport programmes. Creating the EFDS may be a convenient mechanism for Sport England in dealing with a touchy, increasingly prominent issue (Thomas and Houlihan, 2000).

Nearly a quarter-century ago UN secretary General Perez de Cuelar said disability was 'a silent emergency.' Yet, many barriers still exist in public and even more especially in private provision and management, in employment discrimination and limited welfare support. Some of the most intractable barriers are, as Sandra Pew, East Midland Initiative Trust (*pers comm*) said 'barriers of feeling' – keeping out disabled people who are too unsure to enter new environments unaccompanied. What seems not to have been accepted generally is that 'not only are inclusive leisure services efficient, all participants can benefit from such services' (Dattilo and Williams, 1999: 452). Thomas (2001: 8) judged that 'disabled people's participation in sport is an attempt to emulate non-disabled values and an example of disabled people's struggle for acceptance in a predominantly able-bodied world.'

The *Life Opportunities Survey* (ODI, 2010) still found large disadvantages for sport via disability:

- 72% of adults with impairments did not join in sports as much as they would like, compared to 52% of those without;
- conversely, 35% said they were too busy to join in sports as much as they would like compared to 71% of those unimpaired the same as adults without impairments.

HMG (ODP/DCMS, 2010) signalled a policy of using the 2012 Games both as a springboard for increasing sports participation and performance, but also for:

- promoting accessible tourism and public transport (e.g., changes to 145 railway stations);
- Promoting health through the 'Be Active, Be Healthy' programme;
- Doubling the 'Access to work' programme to £138m.

Despite this, more research and evaluation of the effectiveness of provision is necessary to ensure future investment is appropriate and productive (Barnes et al., 1999). Current debates about disability benefits highlight the particular extremes of isolation and costs which poor disabled people bear. But this has not been adequately reflected in SEx literature, where much of the discourse seems to have focussed on social insertion through employment – the SID discourse (p 14), not a real option for many disabled people; and in sport and recreation literature the discourse is sporadic. Despite forming the EFDS, there is not yet a coherent policy of provision for disabled people's sport.

9   Sport and youth delinquency and crime

So long as there is neither school nor work, mischief fills the empty hours
(Burt, 1925: 29)

Total recorded crime has been falling in most countries since 1995 (Flatley et al., 2010), but concerns about youth remain prominent, with 1,000,000 youngsters coming into contact with the justice system each year (Lockhart, 2009). In the first section of this chapter, we examine the background to youth justice and offending, then we review the links between sport and prevention or rehabilitation of young offenders, terminating in a new synthesis by McCormack (2000). After reviewing recent evaluations of schemes in Britain and elsewhere, there are case studies of local primary and tertiary interventions, and a national one.

Introduction: youth and crime – the facts

Rebellion of youth has been a problem to every older generation; even when it was a social problem and incurred significant communal costs, it was often excused by Burt's or some other version of the old adage 'the devil makes work for idle hands.' 'Rational recreations' were devised by the middle classes to prevent mass urban workforces getting into debauchery (Bailey, 1987). After the inner city riots of the late 1970s, the same idea was basic to the Scarman report (1982) and Action Sport projects. Part of society with 'time on its hands' is unemployed people, especially jobless youngsters. Glyptis (1989) conclusively showed that constructive recreational programmes could not replace the role of work in filling time, providing a structure to life, or produce income and offer equivalent rewards. If delinquency is linked to factors other than boredom, like a need to achieve status, this may question the validity of sport and recreation provision in preventing it.

The proportion of young people in Britain's population has declined over the last 150 years. The 15–19s reduced by a quarter in the 1980s, though non-white minorities have much higher proportions of youth, making them more culturally diverse than ever before, with consequences for adolescent lifestyles and culture, a phase Hendry (1993: 1) described as 'a time set aside for waiting, developing and maturing and for accomplishing the rites of passage between childhood and adult status.' He suggested adolescence is now a longer stage in the lifecycle, with youth entering puberty earlier, being more exposed through media to society's consumption, problems and dilemmas, and leaving later for adulthood involving jobs, financial independence and leaving home. Hendry (1993) in research with 10,000 Scottish youth, related adolescent leisure as a series of foci: at age 13 young people are very interested in groups, clubs and organised activities, by 15 more likely to be involved in casual leisure activities – 'hanging around'; by 17, more influenced by commercial leisure. Observation suggests these changes have moved even earlier.

The Crime and Disorder Act 1998 defined antisocial behaviour as 'acting in a manner that caused/was likely to cause harassment, alarm or distress.' Local partnerships were set up to discourage it, and two-year court Orders (ASBOs) created; a one-day count in 2003 equated to 13.5m incidents a year (Home Office, 2004a). Between 1999 and 2008, 17,000 ASBOs were issued, 40% to under 18s, nine out of ten to boys (Ministry of Justice *statistics*, 28 July 2010). In the minds of the press and public this has become a threatening form of behaviour: 28% of adults perceived it as problematic (Wood, 2004). As issue rates fell and breaches rose, the Coalition replaced ASBOs in February 2011 with new Orders they said would be 'more flexible.'

Some young offenders acknowledged the importance of leisure, 13% saying sports provision would prevent others offending Audit Commission (1996). This could support the idea of better leisure education, within the citizenship part of school curricula, as argued by Bacon (1981) and Roberts (1983: 58):

> Are today's young people being better prepared for their futures?…we have still not developed effective means of delivering recreational interests to all young people, especially girls, and male and female early school leavers, mainly from working-class homes.

Roberts (1996) suggested young people had a better grounding of sport in schools, better facilities and more money, and hence participated more than their predecessors. We shall see below how far this is true of those at risk or having offended. Policy Action Team 10 (DCMS, 1999: 23) claimed purposeful sport could reduce offending, as did Culture Secretary Tessa Jowell four years later when summer SPLASH schemes showed local immediate reductions in crime of 5.2% (DCMS *Press Release* 13 January 2003).

Around 2000 there were concerns about the levels of truancies and exclusions from school (ONS, 2000), of unemployment (up from 13% in 1981 to 16% in 1991 for 16–17 year olds and to 22% in 1999, but much higher amongst the unqualified, and often twice as high amongst ethnic minorities. Hence, Tony Blair introduced the New Deal package of training with subsidies for employers for short-term job creation, criticised as a stopgap. Rising rents and purchase prices for housing made it increasingly difficult for young people to find independence, often leading to frustration that was only alleviated by theft.

Furthermore, more young Britons are unlikely to experience a stable nuclear family background, Smith (1992: 10) estimating that one in five children would experience parental divorce by age 16. The home setting for youngsters at-risk has also deteriorated from 1979, when 18% of children were living close to or in poverty, to 30% in 1987 (Smith, 1992: 13). *Social Trends* (ONS, 2000) reported that almost half of children living with non-working single parents and other benefit groups were in the bottom fifth of families by disposable income in 1997–8. Substantial numbers of young people also spend their youth in local authority care, often involving regular moves, reducing the opportunities for them to develop stable relationships and lifestyles.

Increased media coverage can be seen as one trigger of growing public concern about the risks and extent of crime, though it exaggerates them and the likelihood of violence. However, some areas, often inner city housing estates, had become crime 'black spots.' Young people aged 16–29, people earning less than £10,000, and from ethnic minorities fear crimes of theft, burglary, mugging or rape more than other groups (Mirlees-Black and Maung, 1994). This public concern about crime led to a common belief that the more lenient sentencing policy advocated during the 1980s was misconceived.

An amended Criminal Justice Act in 1994 increased the powers of courts to incarcerate young offenders, controversially providing the means through building new secure units. What are the facts? Over half the crimes solved in 1987 were traced to an offender younger than 21. Criminal statistics suggested that recorded crime rose by 900% from 1950 to 1991. Meanwhile, the number of convictions fell from 555,000 in 1980 to 509,000 in 1990 (Home Office, 1992). In *Misspent Youth,* the Audit Commission suggested that

> A disproportionate amount of crime is committed by young people, especially young males. In 1994, two out of every five known offenders were under the age of 21, and a quarter were under 18.
>
> (Audit Commission, 1996: 12)

In 2006, three-quarters of 10–25s had committed none of the 20 core offences identified; one in 10 had committed one of the serious offences, and one in 14 were frequent offenders (6+ times a year); the most common individual crimes were handling stolen goods, followed by fighting, and then burglary and theft for boys and shoplifting and vandalism for girls. In contrast, car crime was a strongly male preserve, according to Cooper (1989). Half that number was in delinquent youth groups peaking at 14–15 years for girls and 14–17 years for boys (see Table 9.1). Drug use was high (45%), compared to non-members (15%). The gangs averaged 16 members, 60% were white only, 30% of mixed race, and only eight per cent Asian or black only. Their most common were using drugs, threats, making graffiti, damaging things and using violence. Factors most strongly associated with group membership were friends in trouble with the police, having

Table 9.1 Youth participation in offending (10–19s) 2005

		Male	*Female*	*All*
% Members of a	All	6	6	
delinquent youth	Aged 12–13	3	6	
group	Aged 14–15	11	12	
	Aged 16–17	11	18	
	Aged 18–19	3	1	
% of offences	Any 'core' offence			21
committed by	a) to property			30
members of a DY	Vehicle related theft			34
Group	Burglary			40
	Criminal Damage			27
	b) any violent offence			25
	Assault with injury			20
	Assault without injury			21
	Robbery			–
	c) any drug selling offence			22
	Any serious offence			23
% of offences	Threatened/frightened people			40
committed by DY	Used force/violence on people			29
Groups	Graffiti			36
	Damaged/destroyed things			31
	Stolen things			24
	Used threats/violence to steal			3
	Carried knives			17
	Carried guns			4
	Used drugs			51
	Sold drugs to others			18
	Other crimes			7

Source: Sharpe, Aldridge and Medina (2006)

run away from home, commitment to deviant peers, having been expelled/suspended from school, and frequent drunkenness (Sharpe et al., 2006). Repeat offending was common for selling drugs, assaults and theft from shops (32, 20 and 17% respectively of frequent offenders). Also strikingly, 31% of boys aged 10–15 and 21% of girls had been a victim of theft or assault in the previous year (Roe and Ashe, 2008). Longitudinal data showed the influence of 'contagion' from siblings or friends who had offended, and emphasized the importance of early intervention, since the onset of offending averaged 12.4 years (Hales et al., 2009).

The proportion of juvenile offenders form a considerable social problem, while there is a second more serious trend: although four-fifths of young offenders will not commit another offence after the first, a minority are responsible for large numbers of reported crimes: 'six per cent of known offenders are responsible for seventy percent of known crime' (Faulkner, 1987: 9). This group became a target for policing and preventive activity. Selected reconviction rates for under-16s and 16–20s offenders born in 1953–38 were (Soothill et al., 2002):

%	Under 16s	16–20s
Boys: aggressive property offences/car crime	88	83
non-violent property/burglary	68	52
vehicle theft	62	43
wounding	60	40
shoplifting	45	34
Girls: versatile offending	21	22
shoplifting	19	17
trust violation	17	14

The point before which a child cannot be held responsible for its actions is legally recognised as the age of criminal responsibility (in Britain age ten). This concept is difficult to define, since children develop at different rates. Crimes committed by people under 17 years, therefore, are treated differently from adult crimes, in juvenile courts. The profile of young offenders in Britain can be summarised as follows:

- *Age* – If rebellious youth is a phase, then crimes will peak and many will not be repeated. In 1991 in England and Wales, young people sentenced for indictable offences numbered 192,000 aged 14–16 and 920,000 aged 17–20 (Home Office, 1993). Webb and Laycock's (1992) study in Manchester and NE England clearly revealed that initial participation in car crime began at 13–15 years, while other types of juvenile offence were committed by younger people, Cooper (1989) demonstrating that shop-lifting peaked at age 13.
- *Gender* – Cooper (1989) identified rates of conviction for boys at seven to ten times higher than for girls. But Graham and Bowling's (1995: 1) study suggested girls were as likely to offend as boys; perhaps they are better at avoiding identification!
- *Ethnic background* – The same research concluded that 'young Asians are less likely to commit offences and/or use drugs than whites and Afro-Caribbeans' (Graham and Bowling, 1995: 1).

In terms of juvenile crime management, approaches to treating young offenders swung between the two poles of punishment/retribution and reformation. The 1956, Ingleby Committee on juvenile courts suggested that 'delinquency might be an indicator of social deprivation' (Pitts, 1988: 1). This connection led to creating family advice centres and a first broad concept of treatment rather than punishment, after which Lord Longford's advocacy led to the idea of therapeutic centres in 1964. Pitts (1988) argued that Harold Wilson's Labour policy sought to depoliticise and decriminalise social issues, in White Papers *The Child, The Family and The Young Offender* in 1965 and *Children in Trouble* in 1968, and then the Children and Young Persons Act 1969.

But a new government in 1970 meant the age of criminal responsibility was not raised to 14 and courts were not prevented from giving custodial sentences in borstals. Another immediate Act formed a new juvenile criminal justice system incorporating social work. In 1973–7 the number of juveniles imprisoned rose dramatically and those referred to social work declined. Penal approaches appeared to have gained control in a 'backlash' against what was seen as ineffectual social work, though Thorpe et al. (1980: 3) argued a 'collusion and cock-up' between policemen, social workers, probation officers, magistrates and social services administrators lead to a failure to implement the 1969 reforms.

In a re-politicisation of juvenile justice, conservative Home Secretary William Whitelaw introduced the 'short sharp shock' for young offenders, with a physically demanding pilot regime in two young offenders institutions imitating American 'boot camps' (showing no benefits, later these were dropped). The 1982 Criminal Justice Act limited imprisonment through Youth Custody Sentences, Community Service Orders, Secure Care Orders for under 16s (in local authority homes), and Night Restrictions (curfews to prevent youngsters from committing offences).

Juvenile court procedures had become complex, tortuous and costly – 'identifying a young offender costs the police around £1,200…[and]…a further £2,500 to prosecute an offender successfully' (Audit Commission, 1996: 44). Young offenders' institutions were criticised as poorly staffed, under-funded, and breeders of hardened criminals, but were still costly – £1,730 per month in closed institutions and £2,071 in open institutions (Cook, 1997: 97), compared to Community Service Orders costing £140, Probation Orders £190 and Supervision Orders £180. Coopers and Lybrand (1994) estimated every criminal event prevented would save the nation £2,300, 50: 50 public and private money.

Regarding concerns over controlling public expenditure, the case for non-custodial sentencing for less dangerous, first-time offenders seems strong. It is weakened, however, by public perceptions that 'the punishment should fit the crime.' Non-custodial sentences do not deliver a 'pound of flesh' in the public's eyes.

Another Criminal Justice Act, of 1991, introduced for young offenders:

- probation orders for 16 year olds (applied to six per cent of youth disposals in 1995);
- curfew orders for offenders from 16 years;
- supervision orders for offenders up to 18 years (12% in 1995);
- allowing them to appear in youth courts until age 18;
- financial penalties and binding over parents of offenders aged 18 and 16 respectively.

(Jason-Lloyd, 1993)

A fresh Labour government launched major changes via the Crime and Disorder Act 1998, based on Home Secretary Jack Straw's belief that:

Today's young offenders can too easily become tomorrow's hardened criminals. For too long we have assumed that they will grow out of their offending behaviour if left to themselves...an excuse culture has developed within the youth justice system. Parents are not confronted with their responsibilities. Victims have no role and the public is excluded.

(cited in Muncie, 1999: 148)

It created a Youth Justice Board to promote good practice via local inter-agency Youth Offending Teams to manage young offenders through Youth Inclusion Programmes. For persistent and serious offenders, it introduced fast-track sentencing and a new way of allocating secure custody places. The Home Secretary adopted as hard a line on offending as his Tory predecessor, building more prisons for adults and juveniles, but Home Office research concluded:

Custody is the most expensive disposal, and is no more successful at preventing offenders obtaining further convictions than other disposals. But it protects the public from the risk of further harm...while the imprisonment lasts, and satisfies the public's need for retribution...In 1994 it was estimated that a 25 per cent increase in the prison population was needed to achieve a one per cent reduction in crime.

(Home Office *Press statement* 21 February 1998)

The concerns over the effectiveness of non-custodial sentences may be one reason behind the greater number of juveniles receiving custodial sentences in Britain (95.3 per 100,000) than in Germany (87.9) and France (84). Twenty three per cent of its prison population is aged under 21, or roughly double the proportions in those countries. Costs to the taxpayer continue to cause concern: young adults 18–24 made up 9.5% of the population but committed a third of all crime, took a third of Probation case loads, and a third of all prison sentences, at a cost of £16.8–20bn a year. A young prisoner cost £50,000 annually, poor value with re-offending still running above seven in ten (Helyar-Cardwell, 2009).

In 2003–4 the estimated costs of crime were £36.2bn, comprising two per cent on anticipation (insurance and security); 78% on consequences (stolen/damaged property, emotional and physical impact on victims, lost output and health services); and 20% in responsive costs (justice system) (Home Office, 2005).

Causes and triggers of youth delinquency, and interventions

McCormack (2000) scoured the sociological (e.g., Giddens, 1997) psychological (e.g., Bynum, 1996) and leisure studies literatures (e.g., Purdy and Richard, 1983) for factors identified in the genesis of/triggers to delinquent acts. There is no space here to summarise these numerous studies, but in her synthesis McCormack differentiated between structural factors in society, and internal factors related to young persons, their values and attitudes, as below, with major examples of sources:

EXTERNAL   Poverty and urban deprivation (Audit Commission, 1996)
Structural Factors Social residential setting (Mays, 1954)
                    Breakdown in public morality
                    Lack of early parental guidance and control
                       (Farrington, 1996)
                    Attempt to conform to negative social labelling
                       (Cohen, 1980; Muncie, 1984)
                                        ↑
                    Peer pressure and group dynamics
                       (Cohen, 1955; Audit Commission, 1996)
                                        ↓
INTERNAL   Expression of boredom or frustration (Scarman, 1992;
                       Clarke and Critcher, 1985; Marshall, 1994)
Agency Factors   Search for status and recognition
                       (Downes, 1966; Cooper, 1989)
                    Search for entertainment and challenge
                       (Webb and Laycock, 1992)
                    Phase of rebellion against society (Mays, 1972).

This shows a range of factors from structural ones to those of personal agency (Giddens, 1982). At one end of this range, West (1967) suggested the welfare state had removed the need to consider poverty (but juvenile poverty rose from 16% in 1961 to 33% in 1992 – Chapter 3). By the 1990s consumerism was placing huge pressures even on poor young people to achieve status via material goods, as Roberts explained:

> there is a contradiction between the 'good life' of cars, motor cycles, audio equipment and fashionable clothing, and the predicaments of young people who cannot afford the bus fares to claim their social security. Should we be surprised if some of these young people use the meagre resources at their disposal to construct contra-cultures within which to preserve some dignity and self-respect?
>
> (Roberts, 1983: 144)

For some young people, this may be restricted to deviance short of law breaking, but for others will result in delinquent behaviour. It is important to avoid labelling young people in ways that make it difficult for them to move on.

The Audit Commission (1996: 57) summarised the contemporary 'risk factors' for delinquency as 'inadequate parental supervision, aggressive or hyperactive behaviour in early childhood, truancy and exclusion from school, peer pressure to offend, unstable living conditions; lack of training and employment; and drug and alcohol abuse.' Witt and Crompton (1997), having surveyed schemes in over 30 places in the US, provided a wider range of risk factors as listed in Table 9.2. The Youth Justice Board enumerated 20 risk factors (six connected to family, four to school, four to community and six to the young person (CtC, 2005)).

Table 9.2 The relationship between risk factors, risk behaviour and health/life compromising outcomes

Risk factors	Risk behaviours	Health/life compromising outcomes
Poverty	Illicit drug use	School failure
Illegitimate Opportunity	Drunk driving	Legal trouble
Models for deviant behaviour	Tobacco Use	Low work skills
Low perceived life chance	Delinquency	Unemployability
Low self esteem	Truancy	Disease/ Illness
Risk taking propensity	Unprotected sex	Early childbearing
Poor school work		Social isolation
Latch key situations		Depression/ suicide
		Amotivation

Source: Crompton and Witt, 1997: 4

A framework is needed to relate interventions to risk, and one widely used was offered by Brantingham and Faust:

> *Primary prevention* – the modification of criminogenic conditions in the physical and social environment at large
> *Secondary Prevention* – early identification and intervention in the lives of individuals and groups in criminogenic circumstances
> *Tertiary Prevention* – prevention of recidivism.
> (Brantingham and Faust, 1976: 284–96).

Different objectives may be sought at each level:

> *Primary*   to improve youth welfare
>
> *Secondary* to promote socialisation (Witt and Crompton, 1997)
>   to provide diversion (e.g., summer schemes – Crime Concern, nd)
>   to deter youth from offending (Lundman, 1993)
>
> *Tertiary*   to allow society to exact retribution
>   to give offenders chance to atone
>   to divert youth from re-offending.

For individuals, crime prevention can be focused at pre-offending and offending individuals through secondary and tertiary interventions. Primary prevention, on the other hand, is directed not at individuals, but at context (physical environments and social structures which encourage crime and delinquency). They can include holiday schemes like SPLASH (Crime Concern, nd) youth club and community centre projects. Delimiting the influences and effects of such schemes is difficult, and until recently few had been evaluated. The case study below evaluates Street Sport in Stoke-on-Trent.

At secondary level, intervention is based on theories of prevention before offending occurs, for example, directed at socialisation (affecting positive attitude development), diversion and deterrence, as demonstrated in a wide range of schemes (e.g., by Witt and Crompton, 1997). Tertiary responses have been most commonly evaluated, since they deal with serious and repeat offenders who incur large social costs. They seek to alter ingrained behaviour, aid self-development and offer a setting for other therapeutic work. They are based commonly on retribution or punishment (Muncie, 1984). However, no form of detention seems to improve attitudes or behaviour on release, since over 70% commit further offences; indeed, such young people frequently develop a serious history of crime. Non-custodial measures (apart from seeking lower costs) aim to give opportunities to atone, to avoid opportunities to offend, to establish better physical and social situations, to learn constructive attitudes and behaviours, and in some cases to make reparation for vandalism or theft. Interventions may include community homes, attendance centres, supervision orders, Intermediate Treatment (which seek to bring 'the young person into contact with some constructive activity' (Muncie, 1984: 56). Comparison between custodial and community routes of correction therefore is not straightforward. The case study below also looks at Solent Sports Counselling.

Interventions can be grouped into four types: three are found in North America and widely across the world – wilderness adventure/challenge programmes, sports, and community-based multiple interventions involving a range of 'constructive leisure' MacKay (1993: 27). To these may be added one much developed in Britain, 'twocking' – taking away a motor car without the owner's consent – that of motor car schemes (Martin and Webster, 1994).

In his review, Coalter (1996) raised the issue that the causal links between delinquency, recreation as an intervention and outcomes were unclear. McCormack (2001) also criticised schemes for having no clear aims or too many vague and overlapping ones, more than they could realistically claim or demonstrate. Having codified origins of delinquency, the modes of sporting and recreational interventions and the objectives of each level of intervention, she was able to provide a new analytic framework that allowed each scheme to be interrogated for its aims and outcomes (Figure 9.1). She tested this by investigating six very different projects, which could all be accommodated in her schema, showing it to be robust.

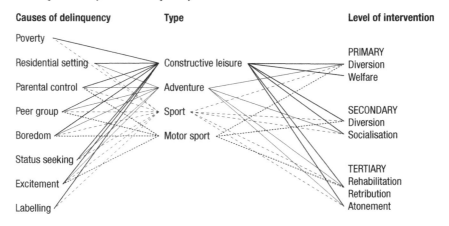

Figure 9.1 A framework to link the causes of delinquency, benefits of recreation and philosophies of intervention

The growing interest in sport as an intervention in youth delinquency

While writing the first edition of this book, coverage of sport and recreation as an intervention grew five or six fold, mostly in the form of literature reviews or surveys of schemes for central or local governments, in Canada (PRFO, 1997; Duck, 1998), the US (MacKay, 1993, Witt and Crompton, 1997), Australia (Potas, Vining and Wilson, 1990), New Zealand (Sullivan, 1998), France (Anstett and Sachs, 1995; Duret and Augustini, 1993), Belgium (de Knop et al., 1997) and the UK (Coalter, 1989b, 1996, Coalter, Allison and Taylor, 2000, Robins, 1990; Utting 1997; Long and Dart, nd; Long and Sanderson, 2001). The flow has slowed since, perhaps because crime rates have fallen, whatever the press write.

The consensus from studies of outdoor recreation and community-based schemes, is:

*   Sport and perhaps outdoor activity increases self-esteem, mood and perception of competence or mastery, especially through outdoor recreation (Sullivan, 1998, Potas, Vining and Wilson 1990, Badenoch, 1998, Barrett and Greenaway, 1995);
*   they reduce self-destructive behaviour (smoking, drug use, substance abuse, suicidal tendencies);
*   they lead to improved socialisation both with peer groups and adults;
*   in most cases where this was investigated, participants enjoy improved academic attendance and performance (Baker and Witt, 1996; Bundrick and Witt, 1998; Witt, 1999, 2000).

But Utting (1997) and Coalter (2007) emphasized there has been insufficient information on which programmes, settings and activities work best, though the small group counselling scheme in Hampshire (Tungatt, 1991) and the one-to-one scheme in West Yorkshire modelled on it (Nichols and Taylor, 1996) suggest that it is the support and counselling that are as important in bringing benefit as the activities, if not more so. Some schemes involved teaching self-restraint in the very activities that one might think would professionalise the deviancy – motor projects for those who had stolen cars or their contents (Martin and Webster, 1994) and martial arts (Twemlow and Sacco, 1998).

Two studies stand out in contrast as presenting mainly negative findings. Trulson (1986) found offenders doing a martial arts programme were more aggressive afterwards. Begg et al. (1996) recorded self-reported delinquent acts after a course for 800 male and 900 female youth aged 15–18 in New Zealand and showed that males with high and females with moderate to high sporting activity were more likely to be delinquent than those with low levels.

The Home Office yardsticks for such interventions seemed to be completion of the programme, and re-offending or recidivism. Attendance at such schemes, whether voluntary or mandated, is often sporadic, with youths experiencing lack of motivation, lack of daily time structure and other distractions, including 'signing on.' Whether community sentence disposals reduce re-offending is less clear, partly because of the difficulty and cost in establishing the true re-offending rate amongst a very mobile population, even given access to the national computerised crime records (Nichols, and Taylor, 1996). MacKay (1993) from American studies, suggested that there was a benefit of reduced recidivism for two to five years after offending, but that thereafter the two rates coalesced, though offences by attenders remained less serious. Tsuchiya (1996), from one to two year recidivism rates in four British schemes, suggested they were very good value for money compared to custody, with its high costs and 79% re-offending rate after two years.

The major problem with all such studies are, first, that the lower levels of delinquency may arise because the attenders self-select and be more likely to offend less. Few studies had quality controls anywhere near Kelly and Baer's (1968) seminal work on 60 offenders and a matched control group. Nichols and Taylor (1996) projected the likelihood of offending for West Yorkshire attenders and suggested that the outcome was lower-than-expected re-offending. Second, such schemes rarely run beyond three months, and some last a matter of days. A sail training week or a mountain expedition may be a life-changing experience in psychological terms, but if the youth returns to the same physical and social complex of deprivation, the pressures, values and conditioning of many years are likely to quickly re-assert themselves.

The constant cry is for longer schemes and prolonged follow-up support, but this happens in only a handful of cases, mainly because of poor public sector support. A claim that some youngsters might become dependent if programmes lasted too long has never been able to be tested in Britain (Taylor et al., 1999). Solent Sports Counselling, praised by the Home Office as a model for Probation services to follow was successively reduced from twelve to eight to four weeks' duration, and then subsumed into a New Deal scheme for unemployed people with little sports content (see below). West Yorkshire Sports Counselling, modelled on Hampshire but delivered one-to-one with serious offenders, was put out to tender and the new private contractor provided only half the contact time, and the specially trained, experienced and recruited team became disenchanted and dispersed (Nichols and Taylor, 1996). Taylor et al. (1999), evaluating 54 UK probation schemes including sport and adventure, reinforced earlier conclusions and warned against seeking to emphasise numbers in throughput before cost effectiveness.

Thus, Coalter agreed with American writers Segrave and Hastad (1985) that 'the efficacy of sport...as an antidote to delinquency is by no means settled, though seven years later he tempered that view and wrote although sport is rarely the solution, in many circumstances and used diagnostically, it can be part of the solution' (1996: 17). Proof of avoiding offending is a form of negative evidence that is very difficult to obtain. The Home Office gave up predictively modelling offending because of its low reliability, in favour of reducing the opportunities to offend (through better design of housing, better locks on cars, community use and surveillance of public spaces etc).

Case study 6: intervening to make a difference? Street Sport, Stoke as a primary intervention and Solent Sports Counselling as a tertiary one

Background to Street Sport and Solent Sports Counselling

In 1994, the City of Stoke-on-Trent made a successful application to the Sports Council to extend detached youth work in Hanley, which had grown from a single worker in 1971 to a team of sixteen in 1986, involving 'a programme of activities including play schemes, play training, community events, establishing residents' associations' (Manager of Community Recreation, 15 July 1997). It then became part of the Leisure Services programme. Street Sport (SS) developed as a 'participation' level intervention, intended to:

> provide an insight into the effectiveness of recreation outreach work on young people in terms of deflecting negative behaviour into constructive activity...offer a valuable indication as to how we can have a significant effect on improving relationships between communities and adolescents in our recreational strategies.
>
> (Leisure and Recreation Committee, 14 February 1995)

The next strategy paper said:

> the greatest chance of achieving success in the development of sporting activity with young people comes from being part of what they do. The activities have to fit in with what already exists using street venues and meeting places.
>
> (Stoke-on-Trent City Council, 1994: 24).

In 1997, the scheme was extended to the whole city. Sessions operated on a drop-in basis, Monday to Friday evenings, with additional day-time sessions throughout school holidays. Portable equipment was carried in a converted van equipped with gas-powered telescopic spotlights. Diary entries and observations suggested average attendance was twelve, or an annual total of 4,200. There was no upper age limit or cut off point. SS was not actively marketed, aiming not to bring more youth out, but rather to provide the recreational needs of youth already there. Thus it directly addressed 'hanging about.' The Community Services Department, responsible for parks and playgrounds, developed Sports Courts (multi-purpose hard areas for football and basketball, with fixed goals, basketball posts and timed lighting for evening use, and a seating area), similar to provision in Bolton.

Hampshire/Solent Sports Counselling (SSC), set up in 1983, was the brainchild of a committed local businessman/magistrate, convinced that many of the youth referred to his court needed support for constructive leisure, and an opportunity to burn up energy through physical activity. It could be seen as protesting against the contemporary lobby for harsher penalties for young offenders. It gained the support of the Manpower Services Commission, and operated initially from a judo hall in Southampton, where young people could drop-in for sessions such as uni-hoc and archery. With evidence from Hants Probation Service, it achieved three years' more security in 1985 as a Sports Council National Demonstration Project, and expanded, with two teams of MSC-funded workers in Southampton and Portsmouth. The distinctive features were an introductory interview to establish recreation interests, assignment to a mentor who introduced attendees to sports and participated with them one-to-one or in small groups. Funding was extended in 1987; and the Sports Council undertook action research involving longitudinal study of individual, which concluded that 'We believe the SSC project has done the ground work...for sport to play a major role in the mainstream work of the Probation Service' (Tungatt, 1991: 87). By 1989, the project was 'mainstreamed' into probation delivery, and promoted as good practice through a national conference. It was frequently a victim of its own success, as shown by comments by two key funders:

> If it's so successful, why don't the Home Office do it, why do we need to be involved?
>
> (Sports Council Southern Regional Director)

> We shouldn't be leading this – let's recommend that the Probation Service takes it on.
>
> (Sports Council's National Director)

By 1990, Hants Probation Service did take over the project; but by April 1992 budget cuts, and concerns about clients' dependence on sports counsellors, the number of sessions per participant was reduced from twelve to eight. During 1995–8 the Probation Service gradually reduced the funding, and sessions were further reduced to four, and the building in Southampton was lost. The administration was moved to Winchester, and in 1997 back to Southampton. In late 1997, facing more severe funding cuts which threatened redundancy for probation officers, Probation decided to incorporate SSC into a main youth referral process, and in March 1998 the Scheme was effectively stopped.

Funding for these schemes was modest; for the first three years it was:

Solent SC	£000	Street Sport	£000
Sports Council grant	67.5	Sports Council grant	120
Hants Probation	309.5	City of Stoke	120

The staffing was for SS in November 1999 two full time and ten casual/part time workers, and for SSC in March 1997 five full time, four on work placements, one administrator, and a manager.

SSC's attendances, including for the key period of evaluation in 1995/6 and 1996/7 are shown in Table 9.3. At its peak, the throughput and completion rates were both substantial, as such schemes go.

Table 9.3 Attendance patterns for Solent Sports Counselling

	1987/8	1988/9	1991/2	1992/3	1995/6	1996/7
Referral	380	380	483	505	636	773
Starts	380	380	323	354	476	581
Completed 4+ Sessions (%)	N/A	N/A	107 (33)	160 (45)	209 (44)	290 (50)
Completed 8+ Sessions (%)			153 (47)	103 (29)	N/A	N/A

Sources: HSC Final Evaluation, 1990; Annual Report 1992/3; Annual Report 1996/7

SS and SSC as interventions

Using the framework established in Figure 9.1, the objectives of the two schemes are shown in Figures 9.2 and 9.3.

SS sessions had several intended outcomes for both youth and their communities: first, to divert them from street corners into positive activity, removing them from peer pressure and other delinquent influences; second, to offer them a new perspective on leisure and provide fun and entertainment; third, for communities, to reduce the perceived threat posed by young people; fourth, to offer education and skill development through adult mentors; finally, to yield outcomes of improved self-confidence, communication skills and changed views of their community and citizenship. As well as confidence, SSC's mentoring process and individually designed programmes aimed to alter leisure behaviour, through better knowledge about local opportunities, and to improve awareness of health and lifestyle choices. The relationships between these two interventions and the causes of delinquency are as shown in Table 9.4.

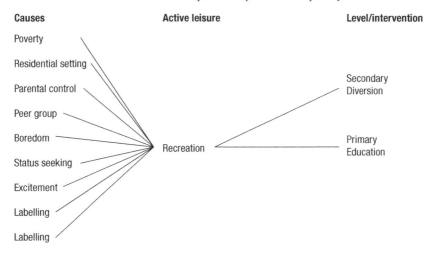

Figure 9.2 Theoretical framework for Street Sport – Stoke-on-Trent

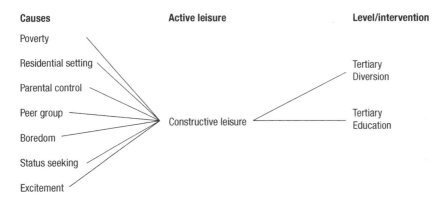

Figure 9.3 Theoretical framework for Solent Sports Counselling Project, Hampshire Probation Service

In both cases the evidence related to participant outcomes. SS had less formal criteria; staff measured success according to numbers attending regularly, whether youngsters saw sessions as fun, whether new faces joined in, and that no friction occurred. SSC produced limited recidivism data during the Sports Council's evaluation, which showed that 'almost half the clients have maintained a trouble-free record since being involved with the project, and a further half-dozen clients appear to have reduced their previous rates of offending' (Tungatt, 1991: 61). SS produced occasional anecdotal evidence related to a general reduction in juvenile crime in the targeted areas. Generally, Stoke police valued any diversion reducing 'calls related to disturbance and vandalism' (Sergeant Taylor, Burslem LPU, September 1999), but could not identify direct links with more serious crimes like burglary, assault and car crime.

Table 9.4 Relationships with causes of delinquency in Street Sport and Solent Sports Counselling

Cause	Street Sport Stoke-on-Trent	Solent Sports Counselling
Poverty	Free/low cost ongoing activities	Low cost, selected activity profile
Setting	Local sessions, Sports Courts	Improved knowledge/access to local facilities
Parents	Community development	Mentors
Peer group	Group sessions	Integration into new groups
Boredom	Activities to target 'hanging around'	New activities
Status	Involvement in community consultation	Client-centred targets for completion
Excitement	No 'buzz,' emphasis on fun	Recreation, some adventure
Labelling	Not 'hanging around'	–
Rebellion	Inclusion in community	General counselling

The young clients, their leisure and the impact of the Schemes

When built in the 1950s, Bentilee was the largest council housing estate in Europe, consisting of a number of 'villages' where recent initiatives sought to engender a stronger sense of community. It suffered from high unemployment, and many young single parents (which partly explained the lack of young women at SS sessions, because of the time needed for childcare). Problems of drug abuse and burglary were so prevalent that some areas were considered 'no-go' for most families.

Some play schemes and youth clubs addressed the needs of younger children, but there was no acceptable provision when they outgrew these (as in Scotland, Hendry, 1993). Some respondents felt the rules at leisure clubs, youth clubs and sports clubs were too strict, but neither was lack of supervision appreciated. This resulted in young people hanging around areas like the shops, annoying residents. A similar situation on the multi-cultural estate of Cobridge was further strengthened by negative media coverage of youth, described as 'young criminals…making life a misery for families on the Grange estate' (*The Sentinel*, 7 September 1999). In the Stanfields estate in north Burslem, three-fifths of residents were aged under 30, 11% faced unemployment, and others low-paid work. Also here was the poorest leisure provision in Stoke, and consequently Stanfields received two SS sessions a week. A large area of open space next to Port Vale Football Club was used during the summer, as was a RedGra all weather pitch at the High School in winter, which had basketball posts and a hard surface suitable for rollerblading.

Besides interviewing staff and local residents, police, school and college staff, observing and having informal discusions with youngsters, McCormack (2000) interviewed 27 young people – 19 males and 18 females, four participants, four spectators, and seven non-participants – involved in a NACRO Moves project for

Year 7 children excluded from school. Twenty were in SS's target ages of 14–18 years. Over half claimed to attend most/every SS session for six months or more. Of SSC's participants, 40 were monitored by McCormack (2000) using questionnaires and entry interviews, and 21 were followed for eighteen months using detailed life history profiles and follow-up records. As expected among offenders on probation, they were generally older, 72% over 21. Of SSC referrals, two-fifths did not attend a session, but of those who did, half completed four sessions and one in seven completed ten or more. While the offending history of this group could not be revealed by the Probation Service, McCormack's respondents had been involved in assault, theft or burglary. With its contextual work, this approximated to Nichols' (2001) call for using a social realist approach.

The constraints on the leisure patterns of these two samples of pre- and post-offending youth had much in common (Table 9.5). Accessibility was defined by Torkildsen (1992) as combining four distinct aspects: physical, social, perceptual and financial. Physical accessibility was cited as a constraint by 35% of the Stoke interviewees; and cost by 70%. An important constraint on young women was their physical safety at night, mentioned in Bentilee and Stanfields. Finally, the perceived accessibility of recreation opportunities was critical. The age difference may explain why transport presented greater problems to the Stoke sample, who generally depended on adults for transport.

After offending, young people became isolated, and lack of information about opportunities and companions became significant influences on their leisure. Although physical ill-health severe enough to preclude participation remained constant, after offending mental health problems, especially depression, became noticeable. These young people were usually unemployed, with few qualifications, and had failed to make the transition to adulthood. The detailed follow-up of some

Table 9.5 Constraints on the young people's participation

Constraint	Hampshire n=21 %	Stoke-on-Trent n=27 %
Cost	46	35
Transport	8	35
Information	25	6
Fear of crime		100 (female)
Confidence	21	16
Peer pressure	8	
Company	38	10
Lack of skills		19
Health problems	8 (physical) 38 (mental)	13 (physical)
Family/work commitments	4	10
Lack of facilities	4	48

SSC clients involved completing life history profiles, mapping their patterns of leisure activities before, during and after the project, and recording related life and offending events, extending Hedges' (1986) model used also by Brodie, Roberts and Lamb (1991). These showed common patterns, of:

- poor support for childhood leisure, and frequent removals, breaking up continuity of attachments to places, people or activities;
- alcohol and/or drug abuse (over 50%);
- spells of mental ill health (40%);
- sporadic or frequent entry and release from institutional care (60%) and custody (23%) .

A typical case was of Martyn, aged 22 (Figure 9.4), who had a long history of petty offences and care (and perhaps abuse); he had been involved in football and swimming coaching before that, and played some badminton while in care. He lived with an older partner in a bedsit in a deprived area of Southampton, both claiming Disability Benefit. His counsellor believed he might have learning difficulties, and was certainly difficult to communicate with. He started swimming and cycling at SSC, and continued with these and badminton afterwards with a volunteer. His bedsit became clean and tidy. After six months contact was lost, but SSC had provided consistent support for his lifestyle choices.

The common middle-class assumption that positive leisure patterns, support and continuity just evolve, cannot be applied to young people with chaotic upbringings. Even amongst regular sports participants, 21–22% of those experienced three or four life transitions during and after school (like taking a gap year, moving to another area, going to college/training or being unemployed, having children, returning to parental home) and 25–34 years of age, compared to half of inactives (YouGov, 2012). The general picture of leisure patterns for young people at-risk or offending demonstrates very impoverished leisure experiences, which previously had been only guessed at (see McCormack, 2005). From both samples there was evidence that these young people lacked the knowledge, skills and confidence to effectively access public leisure opportunities. They lacked role models of positive leisure patterns and had experienced little support in developing and sustaining sports activity.

If the benefit of reduced boredom was to result in less re-offending, sustained changes to leisure patterns were required. Attendances at SS sessions (all for football) in Stanfields and Bentilee demonstrated that many young men aged 14–20 were diverted from hanging about on the streets, and seven in ten rated their football game as SS' most important feature. In Stanfields the workers facilitated setting up and equipping a junior league soccer team. One player, with drug abuse problems, unemployment and crime attended open sessions regularly over four years, and appreciated the lack of pressure. This gentle approach helped him to survive difficult years.

AGE

LIFE EVENT	10	11	12	13	14	15	16	17	18	19	20	21	22	23	24	25
Probation												X	X			
Alcohol																
Care	X	X		X	X											
Custody										X						
Employed								X								
Excluded		X	X													
Psy. Hospital											X					
Move			X		X		X		X		X					
Relationship									X					X		
School	X			X												
Sports Counseling														X		
Training																
Truant		X														
Unemployed							X	X	X	X	X	X	X			
Age Now													X			

LEISURE	10	11	12	13	14	15	16	17	18	19	20	21	22	23	24	25
Cinema																
Pubs / Bars						▬	▬	▬	▬	▬	▬	▬	▬			
Gambling																
TV / Video	▬	▬	▬	▬	▬	▬	▬	▬	▬	▬	▬	▬	▬			
Live Music																
Gardening																
DIY																
Night Clubs							▬	▬	▬	▬	▬	▬				
Pub Quiz																
Shopping																
Computer Games																
Car Repairs							▬	▬	▬	▬	▬	▬				
Other																

SPORT / RECREATION	10	11	12	13	14	15	16	17	18	19	20	21	22	23	24	25
Football	▬	▬	▬	▬												
Golf																
Rugby																
Walking																
Cycling	▬	▬	▬		▬	▬	▬	▬					▬			
Swimming	▬	▬	▬	▬												
Weights								▬	▬	▬						
Keep Fit																
Darts																
Snooker																
Boxing																
Badminton	▬	▬	▬	▬	▬	▬	▬	▬	▬	▬	▬					
Squash																
Fishing																
Mountain Bikes																
Martial Arts																
Running																
Basketball																
Skateboarding																

Figure 9.4 Leisure life history chart for Martyn

The diversion from the prevalent 'hanging about' was important to the youngsters, as well as residents:

> I don't hang around on the streets as much any more, in summer I prefer to play sport in the parks, in winter I only go out now if my friends are there.
>
> (Lindsey, aged 16, Stanfields, September 1999)

Macdonald and Shildrick (2007), in a study of similar deprived youth in Teesside, graphically describe this as 'pinballing' around the estates. Participants made greater use of parks, and took part in tennis, snooker, golf, rounders, cinema, pubs and play schemes. They wanted to participate primarily to socialise and for enjoyment; competition and exercise were secondary motivations.

In contrast, in SSC, diversion was a long-term objective combined with leisure education. Seventy per cent of the sample had joined as a conscious decision to improve their health and fitness, which often needed longer than the standard four sessions – 'completers' averaged eight sessions. There was little evidence of constructive leisure before starting SSC, half having never visited a leisure centre, and only eight per cent had joined clubs, mostly for snooker or gambling. For example, Stuart, aged 25, had a complicated history of serious offending, suffered depression, but after ten sessions reported sustained changes to his leisure, continuing to attend a bridge club, play bowls and mix outside the pub. Nine of ten completers reported an intention to continue participating, and four in five to use leisure centres. The success of SSC in changing leisure behaviour can be seen by reviewing patterns during the year after completion, shown in Table 9.5. Ninety per cent who completed four sessions had tried at least two activities, and after six months two-thirds were still participating in activities introduced by SSC. Drop-out at 12 months was often related to new work commitments, which themselves could be considered successful outcomes.

Many respondents reported that the care system provided little continuity of support for their leisure, and those remaining in school reported a sports delivery system that encouraged only those showing keen-ness and talent. This left many of these youth lacking a sense of direction in their free time, mainly hanging around on the streets, supplemented later by visiting pubs and clubs.

Perceptions of the SS and SSC schemes

The young SS participants saw it primarily as a means of playing football, and of making friends:

> Street Sport is great...I don't get to play a game anywhere else...the rest of the week it's just kick around with mates.
>
> (Male aged 18, Bentilee, July 1999)

I play for the team now and train more seriously with them but I still like to come here to meet my mates and have a bit of fun.

(Male aged 17, Stanfields, July 1999)

Overall the perceptions of the young participants of SS can be summarised thus:

- Unemployment was a prime concern for all.
- They needed places to meet where there was no conflict with older residents and the police.
- They were concerned about crime in their communities, many feeling threatened by the violence they witnessed.
- The weekends and school holidays were identified as key times when they needed something to do.
- Much free time was spent hanging around with peers, a situation they thought increased risks of juvenile crime, drug and alcohol abuse.
- Generally they needed adult support to create effective sports and leisure opportunities.
- Sports participation was low, and the range of activities very limited, skateboarding and BMX being the most common alternatives to football.
- Knowledge of the Recreation Key discount scheme was low.
- Even in childhood, parents had little input into their leisure, siblings and peers being the most common mentors.
- Many activities on offer were team- or course-based, aiming at performance level sport, but many youths wanted to play sport simply for fun and relaxation.
- They liked SS because it was informal, friendly, regular, free and close to home.
- They would like more frequent SS sessions, as once a week left much empty time.

But how was SS seen by non-participants and the community? At Bentilee's Willfield Community Centre, a 17 year-old young women regarded it as a weekly football session for young men, and a youth worker regarded it as another 'limited quick fix solution to a complex problem' (May, 1999). The head teacher at Haywood High School felt it had reduced vandalism in the school grounds. The police believed it had played an important role in reducing community tension, yet felt it should run alongside holiday play schemes, a time of increased crime risk. Community workers in Stanfields regarded it positively, but only as a short-term diversion for young men that did not address young girls' needs.

Perceptions of SSC's completers of over four sessions varied: Dean, who at 22 had numerous convictions including custody for firearms offences and spent ten sessions with his counsellor, thought no changes were needed. Of his SSC experience he said, 'I loved it'; Jason enjoyed four sessions, but after 12 months was no longer involved in sport, citing cost, a lack of equipment and companions. Colin cited conflict with uncertain shift patterns in his job at MacDonalds. Others with mental health problems, like David, saw SSC as another hurdle rather than a help: 'I'm having enough problems keeping the basics together, I am not ready for this sort of Scheme.' But Matt played badminton regularly, helping rebuild his self-esteem, and after 12 months added regular football and fencing, reporting: 'I found the benefits to be immense [including] increased health and fitness, also an increase in self-esteem and self-confidence.' Inevitably, some were not interested, including eight who failed to complete their programmes.

The relationship with the sports counsellor was reported to be of primary importance in all 21 individual cases: 'my sports counselling officer was very good and he did everything possible to help me' (Client P7, spring 1997). Among completers, the only criticism was that counsellors were too busy to offer sufficient time. Ending the programme was an issue for SSC; staff had to plan from the first interview for 'exit routes' that would allow continued participation, via integration into clubs, increasing participants' confidence in accessing venues, selecting volunteer support, and integration into drop in sessions.

Participants' perceptions of SSC can be summarised as:

- Generally they liked and valued it.
- Its most important aspect was the support of the sports counsellor, more important for three-quarters of them than the activities offered.
- Most wanted more sessions, even if they needed no more to satisfy the requirements of the counselling process.
- After six months, two out of three were still participating in activities introduced by SSC.
- After six months, two out of three reported improved health and well-being.
- Perceived benefits were improved knowledge of leisure facilities and confidence to use them, improved self-esteem, and some reduction in boredom.
- Improved perception of leisure opportunities benefited other family members.

Changes in personal factors among the Solent follow-up sample are shown in Table 9.6. This shows that the Scheme had positive impacts on boredom and the former lack of adult role models. The fixed-length contact in Solent and the single weekly session in SS were both perceived by youths as significant limitations.

Table 9.6 Solent Sports Counselling – patterns of continued participation

Past leisure patterns % (N=21)	Intended to continue at exit stage	Playing after 6 months	Playing after 12 months
Previous leisure centre use	100	67	58
Non participant	75	67	33
Total	88	67	46

Table 9.7 Changes in personal factors among Solent Sports Counselling follow-up sample

Factor (%)	Much better	Better	No change	Worse	Much worse
Self image	14	64	21	–	–
Relationship with authority figures	57	–	43	–	–
Knowledge of local leisure facilities	14	57	29	–	–
Attitude to health & fitness	21	50	29	–	–

Nonetheless, most clients felt that there had been an improvement in one or more of their self-image, relationship with authority figures, knowledge of local leisure opportunities, and/or their attitudes to matters of health and fitness (Table 9.7).

Managing such interventions

SS and SSC shared six important features:

1   Dedicated, consistent managers (Robins, 1990: 91), with clear vision and strong leadership to give projects the direction and backing to survive once initial funding stopped;
2   Start-up funding committed for three years, subject to monitoring;
3   Staff members with good inter-personal skills and empathy with young people, whether in group work as in SS, or one-to-one as in SSC;
4   Strove to provide local, affordable and popular recreations;
5   Participants who were volunteers and consulted on activity provision; and
6   Made attempts to evaluate and produce evidence of performance related to aims and outcomes.

Both schemes, however, had limited attraction for girls and young women, not through lack of female leaders, but through the activities on offer. The female worker appointed to SSC commented 'it's all weights and football, there's no mention of aerobics or netball, women see that and decide it's not for them' (Counsellor C, April 1997). Kevin Sauntry in Stoke fought for and pursued over many years a 'style of community recreation I believe communities want and value' (interview, June, 1997), but relied on his team of skilled managers and workers to deliver it. Keith Waldman in Hampshire led SSC from its birth in 1984 to its demise in 1998, had a team with much less hierarchy, and direct 'hands on' delivery, but increasingly had to work within the structures and priorities of the Probation service.

The evidence supports SS as an example of primary intervention, which achieved both community development and diversion for mainly male youngsters at-risk of offending. At tertiary level, SSC showed that community integration was more difficult to achieve, since many community groups resist the integration of known offenders, who can be unsure or impatient about getting involved in groups or organisations. This suggests that primary intervention more effectively integrates young people into their communities and addresses issues of labelling, status and a need to belong.

Impacts on the causes of delinquency

With reference to Figures 9.2 and 9.3 (see p 175), these case study schemes demonstrated the following effects on particular causes of delinquency.

- *Poverty* – Both Schemes operated with low charges, and SSC clients could use a discount Leisure Card (see Chapter 3) to combat a significant financial barrier. However, removing cost constraints alone was not sufficient to establish participation.
- *Residential setting* – SS helped communities to create sports courts in local areas, using waste ground and other open spaces, and this improved both the setting and residents' perceptions of the scheme. Concentrating locally, SSC altered the youths' perceptions of local opportunities and reduced negative influences by introducing legitimate activities.
- *Parental support* – Seventy-five per cent of SS participants felt the contribution of the sports counsellors was a vital aspect. As one said, 'the sports leaders were great, they never pushed an issue or passed judgement but were there every week for us' (Cobridge former participant aged 21, September 1999). Even SSC's counsellors' short-term work provided the personal support and advice lacking in most of its clients' lives. At the time of conviction, 21 year old Scott's view of leisure was a hedonistic search for excitement prompted by extreme boredom and frustration. Over ten sessions, his mature sport counsellor was able to provide a positive role model missing in his earlier life, and Scott reported sustained participation in weight training and swimming, and did not offend in the year after attending SSC.
- *Peer group* – SS worked with the peer group as a whole: '[the staff] helped us to form a football team, we have now played for two seasons and are a strong team on and off the field...we needed their help to get motivated' (footballer aged 17, Stanfields, July 1999). SSC introduced participants to new leisure activities, but not necessarily to new peers or friends.
- *Boredom* – Here the most obvious results were seen, though less significant for SS where 92% of the participants aged under 17 reported extreme boredom outside the weekly sessions and in school holidays. Of SSC's Phase Two sample, seven out of eight felt it had reduced their boredom, a view sustained during the 12 month follow up.

There was no evidence to suggest that either scheme offered a sustained impact on status-seeking behaviour or a search for excitement. However, individual SSC participants reported sustained improvements in their improved self-image (74%), relationships with authority figures (57%), and attitudes to health and fitness

(71%), all of which contributed to greater self-confidence, and reduced their need to achieve status.

Although some previous studies contained individual participants' profiles and a general analysis of their offending backgrounds (Tungatt, 1990; Nichols and Taylor, 1996) there has been no attempt to analyse the existing leisure patterns of young people joining schemes, or to examine how these emerged and were modified. The results showed SS as an example of primary level intervention that achieved both community development and diversion for young people (mainly male) at risk of offending, and reached influential peer groups. In contrast, at tertiary level, SSC showed community integration was more difficult to achieve. This suggests that primary intervention may more effectively integrate young people into their communities and address the issues of labelling, status and a need to belong, whereas individual sessions are needed for alienated and labelled individuals in post-offending schemes.

In summary, six points can be made.

1   *Research and evaluation methods* – The framework developed in Figure 9.1 proved robust across six schemes. For the offenders, the life history charts proved a very useful tool as a framework for the periodic interviews, as a way of relating changing activity profiles, and a help to counsellors in devising a personal activity plan for each client. Nonetheless, it is true that most schemes do not have built-in evaluation (Smith and Waddington, 2004); below I show Positive Futures as an exception.

2   *Cost and efficacy* – The reported average cost of tertiary interventions in 1998/9 was £379 per place, which led to a cost per completion of £730 (Taylor et al., 1999). This would provide an average of 11 sessions of four hours' duration. The cost of one person attending SS for two hours a week for a year in 1997 (100 hours) was approximately £290, demonstrating a potential cost advantage of primary intervention.

3   *Support from schools and adults* – It is clear that the National Curriculum provided a poor social education framework to develop the skills and confidence to access local leisure, and the SSC life history profiles demonstrated the almost complete lack of adult support and mentors in developing constructive leisure compared to those of children with average participation rates (Chapter 4).

4   *Benefits from appropriate activity or counselling?* – A common theme in intervention schemes is that the activities at some point must give the same 'buzz' as offending – e.g., in abseiling, tall ship racing or go-karting. McCormack's findings, however, suggested this is less important, in terms of sustained diversion, than the process of skills development. Activities were not rejected for lack of 'buzz,' but because of barriers of cost, and physical, social and managerial access. SSC clients had particularly impoverished leisure lifestyles, and so the offers were beneficial for most who stuck with the course. If pushed to judgement, both McCormack (2000) and this author would say that it is the availability of a mentor who listens without judging,

who can be a role model and playing companion was the most significant factor in tertiary schemes.

5   *Timing and durability* – The timing of such interventions is clearly crucial, since many other factors in young people's lives alter at different stages. The schemes demonstrated that primary provision can effectively address groups, which significantly reduces the cost per participant, and so ongoing support can be afforded. Sustained skills development should be possible, since such youngsters do not need to develop independent exit routes. Tertiary provision was shown to require significant one-to-one counselling, thus increasing the individual cost and reducing the potential for ongoing support. With very mobile populations like offenders establishing exit routes or follow-up may be difficult. Joliffe and Farrington's (2007: 9) overview of 18 studies was less positive, suggesting 'mentoring was a promising but not proven intervention.'

6   *Involving the youngsters and the community* – The important act of community integration was more easily achieved by primary intervention. By the time young offenders justified tertiary intervention, official criminal labels or records made integration difficult, and sports clubs generally resisted membership by known offenders, although pub football teams and running clubs were more welcoming. Even more important is involving the youth in designing the programmes.

Giddens (1982) suggested structure and agency have equal importance in dictating individual actions. The outcomes reported from both Schemes concentrated on personal (agency) factors, although the positive role models provided by each and the improved perceptions of young people of local leisure opportunities may address some external causes. This supports Coalter's conclusion (1996) that active leisure interventions may be part of, but are unlikely to provide a total solution to juvenile delinquency.

Case study 7: Positive Futures (PF)

In 2000, the Home Office (HO) Drugs Directorate – with several partners including Sport England and the Football Foundation and numerous locals, especially Youth Offending Teams (YOTs) and Youth Improvement Programmes (YIPs) – set up Positive Futures across England. It was intended to promote sport and physical activity, reduce drug abuse, and modify lifestyles. It was targeted at the 50 most vulnerable and at-risk youth aged 10–19 in each of the one-fifth most deprived areas, though as the programme wound on, a wider range of youth were referred from schools, or self-referred. It was monitored by MORI and from 2004 evaluated by Substance. By the end of Phase 1, in 2003, there were 63 projects – 17 of which were in high crime areas – with a combined annual budget of £3.9m. It involved 26,000 youth, an average of 420 per scheme, more than nine out of ten were under 17 and almost one in five were from BMEs. Phase 2, in 2003–06 comprised a further 37 projects together with 19 funded by a further £15m from the HO and FF. Four in five youngsters took part in sport, notably football and basketball, one in 11 in educational activities (notably arts and anti-drug advice), and one in 12 in recreations (outdoor pursuits and trips).

- In the report *Cul de sacs and Gateways* (HO, 2002: 4) PF was described as a 'relationship strategy, based on the principle that engagement through sport and the building of mutual respect and trust can provide cultural "gateways" to alternative lifestyles.' The crucial mentor/leader was a community sports coach. A particular case was made for the ability of football to build relationships through team working. This report looked forward in Phase 2 to more secure funding, better support from regional agencies, focussing on 17–19s (because most youth contacted had been 10s–16s), to developing a training element, and better monitoring and evaluation.
- Sport England's evaluation of the 24 projects it co-funded (Chapman, Craig and Whaley, 2002) showed: (i) increases in participation, ranked by stakeholders at 4.6 out of 5, with adherence of 78%, demonstrating the importance of sport as a 'hook' for youth (see Nichols, 2007); (ii) youth offending reduced by 15–70% in 12 schemes over 2001, rated 4.1 out of 5; (iii) only a quarter of attenders were girls; but (iv) produced only 'unsure' progress in reducing drug abuse (rated at 3.4).
- Crabbe et al. (2005) looked at case studies of organisation which they classified thus:

Type	Organisation	Approach	Example
Community based	Voluntary	Radical, innovative and participant focused	Calderdale North Liverpool Southwark
Local authority	Statutory	Traditional, formulaic, 'top down'	Sefton Leeds
Hybrid	Partnership	Pragmatic	Keighley Wandsworth

They argued that PF should not be driven by referral routes but use 'flexible, pragmatic outreach approaches'. Two schemes made useful links with Premiership football clubs.

- *End of Season Review* (HO, 2006): by 2005 109,000 youths were involved; 17–19s were now 18% and girls one in three; 24 sports were in the programme, including adventure activities like abseiling; 600 youths had obtained jobs; 500 were volunteering, 700 had returned to school and 1,700 were doing better in school; 4,000 had signed up for some form of training; and leaders reported 2,000 having better relations with their peers and 1,200 with their families; but only now were a logbook and other monitoring devices being piloted.
- Crabbe et al. (2006a) found no ready-made model for partnerships, but voluntary sector forms were often more flexible and appropriate than imposed

forms. When looking at PF's impact they concluded (Crabbe et al. 2006b: 3) 'projects working with fewer participants are more likely to have a significant impact on a higher proportion of those they work with than projects working with large numbers.' A striking conclusion was that PF can also provide physically and emotionally safe places in 'danger zones of racialised and territorial conflict'(2006b: 4).

• They also concluded that the value of sport 'can only be realised within a social and personal developmental approach' (Crabbe et al., 2006c: 4), and frontline grassroots youth work experience was necessary to handle the contrasting nature of both diversionary and developmental work; curiously they recommended an intermediary agency between the national drivers and local deliverers.

In 2008, the Home Office decided to cease managing PF. The programme was put out to tender and 91 projects were handed over to Crime Concern, renamed Catch 22 (which in 2011 was to incorporate Fairbridge's programmes) with funding until 2011. *Taking it on* (HO/Substance 2008) recorded 60,000 youth involved, 22% female, now 54% from BME groups, and two-thirds self-referred. A quarter were moving to positive training, volunteering outcomes, and contributing to national strategies for children, youth, drugs, youth and crime action plans, and six allied Public Service Agreements. Football still occupied a third of sessions, but more were multi-sport, and for fitness and dance. It records specific acts of protection by PF against 20 risk factors for disadvantaged communities identified by the Youth Justice Board (2008: 20–1). Nine regional support officers had been appointed. In 2009, a *Girls Get Moving* fitness week had been introduced to encourage them.

The sustained support for a decade is to be applauded, but in the recession, what will happen in 2011–12? As with so many local programmes, politicians and senior civil servants who are always looking for new messages and programmes, might see it as 'done that, demonstrated that.' While this substantial effort and millions of pounds confirmed most strongly all the lessons Nichols and McCormack drew out, it added only modest further understanding. With Sport Development Officers poorly lead and represented nationally, ironically PF did more for coaching than community sports development.

Midnight basketball and other recent schemes

More recently, Nichols (2007) collated ten of his studies of sports and crime schemes, based on process analysis using scientific realism (Pawson, 2006; Weiss, 1998) to produce a theory of change. He developed a typology combining three levels of risk with three forms of intervention, using a wide range of research methods, viz:

Risk level / intervention	Tertiary – high risk	Secondary– medium risk	Primary – low risk
Pro-social development	Southtown Positive Futures West York Sports counselling ® Haffoty Wen 14 peaks ®	Fairbridge Clontarf, Australia	SPLASH long term
Deterrance			Northtown Parks for All SPLASH on school sites
Diversion		Southtown Summit	Ordinary SPLASH LA holiday schemes

Most of the schemes were short-term and small-scale. Only two, marked ® in the chart, had data on re-offending. He identified intermediate outcomes (like increased fitness, self-confidence, new peers, social responsibility) on the way to longer-term, more 'slippery' outcomes. The SPLASH schemes he examined often worked best in areas with poor youth leisure provision (see Cap Gemini, 2003). But he found little evidence of strong social capital development, like forming new friendships or involvement in exciting alternatives to crime.

In the US, a retired systems analyst, Standifer, was convinced that young black Americans needed some option in the high crime times of 10pm–2am, and created Midnight Basketball (MB) leagues offering education and other workshops and attended by the police. From a pilot in Chicago in 1989, MB grew to scores of programmes in the 1990s, some supported by the Federal Housing and Urban Development department. This led Pitter and Andrews (1997) to characterise it as part of the 'social problems industry,' working with underserved youth. Hartmann's (2001) analysis was that basketball was racially coded as black (many of its locales were black-dominated, giving the Republicans in 1994 a handle for opposing a bill including funding). Yet many of its proponents and operators, perhaps naively, saw it was just a helpful programme that the youth could afford in a capitalist system that priced them out of many recreations. Hartmann and Depro (2006) then sought to see if there were benefits from reduced crime, at a time when violent and property crimes were falling nationwide, concluding there was a statistically (5%) significant greater drop in property crime in MB cities. Coalter (2007: 110–12, 130–1) would describe this as an example of the 'sport plus' (other services and benefits) approach.

Urban Stars, funded by the Laureus Foundation, is similar to PF and offers football, boxing, weightlifting, basketball and dance and education/training to 'vulnerable' youngsters aged 13–19. Set up in three London Boroughs – Coventry and Birmingham and South Gloucestershire – where Parker et al. (nd) undertook 200 interviews and 20 focus groups, it was extended in 2011 to four other cities including Belfast and Glasgow. The unusual feature was that the Gloucestershire site was a Young Offenders Institution, while Urban

Stars involved 165 individuals. Urban Stars showed the same physical social and economic benefits already described here and educational/training successes, all of which changed the young men's and women's attitudes to their abilities and futures. They also demonstrated the crucial value of well-trained, empathetic coaches/mentors, and effective partnerships

The Chief Leisure Officers (CLOA/NCF, nd) championed such schemes with 15 examples. Projects continue to be formulated like newly-branded exercise programmes, get funding, and are heralded as a wonderful new invention when, in fact, they add little to knowledge or practice: after pilots showed short-term reductions in crime, Kickz was rolled out for three years with 11 Premiership and 91 Football league clubs offering soccer sessions in disadvantaged areas three nights a week, year-round, funded by the Football Foundation (£4.7m), Premier League (£1m) and Metropolitan Police (£3m) (*Recreation* Oct 2007: 8); Street League offers soccer for men and women over 16 in England and Scotland (Press Release, 26 August 2003).

Conclusions

Pantazis, Gordon and Levitas (eds, 2006: 277) wrote there is 'a relationship between poverty and social exclusion and risks of victimisation and disorder, as well as fear of crime.' It is easy to agree with CLR (2001) that 'there are strong theoretical arguments for a potentially positive contribution which sport can make to the propensity to commit crime,' from psychology, sociology, criminology, education and leisure studies. The fact is that schemes have often lacked focus in objectives and outcomes. Providers have also not been concerned to measure these until recently. Nor has there been any real baseline data about the sport and leisure behaviour of youngsters beyond national samples in which at-risk or offending youth are an indistinguishable minority. The SSC case study showed in a new and striking way that amongst the generally poor childhood of young offenders, leisure education was non-existent, frequent moves of house or care and of schools and limited parenting resulted in really impoverished leisure, with little or no adult support. It produced what McCormack (2000) rightly called 'a leisure underclass'.

So it can be truly said that many large-scale diversionary projects have 'vague rationales, overly-ambitious objectives and a relatively unsophisticated understanding of the variety and complexity of the causes of criminality and an absence of robust intermediate or final outcomes' (CLR, 2001: 27). The SS case study shows how difficult it is to get such data, but that the youth, the sports leaders, and the community all recognise tangible outcomes, which researchers must try to tease out from multi-sponsor, multi-strand schemes. Positive Futures and Urban Stars have tried to diligently monitor outcomes. Coalter monitored seven schemes over five years, 2004–9, funded by £3m from Comic Relief, many of which exhibited the shortcomings already demonstrated in this chapter, and were 'ill-defined interventions with hard to follow outcomes.' (2011: 5) He used programme theory based on Witt and

Crompton's (1997) protection factors mentioned above and Pawson's (2006) scientific realism, which required a clear specification of aims and outcomes, identifying necessary and sufficient conditions for success, a clear theory of behavioural change, and above all an adequate understanding of the youth's needs (Figure 9.4).

Because regular offenders incur such large costs, in terms of both their crimes and their treatment, interventions with offenders have received relatively more attention but with little better measurement. In part this is because of lack of longitudinal data, and of control groups, but also of a lack of medical style, 'double-blind' treatments which few actors in the British juvenile justice system are likely to agree to.

Few interventions have been costed; Tsuchiya (1996) suggested that community schemes were almost certainly less costly than any form of incarceration. These young lives of impoverished leisure and vandalism or crime do not develop overnight, yet schemes of a few weeks' duration are expected to reverse these 'supertanker' tendencies. Media and political scepticism, and budget pressures have either reduced the length of interventions as in SSC or transferred management, as in West Yorkshire Sports Counselling to a commercial contractor (Nichols and Taylor, 1996). Outside Positive Futures, the commitment shown in SS and Fairbridge schemes is uncommon.

CLR usefully summarised such issues:

> Evidence suggests that outreach approaches, credible leadership, 'bottom-up' approaches and non-traditional, local provision appear to have the best chance of success with the most marginal at-risk groups. A needs-based youth work approach may be more appropriate than a product-led sports development approach. Sport appears to be most effective when combined with programmes that seek to address wider personal and social development...diversion must be complemented by development.
>
> (CLR, 2001: 27–8)

The Audit Commission's (2009a) review produced an excoriating analysis and judgements which reinforce these conclusions. A 16 year old in the criminal justice system cost £200,000, but only £50,000 in support to stay out – £113m could be saved if only one in ten was kept out of further trouble. While sport and leisure 'have an important role in preventing anti-social behaviour' (p4):

- the funding system was wasteful, inefficient and bureaucratic – 'a dog's breakfast' said the Commission's chairman, with youth workers spending up to a third of their time chasing money from many unco-ordinated sources; central government should improve this;
- many projects were short term, averaging only £15,000–£47,000, with no follow-up money; commissioners should give preference to the long term;

- young people want activities that are cheap, 'cool' and easy to access, but are rarely asked for their ideas;
- more activities are needed for girls;
- high one-to-one inputs and enforcement action (like the Solent and West Yorks schemes) should be targeted to few young people for whom low-cost preventive activities have not worked.

10 Rural and urban perspectives on exclusion from sport

In this chapter I explore particular manifestations of exclusions in town and country, beginning with the more neglected topic of exclusion in rural areas and countryside recreation. With a politician's conviction, Sports Minister Richard Caborn said 'we now know that sport and arts can contribute to neighbourhood renewal' (Tackling Regeneration through sport conference, Nottingham 4 December 2001).

Rural England – idyll or exclusion?

Fourteen million English people live in rural areas, two-fifths in remote areas, 27% of whom (3.8m) do not have a car. Of 75 districts DEFRA identified as having significant economic and social disadvantage, 45 were remote (RERC, 2004). Some rural areas within commuting distance of urban labour markets in southern regions are amongst the fastest growing in economy and population. Other remote and upland areas continue to lose people, especially of working age, and because of severe competition from cheaper overseas food sources and cuts in government and EU farming subsidies, supporting services to and in villages has become increasingly difficult. Consequently, it can be said that:

> The myth of a rural idyll leads to misconceptions about the countryside, with many people finding it difficult to believe that social exclusion exists in green and pleasant surroundings.
>
> (Rural Media Company, 2000: 5)

Nothing could be further from the truth. Rural areas have somewhat fewer poorer households than urban areas (16 cf. 23% with 20 cf 29% poor children – DEFRA, 2013), but suffer from spatial disadvantage through dispersion over wide areas, leading to higher threshold costs for transport and services including sport and leisure. But they may find severe social polarisation occurring in settlements growing through 'counter urbanisation,' because of the greater purchasing power of incoming retirees, urban commuters, or 'telecottagers'. *The Times* (*Times Money* 17 September 2011: 70–1) suggested there was a rural premium of £5,000 a year for country dwelling (comprising: energy £1,000, £851 running a car, mortgage £2,000, £198 public services and £1,000 broadband costs).

Cloke, Milbourne, and Thomas (1994) were perhaps the first to explode the myth of the rural idyll, with studies in 12 areas of England and Wales making clear the extent of poverty, shortage of affordable housing, low incomes and limited job opportunities, poor access to cars (especially for women), scant public transport, few shops and pubs, and the misguided appeal of close-knit communities co-existing with crushing isolation. The bulk of those at risk of transport poverty are in rural areas (Sustrans, 2012). A third of retirees live in rural areas, reaching one in five in remote areas, but only 15% are young and one in three people have no qualifications. Eighteen per cent have limiting long-term illness. So there is a greater dependency on self-employed income, pensions and investment (CRC, 2006, 2007).

Unsurprisingly, those least likely to move off low income were single-parent families, families with no earner, and single pensioners; those most likely to do so had good educational qualifications (Dunn et al., 1998), but many did not climb far out of poverty. The CRC (2008: 5) averred that labour market conditions 'condemns [rural communities] to marginalisation against the greater economic power of the towns.' Nonetheless, overall, rural households spent 15% more a week than urban ones on recreation and culture (Pateman, 2011: 46).

The New Policy Institute (2000) divided English districts into remote rural (66, with 5.6m people, accessible rural (104 with 10.8m), and urban (the remainder with 33.1m). Its findings, adding to those above, are summarised in Table 10.1. Clearly, the urban areas had more concentrated deprivation than the rural ones, but there were more people in the lowest 10% of income in the latter, with the remote areas more deprived than the accessible. Similar patterns were found for heads of households receiving means-tested benefits, children in low-income households, unemployed people wanting paid work, and those with no educational qualifications. Rural areas had more older people dying in the winter. Fuel poverty (p 17) was higher in rural areas (34% compared to 16% in towns), because two in five households were not on the gas grid and so relied on more expensive fuels, while only half of rural people had an hourly bus service within 13 minutes' walk (DEFRA, 2013).

Brown (1999) reviewed provision of care in eight counties, reporting:

- a lack of choice, leading to people refusing services;
- some rural care services being less accessible than in towns;
- use of inappropriate services because they are local/convenient;
- reliance on historic provision even when it does not reflect known need.

One issue is that some of those elderly or low paid who are poor, nevertheless feel that there are non-monetary benefits from living in the country, yet a high proportion do not claim welfare payments to which they are entitled (Cloke et al., 1994). One of the issues all gave high priority to was choice of employment and amenity for young people.

Table 10.1 Some indicators of poverty and exclusion in English rural areas

Indicator	Remote rural		Accessible rural		Urban	
	%	mill.	%	mill.	%	mill.
% Households below 50% of average GB income	22	1.24	19	2.03	27	8.76
% children in low-income households	29	0.35	24	0.55	39	2.90
Receiving means-tested benefits	10		8		14	
Adults with no qualifications						
men	15		12		16	
women	19		17		21	
Unemployed adults wanting work	10		8		12	
Excess winter deaths						
men	20		21		20	
women	25		25		23	
Reliant on state pension/Income support	23		17		19	
couples	42		29		34	
men	52		49		50	
women						
Over 65s helped to live at home by Social Services	59		63	·	81	

Source: New Policy Institute (2000)

Sport and leisure services and participation

Lack of leisure and entertainment for rural Scottish youth was emphasized by Pavis, Platt and Hubbard (2000), pointing out that some of their deprivation was disguised by living in parental homes, usually subsidised. Such challenges are exacerbated by a paucity of a wide range of community services and amenities (Spilsbury and Lloyd, 1998). In 1998, these deficits were recorded as in Table 10.2. The only improvement was in nursery and playgroup provision, in the hope of enabling higher female employment, much of which is in tourism and services which are often seasonal and/or low paid.

The Rural Services Network (2011) recorded use of parks and open spaces by 66–88% of rural residents, and of sport and leisure centres by 32–58%, with respective satisfaction levels of 69% and only 46%.

Children in rural areas often have little space for play, especially in areas of arable farming, and feared threats from bullies and gangs of older children as much as those in cities. They also had surprisingly constrained limits on the distance they could roam unsupervised from home. In rural Northamptonshire, there were widespread complaints from youth older than thirteen about 'nothing to do' and lack of involvement in deciding priorities for local amenities (Matthews

Table 10.2 Lack of services in rural areas 1991, 1994 and 1997

Service %	1991	1994	1997
General store	41	42	42
Post Office	42	43	43
Village hall/community centre	30	29	28
Public house	N/A	30	29
Daily bus	72	71	75
Minibus/social car scheme	89	91	92
Private child nursery	93	90	86
Library (permanent or mobile)	12	16*	12
Sports field	52	N/A	50
Women's Institute branch	39	N/A	41
Youth club	67	N/A	68

* Regarded as a rogue/unreliable figure

et al., 2000). For older children, the issues are 'just somewhere to go in the evenings, like a new café or something, just where we could all be,' improved local facilities (including school swimming pools open to the public, more flexible opening hours generally), and more accessible and affordable transport (Hedges, 1999: 7, 49).

A report on social exclusion and transport pointed out that on average people travelled five times as far in a year as they did around 1950. The report also showed that while 'transport poverty' in towns affects youth under driving age in particular as well as women at night, disabled and older people, in rural areas it affects a much wider range of people 'because access to most facilities is almost impossible in some areas without a car, who are socially excluded...since they cannot fully participate, i.e., behave as the vast majority of society behaves.' Having studied 19 areas, the same report concluded 'there appear to be clear connections between transport and social exclusion' (DETR, 2000a). Sixty-four per cent of rural dwellers felt that public transport was bad in 1997–9 compared to 17% in suburbia, and nine per cent in towns (Todorovic and Wellington, 2000: 8). Although 22% of rural households had no car, the poorest tenth of the population are twice as likely to own a car of necessity as their metropolitan cousins. Country households with the lowest fifth of incomes travelled about 25 miles a week to shop, compared to 12 miles for their urban equivalents; rural old age pensioners spent 75% more on petrol a week than their urban counterparts, and the gap was even greater between the two groups of unemployed people (Boardman, 1998).

The powerful convenience of the car is shown by the fact that the numerous weekend and summer bus and train schemes to provide access to the countryside nearly all need subsidy; but some extend regular scheduled services e.g., the Kirklees Wildbus (Glyptis, Collins and Randolph, 1995). While limited diversions of passengers from cars may be possible for journeys-to-work, school, or shop, the dispersed nature of leisure destinations and the marginal cost and convenience of carrying children, picnics, pets, toys, and sports equipment makes it more difficult to persuade pleasure seekers to transfer. The 'car culture' (Linadio, 1996) is very strong.

In terms of recreational visits, the English Leisure Visits Survey 2005 (Research International, 2007) showed while 63% of adults had made a leisure visit to the countryside or coast, this was 11% down on 2002–3, though because of an increase in trip spending, their value stayed almost level. Walking and walking the dog (especially for DE groups at 24%) took the lion's share of activity, followed by cycling, while sports were minority activities at 11%. Eighty-eight per cent of trips were made by whites, four per cent by Asians, three per cent by blacks and two per cent by mixed ethnic groups, showing little change despite the Diversity review (CA, 2002) and strategy. When Natural England (NE) took over the survey, it changed the method from telephone to face-to-face interviewing, and some questions. NE (2010) reckoned the total volume had increased by seven per cent over 2005, allowing for a 2.9% increase in the population. But DE social groups continued to be low visitors (24%, with 47% not visiting). The recession had led to a major retreat from overseas holidays, and an increase of 18% in domestic trips over 2008 (CRC, 2010). In comparison, it had been suggested that visits to US National Parks were declining, but More et al. (2009) showed this was only 1.5%, mostly among 34–5 year olds, with increases by over-65s and people with incomes below $20,000 a year (maybe pensioners), a marked decline by African Americans and a noticeable one by Asian Americans.

Roebuck (2009) extrapolated Active People 2 data to suggest that 6.2m people participated in countryside sport, rising to 8.85m including recreational cycling, and hugely to 24m if including walking for recreation (the most popular countryside activity). He showed these activities were strongly gendered (64% male), socio-economically and ethnically skewed (24.1% for professionals/managers compared to 13.1% for semi- and un-skilled workers, and twice as much by whites compared to BME groups). Correlation with the Index of Multiple Deprivation (Figure 10.1), however, was modest, implying that there are other factors affecting participation. Like most sports distributions, participation declined with age though less so than for urban sports:

% participation in last month by age groups			
15–24 years	19.1	75–84 years	5.8
45–54 years	16.1	over 85 years	2.0

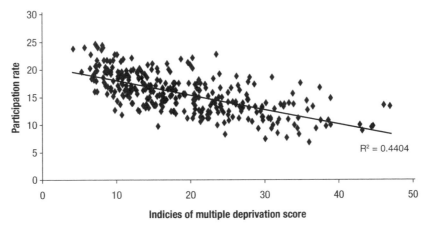

Source: SE Active People 2 database

Figure 10.1 Correlation between deprivation and participation in countryside sport

The Countryside Agency, perhaps rather tardily, had woken up to the fact that countryside visiting was dominated by affluent white people, and in response to DEFRA, commissioned the Diversity Review (CA, 2002) considering options (OPENspace, 2003) which, unsurprisingly, recommended:

- better data on excluded groups (young and older people, low-income and inner city groups including women, BME and disabled groups; a start had been made by a specific qualitative study, BEN, 2003);
- partnerships in providing arts, sport and environment projects;
- inclusive design of facilities (the Sensory Trust, 2005 reviewed the barriers and proposed standards and action plans, and Natural England 2007 offered personal case studies);
- community engagement;
- implementation of a monitoring and evaluation framework.

Uzzell, Leach and Kelay (2004) gathered providers' perceptions about under-represented groups, as follows: BME 47%, inner city dwellers 30%, disabled people 16%, low-income groups 14%, young people nine per cent, women five per cent, and the elderly five per cent. Four Diversity action research projects were commissioned and the results are summarised in Table 10.3. Responses by participants and managers included:

> The Disabled Access Forum was responsible for all the changes...We've doubled the length of our easy access paths and we've got two Trampers [all terrain vehicles].
> (Tim Bell, Shorne Woods Country Park, Stepping out project)

Sometimes I don't fancy going and yet, when you come back you think, wow that was fantastic.

(Coventry, Stepping Out participant)

For children, it doesn't matter what race or ethnicity, and they don't look at anybody's colour of their skin. It's great that children can just play.

(Beyond the Boundary participant)

All organisations from Bradford…noticed differences. They started as cricket clubs, but…have taken more responsibilities on, looking at the more social aspects of how families can be involved.

(Taj Butt, Bradford City Council, Beyond the boundary)

An accompanying policy review said 'the difficulty that structures have with managing difference…may lead to inequality. Therefore, by addressing equality issues, one is inescapably faced with diversity' (CA/EN, 2005: 4). The review concluded that while awareness had increased, action was still modest: of a wide range of projects, only a few targeted ethnic minorities (15%), older people and low-income groups (3% each), and disabled people (7%). After consultation, DEFRA (2008) produced a working group and action plan *Outdoors for all?* Belatedly, the Countryside Council for Wales commissioned a similar review

Table 10.3 Diversity action research projects

Project, purpose, participants	Engage with countryside	Involved in project design	Impact on host, partners	Comment
Beyond the Boundary – cricket and other activities for W Yorks inner city Asian youth – 620 participants, 243 youths, 470 other activities	Yes		Yes	Widened horizons – see quotation- Dales National Park new project 'Go Dales'
By all Means – access to routes and sites in Kent for disabled people – 1,500 plus carers	Yes	Yes	Yes	
Finding common ground – linking inner city Plymouth women with rural people – 1000	Yes, after slow start		Yes	Not long enough for links to become friendships
Stepping out – visiting parks, open spaces for Coventry people with mental health issues – average six per trip	Yes, once carers involved		Yes	

(Open Space, 2008), covering people with low educational attainment; and so did the Forestry Commission, identifying ignorance about use of woods by disabled children, faith groups and people of differing sexual orientations, and of practice know-how (Ambrose-Oji, 2009).

GHK (2005) estimated the use value of tourism and recreation at £5bn of a countryside total of £7.5bn, generating 192,000 jobs; in 2011 they revised figures, suggesting that recreation in the countryside was conservatively estimated at £20bn and fishing at £1bn compared to £7bn for agriculture and £2bn for forestry (HMG, 2011). HMG suggested more efforts should be made to reconnect adults and children with nature. Subsequently, Natural England (2009) exemplified that people living within 500m of accessible greenspace were 24% more likely than those farther away to meet the health benefit threshold (3x30 minutes vigorous exercise per week), suggesting just a one per cent reduction in sedentary people would cut morbidity and mortality costs by £1.4bn. The largest benefit from the forest estate was recreation, estimated at £160m a year (averaging £4 per visit), which would rise to £260m under a policy scenario focussed on it (EFTEC, 2010).

In terms of the four societal systems distinguished by Commins (1993, see pp 11–2), Shucksmith and Chapman (1998) identified failures in Scotland in three (legal, labour market and welfare) that lead to family and community exclusion:

- a sense of powerlessness and distance from policymakers;
- very few openings for graduates to be retained locally, and little or no housing for rent, especially in the public sector;
- low benefits take-up, a lothness to seek official help;
- isolation of older people whose younger kin have left the area to seek work.

Three sources gave details of schemes to combat exclusion lead by municipalities and voluntary organisations. Streich (1999) reviewed *Alternatives to the bus shelter* for young people, and identified a range of modestly-costed mobile and fixed leisure projects. In similar vein, the Local Government Association (1998) stressed the important co-ordinating and leading role local authorities play in combating exclusion, starting with anti-poverty strategies (see pp 38–9). Slee, Curry and Joseph (2001) examined 12 cases promoting social inclusion: three for disabled, six for youth, five for ethnic minorities; and identified seven key drivers of inclusion:

1 *Community driven* – giving ownership, more sustainable than 'top-down' schemes
2 *Empowering beneficiaries* – improving self esteem, not just diversionary fun
3 *Making social cohesion an objective* – while respecting cultural diversity
4 *Driven more by partnerships* – than a single organisation, sharing expertise
5 *Developed by specialist outreach staff* – in conjunction with countryside rangers
6 *Measured qualitatively* – and not just by numbers of attenders, and
7 *Effectively marketed.*

Projects were limited by finance, and sometimes by users growing dependent on providers, a situation very difficult to avoid with, for example, clients suffering from long-term conditions like mental illness (as in the Peak Park walks). Something not remarked on was that sustained action (20 years in the Mendip project) might be thanks to a committed lead agency, municipality or private bodies like the National Trust, Fairbridge or Alvis Brothers farmers. Such points were reiterated by the Carnegie Rural Development Commission, reviewing leisure centres in Scotland, a community club in Ayrshire, a village hall in Lancashire and an activity centre for 'oldsters' in Virginia, US adding 'local people must be the guiding force' (MacLean and Clunie, nd: 5).

Blair's New Labour government strongly believed capital accumulation and social cohesion can co-exist. Its vision in the White Paper *Our Countryside: the future* was four-fold:

- A living countryside, with thriving communities and access to high quality public services.
- A working countryside, with a prosperous and diverse economy, giving high and stable levels of employment.
- A protected countryside, in which the environment was sustained and all which we can enjoy.
- A vibrant countryside which can shape its own future and whose voice is heard by government at all levels.

(DTR, 2000b)

It made little mention of exclusion, but covered SureStart pilots for pre-schoolchildren, Connexions services for 16–19s, 70–100 new spaces for sports and arts projects and £25m from the Neighbourhood Renewal Fund for poorest areas; it is not clear how much was delivered and whether benefits reached the excluded or were claimed by the better-off majority. Perhaps feeling rural areas were getting fewer projects, in 2010 Sport England launched a £10m grant round the first awards, for three types of projects, as shown in Table 10.4.

In rural areas, as in urban, there has been a move from government-led/driven policies to a broader base of governance (Woods and Goodwin, 2003), but hampered by the way poverty and affluence co-exist (Schucksmith, 2001a), by the marginalisation of community and voluntary groups with their 'bottom up' approaches, and because sport and recreation are seen as less important than the 'usual suspects' of housing, agriculture, education and transport.

Table 10.4 Sport England rural themed grants

Project	Funding (£m)	Details of 3 year programme
Games		
Derbys Village Games	0.60	12,000 in 60 events, with 600 volunteers
Norfolk Village Games	0.58	9,000 in 100 teams, 1,000 new members, 140 coaches
Activity programmes		
Devon Active villages	0.60	13,000 in 156 villages
Cycle Suffolk	0.37	2,000 children, 2000 adults and 220 disabled
SW Lakes Outdoor 'n' Active	0.18	Water sport opportunities Devon, Cornwall, Somerset
Re-active8, Get back into	0.18	Coaching for 50+ in N/central Beds
Facilities & transport		
Newquay sports hub	1.68	Centre for 15,000 in deprived area
Old Northants village hall	0.03	Improve changing for teams & badminton, yoga
Bridport LC	0.30	Upgrade changing, appeal to women, girls, 55+
Hunts DC, Dash	0.23	Transport to help 8,000 residents in 17 villages

Sport and exclusion in urban England

Two types of urban area are commonly labelled 'deprived,' as recognised by the EU (EU *Official Journal* C, 180/6, 1994). First, are inner suburbs born of horse-drawn trams, with mixed uses including industries, many of which have been overtaken by third world, cheap-labour manufacture or moved out to more efficient urban fringe or small-town, single-storey sites. Here, poor housing, unemployment and low pay combine with ethnic frictions, often poor health and high crime, and some areas of high value which have been 'gentrified.' Second, are outer suburbs of overwhelmingly public housing, both high and low rise, with limited employment, shops, services and leisure and entertainment provision (like the Stoke-on-Trent estates, see pp 172–3). Comparisons of income above and in Chapter 3 show that the urban poor are poorer than their rural counterparts.

Robson et al. (2001) remarked on the growing rather than narrowing north–south divide in economic performance, making a contrast with the relatively even GDP of French provincial cities relative to Paris (Toulouse, Nantes, and Bordeaux at 61%, compared to Leeds and Liverpool at 51 and 50% of London's), wrote of a pressing need to link the prosperity of city centres to surrounding areas of impoverished households. From data on 60 cities, Lee, Sissons and Jones (2013) found the most unequal were London and its southern neighbours (Watford, Luton, Bracknell, Reading Guildford, Aldershot) and the most equal in the north and west (Sunderland, Cardiff, Peterborough) with few a high earners; while many would seek to attract high earners, this would grow inequality which was likely to increase under current trends. Seeing few policy levers on inequality, they suggested urban policymakers should focus on their deprived residents needs.

There is a vague presumption that richer areas have better sports and leisure provision, or have access to them by virtue of high car ownership. Amazingly, this has not been proven yet, beyond a small-scale attempt in two adjacent estates in Stockton-on-Tees (Boothby et al., 1981). Because of the difficulty of identifying and mapping small, public, private and voluntary operations; even Sport England's Facilities Planning database and Model ignores most of this. From their study of facilities in three sectors in six cities, Brodie, Roberts and Lamb (1991: 66–67) showed modest differences in participation in 1986–8: middle-class people were more likely to play four or more sports (25% c.f. 16%), and more likely to have increased the sports they played (38% compared to 33%). Slightly more working-class players were likely to give over eight hours a week to their sport (31% cf. 26%), but more had not changed their participation (40% cf. 36%). Brodie and Roberts (1992: 58) commented that larger gaps were found amongst the two groups of women than men.

What is remarkable in the burgeoning geographical, planning, economic and sociological literature on regeneration and urban management is how little it mentions sports, arts or leisure. Concern about recreation in the inner cities first welled up around the riots of 1977, in addition to the concerns for particular groups (then described as 'deprived of opportunity' rather than 'excluded' – disadvantaged youth, elderly, disabled, women and immigrants, DOE, 1977: 31). At that time, the needs of BME citizens were not identified, nor was poverty an issue. The Sports Council Advisory Group had alerted it to the needs of inner cities (Collins, 1977), the Greater London and South East Council (1983) characterising them as 'special areas requiring special measures.' For a few years, government put more money indirectly into urban sport and recreation through the Urban Programme (in 1982–3 £9.5m on sport and £8.5m on leisure and recreation) than the Sports Council did for the whole country (with £10m).

Yet again, the remedies suggested by Minister for Sport, Colin Moynihan, were not radically different (DOE, 1989), except that they advocated demonstration projects attractive to the private sector. Some recommendations not actioned were:

- schools devoting ten per cent of curriculum time to PE and sport (if anything the hope for two hours a week had receded);
- priority to training primary teachers (taken up in small part by the Youth Sports trust's TOPs programme in the late 1990s);
- new schemes for community use of schools (never widely taken up until the School Space initiative for primary schools after 2001);
- private-sector funding (finally developed through a few Public Finance Initiatives and Public-Private Partnerships 10–20 years later);
- schemes for older people with non-sporting agents like Age Concern (unaccountably given no priority by Sport England pp 116, 250).

During the 1990s, features of urban leisure provision were 'leisure boxes', ice rinks, multiscreen cinemas, food courts and interactive amusement halls; a few were located in major city centre regeneration schemes but many more in what Evans (1998) called the 'pleasure periphery,' accessible only by car and there fore virtually inaccessible to many inner-city residents until planning guidance was revised to give town centres priority (DETR, 1996). Concern shifted from remedying social ills to generating jobs and income: the value of major events were extolled, in the most exaggerated form by 'civic boosterism.' Yet even after initial embarrassments of underestimated costs and overestimated sponsorship for the World Student Games, the City of Sheffield gained benefits from a stream of major events (Price, 1999), and even small events in smaller places bring benefits when well planned (Collins and Jackson, 1998). UK Sport analysed benefits from both spectator/media-driven and competitor-driven events, to help bidding cities better estimate the benefits (UKS, 1999). By the time of the London Olympics in 2012, venues were planned and built in good time and to budget, and for after-use on site or elsewhere.

City Challenge regeneration projects produced evaluation reports, like for the West End of Newcastle (Robinson, nd) where £37.5m was invested in housing, new shops and employment, education, a credit union, a health resource centre, and crime prevention. Sport and leisure elements were improved open spaces, a community (Asian) festival was held, programmes for all ages were run, and arts and culture subsequently became much more important to Newcastle-Gateshead's regeneration (Miles, 2005). Remarking that in urban schemes, young people rarely had a say in decision-making, even when they were the beneficiaries, Fitzpatrick, Hastings and Kintrea (2000: 506–7) commented 'effective... involvement is undermined by both the disadvantaged material position of many young people, and the nature of intergenerational relationships whereby young people are systematically subordinated to adults.'

DETR's Index of Local Conditions combined eleven measures of deprivation, was criticised for not distinguishing deprived rural areas, and for over–emphasising London (Lee and Murie, 1998). The revised Index of Multiple Deprivation used 12 indicators at district scale. The 88 most deprived districts were shown to be:

- 14 in the Northern region, including Tyne and Wear and Teesside;
- 21 in the North West, including two in Cumbria;
- 8 in West and South Yorkshire, and Hull;
- 5 in the West Midlands conurbation and Coventry and Stoke;
- Nottingham and three other districts in the north of the county, and Derby and Leicester;
- 19 London boroughs
- Great Yarmouth and Luton in the East;
- Southampton, Portsmouth, Hastings and Brighton and Hove in the South East;
- Bristol, Plymouth, Kerrier in the South West.

(SEU, 2001a)

Change since 1991 had been small, with 46 of the worst 50 districts the same. Areas relatively improved included Leeds, Salford and some other northern metropolitan districts.

In colliery areas, Bennett, Hudson and Beynon (2000: 81) emphasised the difficulty of replacing higher-income coal jobs in a service-based economy, and the importance of local community development projects which helping people feel 'included, needed and valuable in places that they feel they are no longer of use.' The English Sports Council lobbied successfully for a mere £4m to enable the Coal Industry Welfare Organisation to help retain and develop Miners' Welfare social and recreation centres, but Gore et al. demonstrated such communities obtained fewer, smaller Lottery grants than other towns, and:

> despite traditions of social solidarity and self help...matching funding and procedures are common across Great Britain, but are suffered harder by coalfields resorts and retirement communities, while they have a lower capability to respond.
>
> (Gore, Dabinett and Breeze, 2000: 54)

Other deprived/declining areas included outer Greater London, Liverpool, and peripheral areas of West Cumbria, East Kent, East Norfolk, West Cornwall. At a smaller scale, pockets of deprivation in less deprived districts show up e.g. North Paddington in Westminster, and Kesteven in Lincolnshire.

Once the Cabinet Office's new Social Exclusion Unit produced *Bringing Britain together* in 1998 (see Chapter 3), there was an agenda for 18 Policy Action Teams (PATs). The Action Team for Sport and the Arts (PAT10) determined it would be the first to report, on:

- best practice in using sport, arts and leisure to engage people in poor neighbourhoods, particularly those who may feel most excluded, such as disaffected young people and people from ethnic minorities;
- how to maximise the impact on poor neighbourhoods of government spending and policies on sport, arts and leisure (DCMS, 1999: 5).

It commissioned research reviews from Collins et al. (1999) on sports and Shaw (1999) on the arts. With case studies, it looked at the sector's contributions to health, crime, employment and education, economic development, stronger communities, and an emphasis on people, not buildings. It identified two reasons why past initiatives had not 'set in motion a virtuous circle of regeneration:

- a tendency to parachute solutions in from outside, rather than engaging local communities, and
- too much emphasis on physical renewal instead of better opportunities for local people.

(DCMS, 1999: 28)

PAT10 (*ibid*: 34) also identified seven barriers to wider contributions to neighbourhood renewal:

1   Too much focus on funders' requirements (inputs and outputs) than on recipients' needs (outcomes).
2   Funding too often short term, rather than a longer period of 'mainstreaming' sufficient to sustain benefits.
3   Arts and sports bodies tending to regard community development as an 'add-on', a secondary activity.
4   Other regeneration bodies regarding sport and arts as peripheral, and regeneration neglecting 'self-help' community capacity building.
5   A lack of evaluation of outcomes for community groups and those at risk of exclusion.
6   Schools not playing a full role in developing participation habits.
7   Poor links between sports and arts bodies and organisations involved in regeneration.

Collins et al. (1999) had stressed poverty as the single largest cause of exclusion which exacerbated factors of gender, age, ethnicity, and disability, but PAT10 decided without explanation to focus on the latter two. It set out nine principles to guide sports and arts in regeneration processes (*ibid*: 40–47):

1   valuing diversity (stressed in relation to ethnicity and disability);
2   embedding local control;
3   supporting local commitment;
4   promoting partnerships where all interests had equal stakes;
5   defining common objectives in relation to citizens' needs;
6   working flexibly as situations changed;
7   securing sustainability, 'for services, not projects';
8   pursuing quality from recreation to the highest professional performances;
9   connecting with the mainstream of arts and sports.

The 18 PAT action plans generated 569 recommendations, some major and involving many agencies. When the government did its promised audit, it had accepted 86% of them, partly accepted or was still considering 12% and had only rejected two per cent; the figures for sport and arts being 40, 7 and nil respectively (DCMS, 2001a).

Pursuing its accountability, SEU (2001a) produced details on actions in response to PAT10. This demonstrated eloquently the very fine-grain and short-term targets to which central policy was then working. It also showed the pace of change expected by government of its partners, to which I shall return in Chapter 12. Kate Hoey, then Minister for Sport, stressed 'the social inclusion agenda is firmly embedded in DCMS policies' (SEU, 2001b: 130–1) for all culture sectors and all the agencies it oversaw, as well as all the Lottery distributors.

PAT10 sought to draw its recommendations to the attention of the other PATs, in particular those on jobs (1 recommendation), anti-social behaviour (8), community self-help (9), schools plus (11), young people (12), learning lessons (16), joining it up locally (17) and better information (18). Nothing specific was picked up except: PAT11 picking up leisure needs in extended school hours (recommendation 3); an extension of Playing for Success (see p 87) (recommendation 5); PAT13 on Shops (SEU, 2000) had comments relating to exclusion and leisure in pointing up the withdrawal of retailing choice, of banks, and public telephones. This was reinforced by Forrest and Kearns (1999: 36) who commented that such trends 'meant that these neighbourhoods were no longer self-sufficient for many of the functions people sought from them.'

A background report to an urban White Paper parallel to the rural one, *The state of England's cities* (Robson et al., 2001: 16, 20–23), identified three important trends:

- a continued strong *urban exodus*, the eight UK conurbations gaining 364,000 people in 1991–7 through net births, and 370,000 through migration from overseas, but losing 543,000 people moving out;
- *dangerous mosaics* of social inequality, only 15 of 50 poverty indicators improving during 1994–9, long-term ill people rising from 3m to 3.6m during 1991–8; while districts with 10% above-average mortality grew from 28% to 39%, and poor children became more concentrated in particular schools, burdening them from meeting improvement targets;
- *the particular impact of deprivation on children,* with 208 wards where more than half lived in households dependent on means-tested benefits; and larger numbers under-performed at school, a problem growing as they aged from six to 15.

The issue of joined-up thinking about social and economic issues had already been stressed by Alcock et al. (1998), while Blowers and Young (2000) criticised town planning for mainly reinforcing market trends, and neglecting social matters.

In 2000, DETR produced another urban White Paper, *Our towns and cities: The future*, with provisions affecting sport and culture as shown in Table 10.5. It said:

A healthy, vibrant cultural, leisure and sporting life enhances cities in a positive way. It helps to create places where people want to be, are proud of and can achieve their potential. It contributes to a city's uniqueness and diversity.

(DETR, 2000B paragraph 6.29)

Table 10.5 Government policy actions for urban sport, 2000

Decisions prior to the Urban White Paper
• Scrapping entrance charges to English national museums and galleries for children and pensioners
• One million visitors to artistic experience under Arts Council of England's New Audiences programme
• Strategic municipal planning via preparing Local Cultural Strategies
• Starting a competition for UK Capital of Culture 2008
New measures 2000
• £130m for Space for Sports and Arts scheme for primary schools in selected LEAs
• National standards for public libraries regarding location, access, opening hours
• DCMS Culture online website
• Extending access to national museums and galleries, free for benefit recipients, disabled and £1 only for all other visitors
Improving access in deprived areas
• New Creative Partnerships for access for every school pupil, £40m over two years
• Commitment by ACE grant holders to extending community impact
• New Sport Action Zones where basic provision falls below 'acceptable standards'
• Reallocation of half Sport England's Community Lottery funds to areas of 'greatest needs'

Source: DETR, 2000

The government claimed to be making £33bn available for major services, of which £200m (0.6%) was for leisure, culture and sport. Action 5 identified five Public Service Agreement targets:

• raise significantly, year on year, the average time spent on sport and physical activity by those aged 5 to 16;
• introduce at least 12 Creative [arts] Partnerships by 2004 targeted on deprived areas;
• increase by 500,000 the number of people experiencing the arts;
• ensure all public libraries had internet access by end 2002;
• increase numbers of children attending museums and galleries by a third by 2004.

These clearly reflected some personal concerns of the Secretary of State, Chris Smith. Despite sports minister Kate Hoey's claim to close relationships with education minister Estelle Morris it was notable that the first target did not confront the continuing decline in curriculum time for PE identified in Chapter 4 (p 63).

Understanding whether areal deprivation affects individuals is an important issue in deciding whether area-based initiatives are worthwhile. McCulloch modelled ward-level effects of deprivation on employment, family finances, social status and likes/dislikes about the neighbourhood, and discovered living in social housing clearly raised the chances of an adverse life outcome (i.e., poor areas compounded disadvantages of poor people). But at ward level area influences on individual outcomes were weak, so that 'it was unclear whether policies should aim at improving neighbourhoods, helping people to move out, or at improving job opportunities' (McCulloch, 2001).

In an update on the 1998 Neighbourhood Renewal strategy, culture, sport and art had a brief mention under improving skills – itemising programmes for priority areas like Sport Action Zones (SAZs), £750m for facilities, and 12 Creative [arts] Partnerships (SEU, 2001b: 39); poor social outcomes in deprived areas suggested services may be worse at meeting residents' needs. Testing whether this reflected greater needs, or a lower starting position, fewer resources, Duffy (2000) identified long lists of services used in deprived and non-deprived areas (Table 10.6). Needless to say, in deprived areas buses, GPs, hospitals, and DSS offices were used more often than in other places, libraries and leisure centres somewhat less.

Walpole and Collins (2010) demonstrated how sport had revived the faith of Braunstone, Leicester's (both a Beacon Council scheme and an SAZ) residents in the city council. Managers of Bradford's Trident scheme (2004) were equally sure of its benefits in an area with 60% BMEs. As a number of area-based initiatives (Chapter11) came to an end, Power (2009: 132) commented that 'spreading the untied resource more thinly over bigger areas will not extend…achievements and may actually cancel out positive impact. Motivation at the local level is hard to sustain without the 'carrot' of extra dedicated funding.' Despite New Deal for Communities resources for 39 areas (£50m per area of 10,000 people) over ten years, seven of which were linked with SAZs, Lawless et al. (2010) found only small changes compared to other areas.

Perhaps because of Sport England's advocacy based on descriptive case studies, DCMS did not commission a report on the impact of sport as they did for arts and culture (Evans and Shaw, 2004). In 2004, it reported on eight examples of partnerships involving sport, remarking 'neighbourhood renewal and sport can be thought of as overlapping worlds each with its own silos of structures, decision-makers and specialist funding streams' (SQW Ltd, 2004: iv), and usefully identified seven key barriers, many not new, viz:

1   Lack of interest in sport by many regeneration bodies.
2   Interventions often lacked focus.
3   Links between the two worlds were often not clearly expressed or understood.
4   Information and incentives to 'bend' mainstream programmes were often missing.
5   Many areas lacked a contextual strategic framework.
6   Mainstream funding agencies were inconsistently involved, exemplifying PCTs.
7   Voluntary sports clubs were difficult to engage.

In all this, and with relatively small financial contributions, it is difficult to see anything but a marginal position for culture, leisure and sport in regeneration, despite numerous benefits identified by Coalter, Allison, and Taylor (2000) and

Table 10.6 Urban leisure-related services used at least once a month

	Deprived areas (%) n=380	Other areas (%) n=3,796
Used more frequently in deprived areas		
Local buses	85	75
Public parks	59	53
Youth and community centres	15	9
GP	51	33
NHS Hospital	14	8
Dept of Social Security	19	9
Used less frequently in deprived areas		
High St banks/Building societies	76	92
Libraries	35	42
Leisure centres	26	33

Source: Duffy (2000)

LGA (2001). Alcock et al. (1998) did recommend DETR to consider allocating resources according to need and not by bidding (an approach that Oatley (1998) persuasively argued always and systematically disadvantaged poor and deprived people because good bids require professional preparation, matching funding and advocacy skills, and time and persistence. Yet, despite new technology, artistic and sporting activities cannot be done virtually, they require the face-to-face contact which is the basis of social capital and of city life. Hall (1998: 1089), crystal-ball gazing, asked whether the future creative city was doomed to comprise 'islands of affluence surrounded by seas of poverty and resentment.'

Byrne (1998: 82), reviewing regeneration in North Shields and Wallsend pointed out that 'community involvement, especially in the more deprived communities is often very fragile and…often far from being an equal partner in most local partnerships,' suggesting that powerful agencies can use community development to camouflage urban land development deals.

Sport England (2001c) wished to maximise benefits from section 106 agreements for betterment contributions from developers under the 1980 Planning Act, linking policy to obesity and a London 2012 legacy, arrangements which yielded £21m in 2006–7 and £31m in 2008–9. The problem is that areas with low growth offer limited opportunities for such agreements; only 21 advisory documents from LAs in Yorks and the NE, compared to 106 in the S and E. In 2012 it produced a Sports Facilities Calculator to identify how many sports halls, pools, indoor bowls centres, and artificial pitches would be needed in major developments under the 2008 Community Infrastructure Levy.

There can be little doubt of the honest desire for change represented in New Labour's documents; the Prime Minister said 'our vision is that within 10–20 years, no one should lose out because of where they live. We want to see people living in our poorest neighbourhoods enjoying the same opportunities to build a decent life which most of us enjoy' (DCMS *Press Release 011*, 15 January 2001).

The Coalition's expenditure cuts fall hard on deprived areas in cities: SIGOMA (LGA, 2010) represents major local authorities, a quarter were in the most deprived tenth, with poorer health, education, more public sector jobs, weaker tax bases and lower revenues, but they had already lost £1.2bn in health funding, £0.6bn 'damping' of Rate Support Grant formula finance, and had £879 less annual finance per pupil than London; and in 2010–11 they were to lose £12.61 per citizen compared with an English average of £8.75.

Lister, Reynolds and Webb (2011) for Shelter suggested that Welfare Reform Bill proposals would make much private rented housing in areas of lower unemployment and better job availability too expensive, pushing people out of a third of England (London, the East, East Midlands, and the southwest) to regions with fewer job prospects in the north, where some homeless were already re-housed, far from their home communities. We look further at such matters in Chapter 12.

11 Policy implementation

Partnerships, stronger citizenship and social capital through sport?

This chapter has to be taken as a very preliminary look at lines of sports policy, for even ten years since it was first written, it is too early to make any mature and sensible judgements about impacts, let alone outcomes; anyone who doubts that should look at DCMS' meta-evaluation of the 2012 Games to spot the numerous holes and guesses despite the consultants' efforts (Grant Thornton et al., 2013). As Ray Pawson (2004) said, in sport one is facing 'ill-defined interventions with hard-to-follow outcomes.' Yet politicians want to be judged by results, however premature, and DCMS, unwisely in my view, in 2001 commissioned research on good practice in inclusory policy for sport; not surprisingly since outcome measures had not been agreed and baseline studies not undertaken, its consultants are struggling to make a satisfactory narrative. In the first section, I look at five aspects of policies that have to be thought through and well-constructed if they are to have any chance making a difference. Then picking up threads from Chapter 2, I examine New Labour's concepts of the Third Way and the crucial role the voluntary sports club system has to play as a communal form of social capital, if that idea is to have any validity, and at structural and attitudinal issues which manifest both strengths and weaknesses in the British system, certainly when compared with others in Europe.

Implementing inclusion policies and programmes

In this section, I will deal with a number of aspects of inclusion policies and programmes:

1 the policy lifespan;
2 outputs, outcomes and their measurement;
3 place and people policies;
4 sustaining programmes;
5 sport cannot go it alone – the importance of partnerships.

1. The policy lifespan

Every new minister or agency chief executive comes into office with an overblown expectation about the scale, volume and speed of change they can exert. Moreover, there is pressure not only to modify and re-badge programmes to give them more appeal and currency; one of the most successful affecting leisure was the programmes that started with the Manpower Services Commission for training and work experience for unemployed youth in the 1980s, which underwent three major transformations before being replaced. PAT10 (DCMS, 1999) and Collins et al. (1999) commented on the problem of both the government and Sport England producing too many programmes – what SEU (1998) together had called 'initiative-itis' – and of removing resources and priority from existing to new programmes too quickly. One respondent to Church et al.'s study argued that:

> sports development is continually inundated by initiatives. One after the other, after the other and often these initiatives are a means to actually secure funding. They're not necessarily the rationale for involvement in these initiatives which based on what you've identified as a result of a local community audit consultation. In other words, you run with an initiative because it offers money, then your priorities get screwed, and suddenly you're actually doing something which doesn't meet the priority needs of your local community
>
> (Church et al., 2002: 18)

There is also a tendency to build new organisations and structures which take time to set up and bed in.

This tendency has three effects – the cost and effort of design and promotion does not pay back its full benefit, if it is a national initiative it never reaches partners slow to respond, and existing partners, especially local authorities, become exasperated or confused by shifting priorities. One of the exceptions to this was the *50+ and all to play for* campaign for sport for older people which was low cost, its documentation proving so useful that it was reprinted three times, and is still manifest in some local programmes even though Sport England long since lost interest in that group (Chapter 6).

Programmes intended to produce attitude and behaviour changes cannot come to fruition quickly or easily. In this author's 41 years of experience of running and evaluating projects, a typical pattern has been:

> *Year 1* – Pilot/demonstration set up, with three-year grant relationships established, market research done, programmes launched; there may be a 'honeymoon' effect of early take-up.
>
> *Year 2* – Programmes may be extended or new partners brought in, usage settles into a pattern; if pleased, sponsors publicise by anecdote or description, and other bodies start to copy (Action Sport for urban youth was a typical example).

Year 3 – Staff see the end of the project, and leave as soon as they can get another job, reducing the capacity to deliver (typically sports for delinquent youth); evaluation, if any, starts, but by now numerous copy-cat schemes create 'noise'. Slow adopters soon cease staff interest.

Year 4 – Some local sponsors 'mainstream' the scheme, but often with reduced resources and with adapted, often narrower aims and methods to accommodate it in host departments or programmes; any evaluation is published with caveats as well as strong points, mostly about outputs and value for money. It is not widely disseminated and readers tend to play down the caveats, because they wish to start their own similar programmes, or move on to new initiatives in pursuit of grants.

Any outcomes of the initial programme will post-date its official operation, and those of its imitators or adopters will only happen in Year 7 onwards. On such a timescale, councillors/ministers and civil servants/staff receiving the outcomes research are usually different from those who commissioned it, and the context for receiving and applying lessons has changed, as have political and professional priorities. This is a wasteful model. The Community Projects Foundation, involved in such work since before Second World War, will only share resources if they are able to be committed for five to seven years. In any case, sustained interests in participation, major changes in athletic performance, or generation of jobs, take seven to ten years to establish.

Collins et al. (1999) pointed out that most grant-aid schemes lasted only for three years, and that Research Councils will often reject applications for outcome research because they believe government sponsors should have committed the resources for evaluation up-front. PAT10 recommended timescales should be extended to at least five years, which gives more of them a fighting chance of achieving outcomes. Of programmes in the last 30 years only Champion Coaching and PESSCL (both Chapter 4), and Positive Futures (Chapter 8) had such a span and only the last was monitored.

On the third issue of new organisation; two comments can be made. First, much or even all of the first year of any programme is taken up with setting up structures and appointing people, as was clear from Active Sports partnerships and Sport Action zones. After four years of lobbying from Sport England and the Coal Industry Welfare Organisation, the Tory government eventually found a tiny sum of money to help some Welfare clubs survive and adapt as community organisations, after their pits closed (Collins and Reeves, 1995). But many trustees had long since lost heart and closed, leaving a need for new investment in buildings and organisations.

2. Outputs, outcomes and their measurement

It has been said many times recently that focus has been over-concentrated on outputs – like the number of projects or partners, the volume of use (not even the number of individual customers or frequency of use) or the number of clients completing a course, rather than the outcomes of personal or social change which are often embodied in policy aims by politicians or senior managers and expected by the media and the public. Coalter (2000: 48; 2011) distinguished *intermediate* outcomes (physiological or mental health, identity and self-esteem, well-being and social learning) from *strategic* ones (such as reduced anti-social behaviour, positive social relationships or involvements in building civic structures, or better educational performances). He asked whether participation must precede inclusion, which is a good question; but evidently this link can work both ways: many sports volunteers start helping in a small way with fundraising and making tea while their children play; but others initially brought along as companions or helpers may become participants.

It is clear that still there is little outcome measurement in any rigorous or reliable fashion (Coalter et al., 2000, Priest et al., 2008). This is partly because of the length of the policy span just discussed, and partly because of the low priority and minute funding available from sponsors. Following Pawson (2006), he argued (Coalter, 2007: 19–23, 2011) that effective evaluation needed a clear *logic model* of the steps and mechanisms of an intervention that link inputs through outputs to outcomes (Figure 11.1). It also needed a *theory of the change* expected, which might be in national policy/system-wide, or in an organisation, or in the behaviour of individuals.

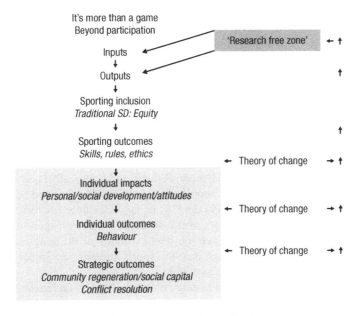

Figure 11.1 Inputs outputs and outcomes according to Coalter

Following Best Value, in 2005–8 a new set of Audit Commission tests for LAs appeared – Comprehensive Performance Assessment; here, sport suffered for lack of indicators compared to libraries; overall six out of ten authorities improved, and those with top scores grew from six per cent to 21%, but with 51 councils still at the basic level 2, this was the weakest sector in CPA (Audit Commission, 2009b). Then the Innovation and Development Agency (IDeA, 2008) produced a development framework for sport and culture and a toolkit. A review of its adoption (ERS, 2010) found it depended on:

- political and managerial leadership – much weakened as these services were 'brigaded' into larger departments of education, community, environment;
- how far performance improvement was embedded in the authority;
- what human and financial resources were available;
- whether sport and culture were a local priority.

Another factor was the extent of support from Non-Departmental Public Bodies, and here Sport England had provided the Active People data and Diagnostic and segmentation tool, and Quest accreditation; all were used by seven out of ten LAs, satisfying nine out of ten, much higher figures than for arts, heritage or libraries.

A revised toolkit was produced, through which LAs could self-assess their services under eight themes and 32 criteria:

1   Leadership
2   Strategy
3   Community engagement
4   Partnership working
5   Resource management
6   People management
7   Service development, marketing and delivery
8   Performance measurement, improvement and learning (IDeA, 2011)

One study I believe shows a long-term outcome was undertaken in the inner cities by Brodie and Roberts (1992; and Brodie, Roberts and Lamb, 1991). They looked at activity patterns of a sample of people using public, voluntary and commercial sports provision in six inner cities in the UK, using interviews, life history charts, and fitness tests to measure changes over a short, 12–18 month span. In fact, the life history analysis, I believe, gave the best evidence of the long-term policy effects of Sport for All, even though in 1995, sports minister Ian Sproat denied to parliament that such evidence was available.

Figures 11.2 and 11.3 show the average number of sports undertaken between the ages of ten and 20 by three age cohorts of men and women. It can be clearly seen that the average number of sports increased in successive cohorts for both sexes. Brodie and Roberts commented:

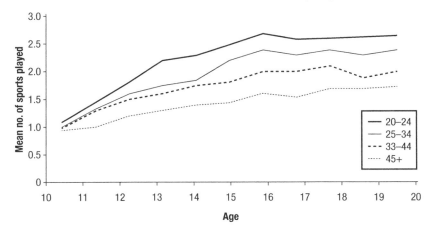

Figure 11.2 Average number of sports played when aged 10–20 by male cohorts

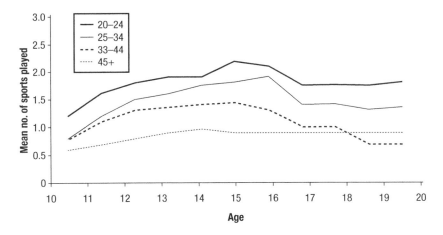

Figure 11.3 Average number of sports played when aged 10–20 by female cohorts

Such an increase is the delayed, but according to our evidence, reliable by-product of introducing higher proportions of successive cohorts of young people to a wide range of sports. If provisions continue to increase in the future – we are confident that the adult participation rate will continue its upward course. This vindicates the liberalisation of the physical education curriculum in schools.

(Brodie and Roberts, 1992: 80–1)

Analysis by Sport England (2013: 14) confirmed that playing only a single sport made people vulnerable to drop-out. I add, however, that while the liberal curriculum might be the genesis, it could only continue because of the growth of an ever-wider range of local public, voluntary club and commercial sport provisions over the same period.

There are difficulties in measurement, as in many social policy areas (Coalter, 2007) – the outcomes are long term, broad, qualitative and affected by many other influences than sport, many groups have been self-selecting and evidence self-reported, control groups and longitudinal studies are rare, difficult and costly to organise, and qualitative data has been scattered and under-rated by policymakers. Also, as Coalter (2001b) commented, there has been a lack of theorisation of the mechanisms by which sport may bring benefits – to whom, under what circumstances and conditions, as Patrikkson (1995: 128) advised the Council of Europe. But one cannot expect the levels of proof that laboratory research produces in medical and physical sciences. Having examined the social impact of library services, Matarasso (1998: 5) wrote 'the decision-making processes of public administration…depend on the balance of probability rather than the elimination of reasonable doubt.'

After all of this, in the real world, evidence of impact is not the only basis decision-makers use; others include personal experience and the opinions of senior colleagues, alongside ideology, value judgements, financial stringency, economic theory, political expedience, intellectual fashions, competing demands and the power and influence of stakeholders (Davis and Howden-Chapman, 1996).

3. Place and people policies

As previously mentioned (see Chapter 2 pp 22–3 and Chapter 3 p 34 and pp 218–20), government has worked through place and people policies. The former used to be operated through a planning process, but under the Thatcher and Major governments became part of a bidding culture, that can be shown to be: profligate in the wasted effort of rejected bids (John, Ward and Dowding, 2004); unfair because it systematically disadvantaging poor areas where the social capital of professional help is scarce (as shown in the coalfields, Gore, Dabinett and Breeze, 2000); and often misguided in that most deprived people are found outside designated areas (Oatley, 1998). Neither is there evidence of economic 'trickle-down' effects from rich to poor, or from poor peripheral to core areas (Smith, 1985).

Powell, Boyne and Ashworth (2001: 253) said that 'attempts to secure greater levels of territorial justice or spatial equity in welfare provision have formed a consistent – if not always coherent – part of government policy for the last 50 years'. The SEU (1998) argued that public spending redistribution focused more on the results than the causes of poverty, and more on regenerating the physical environment than the prospects of residents. Powell and colleagues said 'this means tackling poor schools, adequate adult skills, lack of job opportunities and childcare, improving health, and providing affordable local leisure activities for children and teenagers' (2001: 251).

HMG listed over 50 Area-Based Initiatives (ABIs), which it reduced, rolling a dozen from several Departments into the Single Regeneration Budget, noting it

Table 11.1 Increases in participation in Barrow and Liverpool Sport Action Zones

Category	Barrow		Liverpool	
	2001–2	*2005–6*	*2001–2*	*2005–6*
All	66	*72*	60	*65*
Aged over 50	53	*60*	36	*48*
Men	72	75	66	*72*
Women	61	*69*	54	59
White	66	*72*	60	*66*
Black/Ethnic Minority	N/A	N/A	56	59
C2DE social group	61	*67*	43	*53*

(Taking part at least four times in average four-week period, including walking); statistically significant at 95% interval in italic)

Source: IPSOS/MORI, 2006 p06

was locally that the greatest 'congestion' of initiatives was felt' (RCU, 2002: 225). As time went on, it became as much a matter of social cohesion as regeneration (Home Office, 2003); Alcock (2004) questioned whether these were a matter of policy or local participation. Nonetheless, the Blair government spawned policy-specific Action Zones for Health and Education, on top of which were local partnerships for crime reduction, community safety, and Beacon and Pathfinder councils to be models of delivery. To this mixture, Sport England added 12 Sport Action Zones and 45 mainly county-based Active Sports partnerships (Sport England, 2001c). There were 12 SAZs, ranging enormously in size, from 11,000 people in Braunstone, south Leicester (see Figure 3.3), through 88,000 in wards in Lambeth and Southwark, to 690,000 in the Nottinghamshire-Derby coalfield, and 852,000 in three Metropolitan boroughs in South Yorkshire. Each had an exchequer-paid manager. IPSOS/MORI's (2006) findings on the impact of four SAZs (Barrow-in-Furness, Liverpool, Bradford and Luton) revealed statistically significant increases in participation in the first two, both deprived areas, especially among over 50s, white people and C2DE (semi-skilled and unskilled groups) but not in the latter two, for reasons they could not diagnose (Table 11.1).

Soon after these results were combined with Sport England's monitoring of grants via the Active Communities Development Fund, (Hall Aitken, 2008) concluded there were 13 critical success factors in driving up participation locally:

1 appoint a highly motivated charismatic leader who can quickly establish credibility;
2 establish clear strategic direction supported by a systematic needs assessment;
3 create a focussed, paid delivery team, engaged with the local community;
4 build strong partnerships in and beyond sport;
5 empower local people through a listening, bottom-up approach;
6 promote local volunteering capacity, while expecting turnover of individuals;
7 invest in facilities but focus on people as keys to success;

8   provide small grants to engender goodwill and trust;
9   ensure communications and marketing are tailored to local groups;
10 run low-cost taster sessions, and ensure progression routes;
11 offer a wide diversity of activities tailored to what works for different groups;
12 make local identity/community work for you – be part of 'us'; not 'them'; and
13 make it last – build a culture of sustainability and self help.

In his foreword (Sport England, 2006), Lord Carter wrote of them:

> In effect there are no real surprises. They all represent good community sports development principles and practices. However, what is highly significant is: firstly, how these factors have been strategically applied together in a concerted and focussed way over a five year period; and secondly, because of our focussed and continued research we can say with confidence that this way of working has led to real participation increases amongst some of our most hard to reach priority groups.

Walpole and Collins (2010) demonstrated that Braunstone SAZ incorporated all of these, after seven year's work that was harder and slower but more successful than the local team ever imagined but that was ultimately more than a job: 'it's about trying to improve people's lives.' These lessons could be used in any small community, they have been known for over half a century to the Community Development movement (Taylor, Barr and West, 2000). The keynote was the personal contact made by SD professionals with citizens, and professionals and residents understanding each are experts in their own sphere who need each other and must talk and listen together frequently. It has to be said that a *leitmotif* of the ConDem coalition is its inability to listen and take notice of citizens' responses to policy ideas.

While area policies are useful political tools for rewarding councils and MPs who support a particular government, or areas that make a good case for special concentrated funding (like the EU's RESIDER, RECHAR funds for economic restructuring in steel, coal, textile and armaments industries). Despite the above-mentioned successes, structural problems remain – of pathologising areas of social exclusion and 'blaming the victims', and neglecting pockets of poverty in affluent places. Alcock (2003: 16) concluded 'area based agency could not combat structural inequality and deprivation and that social and economic policies were also needed to address these broader social forces and the power structures that maintained them.'

4. Sustaining programmes

Apart from too-frequent cycling of programmes for political novelty, there is the issue of trying to ensure that each is a good sustained investment. For example, of the Sports Council's demonstration projects, the Active Lifestyles project in Coventry schools had a long follow-up and demonstration effect, whereas the successful women's sports promoters inside Cambridgeshire's Women's

Institutes, could not be 'mainstreamed' because the WI saw no feasible structure for employing a paid promoter in every county.

It seems likely that sustained inclusion is more likely when:

- local people 'own' the work and take active leadership roles – that is, it is driven 'bottom-up' and not 'top-down';
- it gives citizens and local agencies personal and civic freedom and confidence to go on;
- a main sponsor commits core funding for others to match or managers to 'lever' contributions; of Slee, Curry and Joseph's (2001) cases of good practice in countryside recreation, those surviving more than a few years had such a sponsor – a District or County council, the National Trust etc.

It is usually very important to develop outreach methods, by Sport Development Officers and other professionals (McDonald and Tungatt, 1991), which may mean training in the skills of community development (Bryant, 2001). Houlihan (2001: 110) averred 'there is considerable potential for sport and recreation professionals to support and facilitate the construction of citizenship as a bottom-up process.'

Lindsey (2008) conceived of three forms of sustainability, for:

- individuals – as in Positive Futures (pp 186–7);
- communities;
- organisations – as in Sport Action Zones.

One associated issue is that effective programmes almost universally have strong, dedicated leadership/entrepreneurial skills, at least in their start-up and consolidation stages (Collins et al., 1999). This need was recognised more than two decades ago by the Minister for Sport's Review Group (DoE, 1989).

5. Sport cannot 'go it alone': the crucial nature of partnerships

Pierre and Peters claimed that the state is:

> restructuring in order to be able to remain a viable vehicle in an era of economic globalisation and increasing sub-national institutional dynamics...the Blair government is to some extent 'decentring-down', arguing for mobilising stake-holders and partners, diversifying delivery forms, seeking participation. But the pattern is still with desire for central control by finance and regulation; it is only a limited move from 'power over' to 'power to', from 'rowing' to 'steering.'
>
> (Pierre and Peters, 2001: 196)

Rhodes (2000), reviewing changes in government in the 1990s, took a stronger line on how far the state had been 'hollowed out' and weakened, using nine aphorisms (Table 11.2). He also drew nine parallel lessons regarding its ability to work through dispersed networks, and felt the biggest problem was for politicians

Table 11.2 From government to governance?

Changes in the 1990s	Lessons of the 1990s
• from government to governance • more control over less • the hollowing out of the state from above (EU) and below (cities) • the weakness of the core executive • unintended consequences (e.g., in marketisation) • the loss of trust (e.g. between clients and contractors in Tendering) • it's the mix that matters • diplomacy and 'hands-off' management • from de-concentration to devolution	• fragmentation limits the centre's command • regulation substitutes for control • external dependence further erodes the executive's ability to act • fragmentation undermines the centre's ability to co-ordinate • knowledge/policy learning has a juggernaut quality, changing problems as policies seek to solve them • marketisation corrodes trust, co-operation and shared professional values, undermining • the networks it only partly replaces • markets, bureaucracies and networks all fail, so, 'if it ain't broke don't fix it' • steering networks needs diplomacy, so hands-off management is the only effective model • decentralisation is a key mechanism for developing holistic government

Source: Rhodes, 2000

and senior civil servants to learn to let go. Taylor (1997) provided one illustration, describing the DNH/DCMS as a body functioning at 'arms-length but hands-on'; officers like David Pickup, Director of the English Sports Council in the late 1980s and early 1990s would agree very much with the second part, but would doubt the first.

In complex modern states, the best sports scheme will not have a widespread or long-lasting effect if promoted by sports interests in isolation. Another 'buzzword' of New Labour was that of partnerships, Atkinson (2000: 1051) calling them 'a holy grail.' The Audit Commission (2009c) wrote of New Labour moving 'from encouraging to mandating' them; Gordon and Hanafin 1998: 20) even spoke of 'partnership-itis.' The literature in Britain is now considerable (e.g., DETR, 1998, Carley et al., 2000), and grows in Europe (e.g., Geddes, 1997). In most current lottery and agency grant-aid schemes, making partnerships is a condition of awards.

The greater the number of partners, the more complex the resolving of resource allocation, and of managers satisfying the expectations of all stakeholders, whose priorities, timescales, styles of operation, may differ. Carley et al. (2000: 25) commented 'partnerships can lose direction or fall apart upon public squabbling between partners who fail to agree a common agenda.' McDonald (2005) in England and Parent and Harvey (2009) in Canada stated the need to make sports partnerships fit the strategic or operational situation. Partners bring differing power and resources to the table. Discussing urban regimes of municipal government and business that seek to use sport and its arenas to generate income, Henry (2001: 18) thought they might neglect social production and have 'significant negative implications for less powerful groups in society.' Taylor (2001) graphically showed how recreational swimming and teaching declined in Sheffield with the closure of local pools after the building of Ponds Forge 50m pool, even while the city attracted lucrative national and international events.

At a national scale, Sport England proposed a single delivery system where two links in the national policy chain were important – County Sports Partnerships (CSPs – Sport England, 2007a) and Community Sports Networks (CSNs, or Sport and Activity Alliances as some were called – Sport England, 2007b). Forty-nine CSPs developed quite sizeable teams, covering facility development, sports development, the local manifestations of PESSCL/YP projects, and training developments; they handled the Active Sports (Enoch, 2010). The DoH even briefly contributed £240,000 to each for promoting physical activity; yet, in 2009, the Coalition wanted to cut them completely as they were considered to be 'expensive,' but they survived, Sport England arguing for and receiving a basic £10m Lottery-funded common 'core offer' plus what they could raise through partnerships ('enhanced services'). MacIntosh (2009) argued that there were tensions and misunderstandings between being a regional advocate and deliverer (e.g., of training for coaches). Charlton (2010) revealed Lancashire CSP's evolution process, producing a tight core and wider linkages, a configuration also found by Lindsey (2006) and Houlihan and Lindsey (2008) in New Opportunities for PE and Sport (NOPES, Chapter 4). Knight Kavanagh and Page's (2005) monitoring of six CSPs found growth in club membership, coaches and the use of club development plans. Community Sports Networks (Sport England, 2007b) were a local reflection of CSPs, bringing a range of stakeholders together; sometimes more than one in large districts. Doherty and Misener (2008) looked at less formal equivalents in Canada. With transfer of health responsibilities to local authorities, the latest partnership is Health and Wellbeing Boards, with unknown potential for sport (NHS Confederation, 2013).

In Chapter 2, I looked at views of citizenship that had evolved since Marshall's (1950) formulation; more recently, he wrote of collective goods and services providing:

A general enrichment of the concrete substance of civilised life, a general reduction of risk and insecurity [and] an equalisation between the more and less fortunate...between the healthy and the sick, the employed and the unemployed the old and the active.

(Marshall, 1992: 33)

These benefits would be conferred by the state on passive citizens. For many, this was far too rosy and cosy a view of the likely future. Giddens (1994) saw a more active but individualised citizenry, a world of 'clever people' capable of constructing their own biographies, challenging 'expert systems' and choosing their own solidarities, including in sport and leisure. Accordingly, Ellison concluded that:

> Citizenship' no longer conveys a universalist sense of inclusion or participation in a stable political community...instead we are left with a restless desire for social engagement, citizenship becoming a form of social and political practice born of the need to establish new solidarities.
>
> (Ellison, 1997: 714)

In this situation there would be winners and losers, while some might adapt to exclusion by choosing to disengage completely as citizens in any public space 'getting on instead with seeking their own satisfactions' (Jordan, 1996: 107), like those who live in squats, do not register to vote or pay council tax or join any club.

Thus if Bourdieu's concept of individual social capital and Putnam's of communal social capital are brought together, people may choose to gather capital in both forms as skills and contributions as consumers and clients and active members, though the pressure of choice and many obligations may make them more catholic and sporadic in their commitments. So we go on to consider the strengths and weaknesses of British sports clubs as a form of communal social capital.

The Third Way and communal social capital in the form of sport clubs

The Third Way and capacity building

Giddens was influential on the Blair government's view of society. His book, *The Third Way,* argued that globalisation, especially of commerce, the growth of individualism in social life, and the growth of ecological threats and concerns required a new framework for social policy in an inevitably capitalist society. This involved active citizens in *a radical centre*, albeit centre-left (Giddens, 1998: 45, 64). This 'Third Way' encompassed values of:

1 equality
2 protection of the vulnerable
3 freedom as autonomy
4 no rights without responsibilities
5 no authority without responsibility
6 a pluralist, cosmopolitan approach to world and scientific issues
7 a philosophic conservatist approach to the natural world.

It required a synergy between commercial, state and self-help sectors, including combating exclusion that 'is not about gradations of inequality, but about mechanisms that act to detach groups of people from the social mainstream'

(1998: 104). It required sustaining welfare spending, responding to greater equality of men and women in income, sexuality and new family structures, acting to halt the middle/upper classes' desertion of public spaces (leading to what Putnam in America tersely called 'private affluence amid public squalor'), and a focus on the social investment state rather than a focus on human capital, or economic maintenance, with education and employment initiatives aimed at the bottom of the social scale. Lister (1998) and Levitas (1998) criticised Giddens for equating inclusion with equality, and inclusion based on paid work, implying that paid work equalled equality of opportunity. Social investments involved a greater role for the third sector through local distribution systems. Temple (2000: 312) suggested the Third Way 'appeared to demand a less centralised and bureaucratic state than we currently have. Will British politicians and civil servants allow such flexibility?' Cameron's succeeding 'Big Society' would claim to do so, with mixed early evidence (Big Society speech, 19th July 2010, retrieved 20 March 2012 from https: //www.gov.uk/government/speeches/big-society-speech).

Closely allied to the idea of social capital is that of *social cohesion*, said to comprise elements of common values and a civic culture, social order and control, solidarity and reduced financial disparities, social networks, and territorial belonging and identity (Forrest and Kearns, 1999: 996 – see Chapter 7). Major cultural and sporting facilities may engender place identity, especially via professional soccer teams. Social networks may be strong, and believed to be strengthened even more by kinship in traditional working-class suburbs and villages, though how far this was objectively so is disputable. Middle-class and affluent people develop many wider and weaker friendship and interest networks/ ties, including for sport, aided by car ownership, which Fukuyama (1999) argued may be more important inpost-modern society. Baubock (2000: 115) suggested 'the most important demand of citizenship is to learn to cope with the plurality that is continuously generated by civil society.'

Capacity building involves skilled workers initially helping local groups to work at their own pace (Taylor, 1992, Chanan, 1999), which may be slower than managers and politicians desire (like many in sport) or are used to when driving programmes. It must be done locally and 'bottom-up' (Coalter, Allison and Taylor, 2000; European Commission, 2000; Coalter 2001a) and may not particularly look outwards (like the 1980s Action Sport and the STARS schemes for unemployed, Rigg, 1986, Glyptis, 1989). Sources of expertise now dispersed were the Community Development Officers who worked in the New Towns in the 1960s and 1970s. As debated in Chapter 9 and below, in deprived areas, human sports infrastructure in terms of clubs may be weaker than in more 'blessed' areas.

Leisure, including sport and the arts, is delivered in all three sectors, though data is much more difficult to get from commercial and voluntary organisations, because they are mainly smaller and more fragmented than public organisations, and only owe accountability to the public when partnerships are formed and grants given. The commercial sector in leisure has grown, and more of leisure has been 'commodified'. Martin and Mason (1998: 33) found that between 1971 and 1996, free time grew by only five per cent on average, but money spent on free time activities grew by 101 and by 91% per head respectively. Allison (2001) pointed out that this commodification made it all the more difficult for marginalised groups to access facilities and services for their leisure.

Sports clubs as communal social capital

Sport is delivered through a wide range of voluntary bodies, but often as part of a spectrum of activities for leisure, education or socialising (residents' and tenants' association, clubs for female, youth, retired, ethnic and disabled groups). But the core of voluntary sport is the sports club movement organised through and regulated by national governing bodies. Although much of it has been established for over a century, little is known about the scale and operation of the club movement compared to the facts about the people and act of individual volunteering. In 1987, Collins had estimated that there were 155,000 clubs in England; Taylor et al. (2003) suggested 106,000; Cox and Sparham's (SRA) sample (2013) weighted up to 151,000. About 43,000 of these were soccer clubs, so if planning for soccer is wrong, it biases the whole and especially the team games sector. Scotland did a more thorough survey of 3,500 of its estimated 13,000 clubs (Allison, 2001). But Germany has been most thorough, surveying a sample of 4,000 clubs every four years (Heinemann and Schubert, 1994). Weed et al.'s (2005) review demonstrated that there was little or no research on VSC facility use, structures, management or multi-sport environments, so below I piece together modest fragments.

English voluntary sports clubs (VSCs) exhibit peculiar features:

- *Parochial origins* – in links with local villages, estates, factories, churches, womens/youth/cultural groups and particularly public houses. The strong links with the military, or urban or rural workers' movements found in many European states never developed with British trade unions. This gives each a social strength, 'a community of like-minded people,' as Heinemann and Schwab (1999: 147) termed it. But it also leads to a tendency to cliquishness, and a skew to internal 'bonding links of social capital – with people 'like us'. Thiel and Mayer (2009) pointed out that to meet members' needs, VSCs do not have to be efficient organisations.

- *An enrolment of 12–14%* – of the population in VSCs was recorded until 2004, lower than, for example, in Germany (29%), Netherlands (26%) or Denmark (36%). In the first edition of this book I suggested this might be because of the strong development of public sector pay-as-you-play provision in the 1960s and 1970s and of commercial provision since then. I implied consequences of a lower income to the English confederation, the CCPR, now Sport and Activity Alliance, and less credibility and influence on government in contrast to the Deutsche Sportbund (German Sports Federation), which is consulted on every piece of new German legislation and runs its own Sports Training College in Berlin. But then the Active People surveys showed 25% in sports or fitness clubs; no one has explained why the earlier figures are lower or the new ones so much higher, though a sizeable part may be due to including a growing number of fitness clubs.

- *Single sports clubs dominate* – and these are small clubs at that (notably soccer clubs), with an average estimated size of 43 members, compared to 118 in the Netherlands, 142 in Denmark, and 306 in Germany. The small size means a strong social bonding, but economic and organisational weakness in that there is limited scope for role specialisation, a growing feature of sports organisations (Slack, 1999), and emphasis on operational tasks like chairman, secretary, fixtures secretary etc at the cost of developmental tasks. It also makes clubs vulnerable to experienced and competent officers leaving and not being able to be replaced.
- *Clubs have been suffering pressures* – from HMG and NGBs to modernise structures, procedures and meet health and safety equity and safeguarding regulations, while being concerned about smaller numbers of aging volunteers and the problems of recruiting members from a never-widening sphere of free time activities (Nichols et al., 2005).
- *Few large, multi-sport club* – unlike in Germany and other countries. Clubs of over 1,000 members comprised only six per cent of Germany's 66,700 clubs in 1991, but a quarter of all affiliated members. Four-fifths of these large clubs offered eight or more sports compared to only four per cent of small clubs (those with fewer than 300 members). They introduced more new competitive and leisure activities, catered more often for the needs of particular groups (e.g., children, disabled, older people) and were four or five times more likely to employ professional managers (Heinemann and Schubert, 1994). Thus they provide both the likelihood of having specialised skills to call on and a secure base for public investment and 'contracted' programmes, whereas only a minority of larger British clubs can offer this. Chapter 4 (pp 70, 229) mentions Sport England's attempts to generate hub and satellite clubs.
- *Only a third of VSC s wanted to be agents of national sports policy* – according to May, Harris, and Collins' (2013) sample; these were the larger (averaging 268 members) better, more formally organised ones; they found a large degree of ignorance, scepticism of interest in club work even from their own NGBs amongst the smaller informal clubs which desired just to play (averaging 28 members) This pattern reflected findings by Taylor et al. (2003) and by Cuskelly et al. (2006) in Australian rugby clubs.

Taylor et al. (2007) asked: should traditional/informal organisations be left to their own fate, or encouraged to change? Sparkes and Collins (2010) described the Amateur Swimming Association's approach to making clubs decide about their future roles and organisation in Swim 21. Moreover, a CCPR survey of clubs found two in five suffering membership and associated income falls in the recession, and suggested that 6,000 might close (CCPR *Press Release* 7 May 2009). But by the 2013 survey, Cox and Sparham (2013) discovered:

- an estimated 151,000 clubs with an average of 82 adult, and 32 non-playing members, with one in ten growing since London 2012;
- despite a third raising membership fees in 2011, the average financial surplus was four per cent, lower than 2007, and half worried about funding;
- one in five owned their facilities, two in five hired from a LA, and three in five had links with schools;
- on average, there were 24 volunteers of whom nine were coaches and two full- or part-time paid staff.

(These figures suggest a lower response from really small clubs, with only 225 soccer clubs in the sample and 24% in the large/over £30,000 income group).

May, Harris and Collins pointed out that if their findings held across the club landscape, there were serious implications for policy, particularly like that in the 2008–11 phase which depended on NGBs and clubs delivering 300,000 new members, which several had failed and which ones were failing to do. HMG consulted the NGBs, but no one had asked the clubs. Also many clubs feel the regulatory burden on the voluntary sector is too great (Centre for Social Justice, 2011, Sport & Recreation Alliance, 2011). Despite the poor performance of NGBs, with schools they remain the core of Sport England's 2012–17 strategy, with local authorities as also-rans (DCMS/Sport England, 2012).

If sport is the largest sphere of volunteering (26% of the total), surely it must be a source of huge social capital? Putnam (2000) thought so for the US, but saw it declining, together with politics and other associations. But Hall (1999), found the UK situation stable, as confirmed by Warde et al. (2003), though they thought there was fragility in poorer communities. In contrast, as the home of participatory democracy, Scandinavia clubs flourished, with Sweden continuing to grow (Rothstein, 2001). On the other hand, as Putnam (2000: 58) pointed out, club membership was not enough, people had to demonstrate active membership to build the internal 'bonding' and the valued external 'bridging' and 'linking' relationships; Putnam (2000: 23) called the former a social 'WD40', a lubricant, the second a 'superglue.' Andrews, Cowell and Downe (2008: 234) found a statistically significant correlation between LAs' performance and the strength of local associational life.

Collins (2005) reviewed evidence to contribute to answering other questions:

- *Is sport good at bonding bridging and linking?* The intimate nature of many British clubs already mentioned suggested that VSCs would be good at bonding and less so at the others; evidence from Andrew (2004) in London, Nichols (2009) in another English town, and Boessenkool (2001) in Holland suggested; in small clubs the activists are tied up in operating the organisation; also more people seem to bring friends into a club rather than make them there; conversely, multinational data on NGBs show they can build good linking capital with government and other stakeholders (Groeneveld, Houlihan and Ohl, 2011).

- *Does social capital vary by region?* Putnam thought it did, and so did Casey for Brittain (2002).
- *Does it vary between rich and poor communities?* data is indifferent, but suggested that it did (Boothby et al., 1982, Bishop and Hoggett, 1986).
- *Can it be created and destroyed?* Yes, just like other capital: Svendson and Svendson (2003) showed how a network of small rural sports centres was created by the Danish equivalent of British Young Farmers to try to retain younger people in villages; conversely, the British government did little in areas of coalfield closure to retain the physical and social capital of Coal Industry Welfare branches – Collins and Reeves (1995).

Recent governments and even Sports Councils have glibly referred to the sports club movement as the 'grass roots' of sport, but have not done the basic research to understand the system and its problems. In 1995, the narrow youth and excellence focus of the White Paper *Sport: Raising the Game*, only asked that more junior sections should be developed. The Blair government's strategy (DCMS, 2000: 13) viewed clubs as a complement to schools and a link to high-level competition, suggesting linking 'satellite' clubs in clusters to 'hub' clubs (an idea that took ten years to realise). Such a two-level scheme is foreign to the British club movement, so it is interesting that over 1,000 satellite clubs (1.3%) have been formed. With large and multi-sport clubs, despite their strengths, there is a danger that they will be beguiled by grantees and sponsors from their help-roots and start operating like pay-as-you-play venues, 'risking if a sport club treats its members as customers it ought not complain if they also act like customers and are no longer willing to volunteer' (Horch, 1998: 15).
   Some conclusions can be drawn:

1 The club movement is a crucial part of the system; it is where sportspeople are contributors and not just paying customers, consuming someone else's products.
2 If it is to play a greater role in helping to meet public policy aims to increase participation of excluded groups, its structure needs strengthening, perhaps in clusters, where administration could be consolidated, and where particular clubs could specialise in working with particular groups or levels of performer. But this requires an unprecedented level of local co-operation. Allison (2001) argued for this, and the Scottish Football Association undertook an experiment to make a cluster of 27 soccer clubs in Ayrshire. Such a change needs to be espoused strongly by Sport England, NGBs, and the SRA to persuade most club members to strategically change.
3 Multi-sport clubs are not a tradition, and there may be limited contexts where new ones could be formed, like where communities are developing in new private housing estates or in redeveloped inner suburbs (analogues of the community development work undertaken in New Towns from 1950–70).

4   Finding time to give to volunteering is a problem in lifestyles with unprecedented choice; and they are expected to be better trained and more 'professional' than any previous generation.

Much more research with a structured sample (as opposed to the SRA's snowball) into the capabilities of the sports club system, similar to that of Germany, and with attention to deprived communities. Quite simply, in Britain, we don't know much. Which clubs are good for public investment? The process is hit-and-miss, or more often first-come-first-served, or shout-loudest.

Finally, governments and agencies should understand the organisations and networks they want to partner with before intervening. The voluntary organisations must remain legally/constitutionally autonomous in any partnership or client relationship with government. If they do not, they will lose their unique self-organised character in which the club members offer an essentially gift relationship with its heartfelt, committed and generous support. As Horch (1998: 50) commented perceptively: 'if sport clubs are only doing the same things in the same manner as commercial sport organisations then politicians and voters will at some stage ask themselves why they should continue subsidising them.' The British club movement has to modernise and adapt, to avoid the mire of continued parochialism, to find its own, appropriate 'Third Way' and not one designed by others.

Case study 8: Street Games

Disadvantaged areas have a weak sporting infrastructure and lower participation. Active People Survey data confirmed this assertion with poor young people only a little over half as likely to be club members, compete, and be coached (Figure 11.4). Young people from low-income families volunteered a quarter less than the English average and at barely half the rate of those in prosperity, and youth volunteering is both gendered and ethnicised. Street Games (SG) adapted Sport England's equity index using *Active People* 2 data – compare Table 4.3 (Figure 11.5).

SG was started by a former SE officer who had been seconded to community programme work in DCLG and the Home Office, and has dedicated herself to working with disadvantaged youth, making sport accessible 'in the right place, at the right price, at the right time and in the right style.' SG addresses two of Sport England's 19 market segments, both mainly urban – Sports Teams Lads (18–25s, 40% not white, 11% of adult men) and Supportive Singles (also 18–25s, 35% not white, eight per cent of adult women). Together they formed 9.6% of adults, a total of 3.8m, 5.8m if their 14–17 year-old siblings were included. The Survey also showed that 69% of low-income youth would like to do more sport.

From its inception in 2007, SG has grown to 120 local projects, attracting 156,000 participants with 1.5m attendances in simple local facilities (sports halls, recreation grounds/parks, multi-use games areas), delivered in a deceptively laid-back but structured fashion. It offers most frequently football, street dance, basketball, Street Cheer or multi-sport sessions, but a host of other activities, in

50%
40%
30%
20%
10%
0%
45.7
28.7
9.3
4.9
42.7
23.9
43.1
22.9
38.6
19.1
Participation 3 × 30
Volunteering
Club membership
Sports tuition/Coaching
Organised competitive sport
Less than £15,599
More than £45,800

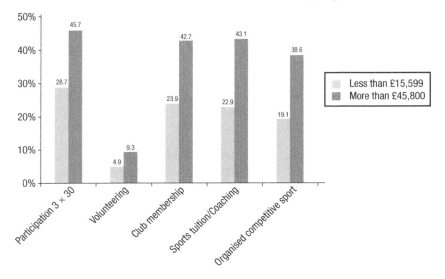

Figure 11.4 Features of sports participation by 16–25s by household income, 2008–9

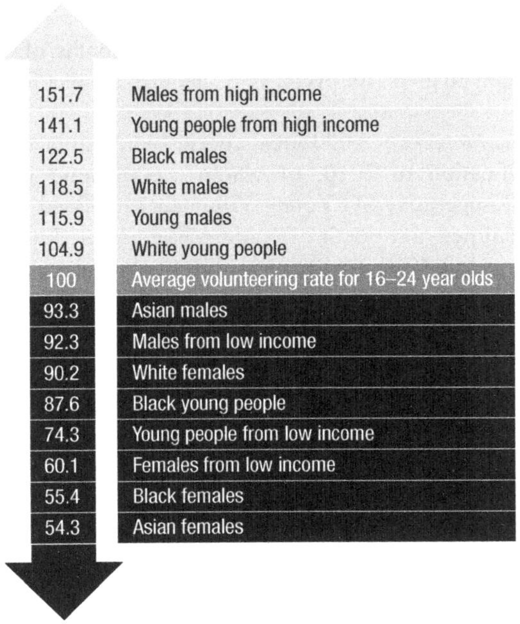

151.7 Males from high income
141.1 Young people from high income
122.5 Black males
118.5 White males
115.9 Young males
104.9 White young people
100 Average volunteering rate for 16–24 year olds
93.3 Asian males
92.3 Males from low income
90.2 White females
87.6 Black young people
74.3 Young people from low income
60.1 Females from low income
55.4 Black females
54.3 Asian females

Sources: Sport England Active People Survey 3 and Street Games, 2009

Figure 11.5 Volunteering Equity Index: regular volunteering by different groups

partnership with, among others, local authorities, NACRO, Youth Offending Teams, NGBs, Sport Leaders UK. It is Action Sport (pp 33, 69, 131, 255) for the twenty-first century. It exceeded all its targets for the first half of its 2008–12 plan (SG, 2008).

It has important features:

(a) *Footie friends* – 'I used to play football with my mates, but this is much better'

(Derbyshire participant)

(b) *Low activity loners* – 'if I wasn't here I'd be bored out of my mind or on the streets, causing no good, if I am honest' (Hastings participant)
– 'it seems highly likely that without SG a significant proportion of low activity loners would barely engage with sport at all'

(SPEAR, 2011)

(c) *More girls participating than many schemes* – 'at first we were scared and shy as there were older girls there and we didn't know how to dance...now it's like a team' (Thanet participant) – £2.3m from the Active Women programme (pp 94–5) will extend this through *Us Girls* in 49 locations

(d) *It retains a good number* – half attended for seven months, of whom four out of five are likely to go on for over a year, and then another 80% for longer

(e) *It develops volunteers* – 8,000 local coaches and volunteers and gained 4,800 qualification to 2010, of whom 2,600 came in through the sponsored Co-operative SG Young Volunteers focussed in hot spots for health inequalities and youth offending; like Street Games and Solent Sports Counselling (Chapter 9) this builds up confidence and self esteem (Craig, 2009)

(f) *Programmes work with NGBs* – Rugby Football league, British (indoor) Rowing, England Athletics Lawn Tennis Association

(g) *It celebrates* – through events and festivals, 200 with 36,000 participants to date but extended through Coca Cola sponsorship, including training academies.

In 2012 SG, was given £20m of Lottery money to deliver 1,000 Doorstep sports clubs, which the four CEO saw as SG's contribution to London 2012 Olympic legacy. Its success can be attributed to clear objectives and a clear theory of behavioural change (Figure 11.6), clear targeting of youth and partners, and intelligent monitoring and evaluation (Anderson, 2011 – compare with Coalter's – p 215 and Figure 11.1). In 2010, it won a bronze in the Chief Medical

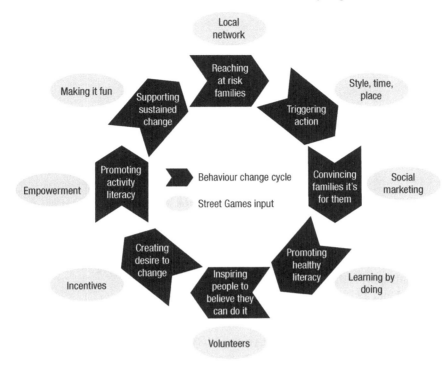

Source: Anderson, 2011

Figure 11.6 Street Games and the behaviour change cycle

Officer's Public Health Awards; Chief Executive Jane Ashworth said 'the same socio-economic barriers that hinder young people's access to sport produce poor health rates, and in particular, rising levels of obesity. We tackle this issue by making sport readily available in a format that engages groups of young people who all too often have to miss out.' (SE *press notice* 25 May 2010).

Conclusions

in the first part of the chapter I made five suggestions for making the implementation of inclusion policies more effective (though they could equally apply to other policy spheres). In the second part I highlighted two major structural changes I believe are needed to make the voluntary sports club movement organisationally stronger for times when it agrees to partner government in tackling the crosscutting issues of lifelong learning, community health and safety, environmental improvement as well as social exclusion. It has to be said, however, that the social benefits sought by New Labour from a more active voluntary sector as part of the Third Way or of Cameron's Big Society cannot be demonstrated by research, not even in European countries where more is known about the form and functioning of the sports clubs.

12 Conclusions

Since 2002–3 when the first edition of this book was written, substantial new literatures have consolidated understanding and updated knowledge, viz:

- how poverty and social exclusion express themselves (Chapter 2);
- levels of income and inequality, especially for children (Chapter 3);
- youth sport and deprivation (Chapter 4);
- sport and gender (Chapter 5);
- multiculturalism and sport (Chapter 6);
- sport and disability (Chapter 8);
- sport for disadvantaged and at-risk youth (Chapter 9);
- sport in urban and especially rural areas (Chapter 10); and
- sport, the voluntary sector and social capital (Chapter 11).

But data is still limited, regarding:

- the dynamics of change in participation and the ability to relate these to demographic change. There was scope to embed a longitudinal panel element in the Active People survey that could measure marginal change in drop-outs and new entrants, but Sport England has not done this;
- good data is still lacking on sport and sexual orientation, and religion/faith, even though these form part of the equality standard; debate on the first is now active (see below).

As background to this chapter it is useful to set the UK in a European context; Table 12.1 shows that the UK lies in the middle ranks, generally between Scandinavia and the Netherlands with higher involvement and south and east Europe with lower (though relative to domestic data, the UK sample seems to have under-represented sports club membership and probably usage and use of sports centres).

Table 12.1 Results of Eurobarometer survey 2009 on sport and physical activity

Item %	EU27	UK	(rank)	Highest, state	Lowest, state
Regularly take sport/physical activity*	31	32	*12*	51 Austria	10 Bulgaria
Never take sport/physical activity	39	32	*10*	56 Bulgaria	6 Sweden
Do not do because sick/disabled	13	22	*1*	22 UK	3 Italy
Not interested in sport/physical activity	42	37	*12*	57 Bulgaria	97 Sweden
Plays in sports centre	8	9	*5=*	15 Italy	3 Romania
Plays in sports club	11	11	*10*	27 Netherlands	2 Greece
Plays in fitness centre	11	8	*14*	31 Sweden	2 Hungary
Plays in park/countryside	48	39	*19*	83 Slovenia	27 Greece
Member sports club	12	9	13	27 Netherlands	2 Romania
Member fitness club	9	14	4	22 Denmark	2 Poland
Member youth/works club	4	4	8	12 Denmark	0 Romania

Source: TNS, 2010

* Note: 4–16 times a month, excluding recreation walking, cycling, dancing 3 Romania

Summary of findings

Chapter 1 included a shortened summary of constraints on people's leisure and the claims made for personal, economic, social and environmental benefits flowing from playing sport. Chapter 2 showed how the Victorian concept of absolute poverty was superceded by the idea of relative poverty as society became more affluent in mid twentieth century, and then of social exclusion as a process. As the Child Poverty Action Group warned, rising national income would not automatically abolish poverty; on the contrary, 'it may well add to the burdens of the poor as more and more things that were once luxuries have become conventional necessities' (Lister, 1990: 51). And so it has proved. Then I summarised a growing volume of data on who is poor and excluded, and sport's relationship to social class, still a reality in contemporary Britain. Finally, I related this discussion to ideas about consumers and citizens.

Chapter 3 pressed home the view that poverty was the core of exclusion, notably for those without work, or on low and insecure incomes on the fringes of the labour market, which includes a disproportionate share of single parents and ethnic minorities, but also several other significant groups, particularly disabled people and elderly without second or index-linked pensions. In common with other advanced nations, the gap between the poorest and the richest has been growing. While for the comfortable/affluent majority, the price of transport, entry or allied costs is not an issue, for the poor groups it either reduces the frequency or precludes many of the sport choices available to most and to their children. Thus leisure facilities and services, public and voluntary, are over-used by those with above-average incomes, a situation unchanged over 20 years, not surprising since governments and their financial watchdogs have pressed for reduced subsidy, which generally has meant above-inflation prices rises, and marketing to the groups most likely to respond. Most sports development programmes targeted at needy groups have shown a good response to effort, notably by Sports Development officers (Hylton and Totton, 2001, Pitchford and Collins, 2010), but such programmes have been generally on a small, local scale that has not shifted the aggregate balance. Case studies 1 and 2 of Leisure Cards show their untapped power as a policy tool and case study 2 of social marketing.

Exclusion of children was the focus of Chapter 4. A quarter of the country's children are currently in poor households, and the UK has one of the lowest-qualified workforces in Europe. These large gaps must be closed if a large minority is not to be disadvantaged in a knowledge-based society, since cohort studies are showing disadvantage continuing into adult life, in incomes and health (Field, 2010; Marmot, 2010). As the National Equality Panel reported: 'economic advantage and disadvantage reinforce themselves across the life cycle, and often on to the next generation. It matters more in Britain who your parents are than in many other countries' (Hills et al., 2010: 36). Though research has not yet been done on status/income and play provision, it is clear that differences in attitudes and participation in sport are established in childhood, in that:

- 'gender-appropriate' play and sports behaviour models are established by the time children attend primary school, to the detriment of girls;
- girls continue to have a limited menu of sports and drop-out earlier than boys;
- disabled and ethnic minority children do not have equal opportunities to their counterparts;
- children from deprived areas take up fewer opportunities to taste, and learn new sports out-of-school, and become club members, as Nottinghamshire's Case Study 3 showed.

These patterns of exclusion carry into performance and elite sport. The government and sports bodies are giving focus and priority to race and disability issues, but the PESSCL/YP programmes (Case Study 4) did not tackle directly poverty/disadvantage issues.

The view that sport was invented by men, and that they are more suited to it is still alive, despite strong challenges by an increasingly empowered women's sports movement. But from childhood onwards girls and women have narrower choice in activities, and fewer opportunities to work as administrators, managers or coaches beyond a basic level, as Tess Kay shows in Chapter 5. While many schemes are mounted to enable more female participation in running as well as playing sport, it has rarely looked at the needs, behaviour or attitudes of the most disadvantaged and excluded; Jeanes' work opens this up, but a greater focus is needed.

Exclusion in older age was the topic of Chapter 6. To constraints on younger people, are added declining physical and sometimes mental capabilities, reduced access to private transport, and an increasing fear of going out at night. Nonetheless, at this phase of life physical and mental benefits from exercise are proportionately greatest and health and welfare expenditure increases almost exponentially. Britain certainly lags behind Scandinavian and other countries and currently has no targeted sport-as-health-prevention policy. This is both extraordinary and perverse. Maintaining mobility and ability to cope better with independent living would be major social boons.

Chapter 7 clearly demonstrated that contemporary British society shows a systematic inequality in almost all spheres of life for BMEs, arising from a lesser share of both economic and social capital, but exacerbated by a still-widespread racist set of beliefs and attitudes, that have been only weakly combated by race relations legislation, and are reflected in both recreational and competitive sport. Football, rugby and cricket in particular are attempting to highlight the problem and mobilise their memberships to eradicate it. Access to leisure and sport is exacerbated by the BMEs' geographical concentration in the inner parts of certain cities and the more limited public, voluntary and commercial provision that *appears* to exist there.

Chapter 8 related to sport for disabled people, and showed how, even in schools and junior clubs, there are great gaps between aspirations and participation, and that provision in mainstream school and clubs is often poorer than for youngsters as a whole. It is policy to 'mainstream' (assimilate) as many disabled children as possible, yes this can perversely separate them from the tailor-made system of competition set up between special schools, and replace it with much more haphazard arrangements. Three-quarters of disabled people depend on welfare benefits and are by definition poor, and social class and gender combine to slash participation compared to non-disabled adults. As the Leicester case study showed (Case Study 5), this operates locally. The Disability Discrimination Act should improve human as well as physical provision, but only slowly, some of society is still locked into the medical or at best the social rather than the empowerment model of disability, and the Coalition's benefit cuts could set back quality of life and sport/exercise participation severely for this group.

Chapter 9 was devoted to growing political and professional interests and a mountain of literature on sport and adventure education that seeks to prevent 'at-risk' young people from falling into crime, and to helping to rehabilitate offenders. Coalter (2001b, 2007, 2013) believed there are strong theoretical grounds for believing sport has benefits for at-risk and offending poorly-funded and short-lived, with little follow-up and support on return to home communities; methodologically, it is morally impossible to undertake medical-type experiments, and funding for longitudinal/before-and-after studies has been rare; in analysis, data and methods have not been powerful enough to unravel the programme effects from the complex of personal and community influences. I reported on Case Study 6 of a primary intervention in Stoke and a tertiary one in Hampshire, while Positive Futures Case Study 7, verified findings from smaller-scale studies, and demonstrated strong learning processes for participants and staff. As the Audit Commission commented, if LAs and others are serious in wanting to tackle this persistent, structural and costly issue, more resource commitment is needed.

Chapter 10 looked at aspects of social and sporting exclusion in country and city. Exclusion in rural areas is less obvious because of smaller numbers more thinly spread, and for the same reasons, policy instruments cost more per head to implement. But recent studies have not shown a lower incidence than in towns. The urban setting has had a long series of mainly geographically targeted prescriptions both for regeneration and recreation. Blair's government, while criticising predecessors for the number of their policy initiatives, produced as many and, demanded action plans on a tight timescale. Harrison (1983: 171) claimed that 'the inverse care law...is valid for almost all forms of public service. Private squalor and public squalor go hand in hand, accentuating each other.' Thus one gets 'postcode discrimination' in sport as much as in other services (Jordan, 1996).

Chapter 11 looked at issues around policy implementation. Firstly, I examined five practical ways to make implementation more effective.

1   Giving organisations and staff a realistic chance of engendering lasting changes and achieving desired outcomes by lengthening policy timespans, not from two or three to five years but to seven or ten, a real test in traditional quadrennial British arrangements of political commitment.
2   Devoting enough resource and intellectual effort to measuring outcomes rather than being satisfied with intermediate outputs, however much they are difficult to define and slippery to measure (Coalter, 2007).
3   Tightening the depth of focus and concentration of effort of both people and place policies, and resisting spreading finance and manpower too thin.
4   Resisting initiative-itis and, once convicted of the rightness of policies, to stick to them long enough to give them a chance of success, despite political attack and economic pressures.
5   Encouraging strong partnerships in tackling cross-cutting issues, but not unwieldy ones; partnership management is only a means, not an end.

In the second half of the chapter, I looked at sport as an expression of citizenship, in the form of voluntary sports clubs. The Blair government acknowledged some shortcomings of sports clubs, in programmes to helping them to improve coaching, accrediting their services to reassure parents and relatives, and more recently, allowing them indirect tax relief through registering as charities. But these actions are based on assumptions about the sector, comprised as it is of overwhelmingly small, single-sport, and in all senses parochial clubs, with little of the structural strength found in large, multi-sport clubs historically more common in some European nations. I suggested two major policy changes – supporting the founding of multi-sport clubs in limited places of new development, and clustering clubs to gain economies of operation without giving up autonomy.

Though this is a concluding chapter, since the Coalition got to work on cutting the role, scope and cost of government, decisions affecting exclusion and sport continue to arrive weekly during editing, and the postlude describes some major changes, most of which, I argue, set back the cause of social exclusion, fairness (Dorling, 2010).

One still-neglected factor in exclusion is of transport. Everyone needs transport and its availability, price and quality limits participation. SEU (2003) reported it excluded jobseekers (40%), students (50%), and access to hospitals and supermarkets for non car-owners (31% and 16% respectively). The BMA (2012: 5) said 'the unintended consequence of increased car use has been the suppression of walking and cycling levels'; while Sustrans (2011) estimated the current 484m walking and cycling trips to be worth £442m. Concession bus and rail schemes brought improved quality of life to elderly users in Scotland (Rye and Mykura, 2009); a 35% increase in use in Salisbury (Baker and White, 2010); and great benefits to users from four deprived areas, especially Wythenshaw in Manchester and Braunstone, Leicester (Lucas, Tyler and Christodoulou, 2009). The DOT (nd) looked at costs of extending concessions for children, youth, older people, disabled and their carers, but Coalition cuts in public finance will ensure these remain a dead letter.

Emerging areas – sport and sexuality, sport for asylum seekers and refugees and sport and religion

All three of these are too scanty to warrant a chapter, though since 2003 the literature on sport and sexuality has developed somewhat, but the other two are still in embryo.

Sport and sexuality

An EU survey of 93,000 LGBT people (FRA, 2013) found 32% had suffered discrimination outside work in the previous year, including sport and fitness – 32% in the UK, 20–32% in Scandianavia and Belgium. Telephone interviews in the UK Integrated Household Survey 2009–10 revealed one per cent identified themselves as gay/lesbian (481,000), 0.5 per cent as bisexual, and 0.5 per cent as 'other' (Joloza, Evans and O'Brien, 2010), 65% under 45, compared to 49% of heterosexuals; women comprised only a third of gay/lesbians, but two-thirds of bisexuals. Griggin and Genasci in Messner and Szabo (1990) said 'because of the extreme negative stigma attached to homosexuality in our culture, many, perhaps most, gay and lesbian people live double lives and are invisible members of our communities.' Regarding sexuality, Lenskyj wrote pithily:

> throughout the century of women's mass sporting participation, femininity and homosexuality have been seen as incompatible with sporting excellence: either sport made women masculine, or sportswomen were masculine at the outset. In the last half century, the term "masculine" has often implied lesbian. Such reasoning reinforced the polarised view of masculinity and femininity, both social and biological, thereby underscoring sex differences and legitimating male supremacy.
>
> (Lenskyj, 1986: 95)

The most comprehensive literature review regarding sport (Brackenridge et al., 2008) made it clear that bisexuality and transexuality were only just being developed (only 20 of 711 items), and there was little evidence of policies and management practices (81 items). More studies focused on lesbian than homosexual sport (e.g., Lenskyj, 1990, Squires and Sparkes, 1996, Clarke, 1998), and few in non-white communities. Underlying prejudices are based on 'homonormativity' (King, 2008) or 'heteronormativity' (Johnson and Kivel in Aitchison, 2007: 94–104). Sport England covers LGBT as part of its equality policy, but it is clear that many organisations have not faced the issue, and some are 'sceptics' or 'resisters.' The first Gay Games were held in the US in 1992, but a similar event happened in the UK only in 2000. A European Gay and Lesbian Sports Federation was founded in 1989, and endorsed the 2009 Copenhagen principle of open sport.

While Clarke (1998) criticised both the Sports Council and DCMS for not identifying gays as a group suffering from exclusion in their national strategies, things have moved on. The Equality Act 2006 included sexual orientation and religion/belief with the other three established forms of discrimination under a single Commission; and Sport England's equity policy made no reference to either. After a 2004 IOC ruling and the passage of the Gender Recognition Act 2004, DCMS (2005) guided sport bodies that transexual people should be able to compete in sports for their acquired gender, but might be restricted or prohibited on grounds of fairness or safety, or if strength, stamina or physique put them at a disadvantage. Nonetheless, Stonewall (Dick, 2009) produced *Leagues behind*, suggesting professional football was 'institutionally homophobic,' with 70% of fans hearing anti-gay language and chants in the previous five years, two-thirds feeling comfortable about a player on their team 'coming out' and over half thought the FA and Premier League ought to do more to tackle abuse. A separate but contentious area is sex typing and testing (Reeser, 2005) for elite competition, sparked by queries about her gender when young South African runner Caster Semenya competed in August 2009; she was later vindicated, but a 2010 IOC meeting of medics could come to no conclusions to guide rulings.

In governments, there has been little recognition let alone support for separate gay sports organisations, for fear of social splintering. The Dutch Ministry commissioned Hekma (1998) to review the Netherlands situation. A third of women and a quarter of men in his sample had experienced some incident, but the low incidence was a result of gay men and lesbians keeping quiet about their sexuality, like King and Thompson's (2001) sample in British clubs. The Dutch National Olympic Committee included sexuality in its anti-discrimination code since 1994. But things are changing:

- a European Gay and Lesbian Sports Federation represents LGBTI interests in the Council of Europe, and will organise Eurogames;
- in the UK Pride Sports organises Pride Games in Manchester, and the Gay Footballers Supporters Network runs league with 16 teams in England and four more in Scotland, Wales and Ireland.

A government initiative led to the five sports councils and major NGBs to sign up to a Charter against Homophobia and Transphobia in Sport (GEO, 2011) and to promote equality, but Lawley (2011: 40) argued major progress will occur only when these issues are dealt with in schools.

Asylum seekers

Asylum seekers migrate as a result of threats or emergencies. In the UK they are found especially in two clusters of towns, each with 12% of the population – diverse conurbations (like Manchester, Birmingham, Bradford and Liverpool) and asylum dispersal towns (like Plymouth, Bolton, Swansea and Rotherham), though arriving in new areas with smaller populations like Lincolnshire can have a marked impact on jobs, housing and health services (Poppleton et al. 2013). The UK has been a magnet for people from all continents. In a ground-breaking study, Amara et al. (2004, 2006) examined top-down policy and bottom-up practice in 13 case studies in Glasgow, Cardiff and the East Midlands, concluding:

- many working in sport had little or patchy appreciation of how sport could help refugees and asylum seekers, and this group often had low priority for funding;
- the emphasis was on provision for men;
- as claimed by Collins (2005), for these groups sport provided bonding capital (as in Derby's Bosnia Herzegovina Community Association, or its Zimbabwean football team), or bridging with other ethnic (Scottish Asian Sport Association, Derby's Madeley Youth Centre programmes for Kurds), or locals (Swansea's World Stars football team or linking capital (Charnwood's Sport Link GP referral scheme).

Leisure Cards seek to attract deprived groups through discounts (Chapter 3); recent data (CIPFA, 2010) showed a tiny minority of four per cent had a specific category for asylum seekers – not surprisingly, in Birmingham, Walsall, Dudley, Bury, Newham, but perhaps less expectedly Lewisham, and Oxford.

A Eurobarometer survey (Euractiv.com Press Release 3 July 2008) suggested that while discrimination based on age, gender, disability, and religion had decreased compared to 2003, 48% of citizens opined discrimination based on ethnicity had worsened –with very much higher figures in Denmark and Netherlands (69 and & 71%, where respectively publishing cartoons of Mohammed and the murder of a right wing politician, Pym Fortuyn had raised the public temperature greatly) but also in Hungary, Italy and Belgium. The arrival of refugees and asylum seekers can rapidly change the ethnic or cultural mix of a community. Sports arts and cultural services including competitions can break down barriers, help self-confidence and aid community and personal development (LGA et al., 2002). There are suspicions about such people being economic migrants, undercutting wage rates and crowding rented housing, but all the evidence is of net benefits to the economy – Dustmann and Frattini (2013) reckoned immigrants from the EEA paid 34% more in taxes than they received in benefits 2001–11, a net contribution of £25bn.

Sport and faith/religion

A reviving area is that of sport and religion. The Protestant churches, beside public schools, played a major role in developing nineteenth century and especially team sport – 'muscular Christianity' (Watson et al., 2005); indeed one in three Premier League clubs originated in churches (Lupson, 2006). Churches had teams and facilities, and helped spread them around the world, notably the Empire/Commonwealth, together with the civil service, the armed forces and the YMCA/YWCA. After 1930, church communities shrank and aged, and sold or converted their sports fields and halls; the consolidation of youth football on Sunday mornings was a body blow to boys, and more recently girls, in junior churches/Sunday schools. But sport being a major attraction to youth, and an interest crossing gender, age and socio-economic boundaries, has been resurging in churches (Parry et al., 2007; Collins and Parker, 2010). Sport chaplaincies are growing in professional clubs (Heskins and Baker, 2006). But work on the churches' social capital through sport – 'faithful capital' (Furbey et al., 2006, CULF, 2006, Baker and Miles-Watson, 2010) – has focussed on welfare, arts and youth work, largely ignoring sport.' Unlike volunteering in general, which ran with social class, Wells et al. (2011) showed how church-based volunteering was oriented to poor areas and social need. Immigration has brought a growth in sporting interest in other faiths, despite Islam being seen as not encouraging female sport and mosques as strongly gendered spaces (Predelli, 2008), multi-sports programmes for both men and women operated in some 37–43% of mosques and Muslim centres (Collins, 2014).

My overall conclusion is that exclusion from sport is real; that at its core is poverty, though we generally have to rely on surrogate measures of socio-economic or social groups. But the pattern of coincident deprivations that add up to exclusion for millions of adults and children are irrefutable. One way of looking at this is to measure the extra impact on participation of social class to other factors like gender, age, ethnicity and disability. Table 12.2 does this, using Sport England's Sports Equity Index, and demonstrates the extent of the effect.

Table 12.2 The extra impact of social class on other factors affecting sports participation

Indexed against males without a disability (60.3% participation=100)			
All DE male	75		
DE without disability	65	DE 16–19	84
White majority, all ages	56	DE 25–29	64
DE ethnic minority	46	DE 30–44	50
DE female	45	DE 45–59	30
DE adult with disability	35	DE 60–69	24

Source: Sport England Equity Index 2002

Why should a substantial minority of citizens and taxpayers have substantially poorer opportunities? Table 12.3 sets out recent and current inequalities in sports participation and in using publicly-funded facilities. The top-bottom gap is substantial, remaining during the recent recession (Roberts, 2013).

Table 12.3 Inequalities in participation in sport – from the 1960s to 2010

%	Visiting sport & leisure centres		Any sport in last four weeks		
	1960s	*1990s*	*1987*	*1996*	*2010–11*
A Professional	20	40	65	63	} 57
B Manager			52	52	
C1 Junior non-manual	44	33	45	47	
C2 Skilled manual	27	20	48	45	} 44
D Semi-skilled	7	8	34	37	
E Unskilled			26	23	
TOTAL			45	46	
Difference between A & E	13	32	40	40	

Sources: English Sports Council, Sport England 1999a; DCMS, 2011

Conclusion: equity, non-participation and exclusion

As Coalter (2000) pointed out, non-participation does not equal exclusion. Since leisure activities are inherently those of choice, and the choice is ever-widening, non-participation may, for many leisure activities be the norm (Slee, Curry and Joseph, 2001: 17). Coalter took Le Grand's argument that exclusion can be said to occur when people want to take part or cannot, or when society suffers, or does not gain communal benefits if people cannot participate (e.g., health services costing more than necessary), or social cohesion is damaged by obvious unfairness. In a similar way, shared amenities – the economist's 'merit goods' such as parks – may not get sufficient use or popular support to be sustained without central or local state intervention. Harland et al. (nd) listed factors affecting non-participation as:

- a general attitude that something is 'boring/not interesting/rubbish' – common amongst youth towards sport, the arts, museums, and libraries, until they are introduced to them by someone with charisma and skill;
- a perceived talent barrier, especially in sport and the arts;
- lack of relevance to them, or of feeling uncomfortable in particular settings;
- negative affective outcomes – embarrassment, anxiety, intimidation (demonstrated by girls regarding PE and sport in Chapter 4, and by many with lower educational attainments in museums and galleries or theatres)

- image barriers – seeing something as not appropriate – 38% of adult respondents to the: the Allied Dunbar National Fitness Survey (SC/HEA 1992).

Of course, data is needed: until recently, it was sparse for tourism, arts and countryside visiting. DCMS' *Taking Part* partly filled the gap for five main sectors (since 2012 for four, sport having been consolidated in *Active People*), while MORI (2001b) and Muddiman et al. (2000) provide some for libraries and museums and Chan and Goldthorpe, (2005a,b) for arts. Resource (2001a,b) and DCMS (2001a,b) argued these subsectors made major contributions to social inclusion. DCMS accepted proposals for more investment in regional and local museums with £2.5m in 200–3 rising to £28m in 2006–7 devoted specifically to social inclusion work, exemplifying Tyne and Wear's museums service which doubled overall attendances during the 1990s and increased the share by people in C2DE groups from 20 to 52%.

Providers can help change some of the attitudes listed above by product modification, enticements to improve access and better promotional methods, but, as shown in Chapter 2, many people are multiply constrained from taking part. The argument has been mounted that in a market-based, if regulated economy, they can chose from a wide range of other leisure activities. But the fallacy of this can be shown in that there is little evidence of this happening on any scale. No single survey covers the full range of leisure, and so I have pieced together evidence from a wide variety of sources (Table 12.4).

Table 12.4 Social inequalities across the leisure spectrum

Activity and social class(SC-NEC)[a]		2005–06 (%)	2009–10 (%)			
			Total	Upper-lower difference	10% least deprived	10% most deprived
Arts	Upper SEC groups	84.4	*82.6*		86.6	
	Lower SEC groups	64.4	64.4	18.2		59.9
Heritage Sites	Upper SEC groups	79.7	79.3		84.2	
	Lower SEC groups	57.1	57.7	21.6		39.8
Libraries	Upper SEC groups	52.1	*43.9*		46.3	
	Lower SEC groups	40.1	*33.6*	9.7		37.6
Museums / Galleries	Upper SEC groups	51.9	*57.0*		63.8	
	Lower SEC groups	28.3	*34.0*	23.0		31.3
Sports	Upper SEC groups	58.6	57.2		58.8	
	Lower SEC groups	43.4	44.0	13.2		49.0

Source: DCMS, *Taking Part* 2005–6 to 2009–10

Note: A Upper = SECs 1–4, Lower = SECs 5–8

A – Participation in the arts, heritage, libraries, museums and galleries and sports sectors 2005–6 to 2009–10 (attending more than once in the last year)(italic indicates significant difference over five years)

(%)	Holidays		Drinking Weekly or Not in more often last year				Going to cinema		Visiting natural sites		GB Pop'n
	All	VFR*	M	F	M	F	in yr	in month	Freq+	Not	
1. AB	33	35	71	61	8	10	72	23	26	26	31
2. C1	32	30					67	22	29	29	27
3. C2	17	16	70	52	11	15	59	17	21	21	24
4. D/E	17	19	57	35	3	23	47	14	24	24	28
Diff 1–4	16	16	14	26	5	13	25	9	2	2	7

Sources: Visit Britain, 2009; Lader and Steel, 2009; Cols 8, 9 British Film Institute, 2010; Natural England, 2010

Notes: *VFR = visiting friends and relatives; +freq = once a week or more often

B – Participation in other popular forms of leisure

Part A shows the gap between professional/managerial groups (SEC 1–4) and routine semi- and un-skilled workers (SEC 5–8) for five sectors, ranging from 10 to 23% – greater between the most and least deprived for arts, museums and galleries and especially heritage, and a statistical decline over five years in arts, libraries and museums, which will now be worsened by the recession. Part B shows the same effect for other popular activities – holidaymaking drinking and going to the cinema and the countryside. So there is no escape from deep social structures in switching activities (see Collins, 2008a).

Widdop and Cutts (2013) used latent class analysis on *Taking Part* data to test classic ideas of 'exclusive' vs 'omnivorous' tastes previously identified in culture (e.g., Chan and Goldthorpe, 2005a,b), identifying five clusters as shown in Table 12.5: classic omnivore and highbrow groups, and lowbrow and fitness active clusters, with distinctive socioeconomic features, especially of femaleness in cluster 2 and age in cluster 4. They point out little has been done to look at whether there are differences among the largest, non-participant group.

To exemplify the matter of holidaymaking: Smith (2001) reported that four in ten British people take no form of holiday, a figure not reduced since 1989 (ETB, 1989). It still has not (Joldersma, 2009), condemning 7m adults to not having a holiday each year, including one in five couples and three-fifths of lone parents; 2.5m children to not even one day at the seaside. Germany, France, Italy, Spain, Portugal, Flemish Belgium, and even Poland, Hungary and Romania have regarded it as something the state should help often via health or welfare organisations (Diekmann and McCabe, 2011); exceptionally, in Britain it is left to two modest charities, the Family Holiday Association and Family Fund, and a trade union, Unison, despite the benefits of family solidarity and self-confidence reaped (Minneart, Maitland and Miller, 2009). Having a holiday is another token of being a normal family, and is very important for being together (51%), getting away from (often depressing and pressing) circumstances (38%), recovering from illness or bereavement (35%), and meeting new people and seeing places (24% – McCabe, Joldersma and Li, 2010).

Table 12.5 Omnivores, actives and non-participants in sport 2005–6

Cluster % feature	1. Classic omnivores 9%	2. Fitness class 27%	3. Lowbrow omnivores 10%	4. Highbrows 13%	5. Non-participants 41%
Above average participation in	All 10 sports	Swim, fit, cyc, racket, jog, advent, water	Swim, fit, cyc, racket, soccer, golf, jog	Cyc, golf, advent, water	nil
Significant socio-economic features, compared to cluster1	Male, Man/prof degree, white, 25–44, own-occ, urban, well-off	Mixed SEC/educ white, Women[17.7] 1-parent, rural, affluent & hard-pressed	Working class, students, male, rented, black-Asian [1.1] urban, moderate/hard pressed	Mixed SEC, own-occ, white, degree, male, ethnic 2.2, older married/no chil 1.4, prosperous	Working class, unempl, older, women, Asian-black, social housing

Source: Widdop and Cutts, 2013

This is not evidence of choosing different options in the supermarket of away-from-home leisure; it is a repeat of limited choice for those with poorer economic and social capital. Sport England has done some research on barriers, but little on non-participants in over 30 years. Yet *Taking Part* 2009–10, showed 36% were just not interested in playing sport, a decrease of only 2% since 1992; knowing better who these people are and where they are could save a lot of abortive marketing effort and money. Slee et al. (2001) cited 28% of people regarding access to the countryside as a priority for government, but the gradient was the reverse of that shown in Chapter 10 where the greatest desire was amongst the DE groups:

% suggesting greater access to the countryside is very important	
AB	15
C1	24
C2	30
DE	41

Muddiman et al. (2000: xi) described libraries as only superficially open to all. They spoke of two models of social inclusion by public library authorities – a 'weak' one of voluntary inclusion, where infrastructure and information change were made and a general invitation to take part issued – and much stronger policies involving targeting, outreach, community development and other interventions. They concluded that, overwhelmingly, the public library service has adopted the first, and weaker of these alternatives showing (2000: 23, 28) that only one in three Library Authorities had strategic inclusion policies and one in two no community outreach projects, and even fewer targeted the most needy or excluded

– the unemployed, prisoners and their families, the homeless, lesbians/homosexuals, refugees, travellers or 'working-class' people.

While I would be marginally less critical of policies for sport centrally and locally, I would say that they have focussed disproportionately on disabled and ethnic minority people (who, along with women, have statutory support), and have played down the poverty issue, including the lack of good transport for non car-owners. In the same way as for libraries, the strong model has costs: it involves affirmative action in intervention, the targeting of resources, outreach work, and positive action to fulfil individual needs. These are conclusions shared by Slee et al. (2001) for countryside recreation, Coalter (2001a) for sport, and Smith (2001) for tourism.

Finally, it is worth pointing out that other researchers in Europe are finding social class gradients in their sport. Van der Meulen, Kraylaar, and Utlee (2001), using a life-history approach with a large sample, showed that better-educated people were less likely to drop out of sport, having been more likely to take it up in the first place. In elite sport, Nagel and Nagel (2001) reported that of 310 high-level competitive athletes in Germany, the proportion from high status backgrounds was 40% compared to 30% from low status backgrounds. This difference was statistically significant for participants in track and field, hockey, swimming, fencing, riding, rowing and sailing; only wrestling, Alpine/Nordic skiing, and cycling showed significant numbers of low-status participants, a noticeably less skewed distribution than for Britain as outlined in Chapter 4.

Virtually every piece of research calls for more research and better understanding. Tiresome though some may see it, this book repeats the litany. Previous work has been too descriptive, atheoretical, short term, output-related, short on in-depth understanding and users' or managers' perceptions, dependent on recall and self-report, and often not realistically grounded in context (Coalter, 2007). Thomas and Palfrey (1996) argued that as well as seeking effectiveness and efficiency, any public sector programme should be scrutinised for:

- equity (treating people with equal needs equally);
- acceptability (approximating to customer/consumer satisfaction);
- accessibility (of information, resources and services);
- appropriateness (relevance to each person's need);
- accountability (to citizens and any other investors);
- ethical considerations (being explicit about values and how conflicts will be resolved);
- responsiveness to consumers (in speed, accuracy and empathy);
- choice (which is a real issue in free time activities like sport and leisure).

They also relate these criteria in an interesting way to the different stakeholders in any policy (Table 12.6), and such an analysis has yet to be done in any full sense for a sport or leisure policy.

Table 12.6 Relationships between evaluation criteria and various stakeholders

Stakeholders / Criteria	Those who pay	Intended beneficiaries	Professionals	Managers	Politicians
Effectiveness		*	*	*	*
Efficiency	*	*	*	*	*
Equity		*		*	*
Acceptability	*		*		*
Accessibility	*		*	*	
Appropriate	*	*		*	
Responsiveness	*	*	*	*	*
Accountability		*	*	*	*
Ethical considerations		*	*		
Choice	*	*		*	

Source: Thomas and Palfrey, 1996

The research agenda is broad, long and will be costly if taken seriously, reflecting affirmative policy actions for excluded people. It was best summarised by Coalter (2001b), thus:

1   *Measuring outputs –*

   • social effectiveness in terms of what kinds of people use facilities and services, and how often;
   • common data for comparisons across the leisure sub-sectors (to improve on Table 12.4!);
   • the nature and extent of non-use, with evidence on reasons for not taking part, and barriers to use, leading to an ability to assess the potential for particular services to address inclusion.

2   *Measuring outcomes –* a more complex and contentious issue of definition and evaluation than for outputs, going beyond enjoyment to developing personal social capital, evidence of evolving confidence and self-esteem (as in the delinquency case study in Chapter 9), impacts on educational performance, local economic benefits and health promotion;
3   *Understanding organisational factors –* including customers' and providers' experiences;
4   *Demonstrating the development of various forms of communal social capital* – which Coalter said would be 'time-consuming and expensive.'

Coalter (2007) developed a process model which sought to distinguish these elements, with outcomes being broad, of public interest and most difficult to measure (see Figure 11.1), as confirmed by the Social Exclusion Unit (2004: 23). Apart from my own endorsement of these ideas, Long and Sanderson (2001: 201) and Rowe (2001) support several aspects, the former speaking of the need to capture any negative side effects.

In the first edition of this book I recorded that Salvation Army/Henley Centre (1999) expected, by 2010:

- living standards for the majority rise by a third in real terms;
- a widening poverty gap, with the top tenth having ten times the income of the bottom tenth;
- greater work pressures on all groups, less able to withdraw from this rat race due to the increasing need to make private provision for their old age;
- fewer family households;
- a vulnerable middle-aged group in a 'care sandwich' will have been created, responsible for dependent children and older people while trying to ensure their own pensions.

Growth in living standards was slower than the Salvation Army anticipated, but the other three have come to pass.

After a world recession and the cuts of a new coalition, I opined (Collins, 2010b) that HMG's strategy for sport was hyper-optimistic, and its tactics for delivery mistaken, as follows:

1 The expectation that sport could bridge the 19-step gap from its position as the fourth most unequal country to the second most equal with Finland (Wilkinson and Prickett, 2009), a richer country with more social equality and three decades of co-ordinated health/sport/physical activity policies, was incredible. Updating the 1999 COMPASS project comparing European sports participation, Gratton, Rowe and Veal (2011) agreed that Britain was still in the middle rank participation group.

2 British participation was lower than Scandinavia but higher than southern Europe. The Minister for Sport quietly dropped his target, and has not replaced it, despite promising something 'more relevant'.

3 As this book has repeatedly shown, after some reductions, social gaps have been begun to widen again, and in sport the social class gap remains stubbornly wide (Rowe, Adams and Beasley, 2004).

4 The Coalition has cut some sports schemes, and by demanding large cuts by LAs condemns sport to larger-than-average cuts and price increases.

5 A policy requiring non-participants to find 120–150 minutes a week for sport and exercise means the only feasible source is to cut TV viewing and get out and be active, a series of decisions needing strong social marketing (like that shown in Birmingham, Case Study 2) which neither DCMS nor Sport England has provided.

6 Obesity among adults and children continues to grow unchecked, with costs of at least £4.7–4.9bn a year (Collins, 2009) and will be the moral panic that takes over this field when the diversion of the Olympics is over.

7 The expectation that NGBs composed of small, single-sport clubs (as shown in Chapter 11) could provide 300,000 new members was mistaken, especially in a cold economic climate; other means are needed.

8   Like most advanced societies, the UK is aging, despite higher birth rates among its newer citizens, yet unlike many of its counterparts, HMG has consistently focussed on youth and ignored the large net gains that can be made from improving the fitness of its older citizens, especially now they are expected to work longer for their pensions.

9   Facility re-investment to replace obsolete venues is insufficient; as it is, LAs now control only half of indoor public facilities on a day-to-day basis, the rest being managed by contractors or increasingly by trusts, as Table 12.7 shows. The Audit Commission (2006, Summary 3) opined none of them 'delivers the best overall value for money, or consistently results in more investment or higher levels of participation. However, in-house services tend to be significantly more expensive.' Surveying LAs' views of the future, King (2012) found three out of five saw their core remit as being facilitator and only one in eight as provider, and most an increasing marginalisation of 'sport for all.' LA expenditure on sport and recreation dropped from £1.4bn in 2010 to £1.1bn in 2012 (Sport England, 2013).

Table 12.7 Public sector sports provision in England and Wales 2009–10

%	In-house/Direct management	Private contractor(s)	Local Trusts, etc.
Indoor sports facilities	49	23	27
Outdoor sports facilities	65	19	16
Golf courses	39	46	15
Sports Development officers	92	4	4

Source: Summarised from CIPFA, 2010

10 Sports participation dropped by four per cent in 1998–2002; Stamatakis and Choudhury (2008) reckoned that 1997–2006 showed increases of only 0.5% for men and three per cent for women, and like Rowe 2004 found no closing of the social class gap; *Active People* showed only a 0.5 increase 2006–8 while the population increased by 1.5%, and thereafter remained static around London 2012. Despite policy, only four of 31 NGBs showed increases in 2009–10, and SE CEO Jennie Price said 'a number of major sports...urgently need to demonstrate their ability to grow participation' (Gibson. O. *Guardian* 16 December 2010).

11 So far as hopes for increasing participation amongst target groups, not one was achieved as *Taking Part* data demonstrated (Table 12.8).

    The UK faces the same challenges as the US, Australia and Canada; increases in elite performance can be managed and afforded but mass participation policies are inconsistent, poorly targeted as to mechanisms, and ineffective (Green, 2007). As could be said of the UK, Australia, Canada or the USA (Nicholson et al., 2011), Sotiriadou, Shilbury and Quick's view of the Australian sport system was:

it places emphasis on the development of junior athletes and their transition to elite. Consequently the participation, development and needs of the general population appear... to receive less attention. [It] under-represents recreational, and health and fitness membership/ participation pathways.

(Sotiriadou, Shilbury and Quick, 2008: 267)

Table 12.8 Taking Part sports participation data 2005–8 (once a month or more often)

	Vigorous sport		Moderate intensity sport	
	% 2007–8	Change from 2005–6	% 2007–8	Change from 2005–6
Black & minority ethnic	52.6	−0.6	21.0	1.8
Limiting disability	30.1	−2.2	9.7	0.2
Lower socio-economic groups	43.8	0.4	16.5	1.3
Females	46.1	−1.6	18.6	0.1

Source: DCMS, 2008

12 the aim of an-Olympic-inspired increase in activity is as unlikely as it has ever been (Brown and Murray, 2001, Coalter, 2004, Weed et al., 2009, Veal et al., 2012) despite the Organising Committee's and HMG's efforts in London.

In the world wide recession, job cuts and with inflation outstripping wage increases, earlier expectations of a growing society of leisure is receding (Veal, 2011, 2012), and Veblen's (1953) case that access to free time was the main means of social differentiation, is substantially weakened – what may distinguish future generations is *how* they use that time.

As was made clear in Chapter 8, the Blair government believed that participation in culture and leisure activity made a contribution towards 'the building and maintenance of social capital' (DCMS, 2001b: 115) 'and [has] a powerful influence...on social exclusion' (DCMS 2001a: 8). The DCMS made valiant attempts to improve access to sport, arts and culture, most directly through abolishing some national museum charges, but also through encouraging inclusion policies in cultural strategies for its Lottery funding bodies, Regional Cultural Consortia and local authorities, and investing in training for Sports Development officers and volunteers (DCMS, 2001a: 8).

Hylton and Totton (2001: 63) concluded 'sport and society both reproduce inequality but they can both also challenge it.' Sport is on the periphery of social exclusion rather than at its core. It is substantially a self-help movement or a consumer product and, apart from some local authorities, largely has kept itself aloof from social problems while partly reflecting them. If sportspeople do not become more involved, it will go on being a mirror rather than an agent of change. Being concerned about the efficiency of the sports delivery process and the effectiveness of programmes is not enough. Social change needs enablers, not just in the public sector. Sport has grown to be a larger part of people's lives and social life in the last 50 years. Yet Chapters 3 to 10 show that the gaps in opportunities for sport have been: slowly closing for most women and some older people; are still large for Asian groups and huge for most disabled people, one-parent families, and many other poor people. Opportunities are inequitable in the Sport England or Rawlsian senses described in Chapter 2.

To be a change agent means working with people and institutions in other sectors with other values, styles of operation and perspectives, and involves compromises and negotiations. Sport can bring joy and achievement for many people who have not had much of either in other spheres of their lives so far – the 'flow experiences' described by Csikszentmihalyi, 'finding delight in what the body can do' (1992: 94–116). Other countries demonstrate to Britain that extending participation and its many benefits *is* possible, even if they still suffer a lesser degree of exclusion.

The messages from this book are simple but profound: sport can be a policy partner and a tool for combating social exclusion. To be effective, it has to be much more people-focussed, and if area programmes are politically necessary, they need to be more tightly focussed for cost-effectiveness. Programmes need to be longer-term, better led, and designed *with* and not just *for* the people and organisations intended to benefit. Sport must be knit with many other aspects of citizenship.

Sport *for all who want it* is still a worthy and worthwhile objective for anyone who believes in a just society and equal opportunities of citizenship, and, I believe, a feasible one. As Donnelly wrote:

> Although sport has been an important agent in the production and reproduction of social inequality, democratising actions on the part of individuals and organisations have sensitised us to sport's potential to be an equally important agent of social transformation for the production of social equality, [and has] the potential to transform individuals and communities in ways that seriously reduce inequalities
>
> (Donnelly, 1996: 237)

Over 30 years ago, Roberts (1977: 25) opined 'consumer sovereignty remains a reality in the leisure market...and one reason is that, to date neither central government nor the local authorities in Britain have developed anything resembling coherent policies...the numerous types of public recreation provision have diverse historical origins.' Substantially, I agree this is still true, despite one Department (DCMS) having oversight over more of the field than its predecessors. He averred that the justifications for state involvement in this constantly changing sphere was threefold: to defend finite resources for the long term (as in National Parks and green belts); to use recreation for expedient other purposes (like improving public health); and to pursue redistributive justice. I think this is still true, though the postlude below will show how little the Coalition cares for the first or third of these. With its values of shared experience, and mutual support, the sports world can leave inclusion to others and be part of the problem of an unequal society, or take hard decisions and demanding steps to be part of the moves to inclusion and be part of solutions, even in current hard times.

Postlude: after the coalition, a deluge?

This brief section seeks to take a look at the short-term impacts that the Coalition's attempts to reduce public expenditure in the aftermath of the banking crash and world recession have made to aspects of and groups in British society, allowing that for sport there has been in 2012 a season of Olympic and other successes (cricket, rugby, Tour de France) from which one would expect at least a short term boost. Is David Cameron's Big Society emerging?

Work

- *Growth in precarious employment* – The Office of National Statistics had suggested that there were 250,000 people on zero-hour contracts (i.e., no guaranteed work), but a Chartered Institute of Personnel Development survey suggested over a million, by one in five employers, with 48% of employers in hotels, leisure and catering having at least one person on such terms (CIPD *Press Release*, 5 August 2013).

Income and poverty

- *Families and children* – despite evidence from the Institute for Fiscal Studies that its benefits outweighed its costs (of £560m and £36m a year administration), the Coalition abolished Educational Maintenance Allowance of £10–£30 per pupil weekly, Secretary of State arguing that there was over 80% deadweight (O'Brien, 2013), yet the Prime Minister said there would be 'little effect' on poor children. The Secretary of State for Communities warned him that capping annual welfare payments at £26,000 per family would add 20,000 families to the homeless in addition to the 20,000 already placed there by other benefit changes (Sparrow, A. *Guardian* 4 July 2011: 1–2). Using 12 indicators, the National Children's Bureau (2013: 1) damningly concluded that 'the inequality that existed fifty years ago still persists...and in some respects has become worse. Unless a new course of action is taken there is a real risk of sleepwalking into a world where inequality and disadvantage are so deeply entrenched that our children grow up in a state of social apartheid'.
- *Youth* – The Prince's Trust (2014) found amongst those Not in Education Employment or Training (NEETS: 430,000 long term) a fifth reckoned they had nothing to live for, two in five said unemployment had led to panic attacks, self-loathing and thoughts of suicide, a fifth of the young women had

self-harmed, one in five had turned to drugs or alcohol for solace, while more than half had no parental role model; there was a real risk of a lost generation.

- *Food poverty* – Cooper and Dumpleton (2013) reckoned that over 500,000 had become reliant on aid from food banks, mostly offered by churches.
- *Income* – Padley and Hirsch (2013: 5) reported that 'the past four years have seen the longest sustained fall in living standards in the post-war era' with more serious impacts on the poorest.
- *New concentrations* – older coastal resorts have high levels of unemployment, poor education and qualifications, and high unemployment, and many small, redundant hotels turned into cheap bed & breakfast accommodation; the Centre for Social Justice (2013) suggested that poverty was attracting poverty with levels of deprivation (failure at school, teenage pregnancy, single fatherhood, addiction, worklessness) as great as inner cities.
- *Myths and truths* – Four major churches (Baptist Union et al., 2013) produced an excoriating critique of myths, which was reinforced by politicians and the press, that blame the poor for their poverty, alleging that 'they' – poor families – are:

Myths	Facts
1. 'lazy and just don't want to work	more poor in work than jobless
2. 'addicted to drink and drugs	under 4% have any addiction
3. 'not really poor – they just don't manage their money properly	poorest spend carefully on essentials
4. 'on the fiddle	0.9% of benefits defrauded
5. have an easy life on benefits	do not meet minimum incomes, halved relative to earnings over 30 years
6. caused the deficit	welfare stable % of tax for 20 years.

Ferragini, Tomlinson and Walker (2013: 5) judiciously concluded 'the existence of such different worlds helps to explain the gulf in understanding and the high level of mistrust…between those who are in poverty and those who are not.'

Women

- Evaluating the UK response in 2008–13 to the 19 articles of the UN Convention on Elimination of all forms of Discrimination against Women, the Women's Resource Centre (CEDAW 2013: 33) reported that 'the government's policies have had a negative impact on many women through the loss of jobs, income and services. Additional measures announced will intensify these losses for all but the richest women.' In the light of Kay's analysis in Chapter 5, this will reduce women's opportunities for sports participation.

Children

- After a decade of shrinkage, and partly as a result of immigration, the numbers of primary and secondary school children are forecast to grow by 20% and 9% respectively 2011–21, demanding more schools and teachers, including PE & sport (DfE, 2013). Despite the CMO (2012) saying 'prevention pays,' Secretaries of State for Education and Health are not listening regarding the long-term costs of inactivity.

Disability

- Of the new fitness-for-work tests, one of its architects, Professor Paul Gregg declared to be 'badly malfunctioning…a complete mess' and in need of revision, having caused 'a huge amount of anguish' (Gentleman, A. *Guardian* 23 February 11: 1–2).

Ethnicity

- Perry (2011) pointed out that services for migrants have already been cut heavily by the Coalition.

Local Authority sport and recreation

- The Audit Commission (2011) reckoned that 47% of the savings LAs need to meet HMG's cuts would come from planning, housing and cultural services, despite them comprising only a sixth of all services, meaning real cuts and price increases.

Sports Participation

- YouGov (2012) gave new insights into meaning and attitudes of young adults to sports participation but only a few into those of non-participants, insufficient to guide effective interventions; life transitions remain the largest reason for dropping out (Sport England, 2013: 13), most of which are not amenable to sports policy, though some transitions provide new opportunities (ibid: 17). The interest in playing varies much less by socio-economic group than actual participation, leading Sport England (2013: 23) to conclude 'as a result this is a key driver for many local authorities.' Maybe the old lesson of taking sport to the people and their doorsteps, tapped by Action Sport in the 1980s and Street Games and Kickz currently, is worthy of further attention. The SRA (2013a) found one in five clubs showed an increase in adult membership over 2011 but only one in ten attributed this to the Olympics; this may partly be the effect of a snowball online sample under-representing small clubs; another sample (2013b) repeated such doubts, but club memberships may be a more reliable legacy than informal participation.

A legacy from London 2012?

*   *For participation* – All previous studies, had shown no benefits from the Olympic Games (e.g., Coalter 2004, and Veal, Toohey and Frawley, 2011), while Pappous (2011) used Eurobarometer data to show an immediate boost in 2004 from 10 to 16% in regular exercisers, but a decline to three per cent by 2009, joint lowest in Europe. Active People 7 showed some 1.5 m more people taking part immediately after the Games than in 2010–11, less so for people in deprived areas, BMEs and 16–24s (suffering worse than most in the recession); eight per cent of both players and non-players claimed to be more interested in sport as a result of the Games (TNS/BMRB, 2012). It is difficult to believe that the short-term boost will outlive the long-term structural inequities.
*   *For disability* – the government (ODI, 2010) talked up a legacy from London 2012 for disabled people, but the most tangible benefits may come from Sport England granting £8m in 2010–12 to recruit and train disabled volunteers, and London Transport's improving access at 164 of its stations.

While life is better in Britain than in Greece, Portugal and Spain and many other countries, this litany suggests that social polarisation is again increasing – indeed may be worse than at any time since Mrs Thatcher was Prime Minister, and that it could take another 20 years to get back to the position of the 1990s. The social divides in health, lifespan and quality of life so graphically illustrated by Marmot (2010, 2011), including sport and leisure, seem unlikely to reduce for a long time,

Figure 12.1 Life expectancy/disability-free life expectancy by neighbourhood income deprivation 1999–2003

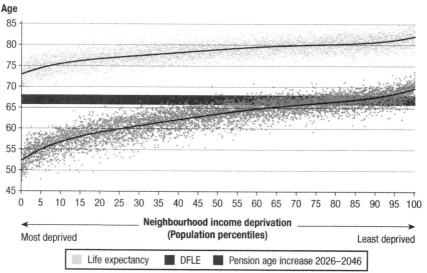

Source: Office for National Statistics

consigning the UK's hopes to improve on its middle rank in sports participation to dust once the Olympic glow has faded.

In the European Year of Social Inclusion, the EU confirmed the role of sport as 'a driver of active social inclusion' (CEU, 2010), with particular reference to accessibility, disadvantage and gender. But in Britain, sport's puny policy leverage (Houlihan and Lindsey, 2013) – what Coalter (2013b: 18) called 'epiphenomenal, a secondary set of social practices dependent upon and reflecting more fundamental structures' is powerless against the structural forces listed above, and one must expect it to suffer inequity and exclusion to at least as great as other sectors of society.

References

Academy of Medical Sciences (2009). *Rejuvenating ageing research*, London: AMS.

Ackcayer, B. (2004). The sport and movement programme of Turkey culture clubs in Cologne, pp. 123. In Leisure tourism and sport conference: Education, integration, innovation 18–20 Mar, Cologne.

Adair, D., Taylor, T. and Darcy, S. (2010). Managing ethnocultural and 'racial' diversity in sport: Obstacles and opportunities. *Sport Management Review* 13.4: 307–12.

Adonis, A. and Pollard, S. (1997). *A class act: The myth of a classless society*, London: Hamish Hamilton.

Age Concern/Commission for Racial Equality (CRE). (1998). *Age and Race: Double discrimination – Life in Britain today for ethnic minority elders*, London: AC/CRE.

Aitchison, C. (2003). From leisure and disability to disability leisure: Developing data, definitions and discourses. *Disability and Society* 18,7: 955–69.

Aitchison, C. (2007). *Sport and gender identities: masculinities, femininities, sexualities*, London: Routledge.

Alcock, P. (1997). *Understanding poverty*, London: MacMillan.

Alcock, P. (2003). 'Maximum feasible participation': lessons from previous wars on poverty. paper to Changing European societies conference Copenhagen 13–15 November.

Alcock, P. (2004). Participation or policy: contradictory tensions in Area-based policy. *Social Policy & Society* 3, 2: 87–96.

Alcock, P. and Craig, G. (1998). Monitoring and evaluation of local authority anti-poverty strategies in the UK. *International Journal of Public Sector Management* 11,7: 553–65.

Alcock, P. et al. (1995). *Combating local poverty: the management of anti-poverty strategies by local government*, Luton: Local Government Management Board.

Alcock, P. et al. (1998). *Inclusive Regeneration: the impact on regeneration of local authorities corporate strategies for tackling regeneration*, Sheffield: Centre for Regional Economic and Social Research.

Aldridge, H. et al. (2011). *Measuring poverty and social exclusion 2011*, York: Joseph Rowntree Foundation.

Allison, M. (2001). *Sport clubs in Scotland*. Research Report 75, Edinburgh: sportscotland.

Alzubadi H. et al. (2013). *Households Below Average Income (HBAI). 1994–5 to 2011–2*, London: Department of Work and Pensions.

Amara, M, et al. (2004). *Sport and multiculturalism* [in the EU], Loughborough: University, Institute of Sport and Leisure Policy.

Amara, M. et al. (2006). *The roles of sport and education in the social inclusion of asylum seekers and refugees: An evaluation of policy and practice in the UK*, Loughborough: University, Institute of Sport and Leisure Policy.

Ambrose-Oji, B. (2009). *Equality and inclusion of social diversity with respect to woods and forests in the UK: An evidence review*, Farnham, Surrey: Forest Research.

American Association of Retired People (2002). *The role of midlife and older consumers in promoting Physical activity through health care settings*, Washington DC: AARP.

American College of Sports Medicine (1998). Position Stand. The recommended quantity and quality of exercise for developing and maintaining cardiorespiratory and muscular fitness, and flexibility in healthy adults. *Medical Science in Sport and Exercise* 30,6: 975–91.

Anders, G. (1982). Sport and youth culture. *International Review of Sports Sociology* 1,17: 49–60.

Anderson, C. (2011). Street Games: doorstep sport. *Leisure Studies Association Newsletter* 88: 57–62.

Anderson, E.M., Clarke, L. and Spain, B. (1982). *Disability in adolescence*, London: Methuen.

Andrew, B. (2004). *Social capital in sport in south London*. Unpublished MSc thesis, Loughborough: University.

Andrews, R., Cowell, R. and Downe, J. (2008). Support for active citizenship and public service performance: An empirical analysis of English local authorities. *Policy and Politics* 36, 2: 225–43.

Anon (2009). *Be Active* report to Birmingham City Council Cabinet July, Appendix A.

Anstett, M. and Sachs, B. (1995). *Sports, jeunesse et logiques d'insertion* [Sports, youth and the logic of insertion], Paris: Ministére de la Jeunesse et des Sports.

Arkenford/Act2 Ltd (2006). *Understanding participation in sport: What determines sports participation among recently retired people?* London: Sport Engalnd.

Arnaud, L. (1996). *Sports policies, ethnic minorities and democracy: a comparative analysis of Lyons and Birmingham*. Paper to 4th EASM congress, Montpellier.

Atkinson, R. (2000). Combating social exclusion in Europe: The new urban policy challenge. *Urban Studies* 37,5–6: 1037–55.

Atkinson, W. (2007). Beck, individualisation and the death of class: a critique. *British Journal of Sociology* 58, 3: DOI10.1111/j.1468-4666.2007.00155.x.

Audit Commission (1989). *Sport for whom?* London: HMSO.

Audit Commission (1996). *Misspent youth: young people and crime*, Abingdon, Oxon: AC.

Audit Commission (1999). *The price is right*, London: AC.

Audit Commission (2003). *Services for disabled children*, London: AC.

Audit Commission (2006). *Public sports and recreation services-making them fit for the future*, London: AC.

Audit Commission (2009a). *Tired of hanging around: Using sport and leisure activities to prevent anti-social activities by young people*, London: AC.

Audit Commission (2009b). *Final score: The impact of the Comprehensive Performance Assessment of local government 2002–08*, London: AC.

Audit Commission (2009c). *Working better together? Managing local strategic partnerships – Cross-cutting summary*, London: AC.

Audit Commission (2011). *Tough times: Councils' responses to a challenging financial climate*, London: AC.

Baas, J.M., Ewert, A. and Chavez, D.J. (1993). Influence of ethnicity on recreation and natural environment use patterns: managing recreation sites for ethnic and racial diversity. *Environmental Management* 17.4: 523–9.

Badenoch, D. (1998). *Wilderness adventure programs for youth at risk.* Paper to 21st biennial ACHPER conference, Adelaide.

Bailey, P. (1987). *Leisure and class in Victorian England: rational recreation and the contest for control 1830–85*, London: Methuen.

Bailey, R., Morley, D. and Dismore, H. (2009). Talent development in PE: a national survey of policy and practice in England. *PE and Sport Pedagogy* 14,1: 59–72.

Baker, C. and Miles-Watson, J. (2010). Faithful & traditional capitals: defining the scope of spiritual and religious capitals: a literature review. *Implicit Religion* 13,1: 17–69.

Baker, D. and Witt P.A. (1996). Evaluation of the impact of two after school recreation programs. *Journal of Park and Recreation Administration* 14,3: 23–44.

Baker, S. and White, P. (2010). Impacts of free concessionary travel: case study of an English rural region. *Transport Policy* 17: 20–6.

Baptist Union et al. (2013). *The lies we tell ourselves: Ending comfortable myths about poverty*, London: Methodist Publishing.

Balloch, S. and Jones, B. (1990). *Poverty and Anti-poverty strategy: The local government response*, London: Association of Metropolitan Authorities.

Barclay, J. (1995). *Inquiry into Income and Wealth,* 2 vols, York: Joseph Rowntree Foundation.

Barnard, H. and Turner. C. (2011). *Poverty and ethnicity: A review of evidence*, York: Joseph Rowntree Foundation.

Barnes, C., Mercer G. and Shakespeare, T. (1999). *Exploring disability: a sociological reader*, Oxford: Polity Press.

Barnes, C. et al. (2000). *Lives of disabled children.* Children 5–16 briefing Stirling: Economic & Social Research Council.

Barrett, J. and Greenaway, R. (1995). *The role and value of outdoor adventure in young people's personal and social development*, Coventry: Foundation for Outdoor Adventure.

Barry, B. (2002). Social exclusion, social isolation, and the distribution of income, pp. 13–22. In J. Hills, J. Le Grand and D. Piachaud (eds). *Understanding social exclusion*, Oxford: , Oxford University Press.

Barton, J., Hine, R. and Pretty, J. (2010). What is the best dose of nature and green exercise for improving mental health? *Environmental Science and Technology* 44,10: 3947–55.

Baubock, R. (2000). Social and cultural integration in civil society, pp. 91–119. In McKinnon, C. and Hampsher-Monk, I. (eds). *The demands of citizenship*, London: Continuum.

Bauman, Z. (1998). *Work, consumerism and the new poor*, Buckingham: Open University Press.

Bayliss, M. (1989). PE and Racism: Making changes. *Multicultural Teaching* 7: 19–22.

Beck, U. (1992). *Risk society: Towards a new modernity*, London: Sage.

Becker, E. and Boreham, R. (2009). *Understanding the risks of social exclusion across the life course: Older Age*, London: Cabinet Office.

Begg, D. et al. (1996). Sport and delinquency: an examination of the deterrence hypothesis: a longitudinal study. *British Journal of Sports Medicine* 30: 335–41.

Bell, B. (2010). Building a legacy for youth and coaching: Champion Coaching on Merseyside 139–66 in Collins, M. (ed). *Examining Sport Development*, London: Routledge.

Bellamy, K. and Rake, K. (2005). *Money, Money, Money: Is it still a rich man's world? An audit of women's economic welfare in Britain today*, London: Fawcett Society.

Bennett, K., Hudson, R. and Beynon, H. (2000). *Coalfields regeneration: Dealing with the consequences of industrial decline*, York: The Policy Press.

Bentley, C. (2008). *Systematically addressing health inequalities*, London: Department of Health.

Beresford, P. (1996). Poverty and disabled people: challenging dominant debates and policies. *Disability and Society* 11,4: 553–67.

Beresford, P. and Croft, S. (1995). It's our problem too. *Critical Social Policy* 15, 2–3: 75–95.

Berghman, J. (1995). Social exclusion in Europe: policy context and analytical framework. In G. Room et al. (eds) *Beyond the threshold: The measurement and analysis of social exclusion* Policy Press: Bristol.

Bernard, M. (ed) (1988). *Positive approaches to ageing: leisure and lifestyle in older age*, Stoke-on-Trent: Beth Johnson Foundation.

Beveridge, W. (1942). *Social insurance and allied services Cmd* 6404, London: HMSO.

Billings, A. and Holden, A. (2008). *Interfaith interventions and cohesive communities: The Burnley project*, Lancaster: The University Dept of Religious Studies.

Birmingham Health & Wellbeing Partnership (2009). *A Pan-Birmingham PA offer*, 27 Feb 2009.

Bishop, J. and Hoggett, P. (1986). *Organising around enthusiasms: Patterns of mutual aid in leisure*, London: Comedia.

Black Environmental Network (2003). *Capturing richness: Countryside visits by black and ethnic minority communities*, Cheltenham: Countryside Agency.

Blair, A. (1999). The Beveridge lecture. Speech at Toynbee Hall, London 18 Mar 1999. Available at: www.number-10.gov.uk/public/info/index.html. [Accessed 25 November 1999].

Blowers, A. and Young, S. (2000). Britain: unsustainable cities, pp. 91–109. In Low, N. et al. (eds). *Consuming cities – The urban environment in the global economy after the Rio Declaration*, London: Routledge.

Boardman, B. (1998). Travel and poverty. *Rural Focus* 10–11.

Boessenkool, J. (2001). Constructing viable sports clubs, pp. 217–45. In Steenbergen, J., de Knop, P., and Elling, A. (eds). *Values and norms in sport*, Oxford: Meyer and Meyer Sport.

Bolton, N. (2010). Promoting participation and inclusion? The free swimming initiative in Wales, pp. 242–59. In M. Collins (ed). *Examining Sports Development*, London: Routledge.

Booth, C. (1882). *Life and labour of the people in London*, London: Macmillan.

Boothby, J., et al. (1982). *A sporting chance? Family, school and environmental influences on taking part in sport*, Study 22, London: Sports Council.

Borrett, N., Kew, F. and Stockham, K. (1996). *Disability, young people sport and leisure paper to WLRA 4th World Congress*. Unpublished. Cardiff July 18–20.

Bourdieu, P. (1978). Sport and social class. *Social Science Information* 18,6: 821–30.

Bourdieu, P. (1985). *Distinction: A social critique of the judgement of taste*, London: Routledge.

Bovaird, T., Nichols, G. and Taylor, P. (1997). *Approaches to estimating the wider economic and social benefits resulting from sports participation*, Birmingham: Aston Business School.

Brackenridge, C. et al. (2008). *A review of sexual orientation in sport*. Research Report 114 Edinburgh: sportscotland.

Bradford Trident (2004). *Sport making a difference in neighbourhoods*. Presentation to Sporting Futures Conference 15 October, Sheffield.

Brantingham, P. and Faust, F. (1976). A Conceptual Model of Crime. *Prevention Crime and Delinquency* 22: 248–96.

Brettschneider, W-D. (1990). Adolescents, leisure, sport and lifestyle, pp. 536–50. In T. Williams, L. Almond and A. Sparkes (eds). *Sport and physical activity: Moving towards excellence*, London: E & F Spon.

Breuer, C. and Wicker, P. (2009). Decreasing sports activity with increasing age? Findings from a 20-year longitudinal and cohort sequence analysis. *Research Quarterly for Sport and Exercise* 80,1: 22–31.

Brewer, M., Browne, J. and Joyce, R. (2011). *Child and working age poverty from 2010 to 2020*, London: Institute of Fiscal Studies.

Brittain, I. (2004). Perceptions of disability and their impact upon involvement in sport for people with disabilities at all levels. *Journal of Sport and Social Issues* 28: 429–52.

British Heart Foundation (BHF). (2003). *Active for later life: Promoting physical activity with older people,* London: BHF.

British Heart Foundation (2009). *Couch kids: the nation's future*, London: BHF.

British Heart Foundation National Centre (2008). *Opening doors to an active life: how to engage inactive communities* Information booklet, Loughborough: The Centre.

British Heart Foundation National Centre (2013). *Making the case for physical activity*, Loughborough: The Centre.

British Medical Association (2012). *Healthy transport=healthy lives*, London: BMA.

British Sports Association for the Disabled (BSAD). (1994). *Short guide to the design of sports buildings*, London: BSAD.

Brodie, D. and Roberts, K. (1992). *Inner city sport: Who plays, what are the benefits?* Culembourg: Giordano Bruno.

Brodie, D., Roberts, K., and Lamb, K. (1991). *Citysport Challenge*, Cambridge: Health Promotion Research Trust.

Brown, A. and Madge, J. (1982). *Despite the welfare state*, London: Heinemann Education.

Brown, A. and Murray, J. (2001). *Literature Review: The impact of major sports events.* Manchester: Metropolitan University, Centre for Popular Culture.

Brown, D. (1999). *Care in the country: Inspection of community care in rural areas*, London: Department of Health.

Brown, G. (1999). Speech to Surestart conference 7 July 1999. Available at: www.hm-treasury.gov.uk/speech/cx70799.html. [Accessed 16 April 2008].

Brownhill, S. and Thomas, H. (1998). Ethnic minorities and British urban policy: A discussion of trends in governance and democratic theory. *Local Government* 24,1: 43–55.

Brundtland, G.H. (2003). In the XXI century poverty still has a woman's face. Available at: www.tierramerica.info/english/2003/0309/igrandesplumas.shtml. [Accessed 25 April 2006].

Bryant, P. (2001). *Social exclusion and sport: the role of training and learning*, London: SPRITO TCL.

Buller, J. (1998). *Bridging the Gap?' An evaluation of Champion Coaching and Performance Squads in Nottinghamshire.* Unpublished MSc thesis, Loughborough: University.

Buller, J.R. and Collins, M.F. (2000). Bridging the post-school institutional gap: Champion Coaching in Nottinghamshire. *Managing Leisure* 5: 200–21.

Bullough, S. (2011). *The importance of student voice.* Presentation to seminar on the Wolfendon Gap Sheffield 9 March 2011, Sheffield: Sport Industry Research Centre.

Bundrick, D. and Witt, P.A. (1998). *College Station after-school programme and time-use study.* Texas A&M University: Department of Recreation, Park & Tourism Sciences.

Burchardt, T. (2006). Capabilities and disability: the capabilities framework and the social model of disability. *Disability and Society* 21,2: 735–51.

Burchell, B. and Rubery, J. (1994). Divided Women: Labour Market Segmentation and Gender Segregation 80–120 in A. MacEwen Scott (ed.). *Gender Segregation and Social Change*, Oxford: Oxford University Press.

Burgess, E. (1967). The growth of the city in E.W. Burgess, R.E. Park and R.D. McKenzie (eds). *The city*, Chicago: Chicago University Press.

Burnett, C. and Hollander, W. (1999). *'Sport for All' versus 'All for Sport': Empowering the disempowered in South Africa* paper to Sport for All congress Barcelona, Nov.

Burt, C. (1925). *The young delinquent*, London: London University Press.

Bynum, J. (1996). *Juvenile delinquency: A sociological approach*, Boston: Allyn and Bacon.

Byrne, D. (1998). Public policy and social exclusion. *Local Economy* 13.1: 81–3.

Byrne, D. (2001). *Social exclusion*, Buckinghamshire: Open University Press.

Cabinet Office (CO). (2000). *Minority ethnic issuers in social exclusion and neighbourhood renewal*, London: Cabinet Office.

Cabinet Office (2001). *Improving labour market achievements for ethnic minorities in British society: a scoping note*. Available at: www.researchonline.org.uk/sds/search/download.do;jsessionid=7BE33A05A47C903C7A9FA4150B3B95F2?ref=T3049. [Accessed 24 February 2014].

Campbell, S. (2000). Change through sport. *Recreation* 59.8: 21–3.

Candler, P. (1999). *Cross-national perspectives on the principles and practice of children's play provision*. Unpublished PhD, Leicester: De Montfort University.

Cantle T. (2007). Race and community cohesion. *Sociology Review* 16,3: 1–6.

Cantle, T. (2008). Parallel lives – the development of community cohesion, pp. 9–19. In N. Johnson (ed). *Citizenship, cohesion and solidarity*, London: The Smith Institute.

Cap Gemini (2003). *Final report*, London: Cap Gemini Ernst & Young UK plc.

Carley, M. et al. (2000). *Urban regeneration through partnership*, Bristol: Policy Press.

Carrington, B. and McDonald, I. (2001). *Race, sport and British society*, London: Routledge.

Carrington, B. and McDonald, I. (2008). The politics of race and sports policy. In B.M.J. Houlihan (ed). *Sport and society*, London: Sage.

Carroll, R. and Hollinshead, G. (1993). Equal opportunities: Race and gender in PE: A case study in J. Evans (ed). *Equality, education and Physical Education*, London: Falmer Press.

Lord Carter (2005). *Review of national sport effort and resources*, London: Sport England.

Casey, T. (2002). *Social capital and regional economies in Britain* Terre-Haut, IN: Rose Hulman Institute of Technology. Unpublished. Available at www.rose-hulman.edu. [Accessed 25 February 2014].

Cashmore, E. (1982). *Black sportsmen*, London: RKP.

Cashmore, E. (1989). *United Kingdom? Race, class and gender since the war*, London: Unwin Hyman.

Cashmore, E. (1996). *Making sense of sports*, 2nd ed, Routledge: , London.

Cavet, J. (1995). Leisure provision in Europe, pp. 49–64. In J. Hogg and J. Cavet (1995). *Making leisure provision for people with profound learning and multiple disabilities*, London: Chapman and Hall.

CEDAW Group (2013). *Women's equality in the UK: A health check,* London: Women's Resource Centre.

CelloMRUK (2010). *Glasgow Household Survey 2010*, Glasgow: Cello.

Central Council for Physical Recreation (CCPR). (1960). *Sport in the community* (The Wolfenden report), London: CCPR.

Centre for Leisure Research (CLR). (1993). *Survey of concession cards in Scotland Final report*, Edinburgh: CLR.

Centre for Leisure Research (1995). *Sport for people with disabilities in the East Midlands*, Nottingham: East Midland Council for Sport and Recreation.

Centre for Leisure Research (1999). *Notes on youth and sport.* Unpublished. Edinburgh: CLR.

Centre for Leisure and Sport Research (2001). *Part of the Game? An examination of racism in grassroots football*, Leeds: Metropolitan University.

Centre for Social Justice (2011). *More than a game: Harnessing the power of sport to transform the lives of young people*, London: CSJ.

Centre for Social Justice (2013). *Turning the tide*, London: The Centre.

Chapman, J., Craig, S. and Whalley, C. (2002). *Positive Futures: A review of impact and good practice, summary*, London: Sport England.

Chan, T.W. and Goldthorpe, J. (2005a). The social stratification of theatre, dance and cinema attendance. *Cultural Trends* 14,3: 193–212.

Chan, T.W. and Goldthorpe, J. (2005b). Social stratification and cultural consumption: Music in England. *European Sociological Review* 23: 1–13.

Chanan, G. (1999). *Local community involvement: A handbook for good practice*, Dublin: European Foundation for living and Working Conditions.

Charlton, A. (2010). A new Active Sports Partnership: Lancashire Sport, pp. 88–104. In M. Collins (ed). *Examining Sports Development*, London: Routledge.

Charrier, D. (1997). *Activités Physiques et sportives et d'insertion des jeunes* [Physical and sporting activities and insertion of youth], Paris: La Documentation Francaise.

Chartered Institute of Public Finance (CIPFA). (1999). (2008). (2009). (2010). *Culture, Sport and Recreation Statistics 2006–7, 2007–8 and 2008–9 Estimates* respectively, London: CIPFA.

Chief Leisure Officers Association/National Cultural Forum (nd). *The role of culture and sport in reducing crime and anti-social behaviour*, Ipswich: CLOA.

Chief Medical Officer (2004). *At least five a week: Evidence of the impact of physical activity and its relationship to health*, London: Department of Health.

Chief Medical Officer (2012). *Our children deserve better: prevention pays*, London: Department of Health.

Child, E. (1985). *General theories of play*, London: Playboard.

Childrens Play Council (CPC). (2000). *Best play: What play provision should do for children*, London: CPC.

Church, A. et al. (2002). *Identifying social, economic and environmental outcome indicators relevant to sport*, Brighton: University of Brighton.

Clarke, A. (1993). Leisure and the elderly: a different world? Paper to LSA conference *Leisure in different worlds*, Loughborough UK 14–18 July.

Clarke, G. (1998). Queering the pitch and coming out to play: Lesbians in Physical Education and sport. *Sport, Education and Society* 3.2: 145–60.

Clarke, J. and Critcher, C. (1985). *The devil makes work*, Basingstoke: MacMillan Education Ltd.

Cloke, P., Milbourne, P. and Thomas, C. (1994). *Lifestyles in rural England*, Rural Research report 18, Rural Development Commission: Salisbury.

Coalter, F. (1989a). Leisure policy: an unresolvable dualism? pp. 115–29. In C. Rojek (ed). *Leisure for leisure*, Basingstoke: MacMillan.

Coalter, F. (1989b). *Sport and anti-social behaviour: a literature review*, Edinburgh: Scottish Sports Council.

Coalter, F. (1990). The politics of professionalism: consumers or citizens? *Leisure Studies* 9: 107–19.

Coalter, F. (1991). Sports Participation: Price or Priorities? *Leisure Studies* 12: 171–82.

Coalter, F. (1996). *Sport and anti-social behaviour: a policy-related review*, Edinburgh: Scottish Sports Council.

Coalter, F. (1998). Leisure studies, leisure policy and social citizenship: the failure of welfare or the limits of welfare? *Leisure Studies* 17,4: 21–36.

Coalter, F. (1999). Sport and recreation in the UK: Flow with the flow or buck the trends? *Managing Leisure* 4: 24–39.

Coalter, F. (2000). Public and commercial leisure provision: active citizens and passive consumers. *Leisure Studies* 19: 163–81.

Coalter, F. (2001a). *Realising the potential of cultural services: the case for sport*, London: Local Government Association.

Coalter, F. (2001b). *Realising the potential of cultural services: Research Agenda*, London: Local Government Association.

Coalter, F. (2004). Stuck in the blocks? A sustainable sporting legacy in A. Vigor and M. Mean (eds.). *After the Gold rush: The London Olympics*, London: Institute of Public Policy Research/Demos.

Coalter, F. (2007). *A wider role for Sport: Who's keeping the score?* London: Routledge.

Coalter, F. (2008). Sport-in-development: Development for and through sport? pp. 39–68. In M. Nicholson and R. Hoye (eds). *Sport and social capital*, Oxford: Elsevier.

Coalter, F. (2011). *Sport conflict and youth development*, London: Comic Relief.

Coalter, F. (2013a). *The social benefits of sport*, Glasgow: sportscotland.

Coalter, F. (2013b). Game Plan and The Spirit Level: the class ceiling and the limits of sports policy? *International Journal of Sport Policy and Politics* 5,1: 3–19.

Coalter, F., Allison, M. and Taylor, J. (2000). *The role of sport in regenerating deprived urban areas*, Edinburgh: Scottish Executive Central Research Unit.

Coalter, A., Duffield, B. and Long, J. (1986). *The rationale for public sector investment in leisure*, London: Sports Council.

Cohen, A.K. (1955). *Delinquent Boys: The culture of the gang*, New York: Collier MacMillan.

Cohen, S. (1980). *Folk Devils and Moral Panics*, 2nd ed, London: Martin Robertson.

Collins, M.F. (1977). *Sport and the inner city*, Research Working Paper 7, London: Sports Council.

Collins, M.F. (1994). Children's Play: 'Little orphan Annie' in the British leisure system, pp. 175–85. In D. Leslie (ed). *Leisure and tourism: Towards the Millennium*, vol 2 publication 52, Eastbourne: Leisure Studies Association.

Collins, M.F. (1996). Sights on sport. *Leisure Management* 15.9: 26–8.

Collins, M.F. (1997). Does a new philosophy change the structures? Compulsory Competitive Tendering and local authority leisure services in Midland. *England Managing Leisure* 2.4: 204–16.

Collins, M.F. (ed). (2002). *Swimming for children from ethnic minorities in Nottingham and Leicester* for Amateur Swimming Association, Loughborough: The University.

Collins, M. (2005). Voluntary sports clubs and social capital, pp. 105–18. In G. Nichols and M. Collins (eds). *Volunteers in sports clubs*, Publication 85, Eastbourne: Leisure Studies Association.

Collins, M. (2008a). Social exclusion from sport and leisure 77–105 in B. Houlihan (ed) *Sport and society: A student introduction*, 2nd ed, London: Sage.

Collins, M.F. (2008b). Leisure cards: Commercial marketing to obtain customer loyalty, or social marketing for disadvantaged groups. *Figure it out, Institute of Public Finance Statistics Bulletin* No.11: 10–3.

Collins, M. (2009). *Some of the large economic and social costs of physical inactivity to Britain.*, London: Council for the Advancement of Arts, Recreation and Education.

Collins, M. (2010a). Social policy and sports policy-meeting the challenge of deprivations, pp. 214–32. In W. Tokarski and K. Petry (eds). *Handbuch Sportpolitik* [Handbook of Sports Policy] Schorndorf: Hofmann.

Collins, M.F. (2010b). From 'sport for good' to 'sport for sport's sake' – not a good move for Sports Development in England? *International Journal of Sport Policy* 2,3: 367–79.

Collins, M. (2011). Leisure Cards in England – an unusual combination of commercial and social marketing? *Social Marketing Quarterly* 17.2: 20–47.

Collins, M. (forthcoming, 2014). Cameron's Big Society, sport and religion, overt or implicit? *Implicit Religion.*

Collins, M.F. and Buller, J.R. (2003). Social exclusion from high performance sport? Are all talented young people being given an equal opportunity of reaching the Olympic podium? *Journal of Sport & Social Issues* 27,4: 420–42.

Collins, M.F and Enoch, N. (2006). *A leisure Card for Derbyshire*, Ilkeston: VAGA Associates.

Collins, M.F. and Jackson, G.A.M. (1998). Economic impacts of sport and tourism, pp. 169–202. In P. de Knop and J. Standeven (eds). *Sports Tourism*, Champaign, ILL: Human Kinetics.

Collins, M.F. and Kennett, C. R. (1998). Leisure poverty and social exclusion: the growing role of leisure cards. *Local Governance* 24.2: 131–42.

Collins, M.F. and Parker, A. (2010). Faith and sport revival in Britain: Muscular Christianity and beyond. *Stadion* 36, 195–212.

Collins, M. F. and Reeves, M. (1995). *From coal industry welfares to community welfares.* Conference paper to CISWO, Mansfield 18 September.

Collins, M.F., Henry, I.P. and Houlihan, B.M.J. (1999). *Sport and Social exclusion.* Report to Policy Action Team 10, London: DCMS.

Collins, M.F., Jackson, G.A.M. and Buller, J.R. (1999). *Leisure for disabled people in Leicester.* Report to City Council. Unpublished. Loughborough: University.

Collins, M.F., Randolph, L. and Sellars, C. (1994). *Service to voluntary sport: Nurturing or starving the grass roots*, Nottingham: East Midland Council for Sport & Recreation.

Collins, T. (1998). Racial minorities in a marginalized sport: Race, discrimination and integration on British Rugby League football, pp. 151–69. In M. Cronin and D. Mayall (eds). *Sporting nationalisms: Identity, ethnicity, immigration and assimilation*, London: Frank Cass.

Colwell, S. (1999). Feminism and figurational sociology: Contributions to understanding of sports, physical education and sex/gender. *European PE Review* 5,3: 219–34.

Commins, P. (ed). (1993). *Combating social exclusion in Ireland 1990–94: a midway report*, Brussels: European Commission.

Commission for Architecture and the Built Environment (2009). *Making the invisible visible: the Real value of open space*, London: CABESpace.

Commission for Racial Equality/Age concern (1998a). *Age and Race: double discrimination – an overview of life for ethnic minority elders in Britain today*, London: CRE/AC.

Commission for Racial Equality/Age Concern (1998b). *Age and Race: double discrimination – education and leisure*, London: CRE/AC.

Commission for Rural Communities (CRC). (2006). *Rural disadvantage: Reviewing the evidence*. Report 31 Cheltenham: CRC.

Commission for Rural Communities (2007). *The state of the countryside 2007*, Cheltenham: CRC.

Commission for Rural Communities (2008). *England's rural areas: Steps to release their economic potential*, Cheltenham: CRC.

Commission for Rural Communities (2010). *The state of the countryside 2010*, Cheltenham: CRC.

Commission on Urban Life and Faith (CULF). (2006). *Faithful Cities*, London: Church House.

Commonwealth of Australia (1999). *Shaping up: A review of Commonwealth involvement in sport and recreation*, Canberra: Commonwealth of Australia.

Community Consultants (1989). *Survey of people with disabilities: Recreational community and leisure needs*, London: Community Consultants.

Communities that Care (2005). *Risk and protective factors*, London: Youth Justice Board.

Cook, D. (1997). *Poverty, crime and punishment*, London: Child Poverty Action Group.

Cooper, B. (1989). *The management and prevention of juvenile crime problems*, London: Home Office.

Cooper, K. and Stewart, K. (2013). *Does money affect children's outcomes? A systematic review*, York: Joseph Rowntree Foundation.

Cooper, N. and Dumpleton, S. (2013). *Walking the breadline: the scandal of food poverty in 21st Century* Britain Manchester: Church Action on Poverty/Oxfam.

Coopers and Lybrand (1994). *Preventative strategy for young people in trouble*, Unpublished. London: C&L.

Council of the European Union (CEU). (2010). Conclusions of 18 November 2010 on the role of sport as a source and driver for active social inclusion. *Official Journal* 3.12.2010 C326/5-7.

Countryside Agency (CA). (2000). *Sense and accessibility* CAX26, Cheltenham: CA.

Countryside Agency (2002). *Diversity Review*, Cheltenham: CA.

Countryside Agency/English Nature (2005). *Diversity Review: Policy and legislation for providers*, Cheltenham: CA.

Cox, L., Coleman, L. and Roker, R. (2006). *Understanding participation in sport: what determines sports participation among 15–19 year-old women*, Trust for the Study of Adolescence, London: Sport England.

Cox, S. and Sparham, P. (2013). *Sports Club survey 2013*, London Sport & Recreation Alliance.

Crabbe, T. et al. (2005). *'Getting to know you': Engagement and relationship building: Case study report*, Sheffield Hallam University.

Crabbe, T. et al. (2006a). *'In the boot room': Organisational contexts and partnerships*, Sheffield: Sheffield Hallam University.

Crabbe, T. et al. (2006b). *Going the distance*, Sheffield Hallam University.

Crabbe, T. et al. (2006c). *Knowing the score: Positive Futures final case study report*, London: Home Office.

Craig, G. (2004). Citizenship, exclusion and older people. *Journal of Social Policy* 33,1: 95–114.

Craig, S. (2009). *Changing the lives of community volunteers (CSGYV year two evaluation)*, London: Leisure Futures.

Crime Concern (nd). *Splash – A guide for scheme organisers*, Swindon: Crime Concern.

Crompton, J. (2011). Using external reference pricing to reduce resistance to leisure service pricing increases. *Managing Leisure* 16,3: 207–15.

Crompton, J. and Witt, P.A. (1997). The roving leader program in San Antonio. *Journal of Park and Recreation Administration* 15,2: 84–92.

Cuskelly, G., Hoyt, R., and Auld, C. (2006). *Working with volunteers in sport: Theory and practice,* London: Routledge.

Csikszmentmihalyi, M. (1992). *Flow: the psychology of happiness,* London: Rider.

Daniel, W. (1968). *Racial discrimination in England,* Harmondsworth: Penguin.

Dattilo, J. and Williams, R. (1999). Inclusion in leisure services delivery, pp. 451–63. In E.L. Jackson and T.L. Burton (eds). *Leisure studies: prospects for the 21st century,* State College, PA: Venture Publishing.

Davis, P. and Howden-Chapman, P. (1996). Translating research findings into health policy. *Social Science and Medicine* 43: 865–72.

Dawson, D. (1988). Leisure and the definition of poverty. *Leisure Studies* 7: 221–31.

Dean, M. (nd). *Growing older in the 21st century,* Swindon: Economic and Social Research.

Deane, J. and Westerbeek, H. (1999). De-ethnicisation and Australian soccer: The management dilemma, pp. 100–104. In *Proceedings* 7th European Congress of Sports Managers 16–19th September Thessaloniki.

de Bosscher, V. et al. (2008). *The global sporting arms race: An international comparative study on Sports Policy Factors leading to International Success (SPLISS),* Oxford: Meyer and Meyer Sport.

de Knop, P. and de Martelaer, K. (2001). Quantitative and qualitative evaluation of youth sport in Flanders and the Netherlands: a case study. *Sport, Education and Society* 6,1: 35–51.

de Knop, P. et al. (1994). Islamic immigrant girls and sport in Belgium. Proceedings 2nd European Congress on Sport Management 241–56.

de Knop, P. et al. (1995). Towards a sound youth policy in the club, *European PE Review* 1,1: 6–14.

de Knop, P. et al. (1996a). *Youth-Friendly Sports Clubs: Developing an effective youth sport policy,* Brussels: VUB Press.

de Knop. P. et al. (1996b). Implications of Islam on Muslim girls' sport participation in Western Europe: Literature review and policy recommendations for sport promotion. *Sport, Education and Society* 1,2: 147–64.

de Knop, P. et al. (1997). Sports stimulation initiatives for underprivileged and immigrant youth in Belgium unpublished paper to conference European Network of Sports Sciences in Higher Education, Bordeaux, 117–23.

Denyer, D. (1997). *Peak Park guided walks.* Unpublished BSc dissertation, Loughborough: University.

Department for Children Schools and Families (DSCF). (2008). *PESSYP: Creating a world class system for PE & Sport,* London: DCSF.

Department for Children Schools and Families (DSCF)./DCMS (2010). *Positive Activities: Good practice guidelines – Delivering sports arts and culture activities as part of the Friday/Saturday night offer,* Annesley, Notts: DSCF.

Department for Culture Media and Sport (1999). *Sport and Arts report of Policy Action Team 10,* London: DCMS.

Department for Culture Media and Sport (2000). *A sporting future for all,* London: DCMS.

Department for Culture, Media and Sport (2001a). *Building on PAT10 Progress report on social inclusion,* London: DCMS.

Department of Culture, Media and Sport (2001b). *Libraries, museums, galleries and archives for All: Co-operation across the sectors to tackling social exclusion,* London: DCMS.

Department for Culture Media and Sport/Strategy Unit (2002). *Game Plan: a strategy for delivering the government's sport and physical activity objectives*, London: DCMS.

Department for Culture Media and Sport (2005). *Transexual people and sport: Guidance for sporting bodies* PP 771, London: DCMS.

Department for Culture Media and Sport (2008). *Taking part: The national survey of culture leisure and sport (complete estimates from year 3*, London: DCMS.

Department for Culture Media and Sport (2011). *Taking part: sports statistics 2010*, London: DCMS.

Department for Culture Media and Sport/Sport England (2012). *Creating a sporting habit for life: A new youth sport strategy*, London: DCMS.

Department for Education (2013). *National Pupil projections* Statistical Release SFR11, London: DfE.

Department for Education and Employment (DfEE). (2000). *Connexions – the best start in life for every young person* Nottingham: DfEE.

Department for Education and Science (DES). (1964). *A chance to share*, London: HMSO.

Department for Education and Science (2003). *Learning through PE and sport: A guide to the PESSCL strategy*, London: DES.

Department for Education and Skills (2004). *Removing barriers to achievement; the government's strategy for Special Educational Needs*, London: DfES.

Department for Environment, Food, and Rural Affairs (DEFRA). (2008). *Outdoors for All? An Action Plan to increase the number of people from under-represented groups who access the natural environment*, London: DEFRA.

Department for Environment Food and Rural Affairs (2013). *Statistical Digest of rural England 2013*, London: Government Statistical Survey.

Department for Transport (nd). *Covering note on WSP Research Report on options for extending the concessionary travel scheme*, London: DOT.

Department of the Environment (DoE). (1977). *Recreation and deprivation in inner urban areas*, London: HMSO.

Department of the Environment (1989). *Sport and active recreation provision in the inner cities: report of the Minister for Sports Review Group*, London: DOE.

Department of the Environment, Transport and the Regions (DETR). (1996). *Town centres and Retailing* Planning Policy Guidance Note 6, London: DETR.

Department of Environment Transport and the Regions (1998). *Building partnerships for prosperity*, London: DETR.

Department of the Environment, Transport and the Regions (2000a). *Index of deprivation* Regeneration Research summary 31, London: DETR.

Department of the Environment, Transport and the Regions (2000b). *Our towns and cities: The future – Delivering an urban renaissance* www.regeneration.detr.gov.uk/policies. Accessed 29 November 2000.

Department of Health (DoH). (2006). *Health Survey for England 2005*, London: DoH.

Department of National Heritage (DNH). (1995). *Sport: Raising the game*, London: DNH.

Department of Social Security (1997). *Social security statistics*, London: DSS.

Department of Social Security (1998). *A new contract for welfare: New ambitions for our country Cm3805*, London: The Stationery Office.

Department of Transport and the Regions (DTR) (2000a). *Social exclusion and the provision and availability of public transport.* Available at: www.mobility-unit.detr. gov.uk [Accessed 2 October 2000].

Department of Transport and the Regions (2000b). *Our Countryside: The future: A fair deal for rural England.* White Paper. Available at: www.detr.gov. [Accessed 7 March 2001].

Department of the Environment, Transport and the Regions (2000c). *Our towns and cities: The future – Delivering an urban renaissance.* Available at: www.regeneration.detr. gov.uk/policies. [Accessed 29 November 2000].

Department of Transport and the Regions (2000d). *Social exclusion and the provision and availability of public transport.* Available at: www.mobility-unit.detr.gov.uk. [Accessed 2 October 2000].

De Pauw, K. and Gavron, S. (1995). *Disability and Sport,* Champaign, Ill: Human Kinetics.

Devine, M.A. (2004). Being a doer instead of a viewer: the role of inclusive leisure contexts in determining social acceptance for people with disabilities. *Journal of Leisure Research* 36,2: 137–59.

Dick. S. (2009). *Leagues behind – football's failure to tackle anti-gay abuse,* London: Stonewall.

Diekmann, A. and McCabe, S. (2011). Systems of social tourism in the EU: a critical review *Current Issues in Tourism.* 14,5: 417–30.

Disability Rights Task Force (DRTF) on Civil Rights for Disabled People (1999). *From exclusion to inclusion,* London: Dept for Education and Employment.

Dishman, R. K. (1995). Physical activity and public health: Mental health. *Quest* 47: 362–85.

Dobbins, M., de Corby, K. and Robeson, P. et al. (2009). *School-based physical activity programs for promoting physical activity and fitness in children and adolescents aged 6–18.* Cochrane database of systematic reviews 1: DOI: 10.1002/14651858.CD007651.

Dobson B. and Middleton, S. (1998). *Paying to care: the cost of childhood disability,* York: Joseph Rowntree Foundation.

Doherty, A. and Misener, K. (2008). Community sport networks, pp. 113–41. In Nicholson, M. and Hoye, R. (eds). *Sport and social capital,* Oxford: Butterworth-Heinemann.

Doll-Tepper, G. et al. (1994). *The future of sport science in the Paralympic movement,* Berlin: International Paralympic Committee.

Donnelly, P. (1996). Approaches to social inequality in the sociology of sport. *Quest* 48: 221–42.

Donnison, D. (1982). *The politics of poverty,* Oxford: Martin Robertson.

Dorling, D. et al. (2007). *Poverty, wealth and place in Britain, 1968–2005,* Bristol: Policy Press.

Dorling, D. (2010). *Injustice: Why inequality persists,* Bristol: Policy Press.

Dorricott, O. (1998). *Social cohesion and sport* paper 98/14. Strasbourg: Council of Europe, Committee for the Development of Sport.

Downes, D. (1966). *The Delinquent Solution,* London: Routledge and Kegan Paul.

Drake, R.F. (1994). The exclusion of disabled people from positions of power in British voluntary organisations. *Disability and Society* 9: 461–90.

Driver, B.L. and Bruns, D.H. (1999). Concepts and uses of the benefits approach to leisure. In E.L. Jackson and T.L. Burton (eds). *Leisure studies: Prospects for the 21st century,* State College, PA: Venture Publishing.

Duck, R. A. (1998). *A report on youth at risk* Toronto: Ontario Ministry of Citizenship, Culture and Recreation.

Duffy, K. (1995). *Social exclusion and human dignity in Europe* Brussels: Council of Europe.

Duffy, R. (2000). *Satisfactions and expectations: attitudes to public services in deprived areas* CASE paper 45, London: Centre for the study of Social Exclusion, London School of Economics.

Dunn, J., Hodge, I., Monk, S. and Kiddle, C. (1998). *Rural Disadvantage: understanding the processes,* Salisbury: Rural Development Commission.

Duret, P. and Augustini, M. (1993). *Sports de rue et insertion sociale* [Street sports and social insertion], Paris: National Institute of Sport and PE.

Dustin, D. L., More, T.A. and McAvoy, L.H. (2000). The faithful execution of our public trust: Fully funding the National Parks through taxes. *Journal of Park and Recreation Administration* 18,4: 92–103.

Dustmann, C. and Frattini, T. (2013). The Fiscal Effects of Immigration to the UK. London: Centre for Research into Migration, UCL.

EFTEC (2010). *The economic contribution of the public forest estate in England*, London: EFTEC.

Elling, A., de Knop, P. and Knoppers, A. (2001). The integrating and differentiating significance of sport, pp. 73–90. In P. de Knop and A. Elling (eds). *Values and norms in sport*, Aachen: Meyer.

Ellison, N. (1997). Towards a new social politics: citizenship and reflexivity in late modernity. *Sociology* 31,4: 697–717.

End Child Poverty (2011). *Child poverty map of the UK*, London: Child Poverty Action Group.

English Federation of Disability Sport (EFDS). (2004). *Count me in! Development Framework 2004–08*, Alsager: EFDS.

English Sports Council (ESC). (1997a). *England, the sporting nation: a strategy*, London: ESC.

English Sports Council (1997b). *Working towards racial equality – a good practice guide for local authorities*, London: ESC.

English Sports Council (1998a). *The development of sporting talent 1997*, London: ESC.

English Sports Council (1998b). *Working towards racial equality in sport: a Good Practice guide for local authorities*, London: ESC.

English Tourist Board (ETB). (1989). *Tourism for all*, London: ETB.

Engstrom, L-M. (2008).Who is physically active? Cultural capital and sports participation from adolescence to middle age: A 38-year follow-up study. *PE and Sport Pedagogy* 13,4: 319–43.

Enoch, N. (2010). Towards a contemporary national structure for youth sport in England 45–71 in M. Collins (ed). *Examining Sports Development*, London: Routledge.

ERS Research Consultancy (2010). *Evaluation of the Culture and Sport Improvement strategy Final Report*, Newcastle: ERS.

Esping-Anderson, G. (1990). *The three worlds of welfare capitalism*, London: Princeton University Press.

European Commission (2000). *Inclusive cities: Building capacity for development*, Luxembourg: EC.

European Commission (2005). *Report on Social Inclusion: in the 10 new member states*, Luxembourg: Publications Office of the European Communities .

European Commission (2007). *White Paper on sport* IP/07/1066 11/07/2007, Brussells: EU.

European Council (2000). *Nice Declaration on the specific characteristics of sport and its social function in Europe*, Nice: EC.

European Foundation for the Improvement of Living and Working Conditions (1995). *For citizens and against exclusion: The role of public welfare services*, Dublin: EFILWC.

European Union (EU). (1994). 180/06 Guildelines for operation programmes or global grants concerning defence conversion (Konver). *Official Journal* C 1 July 18–22.

Eurostat (2010). *Comparing poverty and social exclusion: A statistical portrait of the EU*, Luxembourg: EU Publications Office.

Evans, G. (1998). Urban leisure: Edge city and the new leisure periphery 113–38 in Collins, M. F. and Cooper, I. S. (eds). *Leisure Management: Issues and applications*, Wallingford: CAB International.

Evandrou, M. and Falkingham, J. (2009). Pensions and income security in later life 157–78 in J. Hills, T. Sefton and K. Stewart (eds) (2009). *Towards a more equal society? Poverty, inequality and policy since 1997*, Bristol: Policy Press.

Evans, G. and Shaw, P. (2004). *The contribution of culture to regeneration in the UK: A review of evidence*, London: , London Metropolitan University.

Fahmy, E. et al. (2011). Poverty and place in Britain 1968–99. *Environment and Planning A* 43: 594–617.

Farrington, D. (1996). Understanding and Preventing Youth Crime. *Social Policy Research* 93: 1–6.

Faulkner, D. (1987). *Community Based Sentencing – The Use of Outdoor Challenge* Sports Council North West, Manchester.

Fawcett Society (2010) Available at www.fawcettsociety.org.uk.[Accessed 27 February 2014].

Ferragini, E., Tomlinson, M. and Walker, R. (2013). *Poverty, participation and choice: the legacy of Peter Townsend*, York: Joseph Rowntree Foundation.

FIFA (2006). *Big Count Survey Report*, Zurich: FIFA.

Field, F. (1990). *Losing out: The emergence of Britain's underclass*, Oxford: Basil Blackwell.

Field, F. (2010). *The foundation years: Preventing poor children becoming poor adults*, London: HM Government.

Fitzgerald, H. and Kay, T.A. (2005). *Gifted and talented disability project*, Loughborough: Institute of Youth Sport.

Fitzgerald, H. and Lang, M. (2009). *Review of the literature on volunteering, disability and sport*, Leeds: Metropolitan University.

Fitzpatrick, S. (2004). *Poverty of place*. Paper to JRF centenary conference, York, 14 December.

Fitzpatrick, S., Hastings, A. and Kintrea, K. (2000). Youth involvement in urban regeneration: hard lessons, future directions, *Policy and Politics* 28,4: 493–509.

Flatley, J. et al. (eds). 2010). *Crime in England and Wales 2009–10* Statistical Bulletin12/10, London: Home Office.

Flintoff, A. and Scraton, S. (2001). Stepping into Active Leisure? Young women's perceptions of active lifestyles and their experiences of school PE. *Sport, Education and Society* 6,1: 5–21.

Fleming, S. (1991). Sport, schooling and Asian male youth culture, pp. 30–57. In G. Jarvie (ed). *Sport, racism and ethnicity*, London: Falmer Press.

Floyd, M.F., Gramann, J.H., and Saenz, R. (1993). Ethnic factors and the use of public outdoor recreation areas *Leisure Sciences* 15: 83–98.

Foster, C., Allender, S. and Cowburn, G. (2005). *Understanding participation in sport: A systematic review*, London: SE.

Football Association (FA). (2002). *Ethics and sport equity strategy*, London: FA.

Forrest, R. and Kearns, A. (1999). *Joined up places? Social cohesion and neighbourhood regeneration*, York: York Publishing Services.

French, D. and Hainsworth, J. (2001). 'There aren't any buses and the swimming pool is always cold!' – obstacles and opportunities in the provision of sport for disabled people. *Managing Leisure* 6: 35–49.

[European Agency for] Fundamental Human Rights (FRA). (2010). *Racism, ethnic discrimination and exclusion of migrants and minorities in sport: A comparative overview of the situation in the European Union* Luxembourg: EU Publications.

[European Agency for] Fundamental Human Rights (2103). *European Union lesbian, gay, bisexual and transgender survey*, Luxembourg: EU Publications.

Freysinger, V. J. (1999). Life span and life course pressures on leisure 353–70 in Jackson, E.L. and Burton, T.L. (eds). *Leisure studies: Prospects for the 21st century* State College, PA: Venture Publishing.

Furbey, R. et al. (2006). *Faith as social capital: Connecting or dividing?* Bristol: Policy Press.

Fukuyama, F. (1999). *The great disruption: Human nature and the reconstitution of social order,* London: Profile Books.

Future Foundation (nd). *It's time. Future forecasts for women's participation in sport and exercise,* London: Womens Sport and Fitness Foundation.

Galbraith, J.K. (1992). *The culture of contentment,* London: Sinclair Stevenson.

Gatward, R. and Burrell, T. (2001). *Adults with a disability and sport National Survey Main report,* London: Sport England.

Geddes, M. (1997). *Partnership against poverty and exclusion?* Bristol: Policy Press.

GfK/NOP (2006). *Understanding participation in sport: what determines sports participation among lone parents,* London: Sport England.

GHK (2005). *Revealing the value of nature.* Report to DEFRA, London: GHK.

Gibson, A. and Asthana, S. (1999). Local markets and the polarisation of public sector schools in England and Wales *Transactions of Institute of British Geographers NS* 25: 303–19.

Giddens, A. (1982). *Profiles and Critiques in Social Theory,* Basingstoke: Macmillan.

Giddens, A. (1991). *Modernity and self-identity: Self and society in the late modern age,* Cambridge: Polity Press.

Giddens, A. (1994). *Beyond Left and Right: The future of radical politics,* Cambridge: Polity Press.

Giddens, A. (1997). *Sociology,* Cambridge: Polity Press.

Giddens, A. (1998). *The Third Way,* Cambridge: Polity Press.

Gilchrist, A. (2004). *Community cohesion and community development: Bridges or barricades?* London: Community Development Foundation.

Gilhooly, M., Hamilton, K, and O'Neill, M. (2002). *Transport and ageing: Extending quality of life for older people via public and private transport,* Paisley: The University.

Glennerster, H., Lupton, R., Noden, P. and Power, A. (1999). *Poverty, social exclusion and neighbourhood: studying the area bases of social exclusion* CASE paper 22, London: London School of Economics.

Glyptis, S. (1989). *Leisure and unemployment* Milton Keynes: Open University Press.

Glyptis, S.A., Collins, M.F. and Randolph, L. (1995). *Place and Pleasure: The sporting claim vol 2 Good practice case studies* Leeds: Yorkshire & Humberside Council for Sport and Recreation.

Glyptis, S., Kay, T. and Murray, M. (1985). *Working with Women and Girls,* Birmingham: Sports Council West Midland Region.

Glyn, D. and Miliband, D. (eds). (1994). *Paying for inequality; the economic cost of social inequality,* London: Rivers Oram Press.

Goodale, T.L. and Witt, P.A. (1989). Recreation, non-participation and barriers to leisure, pp. 421–49. In E.L. Jackson and T.L. Burton (eds). *Understanding leisure and recreation: Mapping the past, charting the future* State College, PA: Venture Publishing, Inc.

Goodin, R.E. (1996). Inclusion and exclusion. *European Journal of Sociology* 37,2: 343–71.

Goodley, D. (2000). *Self advocacy in the lives of people with learning difficulties: the politics of resilience*, Buckingham: Open University Press.

Gordon, P. and Hanafin ,T. (1998). Hands across the divide. *Health Management*, October: 20–1.

Gordon, D. and Pantazis, C. (eds). (1997). *Breadline Britain in the 1990s* Aldershot: Ashgate.

Gore, A., Dabinett, G. and Breeze, J. (2000). *The coalfields and the Lottery Phase 2*, Sheffield: Centre for Regional Economic and Social Research, Sheffield Hallam University.

Government Equalities Office (GEO). (2011). *Sports Charter*. Available at: www. equalities.gov.uk/news/sports_charter.aspx. [Accessed 25 February 2014].

Graham, J. and Bowling, B. (1995). *Young People and Crime*, London: Home Office.

Grant Thornton et al. (2013). *Meta-evaluation of the impacts and legacy of the London 2012 Olympic and Paralympic Games*, London: Department of Culture Media and Sport.

Gramann, J.H. and Allison, M. (1999). Ethnicity, race and leisure, pp. 283–97. In Jackson, E.L. and Burton, T.L. (eds). *Leisure Studies: Prospects for the 21st century* State College, PA: Venture Publishing, Inc.

Gratton, C. (1996). *Position paper on sporting performance and excellence*. Unpublished paper. Sheffield: Sheffield Hallam University.

Gratton, C. and Taylor, P. (1985). *Sport and recreation: an economic analysis*, London: E & F Spon.

Gratton, C. and Taylor, P. (1994). *The impact of variations in charges on usage levels in local authority facilities,* Research Digest 34, Edinburgh: Scottish Sports Council.

Gratton, C., Rowe, N. and Veal, A.J. (2011). International comparisons of Sports participation in European countries: an update of the COMPASS project. *European Journal of Sport and Society* 8,1–2: 99–116.

Greater London and South East Council for Sport and Recreation (1983). *Special needs, special measures: sport and recreation in, London's inner city*, London: GLSECSR.

Green, K., Smith, A. and Roberts, K. (2005). Young people and lifelong participation in sport and PE: a sociological perspective on contemporary PE programmes in England and Wales. *Leisure Studies* 24,1: 27–43.

Green, M. (2007). Olympic glory or grassroots development? Sports policy priorities in Australia, Canada, and the United Kingdom 1960–2006. *International Journal of the History of Sport* 24,7: 921–53.

Greendorfer, S. (1983). Shaping the female athlete: the impact of the family, pp. 135–56. In M.A. Boutilier and L. San Giovanni (eds). *The Sporting Woman* Champaign, Ill: Human Kinetics.

Greenfield, B.J. and Senecal, J. (1995). Recreational multifamily therapy for troubled children. *American Journal of Orthopsychiatry* 65,34: 34–9.

Gregg, P., Harkness, S. and Machin, S. (1999). *Child development and family income,* York: York Publishing Services.

Grimshaw, P. and Prescott-Clarke, P. (1978). *Sport school and community*. Research working paper 9, London: Sports Council.

Groeneveld, M., Houlihan, B. and Ohl, F. (2011). *Social capital and sport governance in Europe,* London: Routledge.

Guett, M. et al. (2011). *All for Sport for All: Perspectives of sport for people with a disability in Europe*, Lyon: European Observatoire of Sport and Employment.

Hales, J., Nevill, C., Pudney, S. and Tipping, S. (2009). *Longitudinal analysis of the Offending Crime and Justice survey 2003–06*. Research Report 19, London: Home Office.

Hall, E. (2004). Social geographies of learning disability: narratives of inclusion and exclusion. *Area* 36,3: 298–306.

Hall, P. (1998). *Cities in civilisation*, London Pantheon Books/Weidenfeld and Nicholson.

Hall, P.A. (1999). Social capital in Britain. *British Journal of Politics* 29: 417–61.

Hall Aitken (2008). *Sport Action Zone Evaluation Final Report*, Manchester: Hall Aitken.

Hansen, K., Jones, E., Joshi, H. and Budge, D. (eds) (2010). *Millennium Cohort Study 4th Survey: Users guide to initial findings*, London: Centre for Longitudinal Studies.

Harada, M. (1999). Ageing and leisure in Japan. *World Leisure and Recreation* 41,3: 30–2.

Harahousou, Y. (1999). Elderly people, leisure and physical recreation. *Greece World Leisure and Recreation* 41,3: 20–4.

Hardman, K. (2008). PE in schools: A global perspective. *Kinesiology* 40,1: 5–28.

Hardman, K. and Marshall, J. (2000). *A worldwide survey of the state and status of school PE*, Manchester: Manchester University.

Harland J. et al. (nd). *Attitudes to participation in the arts, heritage, broadcasting and sport: a review of recent research*. Unpublished report to Dept of National Heritage, Slough: National Foundation for Educational Research.

Harrison, P. (1983). *Inside the inner city*, Harmondsworth: Penguin.

Hart, G. and Kung, S.P. (2011). *Participation in sport and recreation activities by 16–19 year-olds in England*. Paper to Wolfenden Gap seminar 9 March, Sheffield.

Hartmann, D. (2001). Notes on Midnight Basketball and the cultural politics of recreation, race and at-risk urban youth. *Journal of Sport and Social Issues* 25,4: 339–71.

Hartmann, D. and Depro, D. (2006). Rethinking sports-based community crime prevention: A preliminary analysis of the relationship between Midnight Basketball and urban crime rates. *Journal of Sport and Social Issues* 30,2: 180–98.

Hawkins, B. (1999). Population ageing: Perspectives from the United States. *World Leisure and Recreation* 41.3, 11–14.

Healey, P. (1998). Institutionalist theory, social exclusion and governance in J. Allen et al. (eds). *Social exclusion in European cities: Processes, experiences and responses*, London: Jessica Kingsley Publishers.

Health Education Authority (1998a). *Physical activity and inequalities*, London: HEA.

Health Education Authority (1998b). *Young and active?* London: HEA.

Health Education Authority (1999). *Physical activity and inequalities*, London: HEA.

Hedges, A. (1999). *Living in the countryside: the needs and aspirations of rural populations CAX 28*, Cheltenham: Countryside Agency.

Hedges, B. (1986). *Personal leisure histories*, London: ESRC/Sports Council.

Heinila, K. (1989). The sports club as a social organisation in Finland. *International Review of Sociology of Sport* 24,3: 225–46.

Heinemann, K. and Schubert, M. (1994). *Die Sportverein* [Sports Clubs] Publication 80 German Federal Sports Institute, Schorndorf: Verlag Karl Hofman.

Heinemann, K. and Schwab, M. (1999). Sports clubs in Germany, pp. 143–67. In Heinemann, K. (ed). *Sports clubs in various European countries* Cologne: Club of Cologne.

Heiser, B. (1995). The nature and causes of transport disability in Britain and how to remove it in Zarb, G. (ed). *Removing disabling barriers*, London: Policy Studies Institute.

Hekma, G. (1998). 'As long as they don't make an issue of it' Gay men and lesbians in organised sports in the Netherlands. *Journal of Homosexuality* 35,1: 1–23.

Helyar-Cardwell, V. (2009). *A new start: Young adults in the criminal justice system, summary*, London: Barrow Cadbury Trust.

Hendry, L. (1992). Sport and Leisure: The not-so-hidden curriculum? pp. 62–87. In J.C. Coleman and C.W. Adamson (eds). *Youth policy in the 1990s – The way forward?* London: Routledge.

Hendry, L. B., Shucksmith, J. S., Love, J. and Glendinning, A. (1993). *Young people's leisure and lifestyles*, London: Routledge.

Henry, I. P. (1993). *The politics of leisure policy*, Basingstoke: MacMillan.

Henry, I. (1999). Social inclusion and the leisure society. *New Political Economy* 4,2: 283–8.

Henry, I. (2001). Postmodernism and power in urban policy: Implications for sport and cultural policy in the European city. *European Sport Management Quarterly* 1: 5–20.

Heskins, J. and Baker, M. (2006). *Footballing lives, as seen by chaplains in the beautiful game*, Norwich: Canterbury Press.

Higgs, J. et al. (2010). *An anatomy of economic inequality in the UK – Summary*, London: Government Equalities Office.

Higgs, P. et al. (2009). From passive to active consumers? Later life consumption in the UK 1968–2005. *Sociological Review* 57,1: 102–24.

Higgins, V. and Ball, R. (1999). Local authority anti-poverty strategies in Scotland. *Public Policy and Administration* 14: 1, 60–75.

Higher Education Funding Council for England (HEFCE). (1997). *The influence of neighbourhood type on participation in Higher Education, Interim report*, London: HEFCE.

Hill, M.S. and Jenkins, S.P. (2000). Poverty among British children: chronic or transitory in J. Micklewright (ed). *Poor children in Europe*, London: Family Policy Study Centre.

Hillary Commission (HC). (1998). *Task force report on Maori sport*, Wellington, NZ: The Commission.

Hills, J, Sefton, T. and Stewart, K. (eds). (2009). *Towards a more equal society? Poverty, inequality and policy since 1997*, Bristol: Policy Press.

Hills, J. et al. (2010). *An anatomy of inequality in the UK: Summary report of the National Equality Panel*, London: Government Equalities Office.

Hills, L. (2006). Playing the field(s): an exploration of change, conformity and conflict in girls' understandings of gendered physicality in physical education. *Gender and Education* 18,5: 539–56.

Hills, L. (2007). Friendship, physicality, and physical education: An exploration of the social and embodied dynamics of girls' physical education experiences. *Sport, Education and Society* 12,3: 335–54.

Hillsdon, M., Jones, A. and Coombes, E. (2011). *Greenspace access, greenspace use, physical activity and overweight* NECR 067, Sheffield: Natural England.

Hindermeyer, O. (ed). (1998). *Les actions de solidarité Bilan 1997* [Actions of solidarity: Review 1997], Paris: Union Nationale des Centres Sportifs de Plein Air.

Hirsch, D. (2008). *Estimating the costs of child poverty*, York: Joseph Rowntree Foundation.

Hirsch, D. (2011). *Minimum Income Standard for the UK 2011*, York Joseph Rowntree Foundation.

Hirvensalo, M., Lampinen, P. and Rantenen, T. (1998). Physical exercise in old age: an eight-year follow up study on involvement, motives and obstacles among persons aged 65–84. *Journal of Aging and Physical Activity* 6: 157–68.

HM Government (2011). *Overarching impact assessment for the Natural Environment White Paper, Natural Choice*, London: HMG.

HM Treasury/DWP/DCSF (2008). *Ending child poverty: Everybody's business*, London: HMT.

Hobcraft, J. (1998). *Intergenerational and life-course transmission of social exclusion: influences of childhood poverty, family disruption, and contact with the police* CASE paper 15, London: London School of Economics.

Hobcraft, J. (2000). *The roles of schooling and adult education in the emergence of adult social exclusion.* Centre for Analysis of Social Exclusion paper 43, London: CASE, LSE.

Hodge, S. et al. (2004). High School general PE teachers' behaviour and beliefs associated with inclusion. *Sport, Education and Society* 9: 395–420.

Holt, R. (1990). *Sport and the British: A modern history*, Oxford: Oxford University Press.

Holman, R. (1978). *Poverty*, London: Martin Robertson.

Home Office (HO). (1992). *Criminal statistics*, London: HO.

Home Office (1993). *Statistical Bulletin 1992,* London: HO.

Home Office (2001). *Community cohesion.* Report of the Review Team chaired by Ted Cantle, London: HO.

Home Office (2002). *Positive Futures: Cul de sacs and gateways*, London: HO.

Home Office (2003). *Community cohesion: Advice for those designing and delivering area-based initiatives*, London: HO.

Home Office (2004). *Defining and measuring anti-social behaviour* D&P report 26, London: HO.

Home Office (2005). *The economic and social costs of crime against individuals and households* Online report 30/5, London: HO.

Home Office (2006). *Positive Futures: End of season review*, London: HO.

Home Office/Substance/Catch 22 (2008). *Taking it on*, London: HO.

Horch, H-D. (1998). Self-destroying processes of sports clubs in Germany. *European Journal of Sports Management* 5,1: 46–58.

Horne, J., Tomlinson, A. and Whannel, G. (1999). *Understanding sport: An introduction to the sociological and cultural analysis of sport*, London: E & F Spon.

Horsfield, G. (2012). *Family spending 2012*, London: Office of National Statistics.

Houlihan, B.M.J. (1991). *The policy and politics of sport*, London: Routledge.

Houlihan, B. (1997). *Sport, policy and politics*, London: Routledge.

Houlihan, B. (1999). *Sporting excellence, schools and sports development: The politics of crowded policy spaces.* Unpublished paper to CRSS-EPER conference on PE and Excellence, Leicester September.

Houlihan, B. (2001). Citizenship, civil society and the sport and recreation professions *Managing Leisure* 6,1: 1–14.

Houlihan, B. and Green, M. (2006). The changing status of school sport and PE: explaining policy change. *Sport Education & Society* 11,1: 73–92.

Houlihan, B. and Green, M. (2008). *Elite sports development: Systems, structures and public policy*, Oxford Butterworth Heinemann.

Houlihan, B. and Lindsey, I. (2008). Networks and partnerships in sports development, pp. 225–42. In V. Girginov (ed). *Management of Sports Development*, Oxford: Butterworth-Heinemann.

Houlihan, B.M.J. and Lindsey, I. (2013). *Sport policy in Britain*, London: Routledge.

Houlihan, B. and Wong, (2005). *Report on 2004 survey of Specialist Sports Colleges*, Loughborough: Institute of Youth Sport, Loughborough University.

House of Commons ODPM: Housing, Planning, Local Government and the Regions Committee (2004). *Social Cohesion* 6th report 2003–04 volume 1. Report HC45-1, London: The Stationery Office.

Humberstone, B. (2002). Femininity, masculinity and difference: what's wrong with a sarong? 58–78 in Laker, A. (ed). *The sociology of sport and physical education: An introductory reader*, London and New York: Routledge.

Hums, M. A., Moorman, A. M. and Wolff, E. I. (2000). *Paralympic athletes inclusion into National Sports Organisations paper to 8th European Sports Management Congress* Sept, San Marino.

Hutson, S, Thomas, J. and Sutton, M. (1995). *Why boys and girls come out to play: Sport and school age children at the transition from primary to secondary education*, Cardiff: Sports Council for Wales.

Hylton, K. (1999). Where are the black managers? *Leisure Manager*, September, 32–4.

Hylton, K. (2009). *'Race' and sport: Critical Race Theory*, London: Routledge.

Hylton, K. and Morpeth, N.D. (2012)., London 2012: 'race' matters and the East End. *International Journal of Sport Policy and Politics* 4,3: 379–96.

Hylton, K. and Totten, M. (2001). Community sports development pp 66–98 in K. Hylton et al. (eds). *Sports development: Policy, processes and practice*, London: Routledge.

Inclusive Fitness Initiative (nd). *Inclusion works out 2008–12* Alsager: English Federation of Disability Sport.

Innovation and Development Agency (IDeA), DCMS and Sport England (2008). *A Passion for Excellence: An improvement strategy for culture and sport*, London: IDeA.

Innovation and Development Agency (2011). *Culture and Sport Improvement Toolkit (CSIT)*, London: IDeA.

Institute of Leisure and Amenity Management ILAM (1997). *Disability Discrimination Act: Issues and guidelines* Factsheet 97/5 Reading: ILAM.

Institute of Sport and Recreation Management ISRM (2000). *Couch kids.* Information sheet 201 Melton Mowbray: ISRM.

IPSOS/MORI (2006). *Understanding the success factors in Sport Action Zones: Final Report*, London: Sport England.

Jackson, E. (1988). Leisure constraints: a review of past research *Leisure Sciences* 10: 203–15.

Jackson, E. (1990a). Variations in the desire to begin a leisure activity: evidence of antecedent constraints? *Journal of Leisure Research* 22: 55–70.

Jackson, E. (1990b). Recent developments in leisure constraint research. *Proceedings of the 6th Canadian Congress on Leisure Research*, Waterloo: Canadian Leisure Studies Association.

Jackson, E.L. (1991). Leisure constraints/constrained leisure Introduction. *Journal of Leisure Research* 23,4: 279–85.

Jargowsky, P.A. (1996). *Poverty and place: Ghettos, barriers and the American city*, New York: Russell Sage Foundation.

Jarvie, G. and Maguire, J. (1994). *Sport and leisure in social thought*, London: Routledge.

Jason-Lloyd, L. (1993). *The Criminal Justice Acts: A Basic Guide*, Huntingdon: ELM.

Jawad, H., Benn, T. and Dagkas, S.(2011). Facilitating participation in PE and school sports for Muslim girls, pp. 203–17. In S. Dagkas and K. Armour (eds). *Inclusion and exclusion through youth sport and PE,* London: Routledge.

Jeanes, R. (2010). 'It lets us be a "normal" family': The value of inclusive play facilities for addressing social exclusion amongst young disabled people and their families 165–84 in M. Stuart-Hoyle and J. Lovell (eds). *Leisure experiences: Space, play and performance Publication109*, Eastbourne: Leisure Studies Association.

Jeanes, R. (2011). Girls and Sport in R. Bailey, and I. Stafford (eds). *Coaching Children in Sport*, London: Routledge.

Jeanes, R. and Kay, T. (2008a). *Evaluation of the Chance to shine Programme: Findings from the Year 2 evaluation*, Loughborough: Institute of Youth Sport.

Jeanes, R. and Kay, T. (2008b). 'She had to buy a football book to do it' Issues in the Leadership of Physical Activity for Girls. *PE Matters* 32–6.

Jeanes, R. and Kay, T. (2008c). *Chance to Shine Evaluation: Examining sustainability*, London: Cricket Foundation.

Jeanes, R. and Nevill, M. (2008). *Evaluation of the Football Foundation Projects: Key Findings and Lessons Learnt.* Institute of Youth Sport report, London: Big Lottery Fund and The Football Foundation.

Jeanes, R. and Magee, J. (2012). 'Can we play on the swings and roundabouts?' Creating inclusive play spaces for disabled young people and their families. *Leisure Studies*, 31,2: 193–210.

Jeanes, R., Musson, H. and Kay, T. (2009). *Evaluation of the Cricket Foundation's Street Chance initiative*, Loughborough: Institute of Youth Sport.

Jerwood, K. and Cook, E. (2010). *Be Active: social marketing in the NHS 2010 presentation*, Birmingham: Birmingham City Council.

John, P., Ward, H. and Dowding, K. (2004). The bidding game: Competitive funding regimes and the political targeting of Urban Programme regimes. *British Journal of Political Science* 34: 405–28.

Johnson, C. Y., Bowker, J. M., English, D. B. K. and Worthen, D. (1998). Wildland recreation in the rural South: an examination of marginality and ethnicity theory. *Journal of Leisure Research* 30,1: 101–20.

Joldersma, T. (2009). *Analysis of demand* [for social tourism]. Paper to conference European Forum of Social Tourism, Malaga 15–17 October.

Joliffe, D. and Farrington, D. (2007). *A rapid evidence assessment of the impact of mentoring on re-offending, a summary.* Online report 11/107, London: Home Office.

Joloza, T., Evans, J. and O'Brien, R. (2010). *Measuring Sexual Identity: An evaluation report*, London: National Statistics.

Jones, L. (1998). Inequality in access to local environments: the experiences of Asian and non-Asian girls. *Health Education Journal* 57, 313–28.

Jones, S.G. (1988). *Sport, politics and the working class: A study of organised labour and sport in inter-war Britain*, Manchester: Manchester University Press.

Jordan, B. (1996). *A theory of poverty and social exclusion*, Cambridge: Polity Press.

Kaplan, M. (1975). *Leisure: Theory and policy* New York: John Wiley.

Kay, T. A. (2000). Sporting excellence: a family affair? *European Physical Education Review* 6,2: 151–69.

Kay, T.A. (2009a). Developing through sport: Evidencing sport impacts on young people. *Sport and Society* 12,9: 1177–91.

Kay, T.A. (2009b). Integration and Migration – Gymnastics and Sports with and for Immigrants. Paper to 1st International Sports Science Congress of the German Gymnastics Federation (DTB). *Facing new challenges: Education, Health Promotion, Integration in Gymnastics and Sports*, Frankfurt, June.

Kay, T. A. and Jackson, G.A.M. (1990). Leisure Constraints 551–62 in T. Williams, L. Almond and A. Sparkes (eds). *Sport and physical activity*, London: E and F N Spon.

Kay, T.A. and Jackson G.A.M. (1991). Leisure despite constraint. *Journal of Leisure Research* 23, 301–313.

Kay, T. and O'Donovan, T. (2004). *Girls in Sport: Final monitoring and evaluation report to Youth Sport Trust and Nike*, Loughborough: Youth Sport Trust.

Kay, T.A. and Brown, S. (2007). *Out of School Hours Learning year 3 report 2006/07*, Edinburgh: sportscotland.

Kearns, A. and Forrest, R. (2000). Social cohesion and multilevel urban governance. *Urban Studies* 57, 5–6: 995–1017.

Kelly, F.J. and Baer, D.J. (1968). *Outward Bound schools as an alternative to institutionalisation for adolescent delinquent boys* Boston: Fandel.

Kennett, C.R. (2002). *Leisure poverty and social exclusion: An analysis of leisure cards schemes in Great Britain.* Unpublished PhD thesis, Loughborough: University.

Kent Sports Development Unit (KSDU). (1999). *Sportslink projects in Kent.* Canterbury: KSDU (mimeo).

Kew, F. (1997). *Sport: social problems and issues,* Oxford: Butterworth-Heinemann.

King, L. and Thompson, P. (2001). 'Limp-wristed, Kylie Minogue-loving, football-hating, fashion victims' Gay sports clubs – providing for male members, challenging social exclusion? 81–102 in G. McPherson and G. Reid (eds). *Leisure and social exclusion,* publication 73, Eastbourne: Leisure Studies Association.

King, N. (2012). *Local authority sport and recreation services in England: Where next?* Manchester: Association for Public Sector Excellence.

King, S. (2008). What's queer about (queer) sport sociology now? A review essay. *Sociology of Sport Journal* 25: 419–42.

Kingdon, J.W. (1995). *Agendas, alternatives and public policies,* 2nd ed, New York: Harper Collins.

Kirk, D. (2005a). Physical culture, lifelong participation and empowerment: Towards an educational rationale for PE 3–27 in A. Flintoff, J. Long and K. Hylton (eds). *Youth sport and active leisure: theory, policy and participation.* Publication 87 Eastbourne: Leisure Studies Association.

Kirk, D. (2005b). PE youth sport and lifelong participation: the importance of early life experiences. *European PE Review* 11,3: 239–55.

Kirk, D. et al. (2000). *Towards girl-friendly PE: The Nike/YST Girls in Sport partnership project,* Loughborough University: Institute of Youth Sport.

Kitchin, R. (1998). 'Out of place', 'Knowing one's place': space, power and the exclusion of disabled people. *Disability and Society* 13,3: 343–56.

Knight Kavanagh and Page (2005). *Active Sports/CSP impact study, year 3* Bury, Lancs: KKP.

Krouwel, A., Boonstra, N., Duyvendak, J. W. and Veldboer, L. (2007). A good sport? Research into the capacity of recreational sport to integrate Dutch minorities. *International Review for Sociology of Sport* 24,2: 165–79.

Lader, D. and Steel, M. (2009). *Drinking: Adults' behaviour and knowledge.* Opinion report 42, London: Office of National Statistics.

Law, C.M. and Warnes, A.M. (1976). The changing geography of the elderly in England and Wales *Transactions, Institute of British Geographers* (new series) 11,4: 453–71.

Lawless, P., Foden, M., Wilson, I. and Beatty, C. (2010). Understanding Area-based regeneration: The New Deal for Communities programme in England. *Urban Studies* 47, 2: 257–75.

Lawley, S. (2011). Sexual orientation and invisibility. *Leisure Studies Association Newsletter* 88: 36–41.

Layard, R. (1997). Preventing long-term unemployment. In D.J. Snower and G. de la Dehasa (eds). *Unemployment policy,* Cambridge: , Cambridge University Press.

Leaman, O. and Carrington, B. (1985). Athleticism and the reproduction of gender and ethnic marginality. *Leisure Studies* 4: 205–17.

Lee, N., Sissons, P. and Jones, K. (2013). *Wage inequality and unemployment polarisation in British Cities,* London: Work Foundation.

Lee, P. and Murie, A. (1998). Targeting deprivation through housing tenure is flawed. *New Economy* 5,2: 89–93.

Leicester City Council (LCC). (1985). *Leisure Pass: Annual Report.* Unpublished. Leicester: LCC.

Leicester City Council (1999). *Services for disabled people*, Leicester: LCC.

Leishman, M. (1996). Gaining access: Disability Discrimination Act. *Leisure Management.*

Lenskyj, H. (1986). *Out of Bounds: Women, Sport and Sexuality*, Toronto: The Women's Press.

Lenskyj, H.J. (1990). Power and play: Gender and sexuality issues in sport and physical activity. *International Review of Sociology of Sport* 25,3: 235–43.

Lester, S. and Russell, W. (2008). *Play for a change: Play, policy and practice – a review of contemporary perspectives,* London: National Childrens Bureau.

Letki, N. (2008). Does diversity erode social cohesion? Social capital and race in British neighbourhoods. *Political Studies* 56: 99–126.

Levitas, R. (1996). The concept of social exclusion and the new Durkheimian hegemony. *Critical Social Policy* 16: 5–20.

Levitas, R. (1998). *The inclusive society? Social exclusion and New Labour*, Basingstoke: MacMillan.

Levitas, R. et al. (2007). *The multi-dimensional analysis of social exclusion*, Bristol: Bristol Institute for Public Affairs.

Levitt, L. (1991). Recreation for the mentally ill, pp. 161–177. In B.L. Driver, P.J. Brown and G.L. Peterson (eds). *Benefits of Leisure State College*, PA: Venture Publishing.

Linadio, M. (1996). *Car culture and countryside change*, London: The National Trust.

Lindsey, I. (2006). Local partnerships in the UK for the New Opportunities for PE and Sport programme: A policy network analysis. *European Sport Management Quarterly* 6,2: 167–84.

Lindsey, I. (2008). Conceptualising sustainability in sport development. *Leisure Studies* 27,3: 279–94.

Lilley, P. (1996). Letter to Paul Coggins, chair of the UK International Year against Poverty Coalition. *Guardian* 15 May.

Lister, R. (1990). *The exclusive society: Citizenship and the poor*, London: Child Poverty Action Group.

Lister, R. (1998). From equality to social inclusion: New Labour and the welfare state. *Critical Social Policy* 18,2: 215–25.

Lister, R. (1999). *Building an Inclusive Society.* Annual Lecture on Social Change, London.

Lister, S., Reynolds, L. and Webb, K. (2011). *The impact of Welfare Reform Bill measures on affordability for low income renting families*, London: Shelter.

Lobo, F. (1998). Young people, employment and leisure. *World Leisure and Recreation 1*: 4–8.

Local Government Association (LGA). (1998). *Tackling rural poverty and social exclusion: The role of local authorities*, London: LGA.

Local Government Association (2001). *All together now? A survey of local authority approaches to social inclusion and anti-poverty*. Research Report 20, London: LGA.

Local Government Association (2002). *Guidance on community cohesion*, London: LGA.

Local Government Association, Home Office et al. (2002). *Guidance on community cohesion*, London: LGA.

Lockhart, G. (ed). (2009). *Less crime, lower costs*, London: Policy Exchange.

Long, J. (2000). No racism here? A preliminary examination of sporting innocence. *Managing Leisure* 5, 121–33.

Long, J. and Dart, J. (nd). *Youth, leisure, sport, crime and community: an annotated bibliography.* Unpublished. Leeds: Leeds Metropolitan University.

Long, J. and Hylton, K. (2000). *Shades of white: an examination of whiteness in sport.* Paper to Leisure Studies conference Glasgow.

Long, J. and Sanderson, I. (2001). The social benefits of sport: Where's the proof? pp. 187–203. In C. Gratton and I. Henry (eds). *Sport in the City,* London: Routledge.

Long, J. and Spracklen, K. (eds). (2011). *Sport and challenges to racism,* London: Palgrave.

Long, J. et al. (1995). *What's the Difference: a study of the nature and extent of racism in rugby league.* Leeds: RFL/CRE/LCC/LMU.

Long, J. et al. (1997a). *Crossing the Boundary: a study of the nature and extent of racism in local league cricket.* Leeds: LMU.

Long, J., Carrington, B. and Spracklen, K. (1997b). 'Asians Cannot Wear Turbans in the Scrum': Explanations of racist discourse within professional rugby league, *Leisure Studies* 16,4: 249–59.

Long, J. et al. (2009). *Systematic Review of the Literature on Black and Minority Ethnic Communities in sport and physical recreation* Leeds: Metropolitan University.

Loughborough Partnership (2005). *School Sports Partnerships: Annual monitoring and evaluation, Loughborough:* Institute of Youth Sport.

Lucas, K. Tyler, S. and Christodoulou, G. (2009). Assessing the 'value' of new transport initiatives in deprived neighbourhoods in the UK *Transport Policy* 16: 115–22.

Lundman, R. (1993). *Prevention and control of juvenile delinquency.* 2nd ed, Oxford: Oxford University Press.

Lupson, P. (2006). *Thank God for Football!,* London: Azure.

Lusted, J. (2011). Negative equity? Amateurist responses to race equality initiatives in English grass roots football. In D. Burdsey (ed). *Race, ethnicity and football: Persisting debates and emergent issues,* London: Routledge.

MacDonald, G. and Leary, M.R. (2005). Why does social exclusion hurt? The relationship between social and physical pain. *Psychological Bulletin* 131,2: 202–23.

Macdonald, I. (2001). Splashing out for young people. *Leisure Manager* 8: 26–7.

MacDonald, R. (1997). *Youth and social exclusion,* London: Routledge.

MacDonald, R. and Shildrick, T. (2007). Street corner society: Leisure careers, youth (sub). Culture and social exclusion. *Leisure Studies* 26,3: 339–55.

MacGowan, H. (1997). The accessibility of Australian Aboriginal people to sport and recreation, pp. 17–28. In M.F. Collins and I.S. Cooper (eds). *Leisure Management: Issues and applications,* Wallingford: CAB International.

Mack, J. and Lansley, S. (1985). *Poor Britain,* London: Allen and Unwin.

MacKay, S. (1993). Research findings related to the potential of recreation in delinquency prevention. *Trends* 30,4: 27–30, 46.

MacIntosh, C. (2009). *County Sports Partnerships – a new regional architecture for Sport Development?* Paper to ISSA conference Utrecht, 15–18 July.

MacLean, H. and Clunie, R. (nd). *Steps to successful community-led service provision in rural areas,* London: Carnegie UK Trust.

Maguire, J. (1988). Race and position assignment in English soccer: a preliminary analysis of ethnicity and sport in Britain. *Sociology of Sport Journal* 5,3: 257–69.

Maguire, J. (1991). Sport, racism and British society: a sociological study of male Afro-Caribbean soccer and rugby Union players, pp. 94–123. In G. Jarvie (ed). *Sport, racism and society,* London.

Majima, S. and Warde, A. (2008). Elite consumption in Britain 1961–2004: Results of a preliminary investigation.*Sociological Review* 56 Suppl1: 210–39.

Mandelson, P. (1997). Labour's *next steps: Tackling social exclusion* Pamphlet 581, London: The Fabian Society.

Marmot, M. (2005). Social determinants of health inequalities *The Lancet.* 365(9464): 1099–1104.

Marmot, M. (2010). *Fair start, healthy lives: Strategic review of health inequalities in England post 2010,* London: The Marmot Review.

Marmot, M. (2011). *Fair society, healthy lives Marmot report 1 year on.* Presentation to BMA press conference, 10 February 2011.

Marshall, A. (1994). (nd). *Young People and Crime.* Unpublished. Leicester: National Youth Agency.

Marshall, G. (ed). (1997). *Repositioning class: social inequality in industrial societies,* London: Sage.

Marshall, T.H. (1950). *Citizenship and social class and other essays,* Cambridge: Cambridge University Press.

Marshall, T.H. (1992). Citizenship and social class. In T.H. Marshall and T. Bottomore (eds). *Citizenship and social class,* London: Pluto Press.

Martin, J. and White, A. (1998). *OPCS surveys of disabled people in GB Report 2 Financial circumstances of disabled adults in private households,* London: HMSO.

Martin, J. P. and Webster, D. (1994). *Probation motor projects in England and Wales,* Manchester: Home Office.

Martin, W.H. and Mason, S. (1998). *Transforming the future: rethinking work and leisure,* Sudbury: Leisure Consultants.

Martinek, T. and Hellison, D.R. (1997). Fostering resiliency in underserved youth through physical activity. *Quest* 49,1: 34–49.

Mason, V. (1995). *Young people and sport in England,* London: Sports Council.

Matarasso, F. (1998). *Poverty and oysters: The social impact of local arts development in Portsmouth,* Stroud: Comedia.

Matthews, H. et al. (2000). Growing up in the countryside: Children and the rural idyll. *Journal of Rural Studies* 16: 141–53.

Mathieson, J. and Summerfield, C. (2000). (eds). *Social focus on young people,* London: Stationery Office.

Mawson, H. and Parker, A. (2013). The next generation: Young people, sport and volunteering 152–165 in A. Parker and D. Vinson (eds). *Youth sport, physical activity and play,* London: Routledge.

Maxwell, H., Taylor, T. and Foley, C.(2011). Social inclusion of Muslim women a in Australian community sport, pp. 15–34. In J. Long, H. Fitzgerald and P. Millward (eds). *Delivering equality in sport and leisure.* Publication 115 Eastbourne: Leisure Studies Association.

May, T., Harris, S. and Collins, M.F. (2013). Implementing Community Sports policy: understanding the variety of voluntary club types and their attitudes to policy. *International Journal of Sport Policy and Politics* 5,3: 397–419.

Mays, J.B. (1954). *Growing up in the city: A study of juvenile delinquency in an urban neighbourhood,* Liverpool: Liverpool University Press.

Mays, J. (1972). *Juvenile Delinquency the Family and the Social Group,* London: Longman.

McCabe, A. et al. (2013). *Making the links: poverty, ethnicity and social networks,* York: Joseph Rowntree Foundation.

McCabe. M. (1993). Family Leisure Budgets: Bringing Body and Soul Together, pp. 150–61. In C. Brackenridge (ed). *Body Matters.* LSA conference proceedings 47.

McCabe, S., Joldersma, T. and Li, C. (2010). Understanding the benefits of social tourism: Linking participation to subjective wellbeing and quality of life. *International Journal of Tourism Research* 12: 761–73.

McConkey, R. and McGinley, P. (1990). *Innovations in leisure and recreation for people with a mental handicap*, Chorley: Lisieux Hall.

McCormack, F. (2000). *Leisure exclusion? Analysing interventions using active leisure with young people offending or at-risk.* Unpublished PhD thesis, Loughborough: University.

McCormack, F. (2001). The policy of outreach interventions for young people to achieve community development and social inclusion through leisure, pp. 7–22. In G. McPherson and G. Reid (eds). *Leisure and social exclusion 73*, Eastbourne: Leisure Studies Association.

McCormack, F. (2005). Impoverished leisure experiences: how can active leisure programmes make a difference? In K. Hylton, J. Long and A. Flintoff (eds). *Evaluating sport and active leisure for young people 88*, Eastbourne: Leisure Studies Association.

McCulloch, A. (2001). Ward level deprivation and wider social and economic outcomes in British Household Panel Study. *Environment and Planning A* 33: 667–84.

McDonald, D. and Tungatt, M. (1991). *National Demonstration Projects – major lessons for sports development,* London: Sports Council.

McDonald, I. (2005). Theorising partnerships: Governance, communicative action and sport policy. *Journal of Social Policy* 34,4: 579–600.

McGregor, S. (1981). *The politics of poverty,* London: Longman.

McGuire, F. (2000). What do we know? Not much: the state of leisure and ageing. *research Journal of Leisure Research* 32,1: 97–100.

McIntosh, P. and Charlton, V. (1985). *The impact of sport for all programmes 1966–84, and a way forward,* London: Sports Council.

McKay, J. (1997). *Managing Gender: Affirmative Action and organizational power in Australian, Canadian and New Zealand Sport,* Albany, NY: State University of New York.

McPherson, B. (1991). Ageing and leisure benefits: a life cycle perspective. In B. Driver, P. Brown and G.L. Peterson (eds). *Benefits of Leisure* State College, PA: Venture Publishing.

McPherson, B. D. (1999). Population ageing and leisure in a global context: factors influencing inclusion and exclusion within and across culture. *World Leisure and Recreation* 41,3: 5–10.

Melnick, M. (1988). Racial segregation by playing position in the English football league: a preliminary analysis. *Journal of Sport and Social Issues* 12,2: 122–30.

Mendola, D., Busetta, A. and Aassve, A. (2008). *Poverty permanence among European youth.* Working Paper 2008–04, Colchester: Institute for Social and Economic Research, University of Essex.

Merkel, U. (1999). Sport in divided societies – the case of the old, the new, and the 're-united' Germany, pp. 139–66. In D. Sugden and A. Bairner (eds). *Sport in divided societies* Brighton/Aachen: Meyer and Meyer.

Messent, P., Long, J. and Cooke, C. (1996) *Care, choice and leisure opportunities in the community for people with learning disabilities 4th WLRA congress Free time and the quality of life in the 21st century.* Unpublished. Leeds: Leeds Metropolitan University.

Messner, M.A. and Szabo, D. F. (eds) (1990). *Sport, Men and the gender order: critical feminist perspectives,* Champaign, Ill: Human Kinetics.

Midwinter, E. (1992). *Leisure: New opportunities in the third age,* Dunfermline: Carnegie UK Trust.

Miles, S. (2005). 'Our Tyne': Iconic regeneration and the revitalisation of identity in Newcastle Gateshead. *Urban Studies* 42,5–6: 913–26.

Miller, P., Gillinson, S. and Huber, J. (2006). *Disablist Britain: Barriers to independent living in Britain 2006,* London: Demos/SCOPE.

Minneart, L., Maitland, R. and Miller, G. (2009). Tourism and social policy: The value of social tourism. *Annals of Tourism Research* 36,2: 316–34.

Minister for Sport's Review Group (MSRG). (1989). *Building on ability,* Leeds: HMSO.

Mirlees-Black, C. and Maung, N. A. (1994). *Fear of crime: Findings from the 1992 British Crime Survey.* Research Findings 9, London: Home Office.

Mizen, P. et al. (2000). *Work, labour and economic life in late childhood.* Children 5–16 Research Briefing 4, Coventry: University of Warwick.

Modell, S.J. (1997). An exploration of the influence of educational placement on the community recreation and leisure patterns of children with developmental disabilities. *Perceptual and Motor Skills* 85: 695–704.

Moore, R. (1986). *Childhood's domain,* London: Croom Helm.

More, T. and Stevens, T. (2000). Do user fees exclude low-income people from resource-based recreation? *Journal of Leisure Research* 32,3: 341–57.

More, T. A., Warnick, R. B., Schuet, M. A. and Kuentzl, W. K. (2009). Changes in National Park visitation (2000–08). and interest in outdoor activities (1993–2008). In *Proceedings of NE Recreation Research Symposium 2009.*

MORI (2000). *Nestle Family Monitor 2000 – Sport and the Family,* London: MORI.

MORI (2001a). *Young people and sport in England 1999,* London: Sport England.

MORI (2001b). *Visitors to museums and galleries in the UK,* London: Resource.

Morris, J. (1989). *Able lives: Women's experience of paralysis,* London: The Women's Press.

Muddiman, D. et al. (2000). *Open to all? The public library and social exclusion,* London: Resource.

Mulder, C., Shibli, S. and Hale, J. (2005). Young people's demand for countryside recreation: A function of supply, tastes and preferences? *Managing Leisure* 10: 106–27.

Muncie, J. (1984). The trouble with kids today. In *Youth and Crime In Post War Britain,* London: Hutchinson.

Muncie, J. (1999). Institutionalised intolerance: Youth Justice and the 1998 Crime and Disorder Act *Critical Social Policy* 59: 147–175.

Murray, C. (1990). *The emerging British underclass,* London: Institute of Economic Affairs.

Murray, C. (1994). *Underclass: The crisis deepens,* London: Institute of Economic Affairs.

Nagel, M. and Nagel, S. (2001). *Social background and top performance sports paper to ECSS Congress* 24–28 July, Cologne.

Nankivell, O. (1988). *Market morality* Audenshaw Research Paper 118, Oxford: The Hinksey Centre.

National Childrens Bureau (2013). *Greater expectations: Raising aspirations for our children,* London: NCB.

National Coaching Foundation (NCF). (1996). *Champion Coaching – the guide,* Leeds: Sports Council.

Natural England (2007). *A Sense of freedom,* Sheffield: NE.

Natural England (2008). *Position Statement on Health and Wellbeing,* Sheffield: NE.

Natural England (2009). *No charge? Valuing the natural environment,* Sheffield: NE.

Natural England (2010). *Monitor of engagement with the natural environment,* NECR049 Sheffield: NE.

Neville, M. (2008). *Evaluation of the New Opportunities for PE and Sport Initiative (NOPES).* Five year report, Loughborough: Institute of Youth Sport.

New Policy Institute (2000). *Indicators of poverty and social exclusion in rural England CAX41*, Cheltenham: Countryside Agency.

NHS Confederation (2013). *Stronger together: how health and wellbeing boards can work effectively with local providers*, London: NHSC.

Nicholl, J.P., Coleman, P. and Williams, B.T. (1993). *Injury in sport and exercise*, London: Sports Council.

Nichols, G. (2001). A realist approach to evaluating the impact of sports programmes on crime reduction 71–80 in G. McPherson and G. Reid (eds). *Leisure and social exclusion* publication 73 Eastbourne: Leisure Studies Association.

Nichols, G. (2007). *Sport and crime reduction*, London: Routledge.

Nichols, G. (2009). Inequality and positional consumption – a fresh insight into debates in leisure studies on time pressure on leisure and volunteering, choosing a work/life balance and the nature of a 'leisure' society. *Journal of Policy Research in Tourism, Leisure and Events* 1: 270–275.

Nichols, G. and Taylor, P. (1996). *West, Yorkshire Sports Counselling; final evaluation* Sheffield: Sheffield University.

Nichols, G. et al. (2005). Pressures on the UK voluntary sport sector. *Voluntas* 16,1: 33–50.

Nicholson, L. (2004). Older people, sport and physical activity: A review of key issues. *Research Digest 99*, Edinburgh: sportscotland.

Nicholson, M., Hoye, R. and Houlihan, B. (2011). *Participation in sport: International policy perspectives*, London: Routledge.

Nixon, H.L. II (2000). Sport and disability, pp. 422–38. In J. Coakley and E. Dunning (eds). *Handbook of Sports Studies*, London: Sage.

Nottinghamshire County Council (1993). *Proposal for the re-launch of STS*, Nottingham: Leisure Services Dept.

Nottinghamshire County Council (1994). *Social Need in Nottinghamshire*, Nottingham: Planning and Economic Development Dept.

Oakley, B. and Green, M. (2000). *Elite sport development systems and playing to win: Uniformity and diversity in international approaches.* Paper to Leisure Studies Association conference Glasgow, July 2000.

Oakley, M. and Tinsley, M. (2013). *Outcomes not just incomes: Improving Britain's understanding and measurement of child poverty*, London: Policy Exchange.

Oatley, N. (ed). (1998). *Cities, competition and urban policy*, London: Paul Chapman.

O'Brien, D. (2013). Drowning the deadweight in the rhetoric of economism: what sport policy, free swimming and EMA tells us about public services after the crash. *Public Administration* 91,1: 69–82.

O'Brien, E. (2005). *Trees and Woods: Nature's health service*, Farnham: Forest Research.

O'Brien Cousins, S. (1995). Social support for exercise among elderly women in Canada. *Health Promotion International* 10,4: 273–82.

O'Brien Cousins, S. (1999). Cross-cultural studies on physical activity, sport and ageing in North America, *World Leisure and Recreation* 41,3: 15–9.

Office for Disability Issues (ODI). (2010a). *Life Opportunities survey 2009–10*, London: ODI.

Office for Disability Issues/DCMS (2010b)., London *2012: a legacy for disabled people*, London: ODI.

Office of the Deputy Prime Minister (ODPM). (2003a). *Community cohesion advice for those designing, developing and delivering Area Based Initiatives (ABIs).: Building cohesion into regeneration and renewal*, London: ODPM.

Office of the Deputy Prime Minister, LGA, NRU, CRE (2003b). *Building a picture of community cohesion*, London: ODPM.

Office of the Deputy Prime Minister (2005). *The state of English cities* 2 vols, London: ODPM.

Office of the Deputy Prime Minister (2006a). *A sure start to later life: ending inequalities for older people – a Social Exclusion Unit final report*, London: ODPM.

Office of the Deputy Prime Minister, Social Exclusion Unit (2006b). *The social exclusion of older people: Evidence of the first wave of the English Longitudinal Study of Ageing* (ELSA)., London: HMSO.

Office of National Statistics (ONS). (2000). *Living in Britain: the General Household Survey,* London: ONS.

Office of National Statistics (2013). *Working and workless households.* ONS Statistical Bulletin 28 August.

OFSTED (2013). *Beyond 2012 – outstanding PE for all,* London: OFSTED.

Oliver, M. (1996a). *Understanding disability: From theory to practice,* Basingstoke: MacMillan.

Oliver, M. (1996b). A sociology of disability or a disability sociology. In L. Barton (ed). *Disability and Society: Emerging issues and insights,* London: Longman.

OPENspace (2003). *Diversity review for the Countryside Agency: Options for implementation,* Edinburgh: College of Art and Heriot-Watt University.

Oppenheim, C. and Harker, L. (1996). *Poverty: The facts,* London: Child Poverty Action Group.

Osberg, L. (1995). The equity/inefficiency trade-off. *Canadian Business Economics* Spring 5.

Ottesen, L., Skirstad, B., Pfister, G. and Habermann, U. (2010). Gender relations in Scandinavian sports organizations: A comparison of the structures and policies in Denmark, Norway and Sweden. *Sport in Society* 13,4: 657–75.

Ouseley, H. (1995, October). *Let's kick racism Newsletter* 2, London: Advisory Group against racism and intimidation.

Oxford City Council (OCC). (1998). *Reports on Flex Card to Leisure Services Committee 12.* Jan and 1 July, Oxford: OCC.

Padley, M. and Hirsch, D. (2013). *Household minimum income standard 2008–9 to 2011–12,* York: Joseph Rowntree Foundation.

Palfrey, C. and Thomas, C. (1992). *Policy evaluation in the public sector,* Aldershot: Avebury.

Pantazis, C., Gordon, D. and Levitas, R. (eds). (2006). *Poverty and social exclusion in Britain: The Millennium survey* Bristol: Policy Press.

Pappous, S. (2011). Do the Olympic Games lead to a sustainable increase in grass roots sport participation? A secondary analysis of Athens 2004. In J. Savery and K. Gilbert (eds). *Sustainability and sport,* Chicago: Common Ground Publishingf.

Parent, M.A. and Harvey, J. (2009). Towards a management model for sport and physical activity community-based partnerships. *European Sport Management Quarterly* 9,1: 23–45.

Park, R.E. (1952). *Human communities,* New York: Free Press.

Parker, A. et al. (nd). *Urban Stars: Sport crime prevention and community action,* London: Laureus Foundation.

Parker, S. (1997). Leisure and culture: consumers or participants? Paper to *Leisure, Culture and commerce,* LSA conference Roehampton, London, July.

Parks and Recreation Federation of Ontario (PRFO). (1997). *The benefits catalogue* Ottawa: CPRA.

Parry, J., Robinson, S., Watson, N. J. and Nesti, M. (eds). (2007). *Sport and Spirituality: An introduction,* London: Routledge.

Pateman, T. (2011). Rural and urban areas: comparing lives, *Regional Trends* 43: 1–77.

Paterson, K. and Hughes, W. (2000). Disabled bodies pp. 29–44. In P. Hancock et al. (eds). *The body, culture and society*, Milton Keynes: Open University Press.

Patsios, D. (2006). Pensioners, poverty and social exclusion, pp. 431–58. In C. Pantazis, D. Gordon and R. Levitas (eds). *Poverty and Social Exclusion in Britain: The Millennium Survey*, Bristol: Policy Press.

Patrickkson, G. (1995). *The significance of sport for society: Health, socialisation, economy: A scientific review*, Strasbourg: Council of Europe Press.

Pavis, S., Platt, S. and Hubbard, G. (2000). *Young people in rural Scotland: Pathways to social inclusion and exclusion*, York: York Publishing Services.

Pawson, R. (2004). *Evaluating ill-defined interventions with hard-to-follow outcome.* Paper to ESRC seminar 'Understanding and evaluating the impact of sport and culture on society'. Leeds Metropolitan University, Jan.

Pawson, R. (2006). *Evidence-based policy: A realist perspective*, London: Sage.

Penney, D. (2000). Physical Education…in what and whose interests? In R.L Jones and K.M. Armour (eds). *Sociology of sport: Theory and practice*, London: Pearson Education.

Penney, D. and Evans, J. (1999). *Policy, politics and practice in Physical Education*, London: E. & F. Spon.

Perry, J. (2011). *UK Migration: the leadership role of housing providers*, York: Joseph Rowntree Foundation.

Philip, L. and Gilbert, A. (2007). Low income amongst the older population in GB: A rural/non-rural perspective on income levels and dynamics. *Regional Studies* 41,6: 735–45.

Phillips C. (2009). Ethnic inequality: another ten years of the same? pp. 179–200. In J. Hills et al. (eds). *Towards a more equal society? Poverty, inequality and policy since 1997*, Bristol: Policy Press.

Philpotts, L. (2013). An analysis of the policy process for PE and school sport: The rise and demise of school sport partnerships *International Journal of Sport Policy and Politics* 5,2: 193–211.

PIEDA (1991). *The economic significance and impact of sport in Scotland*, Reading: PIEDA.

Pierre, J. and Peters, B.G. (2001). *Governance, politics and the state*, Basingstoke: MacMillan.

Pitchford, A. and Collins, M. (2010). Sports development as a job, career and training, pp. 259–88. In Collins, M. (ed). *Examining Sports Development*, London: Routledge.

Pitter, R. and Andrews, D.L. (1997). Serving America's underserved youth: Reflections on sport and recreation in an emerging social problems industry. *Quest* 49: 85–99.

Pitts, J. (1988). *The Politics of Juvenile Crime*, London: Sage.

Platt, L. and Noble, M. (1999). *Race, Place and poverty: ethnic groups and low income distributions*, York: York Publishing Services for the Joseph Rowntree Foundation.

Platt, L. (2009). *Ethnicity and child poverty.* Research Report 570, London: Dept of Work and Pensions.

Poinsett, A. (ed). (1996). *The role of sports in youth development.* Report of Carnegie Corporation meeting 18.March 1996, New York: CC of New York.

Polley, M. (1997). *Moving the goalposts: a history of sport and society since 1945*, London: Routledge.

Poppleton, S. et al. (2013). *Social and public service impacts of international migration at the local level.* Research Report 72, London: Home Office.

Potas, I., Vining, A. and Wilson, P. (1990). *Young people and crime: costs and prevention*, Canberra: Australian Institute of Criminology.

Powell, M. (ed). (1999). *New Labour, new welfare state? The 'Third Way' in British social policy*, Bristol: Policy Press.

Powell, M., Boyne, G. and Ashworth, G. (2001). Towards a geography of people poverty and place poverty. *Policy and Politics* 29.3: 243–58.

Power, A. (1997). *Estates on the edge: the social consequences of mass housing in Northern Europe*, Basingstoke: MacMillan.

Power, A. (2009). New Labour and unequal neighbourhoods 115–33 in J. Hills, T. Sefton and K. Stewart (eds) (2009). *Towards a more equal society? Poverty, inequality and policy since 1997*, Bristol: Policy Press/Joseph Rowntree Foundation.

Predelli, L.N (2008). Religion, citizenship and participation: A case study of immigrant Muslim women in Norwegian mosques. *European Journal of Women's Studies* 15: 241–60.

Pretty, J. et al. (nd). *A countryside for Health & Wellbeing: executive summary*, Sheffield: Countryside Recreation Network.

Price, P. (1999). New sports facilities as the catalyst for urban regeneration in 1998. *Conference proceedings*, 261–70, Melton Mowbray: Institute of Sport and Recreation Management.

Price Waterhouse Coopers (PWC). (2010). *Evaluation of the impact of free swimming Year 1 Report*, London: PWC.

Priest, N. et al. (2008). *Interventions implemented through sporting organisations for increasing participation in sport (review)*. New York: Cochrane Library/J Wiley & Sons Ltd.

Purdy, D. and Richard, S. (1983). Sport and juvenile delinquency: An examination and assessment of four major theories. *Journal of Sport Behavior* 6,4: 179–93.

Puranaho, K. (2000). *Why only the rich can play?* Paper to 8th Congress of the European Association of Sports Management, San Marino.

Putnam, R.D. (2000). *Bowling alone*, New York: Simon and Schuster.

Putnam, R.D. (2007). E Pluribus Unum: Diversity and community in the 21st century *Scandinavian Political Studies* 30,2: 137–74.

Qualifications and Curriculum Authority (1999). *Analysis of educational resources: Resources for PE 5–16*, London: QCA.

Quick, S., et al. (2008). *School sport survey 2007–8*. Research Report DCSF-RW063, London: Department for Children Schools and Families.

Quick, S., Simon, A. and Thornton, A. (2010). *PE and Sport survey 2009–10*, Research report DFE RR032, London: Department for Education.

Rabiee, F., Robbins, A. and Khan, M. (2008). *An evaluation of the short term impact of the Gym for Free scheme on health & wellbeing of residents in Ladywood*, Birmingham: Birmingham City.

Ravenscroft, N. (1993). Public leisure provision and the good citizen. *Leisure Studies* 12: 33–44.

Ravenscroft, N. (1996). Leisure, Consumerism and active citizenship in the UK. *Managing Leisure* 1: 163–94.

Ravenscroft, N. (1998). The changing regulation of public leisure provision. *Leisure Studies* 17: 138–54.

Ravenscroft, N. and Markwell, S. (2000). Ethnicity and the integration and exclusion of young people through park and recreation provision. *Managing Leisure* 5: 135–50.

Rawls, J. (1971). *A theory of justice*, Cambridge, Mass: Harvard University Press.

Rees, C. R. and Miracle, A. W. (2000). Education and sports, pp. 277–90. In J. Coakley and E. Dunning (eds). *Handbook of sports studies,* London: Sage.

Reeser, J.C. (2005). Gender identity and sport: Is the playing field level? *British Journal of Sports Medicine* 39: 695–9.

Regional Coordination Unit (RCU). (2002). *Review of Area-Based Initiatives,* London: Office of the Deputy Prime Minister.

Research International (2007). *English Leisure Countryside Visits Survey,* Sheffield: Natural England.

Resource (2001a). *Using museums, galleries, archives and libraries to develop a learning community: A strategic plan for action,* London: Resource.

Resource (2001b). *Renaissance in the regions: A new vision for England's museums,* London: Resource.

Rhodes, R.A.W. (2000). *Transforming British government Volume 1: Changing Institutions,* Basingstoke: MacMillan/ESRC.

Rigaux, N. (1994). *La perception de la pauvreté et de l'exclusion sociale en Europe [The perception of poverty and social exclusion in Europe].* Eurobarometer 40 Brussels: European Commission.

Rigg, J. (2006). Disabling attitudes: public perceptions of disabled people, pp. 213–37. In Park, A. et al. *Perspectives on a changing society,* London: Sage.

Rigg, M. (1986). *Action sport: An evaluation,* London: Sports Council.

Riordan, J. and Kruger, A. (eds). (1999). *The story of worker sport* Champaign, Ill: Human Kinetics.

Roberts, K. (1977). Leisure and lifestyles under welfare capitalism, pp. 19–37. In M. Smith (ed). *Leisure and urban society* Publication 6 Eastbourne: Leisure Studies Association.

Roberts, K. (1978). *Contemporary society and the growth of leisure,* London: Longmans.

Roberts, K. (1983). *Youth and Leisure,* London: George Allen and Unwin.

Roberts, K. (1996). Young people, schools, sport, and government policies. *Sport Education and Society* 1,1: 47–57.

Roberts, K. (1999). *Leisure in Contemporary Society,* Wallingford, Oxon: CABI Publishing.

Roberts, K. (2013). *Social class and leisure in recent recessions.* Paper to LSA conference, *Re-classing leisure* Salford July 8–9.

Roberts, K. and Brodie, D. (1992). *Inner city sport: Who plays, what are the benefits?* Culembourg: Giordano Bruno.

Roberts, K. and Fagan, C. (1999). Young people and their leisure in former communist countries: four theses examined. *Leisure Studies* 18: 1–17.

Roberts, K. and Parsell, G. (1994). Youth cultures in Britain: the middle class takeover. *Leisure Studies* 13: 33–48.

Robins, D. (1990). *Sport as Prevention,* Oxford: Centre for Criminological Research, University of, Oxford.

Robinson, T. (nd). *The City Challenge programme in South Newcastle,* Newcastle on Tyne: Newcastle University.

Robson, B.T, (2001). *Slim pickings for the cities of the north.* Email from author 2 Mar 2001.

Roche, M. and Annesley, C. (1998). *Comparative social inclusion policy in Europe: Report 1 Contexts,* Sheffield: SEDEC Coordination Centre, Sheffield University.

Rodger, J. and Cowen, G. (2006). *Final evaluation of Connexions Smart Card* Research Report 614, London: Department for Education and Employment.

Rodgers, H.B. (1977). *Rationalising sports policy* Strasbourg: Council of Europe.

Rodger, J. and Cowen, G. (2006). *Final evaluation of Connexions Smart Card.* Research Report 614, London: Department for Education and Employment.

Roe, S. and Ashe, J. (2008). *Young people and crime: Findings from the 2006 Offending, Crime and Justice Survey.* Statistical Bulletin 09/08, London: Home Office.

Roebuck, M. (2009). Participation in sport and active recreation in the countryside. *Countryside Recreation* 17,1: 7–9.

Roll, J. (1992). *Understanding poverty*, London: Family Policy Studies Centre.

Room, G. (1993). *Anti-poverty research in Europe*, Bristol; school for Advanced Urban Studies.

Room, G. (ed). (1995). *Beyond the threshold: the measurement and analysis of social exclusion*, Bristol: Policy Press.

Rothstein, B. (2001). Social capital in the Social Democratic welfare state, *Politics and Society* 29,2: 207–41.

Rowe. N. (2001). *The social landscape of sport – recognising the challenge and realising the potential.* Paper to regional conferences, London: Sport England.

Rowe, N., Adams, R. and Beasley, N. (2004). Driving up participation in sport: the social context, the trends, the prospects and the challenges, pp. 4–11. In *Driving up participation in sport,* London: Sport England.

Rowe, N. and Champion, R. (2000). *Sports participation and ethnicity in England – National survey 1999–2000 Headline findings*, London: Sport England.

Rowntree, B. (1901). *Poverty: A study of town life*, London: MacMillan.

Rudd, P. and Edwards, K. (1998). Structure and agency in youth transitions: Student experiences of vocational FE training. *Journal of Youth Studies* 1,1: 39–62`.

Rudolf, M. (nd). *Tackling obesity through the Healthy Child programme*, Leeds: Leeds Community Healthcare.

Rural Evidence Research Centre (RERC). (2004). *Social and economic change and diversity in rural England*, London: Dept for Environment, Food and Rural Affairs.

Rural Media Company (2000). *Not seen, not heard? Social exclusion in rural areas CA49*, Cheltenham Countryside Agency.

Rural Services Network (2011). *The state of rural public services 2011.* Available at: www.rsnonline.org.uk. [Accessed 15 October 2013[.

Rutter, J. and Latorre, M. (2009). Migration, migrants and inequality, pp. 201–20. In J. Hills et al. (eds). *Towards a more equal society? Poverty, inequality and policy since 1997*, Bristol: Policy Press/Joseph Rowntree Foundation.

Rye, T. and Mykura, W. (2009). Concessionary bus fares for older people in Scotland – are they achieving their objectives? *Journal of Transport Geography* 17: 451–6.

Salvation Army/Henley Centre (1999). *The paradox of prosperity*, London: Henley Centre for Forecasting.

Sasidharan, V. et al. (2006). Older adults' physical activity participation and perceptions of wellbeing: Examining the role of social support for leisure. *Managing Leisure* 11: 164–85.

Savage, L. (2011). *Snakes and ladders: who climbs the rungs of the earnings ladder?* London: Resolution Foundation.

Savage, M. (2000). *Class analysis and social transformation*, Buckingham: Open University Press.

Savage, M. and Egerton, M. (1997). Social mobility, individual ability and the inheritance of class inequality. *Sociology* 31,4: 645–72.

Saveedra, M. (2009). Dilemmas and Opportunities in Gender and Sport-in-development, pp. 124–55. In R. Levermore and A. Beacom (eds). *Sport and International Development* Basingstoke: Palgrave Macmillan.

Save the Children (2011a). *The UK poverty rip-off: The poverty premium 2010,* London: StC.

Save the Children (2011b). *Severe child poverty: Nationally and locally,* London: StC.

[Lord] Scarman (1982). *The Scarman Report,* London: Penguin.

Scharf, T., Phillipson, C. and Smith, A.E. (2005). Social exclusion of older people in deprived urban communities. *European Journal of Ageing* 2: 76–87.

Scheerder, J., Taks, M. and Vanreusel, B. (2005). Social changes in youth sports participation styles 1969–99: the case of Flanders. *Sport Education & Society* 10,3: 321–41.

Schweinhart, L. and Weikart, D. (1997). *Lasting differences: The High/Scope pre-school curriculum project through age 23,* Ypslanti, MI: High/Scope Press.

SCOPE (2005). Time to get equal in volunteering: *Tackling disablism,* London: SCOPE.

Scott, J. (1994). *Poverty and wealth: Citizenship, deprivation and privilege,* London: Longman.

Scott Porter Research and Marketing Ltd (2001a). *Sport and ethnic minorities: Aiming at social inclusion.* Research Report 78, Edinburgh: Sportscotland.

Scott Porter Research and Marketing Ltd (2001b). *Sport and people with a disability: aiming at social inclusion.* Research Report 77, Edinburgh: Sportscotland.

Scottish Household Survey (SHS). (2013). *Scotland's people,* Edinburgh: Scottish Government.

Scraton, S., Magee, J., Caudwell, J. and Liston, K. (1999). 'It's still a man's game?' *International Review for the Sociology of Sport* 34,2: 99–111.

Scraton, S., Bramham, P. and Watson, B. (2000). 'Staying in' and 'going out': Elderly women, leisure and the postmodern city, pp. 101–20. In S. Scraton (ed). *Leisure, time and space: meanings and values in people's lives.* Leisure Studies Association publication 57, Eastbourne: LSA.

Searle, C. (1993). *The BOA athlete report – 25 ways to put the Great back into sporting Britain,* London: British Olympic Association.

Segrave, J. and Hastad, D. N. (1985). Three models of delinquency. *Sociological Focus* 18,1: 1–17.

Seigenthaler, K.L. and Vaughan, J. (1998). Older women in retirement communities: perceptions of recreation and leisure. *Leisure Sciences* 20: 53–66.

Semour, L. (2003). *Nature and psychological well-being.* Research Report 533, English Nature: Peterborough.

Sensory Trust (2005). *By all reasonable means: Inclusive access to the outdoors for disabled people.* Report 215, Cheltenham: Countryside Agency.

Seppanen, P. (1982). Sports Clubs and parents as socialising agents in sport *International Review of Sports Sociology* 1,17: 79–90.

Shah, H. (2008). Solidarity in a globalised society – implications for education 64–70 in N. Johnson (ed). *Citizenship, cohesion and solidarity,* London: The Smith Institute.

Sharkey, P. (1996). Equal Rights *Recreation* Nov.

Sharp, C. et al. (1999). *Playing for Success: An evaluation of the first year.* Research Report 167, London: Department for Education and Employment.

Sharp, C., Schagen, I. and Scott, E. (2004). *Playing for Success: The Longer Term impact,* Research Report 593, London: Dept for Education and Skills.

Sharpe, C., Aldridge J. and Medina, J. (2006). *Delinquent youth groups and offending behaviour: Findings from the 2004 Offending Crime and Justice survey.* Online Report 14/06, London: Home Office.

Shaw, P. (1999). *The Arts and Neighbourhood Renewal Literature review on the arts and social exclusion to inform the work of Policy Action Team 10.,* London: DCMS.

Shucksmith, M. and Chapman, P. (1998). Rural development and social exclusion. *Sociologica Ruralis* 38,2: 225–42.

Shucksmith, M. (2001a). *Development and ruralities in Europe.* Paper to a meeting of the ADPR (Portuguese Association for Regional Development): Vila Real.

Schucksmith, M. (2001b). *Exclusive countryside? Social inclusion and regeneration in the countryside,* York: Joseph Rowntree Foundation.

Slack, T. (1999). *Understanding sports organisations,* Champaign, Ill.: Human Kinetics.

Sleap, M. (1998). *Social issues in sport,* Basingstoke: MacMillan.

Slee, W., Curry, N. and Joseph, D. (2001). *Removing barriers, creating opportunities: Social exclusion in countryside leisure in the UK,* Cardiff: Countryside Recreation Network.

Smith, A. (1812). *The wealth of nations,* Harmondsworth: Penguin.

Smith, A. and Leech, R. (2010). Evidence, what evidence? Evidence-based policy making and School Sport Partnerships in NW England. *International Journal of Sport Policy* 2,3: 327–45.

Smith, A. and Waddington, I. (2004). Using 'sport in the community' schemes to tackle crime and drug use among young people: Some policy issues and problems. *European Physical Education Review* 10,3: 279–98.

Smith, D.M. (1985). *Geography, inequality and society,* Cambridge: Cambridge University Press.

Smith, F. (2000). *Child-centred after school and holiday childcare.* Children 5–16 Research Briefing 10, Uxbridge: Brunel University.

Smith, F. and Barker, J. (2001). Commodifying the countryside: the impact of out-of-school care on rural landscapes of children's play. *Area* 33.2 169–76.

Smith, M. (1992). *The Changing Position of Young People.* Conference Notes, City Challenge, London.

Smith, R. (2001). Including the forty per cent: Social exclusion and tourism policy, pp. 141–53. In G. McPherson and M. Reid (eds). *Leisure and social inclusion: Challenges to policy and practice.* Publication 73, Eastbourne: Leisure Studies Association.

Social Exclusion Unit (SEU). (1998). *Bringing Britain Together,* London: Cabinet Office.

Social Exclusion Unit (2000). *Report of PAT 13 on shops,* London: SEUs.

Social Exclusion Unit (2001a). A *National Strategy of Neighbourhood Renewal: Policy Action Team Audit,* London: SEU.

Social Exclusion Unit (2001b). *A new commitment to Neighbourhood Renewal: National Strategy Action Plan,* London: SEU.

Social Exclusion Unit (2003). *Making the connections: final report on transport and social exclusion,* London: SEU.

Social Exclusion Unit (2004). *Tackling social exclusion: Taking stock and looking forward,* London: SEU.

Social Exclusion Unit Task Force (SEUTF). (2008). *Aspiration and attainment amongst young people in deprived communities,* London; Cabinet Office.

Soothill, K., Francis, B. and Fligelstone, R. (2002). *Patterns of offending: A new approach* Findings 171, London: Home Office.

Sotiriadou, K., Shilbury, D. and Quick, S. (2008). The attraction, retention/ transition and nurturing process of sports development: some Australian evidence. *Journal of Sport Management* 22, 247–72.

Spaaij, R. (2011). *Sport and social mobility: Crossing boundaries,* London: Routledge.

Sparkes, D. and Collins, M. (2010). Managing development in club sport: The ASA and Swim 21 167–89 in M. Collins (ed). *Examining Sports Development,* London: Routledge.

Speakman, L. and Lowe, P. (2006). *The Ageing countryside: Growing older in rural England*, London: Age Concern.

Special Interest Group of Municipal Authorities (SIGOMA). (2010). *All in this together*, London: SIGOMA/LGA.

Spilsbury, M. and Lloyd, N. (1998). *1997 Survey of rural services*, Salisbury: Rural Development Commission.

Sport and Recreation Alliance (2011). *Red card to red tape: How clubs want to break free*, London: SRA.

Sport and Recreation Alliance (2013a). *Sports Club survey 2013*, London: SRA.

Sport and Recreation Alliance (2013b). *Olympic Games and Paralympic Games: Legacy survey*, London: SRA.

Sport England (1999a). *The value of sport*, London: SE.

Sport England (1999b). *The value of sport to local authorities*, London: SE.

Sport England (1999c). *The value of sport to regional development*, London: SE.

Sport England (1999d). *The value of sport to health*, London: SE.

Sport England (2000). *The use and management of sports halls and swimming pools in England 1997*, London: SE.

Sport England (2001a). *Making English sport inclusive: Equity guidelines for governing bodies*, London: SE.

Sport England (2001b). *Young people with a disability and sport: headline findings*, London: SE.

Sport England (2001c). *Sport Action Zones: Summary report on the establishment of the first 12 zones*. Available at: www.sportengland.co.uk. [Accessed 22 November 2001].

Sport England (2002). *No limits: Sport England's equity policy*, London: SE.

Sport England (2004). *The Framework for sport in England: A vision for 2020*, London: SE.

Sport England (2005). *Sport Equity index*. Available at: www.sportengland.co.uk. [Accessed 10 August 2009].

Sport England (2006). *Sport playing its part: the contribution of sport to meeting the needs of children and young people*, London: SE.

Sport England (2007a). *Policy statement: the delivery system for sport in England*, London: SE.

Sport England (2007b). *Community Sports Networks*, London: SE.

Sport England (2008a). *Strategy 2008–11*, London: SE.

Sport England (2008b). *Impact: Innovation working in communities, increased participation, Sport Action Zones, ACDF, Magnet Fund, in 3D: Driving change, Developing partnerships, Delivering outcomes*, London. Available at: www.sportengland.org. [Accessed 10 August 2008].

Sport England (2009). *Active People Survey 2008–09*, London: SE.

Sport England (2012). *A sporting habit for life 2012–17*, London: SE.

Sport England (2013). *How we play – the habits of community sport*, London: SE.

Sport England (nd). *Satellite club guide*, London: SE.

Sport England and Youth Sport Trust (2009). *PESSYP: A guide to delivering the five hour offer*, London: SE.

Sport Physical Recreation and Activity Research Centre (SPEAR). (2011). *Street Games Additionality evaluation*, Canterbury: Christchurch Canterbury University.

Sport Structures (2005). *Identification of workforce and volunteer profiles within sports organisations*, Sutton Coldfield: SS.

Sporting Equals (2001). *Achieving racial equality: a standard for sport.* Information sheet, Melton Mowbray: Institute of Sport and Recreation Management.

Sports Council (1982). *Sport in the community: The next ten years,* London: SC.

Sports Council (1988). *Annual Report 1987–88,* London: SC.

Sports Council (1993). *Sport in the 90s: New Horizons,* London: SC.

Sports Council (1994a). *Black and ethnic minorities in sport: Policy and objectives,* London: SC.

Sports Council (1994b). *Guidance Notes: Access for disabled people,* London: SC.

Sports Council (1994c). *Black and ethnic minorities in sport: Policy and objectives,* London: SC.

Sports Council (1995). *Running Sport-starting a junior section,* London: Sports Council.

Sports Council/Coventry City Council (1989). *Active lifestyles: an evaluation,* Coventry/CCC.

Sports Council/Health Education Authority (1992). *Allied Dunbar national fitness survey, main report,* London: SC/HEA.

Sports Council (NW). (1991). *Sport and Racial Equality* Factfile 3 Manchester: SC.

Sports Council (Y&H). (1995a). *Sharing good practice: sport and black & ethnic minorities – 'Is it cricket?',* Leeds: SC.

Sports Council, Yorkshire & Humberside (1995b). *Sharing good practice: sport for people with Disabilities,* Leeds: SC Women and sport.

Sports Council for Wales (SCW). (nd). *Time out: Is PE out of time and out of resources?* Cardiff: SCW.

Sports Council for Wales (2013). *School sport survey 2013,* Cardiff: SCW.

Spracklen, K., Long, J. and Hylton, K. (2006). Managing and Monitoring Equality and Diversity in UK Sport. *Journal of Sport and Social Issues* 30,3: 289–305.

Spring, E. (2013). *Disabled people's lifestyle survey,* Loughborough: English Federation for Disability Sport.

Squires, S.L. and Sparkes, A.C. (1996). Circles of silence: Sexual identity in Physical Education and sport. *Sport, Education and Society* 1.1: 77–101.

SQW Ltd (2004). *Joint working in sport and neighbourhood renewal.* Research Report 9, London: Office of the Deputy Prime Minister.

Stamatakis, E. and Choudhury, M. (2008). Temporal trends in adults' sports participation patterns in England between 1997 and 2006: The Health Survey for England. *British Journal of Sports Medicine* 1–8.

Stassen, B. (ed). (1996). Sports de proximité et d'aventure, outils d'insertion sociale [neighbourhood and adventure sports, useful in social insertion]. *Sport* no.155, Brussels: Ministere de la Culture et des Affaires Sociales.

Stead, D. and Swain, G. (eds). (1987). *Youth work and sport,* London: Sports Council/ NYB/NCVYS.

Stebbins, R. (1997). Casual leisure: a conceptual framework. *Leisure Studies* 16.1, 17–25.

Stedman-Jones, G. (1971). *Outcast, London: A study in the relationship between the classes in Victorian society,* Oxford: Oxford University Press.

Stodolska, M. and Jackson, E.L. (1998). Discrimination in leisure and work experienced by a White ethnic minority group. *Journal of Leisure Research* 30.1: 23–46.

Stoke-on-Trent City Council (1994). *Sport and Recreation – Towards the Millennium: a strategy for leisure provision in Stoke-on-Trent,* Stoke: STCC.

Stoneham, J. (2001). Making Connections for accessible greenspaces. *Countryside Recreation* 9.1, 14–16.

Street Games (SG). (2008). *Strategic Plan 2008–12,* London: SG.

Street Games (2009). *How race, gender and income affect volunteering rates.* Briefing paper 6, London: SG.

Streich, L. (1999). *Alternatives to the bus shelter: Imaginative ways to make it happen for young people in rural areas,* Leicester: Youth Work Press.

Su, F. and Bell, M.G.H. (2009). Transport for older people: characteristics and solutions, *Research in Transportation Economics 25,* 46–55.

Sugden, J. and Tomlinson, A. (2000). Theorising sport and social class, pp. 309–21. In J. Coakley and E. Dunning (eds). *Handbook of sports studies,* London: Sage.

Sullivan, C. (1998). *The growing business of sport and leisure: an update,* Wellington, NZ: Hillary Commission.

Sustrans (2011). *So simple. Making smarter travel choices, possible desirable, inevitable Annual Review 2011,* Bristol: Sustrans.

Sustrans (2012). *Locked put: Transport poverty in England,* Derby: Sustrans.

Sutton, E. (2008). The state of play: Disadvantage, play and children's well being, *Social Policy & Society* 7.4: 537–49.

Svendson, G.L. and Svendson, G.T. (2003). *The creation and destruction of social capital,* Cheltenham: Edward Elgar.

Tabbush, P. and O'Brien, E. (2003). *Wellbeing: Trees woodlands and natural spaces,* Farnham: Forest Research.

Tackey, N.D., Barnes, H. and Khambhaita, P. (2011). *Poverty, ethnicity and education,* York: Joseph Rowntree Foundation.

Talbot, M. (1989). 'Being herself through sport'. Paper to the Leisure Studies Association Conference *Leisure, Health and Wellbeing,* Leeds.

Taylor, A. (1997). 'Arms length but hands on': Managing the new governance: The Department of National Heritage and cultural policy in Britain. *Public Administration* 75 441–66.

Taylor, A. H., Cable, N. T. and Faulkner, G. (2004). Physical activity and older adults: a review of health benefits and the effectiveness of interventions. *Journal of Sports Sciences* 22,703–25.

Taylor, D.E. (1992). *Identity in ethnic leisure pursuits,* San Francisco: Mellen Research University.

Taylor, M. (1992). *Signposts to community development,* London: Community Projects Foundation.

Taylor, M. Barr, A. and West, A. (2000). *Signposts to Community Development,* 2nd ed, London: Community Development Foundation.

Taylor, P. (2001). Forecasting in C. Gratton and I. Henry (eds). *Sport in the city,* London: Routledge.

Taylor, P. and Kung, S.P. (2010). Use of public sports facilities in England *Sport et Citoyenet*te 12: 12.

Taylor, P. and Page, K. (1994). *The financing of local authority sport and recreation: a service under threat?* Melton Mowbray: Institute of Sport & Recreation Management.

Taylor, T. and Toohey, K. (1996). Sport, gender and ethnicity: an Australian perspective, *World Leisure and Recreation* 38,4: 35–7.

Taylor, T.L. & Toohey, K.M. (2002). Behind the veil: exploring the recreation needs of Muslim women. *Leisure/Loisir* 26, 1/2: 85–105.

Taylor, P., Crow, I., Irvine, D. and Nichols, G. (1999). *Demanding physical programmes for young offenders under probation supervision.* Research Findings 91, London: Home Office.

Taylor, P. et al. (2003). *Sports volunteering in England 2002,* London: Sport England.

Taylor, P. et al. (2004). *Widening access through facilities.* Report to Sport England, Sheffield: Sports Industry Research Centre.

Taylor, P. et al. (2007). Facilitating organisational effectiveness among volunteers in sport. *Voluntary Action* 8,3: 61–78.

Taylor, W., Baronowski, T. and Rohm Young, D. (1998). Physical activity interventions, in low income ethnic minority and populations with disability. *American Journal of Preventative Medicine* 15.4, 334–43.

Telama, R. (2006). Participation in organised youth sport as a predictor of adult physical activity: A 21-year longitudinal study *Pediatric Exercise Science* 18,1: 76–88.

Temple, M. (2000). New Labour's Third Way: pragmatism and governance *British Journal of Political and International Relations* 2,3: 302–25.

The Poverty Site (2010) Poverty.org. Available at: www.poverty.org.uk/07/index. shtml?2#why. [Accessed 20 September 2010].

Thiel, A. and Mayer, J. (2009). Characteristics of voluntary sports clubs: A sociological perspective. *European Sport Management Quarterly* 9,1: 81–98.

Thomas, N. (2001) *Sports policy for disabled people.* Unpublished, Stafford: Staffordshire University.

Thomas, N. and Houlihan, B. (2000). The development of sports policies for disabled people in England: issues for the new Millennium. Paper to Paralympic conference, Sydney.

Thomas, N. and Smith, A. (2009). *Disability, sport and society: An introduction,* London: Routledge.

Thomas, P. and Palfrey, C. (1996). Evaluation: Stakeholder-focused criteria. *Social Policy and Administration* 30,2 125–42.

Thomson, I. (1998). *Sport in Denmark,* Edinburgh: Scottish Sports Council.

Thomson, R. and Beavis, N. (1985). *Talent identification in sport,* Otago NZ: Faculty of PE.

Thorpe, D., Smith, D., Green, C. J. and Paley, J. H. (1980). *Out of Care: the Community Support of Juvenile Offenders,* London: George Allen and Unwin Ltd.

Thorpe, R. and Collins, M. (2010). Sport and higher Education Participation and excellence, pp. 105–119. In M. Collins (ed). *Examining Sports Development,* London: Routledge.

Tiessen-Raaphorst, A. and Breedveld, K. (2007). *Sport in the Netherlands: A short introduction.* The Hague: Social and Cultural Planning Office.

TNS (2010). *Sport and Physical Activity.* Special Eurobarometer survey 334, Brussels: TNS.

TNS/BMRB (2012). *Inspiring a generation: A Taking Part report on the 2012 Olympic and Paralympic Games,* London: TNS/BMRB.

Todorovic, J. and Wellington, S. (2000). *Living in Urban England: Attitudes and aspirations,* London: Dept of the Environment, Transport and the Regions.

Tomlinson, A. (1986). *'Playing away from home':* Leisure, access and exclusion. In P. Golding (ed). *Poverty and exclusion,* London: Child Poverty Action Group.

Tomlinson, A. (1991). Leisure as consumer culture. In D. Botterill and A. Tomlinson (eds). *Ideology, leisure policy and practice.* Publication 45, Eastbourne: Leisure Studies Association.

Torkildsen, G. (1992). *Leisure and recreation management,* London: E and F Spon.

Townsend, P. (1979). *Poverty in the UK: A survey of household resources and standards of living,* London: Penguin.

Townsend, P. (1987). Disadvantage. *Journal of Social Policy* 16, 125–46.

Townsend, P. (2010). The meaning of poverty. *British Journal of Sociology* DOI: 10.1111/j.1468-4446.2009.01241.x.

Townsend, P. and Abel-Smith, B. (1965). *The poor and the poorest,* London: Bell.

Trulson, M. (1986). Martial arts training: a 'novel' cure for juvenile delinquency. *Human Relations* 39.12, 1131–40.

Tsuchiya, M. (1996). Recreation and leisure programmes for delinquents: the non-custodial option, pp. 287–302. In M.F. Collins (ed). *Leisure in industrial and post-industrial societies* Eastbourne: Leisure Studies Association.

Tungatt, M. (1990). Everybody Active project, pp. 328–38. In C. Williams, L. Almond and A. Sparkes (eds). *Sport and physical activity,* London: E & F Spon.

Tungatt, M. (1991). *Solent Sports Counselling Final Evaluation Report,* Manchester, Sports Council, Research Unit North West.

Twemlow, S. W. and Sacco, F. C. (1998). The application of traditional martial arts practice and theory to the treatment of violent adolescents. *Journal of Leisure Research* 30.3, 356–79.

UK Sport (UKS). (1999). *Major events: The economics,* London: UK Sport.

UK Sport (2001). *World Class: The athlete's view,* London: UKS.

UK Sport (2009). *Home Advantage: the performance benefits of hosting major sports events,* London: UKS.

UK Sport (2007). Women *in sport 2006 Monitoring the strategic framework,* London: UK Sport.

UK Sport/Sport England/CONI (1999). *Compass 1999: Sports participation in Europe,* London: UK Sport.

UK Sport/Women's Sport Foundation (2003). *Framework strategy for women,* London: UKS.

Urban Regeneration and Greenspace Partnership (URGP). (2010). *Benefits of green infrastructure,* Farnham: Forest Research.

Utting, D. (1997). *Reducing criminality among young people: a sample of relevant programmes in the UK,* London: Home Office.

Uzzell, D., Leach, R. and Kelay, T. (2004). *What about us? Diversity review evidence: changing perceptions: provider awareness of under-represented groups,* Guildford: Surrey University.

Van Campen, C. (ed). (2008). *Values on a grey scale,* The Hague: Netherlands Institute for Social Research.

Van der Meulen, R., Kraylaar, G. and Utlee, W. (2001). *Lifelong on the move: An event analysis of attrition in on-elite sport paper to ECSS Congress,* 24–28 July, Cologne.

Van Tuyckom, C., Scheerder, J. and Bracke, P. (2010). Gender and age inequality in regional sports plans: A cross-national study of 25 European countries. *Journal of Sports Science* 28,10: 1077–84.

Vanhuysse, P. (2013). *Intergenerational justice in aging societies: A cross-national comparison of 29 OECD countries,* Gutersloh: Bertelsmann Foundation.

Veal, A.J. (2011). The leisure society I: myths and misconceptions 1960–79. *World Leisure Journal* 53,3: 206–27.

Veal, A.J. (2012). The leisure society II: the era of critique 1980–2011. *World Leisure Journal* 54.2: 99–140.

Veal, A.J., Toohey, K. and Frawley, S. (2012). The sport participation legacy of the Sydney 2000 Olympic Games and other international sporting events hosted in Australia. *Journal of Policy Research in Tourism Leisure & Events* 4,2: 155–84.

Veit-Wilson, J. (1998). *Setting adequacy standards* Bristol: Policy Press.

Veblen, T. (1953). *The theory of the leisure class* New York: American Library.

Verma, G. K. and Darby, D. S. (1994). *Winners and Losers: Ethnic minorities in sport and recreation,* Brighton: Falmer Press.

Voluntary Action Leicester (1998). *Directory of Voluntary Groups in Leicester* Leicester: VAL.

Vuori, I. et al. (eds) (1995). *The significance of sport for society: health, socialisation, economy,* Strasbourg: Council of Europe Press.

Wade, E. (1987). *Bridging the gap: A scheme to stop school leavers dropping out of sport*, London: Sports Council.

Walker, A. (1982). *Unqualified and underemployed*, Basingstoke: Macmillan.

Walker, A. and Walker, C. (1997). (eds). *Britain divided: The growth of social exclusion in the 1980s and 1990s*, London: Child Poverty Action Group.

Walker, A., Barnes, M., Cox, K. and Lessof, C. (2006). *New Horizons Research Programme Think Piece: Social exclusion of older people: Future trends and policies*, London: Department of Communities and Local Government.

Walker, R. (1995). The dynamics of poverty and social exclusion. In G. Room et al. (eds). *Beyond the threshold: The measurement and analysis of social exclusion* Bristol: Policy Press.

Walker, R. and Park, J. (1997). Unpicking poverty in C. Oppenheim (ed). *An inclusive society*, London: Institute of Public Policy Research.

Wallace, E. et al. (2009). *Extended school survey of schools pupils and parents.* Report RR068, London: Ipsos MORI for DSCF.

Walpole, C. (2012). *Evaluating a different approach to sports volunteering by young people.* Paper to European Sport Development Network, Sheffield Sept 5.

Walpole, C. and Collins, M. (2010). Sports development in microcosm: Braunstone Sport Action Zone 190–210 in M. Collins (ed). *Examining Sports Development,* London: Routledge.

Warde, A. and Bennett, T. (2008). A culture in common: the cultural consumption of the UK managerial elite. *Sociological Review* 56, Suppl 1.

Warde, A. et al. (2003). Trends in social capital: Membership of associations in Great Britain, 1991–98. *British Journal of Social Policy* 33: 525–34.

Waring, A. and Mason, C. (2010). Opening doors: Promoting social inclusion through increased sports opportunities. *Sport in Society* 13.3: 517–29.

Watson, N. et al. (2000). *Life as a disabled child: a qualitative study of young people's experiences and perspectives*, Edinburgh: University of Edinburgh.

Watson, N.J., Weir, S. and Friend, S. (2005). The Development of Muscular Christianity in Victorian Britain and Beyond. *Journal of Religion and Society* 7,1: 1–25.

Webb, B. and Laycock, G. (1992). *Tackling car crime: The nature and extent of the problem*, London: Home Office.

Weed, M. et al. (2005). *Academic Review of the Role of Voluntary Sports Clubs Institute of Sport & Leisure Policy*, Loughborough University: Sport England.

Weed, M. et al. (2009). *A Systematic Review of the Evidence Base for Developing a Physical Activity and Health Legacy from the, London 2012 Olympic and Paralympic Games*, London: Department of Health.

Weiss, C. (1998). *Evaluation* NJ: Prentice Hall.

Wells, P. et al. (2011). *A Big Society in, Yorks and Humber?* Sheffield: Centre for Economic and Social Research, Sheffield Hallam University.

West, D. (1967). *The Young Offender*, London: Penguin Books.

West, P.C. (1984). Social stigma and community recreation participation by the mentally and physically handicapped. *Therapeutic Recreation Journal* 18.1, 40–9.

Wetherby, A. (1998). *Disability Discrimination Act Facilities Factfile*, London: English Sports Council.

Whitson, D. (2002). The embodiment of gender: Discipline, domination and empowerment 227–39 in S. Scraton and A. Flintoff (eds). *Gender and sport: A reader*, London: Routledge.

Widdop, P. and Cutts, D. (2013). Social stratification and sports' participation in England. *Leisure Sciences* 35,107–28.

Wilkinson, R. (1998). What health tells us about society. *Institute of Development Studies Bulletin* 29.1, 77–84.

Wilkinson, R. and Prickett, K. (2009). *The Spirit level: why more equal societies nearly always do better*, London: Allan Lane/Penguin Press.

Williams, T. (1988). *Issues of integration, participation and involvement in physical education and sport.* Working Paper 1 EveryBody Active project, Sunderland: Sunderland Polytechnic.

Wilson, G.D.H. and Hattingh, P.S. (1992). Environmental preferences for recreation within deprived areas: The case of black townships in South Africa. *Geoforum* 34.4, 477–86.

Wilson, W.J. (1997). *When work disappears: The world of the new urban poor*, New York: Alfred Knopf.

Witt, P. (1999). Evaluation of the 1998–99 Neighborhood Teen Program of Austin Parks and Recreation Department. Email correspondance with author, 17 July 2000.

Witt, P. (2000). *Differences between after-school programme participants and nonparticipants.* Available at: http://rptsweb.tamu.edu/Faculty/Witt/wittpub12.htm [Accessed 9 May 2003]

Witt, P. and Crompton, J. (1996). *Recreation Programs that Work for At Risk Youth: The Challenge of Shaping the Future*, Pennsylvania: Venture Publishing.

Witt, P.A. and Crompton, J. (1997). The protective factors framework: a key to programming for benefits and evaluating for results. *Journal of Park & Recreation Admin* 15.3, 1–18.

Women's Resource Centre (2013). *Women's Equality in the UK – A health check* plus Appendix 25 Women & sport (online)., London: WRC.

Womens Royal Volunteer Service (2011). Gold Age pensioners: Valuing the socio-economic contribution of older people in the UK, London: WRVS.

Women's Sport and Fitness Foundation (WSFF). (2008). *Women in sport: Unlocking the potential*, London: WSFF.

Women's Sport and Fitness Foundation (2009). *Sweat in the City*, London: WSFF. Available at: www.wsff.org.uk/system/1/assets/files/000/000/262/262/cc837836e/original/11308_SitC_Report_latest2.pdf. [Accessed 24 February 2014].

Women's Sport and Fitness Foundation (2010). *Young women and girls sport and physical activity*, London: WSFF.

Wood, A., Downer, K. and Toberman, A. (2011). *Evidence review of smart card schemes in local authorities.* Research Report 738, London: Department for Work and Pensions.

Wood, M. (2004). *Perceptions and experiences of antisocial behaviour* Findings 252, London: Home Office, Youth Justice Board et al. (nd). *Antisocial behaviour: Guidance to Youth Offending Teams*, London: YJB.

Woods, M. and Goodwin, M. (2003). Governance and policy in rural areas, pp. 245–52. In P. Cloke (ed). *Country visions* Harlow: Pearson.

Yates, L. et al. (2008). Modifiable factors associated with survival and function to age 90 years. *Arch Intern. Med* 168, 3: 284–90.

YouGov (2012). *How to develop a sporting habit for life*, London: Sport England.

Youth Sport Trust (YST). (2000). *Know the score: Evidence to support the impact of the Sports College network, Loughborough*: YST.

Youth Sport Trust/Nike (2001a). *Girls in Sport*, Loughborough: Youth Sport Trust.

Youth Sport Trust/Nike (2001b). *Evaluation of girls and sport project*, Loughborough: Youth Sport Trust.

Zaidi, A. and Burchardt, T. (2003). *Comparing incomes when needs differ: equivalisation for the extra costs of disability* Centre for Analysis of Social Exclusion. Paper 64, London: London School of Economics.

Author index

Subject index

Page numbers in **bold** indicate Tables and page numbers in *italic* indicate Figures.

Lightning Source UK Ltd.
Milton Keynes UK
UKOW07f2041010315

247064UK00001B/15/P

Lightning Source UK Ltd.
Milton Keynes UK
UKOW07f2041010315

247064UK00001B/15/P